SEXUAL POLITICS

Sexual Politics

*Sexuality, Family Planning, and the British
Left from the 1880s to the Present Day*

STEPHEN BROOKE

OXFORD

UNIVERSITY PRESS

OXFORD
UNIVERSITY PRESS

Great Clarendon Street, Oxford OX2 6DP

Oxford University Press is a department of the University of Oxford.
It furthers the University's objective of excellence in research, scholarship,
and education by publishing worldwide in

Oxford New York

Auckland Cape Town Dar es Salaam Hong Kong Karachi
Kuala Lumpur Madrid Melbourne Mexico City Nairobi
New Delhi Shanghai Taipei Toronto

With offices in

Argentina Austria Brazil Chile Czech Republic France Greece
Guatemala Hungary Italy Japan Poland Portugal Singapore
South Korea Switzerland Thailand Turkey Ukraine Vietnam

Oxford is a registered trade mark of Oxford University Press
in the UK and in certain other countries

Published in the United States
by Oxford University Press Inc., New York

© Stephen Brooke 2011

British Library Cataloguing in Publication Data

Data available

Library of Congress Cataloging in Publication Data

Data available

Typeset by SPI Publisher Services, Pondicherry, India
Printed in Great Britain
on acid-free paper by
MPG Books Group, Bodmin and King's Lynn

ISBN 978–0–19–956254–1

1 3 5 7 9 10 8 6 4 2

To Theo and Amy

Acknowledgements

The first debts I owe for this book are material ones. The Social Science and Humanities Research Council of Canada provided me with a major grant in 1997 to begin the work and I am very grateful for its support. Smaller but no less valuable grants came from the European Council and York University. I was very fortunate to hold a York Research Fellowship for the book's last stages and I thank the York Faculty of Arts for its generosity in this regard.

During the writing of this book, I was extremely fortunate to benefit from the generosity of two institutions. In 2005, I worked on the book in the most beautiful surroundings imaginable thanks to the Rockefeller Foundation and its Study Centre at the Villa Serbelloni, Bellagio, Italy, where Pilar Palacia was a gracious host. I still miss my polenta hut with its lovely view of the gardens and mountains of Lake Como. I was also lucky to enjoy the munificence of Massey College in 2007–8 and I would like to thank the Master, John Fraser.

Over the years, I have benefited from excellent research assistance from many students; I would like to thank, in particular, Amanda Bidnall, Amanda Crocker, Joe Buscemi, and David Cousins. Archivists and librarians are the often-unsung heroes and heroines of academic research and I would like to acknowledge the particular help of Mieke Izjermans of the Institute for Social History, Amsterdam, Sue Donnelly and the staff at the London School of Economics, and the staff at the Women's Library, London. Lesley Hall at the Wellcome Library provided much advice on sources and has always been a fount of expertise on sexual politics.

I would also like to thank Rupert Cousens, Seth Cayley, and Stephanie Ireland at Oxford University Press for guiding this book through to publication with such efficiency and sense.

My greatest debts are personal ones. Geoff Eley, Claire Langhamer, Matt Houlbrook, Matthew Hilton, Selina Todd, Sonya Rose, Hera Cook, Seth Koven, Chris Waters, and Marc Stein provided invaluable encouragement at particular points in the writing of this book. I am very grateful to Claire Langhamer and Lucy Robinson for reading and commenting on particular chapters. My friends and colleagues Thabit Abdullah, Judith Allen, Peter Bailey, Bettina Bradbury, Gillian McGillivray, James Cypher, Audrey Pyée, Jim Cronin, Philippa Levine, Deborah Gorham, Peter Weiler, Greig Dymond, Molly Ladd Taylor, Su Lin Lewis, Kenneth O. Morgan, Clare Brant, Marlene Shore, Ben Lander, Christine Grandy, Deborah Gorham, Anne-Marie Rafferty, Damian Tarnopolsky, Mark Schatzker, Bill Wicken, Nick Rogers, Jeanette Neeson, Judith Carney, Erika Stokes, Chris Elson, Catherine Ellis, Amy Bell, and Stephen Heathorn have helped me in many different ways. York University's Department of History has been a collegial and stimulating home to me since 1999. Much of my writing in 2008 and 2009 was done at the Linnux Café and I am grateful to David and Lena for cappuccino, muffins, bagels, and the view of Grace and Harbord Streets. In the spirit of a book, at least in part, about reproduction, I want to express my appreciation to the brilliant staff at Montrose Childcare Centre, especially Lixia Hong, Rob Zimmer, Cheryl Clifford, Lisa Marino, and Nancy Crispim. Over the decade or more it took to write this book, the work of Denis Johnson, Aimee Mann, McCoy Tyner, Frederick Davidson, Barry Wordsworth, and James Richardson provided consistently good company. That decade of writing would not have ended without the help of Jo Kanfner.

Glen Jeffery provided me with a home in London literally and metaphorically. I cannot thank Glen and his sons Jack and Tom enough for their unstinting hospitality and, more importantly, for their friendship. I am similarly grateful to Anita Avramides, Aidan and Annie Gaule, and David and Helen Constantine, who provided sustenance, fun and warmth in Oxford. I am very fortunate indeed to have Becky Conekin and Kate McPherson as inspiring colleagues and wonderful and supportive friends. Martin Francis has been a dear comrade in the historical life for twenty-five years. I could not hope for a funnier, smarter, and more loyal companion on that journey.

Though I have stopped her a number of times from telling me too much about her own reproductive practices in 1940s' and 1950s' England, my mother Mary has always been a source of love, as have my brother Richard, my sister-in-law Leena, my niece Vivi, and my nephews Samuel and Daniel. I wish that four people were here to celebrate the completion of this book: John Brooke (1926–2004), Kenneth Black (1924–2007), Ewen Green (1958–2006), and Larry Stokes (1940–2007).

The last and most important thanks are the simplest. Amy and Theo have shown me what is most important and what is most precious. This book is small recompense for that gift, but it is to Amy and Theo that it is dedicated with my deepest love.

Table of Contents

List of Illustrations

List of Abbreviations

ACLW	Annual Conference of Labour Women
ALRA	Abortion Law Reform Association
AUEW	Amalgamated Union of Electrical Workers
BMA	British Medical Association
BPAS	British Pregnancy Advisory Service
CAC	Campaign Against Corrie
CHE	Campaign for Homosexual Equality
CLP	Constituency Labour Party
CLPD	Campaign for Labour Party Democracy
CLRC	Criminal Law Review Committee
CO-ORD	Coordinating Committee in Defence of the 1967 Abortion Act
CP	Communist Party
CPGB	Communist Party of Great Britain
CWO	Chief Woman Officer, Labour Party
EMWWA	East Midlands Working Women's Association
FPA	Family Planning Association
FWG	Fabian Women's Group
GLC	Greater London Council
GLF	Gay Liberation Front
GLG	Gay Labour Group
GWP	Gay Rights Working Party
HFE	Human Fertilisation and Embryology
HLRS	Homosexual Law Reform Society
ILEA	Inner London Education Authority
ILP	Independent Labour Party
IMG	International Marxist Group
IS	International Socialists
LARC	Labour Abortion Rights Campaign
LCC	Labour Coordinating Committee
LCGR	Labour Campaign for Gay Rights
LCLGR	Labour Campaign for Lesbian and Gay Rights
LTC	London Trades Council
MEP	Member of the European Parliament
M-O	Mass-Observation
MFGB	Miners' Federation of Great Britain
MWF	Medical Women's Federation
NAC	National Abortion Campaign
NALGO	National Association of Local Government Officers
NEC	National Executive Committee
NFRB	New Fabian Research Bureau
NJACWER	National Joint Action Committee for Women's Equal Rights
NJCWWO	National Joint Committee of Working Women's Organizations
NLWAC	National Labour Women's Advisory Committee

NUM	National Union of Miners
NWHRC	North Western Homosexual Reform Committee
PLP	Parliamentary Labour Party
RCOG	Royal College of Obstetricians and Gynaecologists
RCP	Revolutionary Communist Party
SDF	Social Democratic Federation
SDP	Social Democratic Party
SJCIWO	Standing Joint Committee of Industrial Women's Organizations
SJCWWO	Standing Joint Committee of Working Women's Organizations
SMA	Socialist Medical Association
SPUC	Society for the Protection of the Unborn Child
SWP	Socialist Workers' Party
TGWU	Transport and General Workers Union
TUC	Trades Union Congress
USDAW	Union of Shop, Distributive and Allied Workers
WACC	Women's Abortion and Contraceptive Campaign
WBCG	Workers' Birth Control Group
WCG	Women's Cooperative Guild
WLSR	World League for Sexual Reform

Introduction
'Your Sex Life is Political'[1]

In November 1937, two married, working-class women, Ivy Roche and Elizabeth Oakes, travelled to London from the industrial East Midlands to appear before a Whitehall inquiry. Facing a committee heavy with the great and the good, Roche and Oakes spoke for 'women who are working, whose husbands are out of work, and . . . working-class people generally'. They argued for the legalization of abortion. To Oakes and Roche, access to legal and safe abortion was a crucial means of preserving women's lives and the working-class family in a period of high unemployment and poverty. Oakes and Roche were not, by any stretch of the imagination, sexual radicals. They were respectable married women representing other respectable married women. Their belief in legalized abortion grew from a desire to protect the working-class home. For them, sexual reform was social reform. Oakes and Roche were representatives of the East Midlands Working Women's Association (EMWWA), a thousand-strong organization of women from Nottingham and Derby. But the EMWWA was 'in *fact*, the Women's Section of the Labour Party'. The Labour women of the East Midlands had asked for, and been refused, formal party representation at the Whitehall inquiry on abortion. Despite this, Oakes, Roche, and their comrades were 'so anxious' to make clear 'conditions here' that a 'non-political Association was formed out of the political body.'[2]

Oakes and Roche gave their evidence, went home to the Midlands and the EMWWA was never heard of again. But this episode tells us much about the ambiguous relationship between sexuality and politics in twentieth-century Britain. For most of the century, the stage for that relationship was not the floor of the House of Commons or the street, but back rooms, front parlours, cafés, and local meeting halls. These were political campaigns waged in the borderlands of what was considered legitimate politics. In 1937, Oakes, Roche, and the women of the EMWWA discovered a truth linking the whole century: the limits of the body politic in dealing with the politics of the body.

Just over two decades later, Allan Horsfall made the same discovery. Horsfall had been born, bred, and lived most of his life in the 'small mining and weaving towns

---

[1] Ken Livingstone, 1981, quoted in John Carvel, *Citizen Ken* (London: Chatto and Windus, 1984), 212.

[2] The National Archive, Kew [TNA], Ministry of Health [MH] 71/23, East Midlands Working Women's Association, Memorandum to Interdepartmental Committee on Abortion, 16 November 1937; MH 71/25, Oral Evidence to Interdepartmental Committee on Abortion of Mrs Ivy E. Roche and Mrs E. Oakes, East Midlands Working Women's Association.

of industrial Lancashire'. After national service, he ended up working as a colliery clerk for the National Coal Board. The Suez crisis politicized him and he became a local Labour councillor in Nelson between 1958 and 1961. Horsfall was a homosexual. In the 1980s, he recalled the restrictions on gay life outside London, limited to the bars of better hotels in Bolton and Manchester. This life, he said, 'served to reinforce the prevailing misconception that homosexuality was something alien to the working class'. Fear of persecution was deep and justified. Horsfall remembered that the licensee of the Union Hotel in Manchester was imprisoned for a year for simply allowing homosexuals to use the hotel bar.[3] But this did not diminish Horsfall's determination to pursue the cause of homosexual rights. Encouraged by the publication of the 1957 Wolfenden Report, in 1960 he put down a motion in his local Labour Party supporting its implementation, with the longer-term aim of getting such a motion to the party's national conference. His initiative prompted a mixture of outrage and obstruction. Myriad excuses were made for not discussing the issue. Horsfall later joked that the only argument not used was that homosexuality would scare away new industry. What particularly depressed Horsfall was how closeted Labour members were, not just with respect to homosexuality, but to any discussion of sex:

> It soon became clear that sex, if it exists at all for these people, exists apart from life—something to be found in the jungle or the rabbit hutch or the farmyard but never, never, perish the thought in the lives of all the decent, respectable hard-working people who send us back to the Town Hall each year.[4]

The treatment of the issue by his local party also confused him. One Labour comrade denied that homosexuality was a political issue: 'I asked him how the individual conscience was to make itself felt, in a matter of legislation, except through political action.'[5]

The present book is an examination of the ambiguous but rich relationship between sexuality and socialist politics between the 1880s and the present day, the uneven landscape on which Ivy Roche, Elizabeth Oakes, and Allan Horsfall found themselves. It explores the intersection of political ideology, party politics, and sexual issues. This is intended not only as a contribution to the political history of sexuality in the twentieth century, but also as a study in the tensions between politics and sexual issues. _Sexual Politics_ highlights the dynamic relationship between class, gender, sexuality, and politics over the twentieth century. The political fate of particular issues, such as homosexual rights and abortion law reform, raises broader questions, such as the nature of the divide between public and private, the place of sexual expression in politics, the relationship between feminist and gay activism and politics, the political purchase of ideas of class, gender, and sexual orientation, and,

---

[3] Allan Horsfall, 'Battling for Wolfenden', in Bob Cant and Susan Hemmings (eds), _Radical Records_ (London: Routledge, 1988), 15.

[4] Allan Horsfall, 'Wolfenden in the Wilderness', _New Left Review_ 12 (November–December 1961), 30.

[5] Horsfall, 'Wolfenden in the Wilderness', 30.

not least, how private relations between individuals, whether of love or sex, become political issues.

The present work examines ideas of sexual relations and emancipation (both heterosexual and same-sex), sexual rights (such as homosexual law reform and gay and lesbian rights), and reproductive politics (notably birth control access and abortion law reform) on the British Left between the 1880s and the early twenty-first century. A principal focus of the book is the Labour Party, though other left-wing groups are discussed. The discussion of venereal disease, sex education, and the legal reform of marriage and divorce are not dealt with in the present book, in part because of space, in part because some of these issues were not covered in detail or consistently by the Left.

The history of sexuality in Britain has already attracted considerable historical attention.[6] There has also been valuable work on women, gender, and the Labour Party up to 1939.[7] There are fewer studies of the link between sexuality and party politics over the entire century. While the history of sexuality, socialism, and working-class politics in nineteenth-century Britain has afforded valuable insights, the twentieth century has been less well-served, with the exception of work by Lesley Hall and Sheila Rowbotham on Stella Browne, Anna Marie Smith and Martin Durham on post-1968 Conservatism, Stephen Jeffery-Poulter on homosexual law reform, and Lucy Robinson on the Left and gay politics.[8] Lesley Hoggart's *Feminist Campaigns for Birth Control and Abortion Rights* (2003) is a

---

[6] See Jeffrey Weeks, *Sex, Politics and Society: The Regulation of Sexuality Since 1800* (London: Longman, 1981, 1989); Frank Mort, *Dangerous Sexualities: Medico-Moral Politics in England Since 1830* (London: Routledge, 1987); Lesley Hall, *Sex, Gender and Social Change in Britain Since 1880* (New York: St Martin's, 2000); Barbara Brookes, *Abortion in England 1900–1967* (London: Croom Helm, 1988); Hera Cook, *The Long Sexual Revolution* (Oxford: Oxford University Press, 2004); Kate Fisher, *Birth Control and Marriage in Britain 1918–60* (Oxford: Oxford University Press, 2006); Matt Houlbrook, *Queer London* (Chicago: University of Chicago Press, 2005); Laura Doan, *Fashioning Sapphism: The Origins of Modern English Lesbian Culture* (New York: Columbia University Press, 2001); Rebecca Jennings, *A Lesbian History of Britain: Love and Sex Between Women since 1500* (Oxford: Greenwood, 2007).

[7] See Christine Collette, *For Labour and Women: The Women's Labour League 1906–18* (Manchester: Manchester University Press, 1986); Karen Hunt and June Hannam, *Socialist Women: Britain, 1880s to 1920s* (London: Routledge, 2002); Pamela Graves, *Labour Women: Women in British Working-Class Politics 1918–1939* (Cambridge: Cambridge University Press, 1994); Martin Francis, 'Labour and Gender', in Duncan Tanner, Pat Thane, and Nick Tiratsoo (eds), *Labour's First Century* (Oxford: Oxford University Press, 2000).

[8] For the nineteenth century, see Barbara Taylor, *Eve and the New Jerusalem* (London: Virago, 1983); Anna Clark, *The Struggle for the Breeches* (London: Rivers Oram, 1996); Denise Riley, *'Am I That Name?' Feminism and the Category of 'Women' in History* (Minneapolis: University of Minnesota Press, 1988). For the twentieth century, see Sheila Rowbotham, *A New World For Women: Stella Browne, Socialist Feminist* (London: Pluto, 1977); Lesley Hall, *The Life and Times of Stella Browne, Feminist and Free Spirit* (London: I. B. Tauris, 2011); Lesley Hall, 'No Sex Please, We're Socialists: The British Labour Party Closes Its Eyes and Thinks of the Electorate', in Jesse Battan, Thomas Bouchet, and Tania Regin (eds), *Meetings & Alcoves: The Left and Sexuality in Europe and the United States since 1850* (Dijon: L'Institut d'histoire contemporain, 2004); Lesley Hall, '"I Have Never Met the Normal Woman": Stella Browne and the Politics of Womanhood', *Women's History Review* 6 (1997), 157–82; Anna Marie Smith, *New Right Discourse on Race and Sexuality: Britain, 1968–1990* (Cambridge: Cambridge University Press, 1994); Martin Durham, *Sex and Politics: The Family and Morality in the Thatcher Years* (Houndmills: Macmillan, 1991); Stephen Jeffery-Poulter, *Peers, Queers and Commons* (London: Routledge, 1991); Lucy Robinson, *Gay Men and the Left in Post-War Britain*

compelling examination, but it does not consider reproductive questions in a wider political, social, or cultural context.[9]

Sexual Politics begins in the 1880s, with the work of socialists and sex reformers such as Edward Carpenter, Karl Pearson, and Olive Schreiner. It ends in 2010 after a consideration of the Labour government's legislation on the age of consent, civil partnership, adoption, Section 28, and the time limit on legal abortions. This broad sweep captures the importance of sexual issues to social and intellectual life in Britain in the 'long' twentieth century, whether we think of the law on issues such as abortion and homosexuality or the association between modern subjectivity and sexual identity and behaviour. The 'revival' of socialism in the 1880s also brought with it an interest in sexual reform that the Left never shrugged off over the next hundred years or more.

This book is structured around several themes. The first is the strong relationship between sexual radicalism and socialism from the late nineteenth century to the early twenty-first century. The book begins with a discussion of the way that socialist writers in the late nineteenth century linked the remaking of sexuality with the remaking of society along socialist lines. Such threads were picked up in the early twentieth century by socialist-feminists such as Stella Browne, Dora Russell, and Naomi Mitchison. The flowering of second wave feminism, gay liberation, and post-1968 left-wing radicalism afforded another glimpse of this tradition. Socialism provided a framework for thinking about radical sexual reform and, in turn, sexual reform generated ideas of radical political change.

A strong relationship between Left politics and sexuality can also be discerned from something more quotidian, but just as profound: the amelioration of the conditions of working-class life through reproductive control. If birth control advocacy had nineteenth-century roots in Malthusianism, eugenics, and sexology, legislative change in the mid-twentieth century has been presented as primarily the fruit of either feminist efforts or effective pressure group politics.[10] This book argues, however, that a mainspring of political action on birth control in the twentieth century was the perception and experience of working-class family life. At critical points, the politics of birth control and abortion were a form of working-class politics. The apprehension of class differences in access to both birth control and legal abortion animated the work of birth control advocates and helped place their advocacy within the context of working-class and Labour politics. The impulse to widen birth control access may have had its roots in Malthusianism, eugenics, and sexology, but it became about the empowerment of working-class women and men and the protection of working-class families. Without rejecting

(Manchester: Manchester University Press, 2007); see also David M. Rayside, 'Homophobia, Class and Party in England', *Canadian Journal of Political Science* 25 (1992), 121–49.

[9] Lesley Hoggart, *Feminist Campaigns for Birth Control and Abortion Rights in Britain* (Lampeter: Edwin Mellen, 2003).

[10] See Hoggart, *Feminist Campaigns for Birth Control and Abortion*; Keith Hindell and Madeleine Simms, *Abortion Law Reformed* (London: Peter Owen, 1971).

the feminist contribution to the history of reproductive politics, *Sexual Politics* situates campaigns for birth control access and abortion law reform more firmly within the context of class politics. This is traced through accounts of particular organizations, such as the Workers Birth Control Group (WBCG), the Fabian Women's Group (FWG), the Women's Cooperative Guild (WCG), the National Abortion Campaign (NAC), the Labour Abortion Rights Campaign (LARC), the Abortion Law Reform Association (ALRA), and the EMWWA, and in the stories of individuals whose work encompassed both socialist or working-class politics and reproductive politics, such as Stella Browne, Lena Jeger, Janet Chance, Kenneth Robinson, Dora Russell, Douglas Houghton, Dorothy Thurtle, and Jo Richardson.

The third theme of the book concerns sexual rights, in particular, rights of sexual expression and orientation. *Sexual Politics* examines the treatment of homosexual rights by socialist thinkers and activists from Edward Carpenter to the gay rights movement of the late twentieth and early twenty-first centuries. The place of rights of sexual expression and orientation in left-wing politics is explored through individuals like Allan Horsfall, Maureen Colquhoun, Bob Crossman, and Peter Tatchell, the campaigns for gay rights within the Labour Party of the 1980s and 1990s, the relationship between Labour and gay rights organizations such as Stonewall, and the treatment of issues such as age of consent, civil partnership, and Section 28 in the early twenty-first century.

To get at these themes, *Sexual Politics* deals with a series of individuals and organizations. But the book has an institution at its centre, the Labour Party, which has been the focal point of socialist and working-class politics since 1918. *Sexual Politics* argues that Labour and sexual reform have had an exceptional and rich, if ambiguous, connection over this period.

This can be seen in a number of ways. First, the politics of sex reform and the politics of the Left have long formed overlapping circles.[11] Many sex reformers and organizations dedicated to dealing with birth control and abortion worked either directly within socialist and left-wing parties such as Labour or indirectly within the ambit of socialism and working-class politics. In the nineteenth century, for example, many of those pursuing the new 'science' of sexology and advocates of birth control, whether from a Malthusian or eugenicist perspective, were also committed socialists.[12] In the 1920s, the WBCG campaigned exclusively within the Labour Party to widen access to contraceptive knowledge. The World League for Sexual Reform (WLSR) was replete with socialist figures. While professing to be 'strictly non-party', the ALRA's strength partly rested on affiliations to Labour

---

[11] A point also clear in wider European socialist politics. See, for example, Gert Hekma (ed.), *Past and Present of Radical Sexual Politics* (Amsterdam: Mosse Foundation, 2004).

[12] See, for example, Sheila Rowbotham and Jeffrey Weeks, *Socialism and the New Life: The Personal and Sexual Politics of Edward Carpenter and Havelock Ellis* (London: Pluto, 1977); Chushichi Tsuzuki, *Edward Carpenter, 1844–1929: Prophet of Human Fellowship* (Cambridge: Cambridge University Press, 1980); Taylor, *Eve and the New Jerusalem*; Chris Nottingham, *The Pursuit of Serenity: Havelock Ellis and the New Politics* (Amsterdam: Amsterdam University Press, 1999); Sheila Rowbotham, *Edward Carpenter: A Life of Liberty and Love* (London: Verso, 2008).

women's sections and local WCGs; there was no such relationship with the Liberal or Conservative parties.[13]

If we look at reproductive politics, there was also considerable discussion of sexual issues within the Labour Party, through formally affiliated organizations such as Labour's women's sections, the WCG, the Fabian Society and the Trades Union Congress (TUC), and the work of groups orbiting within the sphere of Labour politics such as the WBCG and ALRA and, later in the century, the NAC, LARC, and the anti-abortion organization, the Labour Life Group.[14] Whether informally or formally, birth control and abortion thus had a place within Labour politics between the 1920s and the 1970s to a degree that is not true of other major parties such as the Conservatives.[15]

Turning to homosexual rights, the work of Edward Carpenter in the late nineteenth century and Allan Horsfall with the North Western Homosexual Reform Committee (NWHRC) in the 1960s are but two illustrations nearly a century apart of how socialism and working-class politics offered one avenue along which the debate over homosexual identity and rights developed. From the 1970s to the early twenty-first century, the Labour Party further proved a sphere for the discussion of issues like gay rights, through figures such as Ken Livingstone and Peter Tatchell and organizations like the Labour Campaign for Lesbian and Gay Rights (LCLGR).

There were, as well, particular moments when Labour politics played a pivotal role in the unfolding of sexual reform in Britain. This includes the WBCG campaign of the 1920s, the intervention of Labour parliamentarians such as Kenneth Robinson, Douglas Houghton, and Lena Jeger in the abortion issue in the 1950s and early 1960s, Robinson and Leo Abse's support for homosexual law reform in the same period, the critical part played in 1967 by the Labour government in facilitating the passage of the Abortion Act, the Sexual Offences Act, the National Health Service (Family Planning) Act, the campaigns (often led by socialist or Labour women) to defend the Abortion Act in the 1970s, Livingstone's Greater London Council (GLC), and the legislative achievements of Labour governments between 1997 and 2010.

Finally, both the discussion of sexual reform and the discussion of socialism over the past hundred years have moved within a similar discursive universe. Ideas of

---

[13] Contemporary Medical Archives, Wellcome Institute, London [CMA], ALRA Papers, SA/ALR/ A.3/6/34, Alice Jenkins to Kathleen Child, 13 May 1957.

[14] See Joni Lovenduski, 'Parliament, Pressure groups, Networks and the Women's Movement: The Politics of Abortion Law Reform in Britain 1967–83', in Joni Lovenduski and Joyce Outshoorn, (eds), *The New Politics of Abortion* (London: Sage, 1986).

[15] The history of women within the Conservative party suggests that birth control was not an issue given much attention by the Conservative women's sections or the party more generally. See Joni Lovenduski, Pippa Norris, and Catriona Burness, 'The Party and Women', in Anthony Seldon and Stuart Ball (eds), *Conservative Century* (Oxford: Oxford University Press, 1994); G.E. Maguire, *Conservative Women: A History of Women and the Conservative Party 1874–1997* (London: Palgrave Macmillan, 1998). In the 1960s, though there was some sympathy for eugenicist arguments for birth control, the Conservatives remained largely hostile to feminist advocacy of abortion. See CMA, BCC, SA/BCC/C.16, Birth Control Campaign correspondence with the Conservative Party.

personal emancipation, the amelioration of material existence (particularly for working-class people), equality, empowerment, community, and fellowship infused arguments for socialism and arguments for sex reform. In specific instances, socialism often provided a language for talking about sex; sex reform similarly afforded a new landscape for thinking about political action. For all these reasons, the development of sexual politics in Britain during the twentieth century often intersected with the particular political context of the Labour Party. This is not to deny the importance of non-party pressure groups, such as the Family Planning Association (FPA) or the Homosexual Law Reform Society (HLRS); it is, however, to assert and explore the link between sexual issues and partisan politics and ideology.[16]

A pattern of tension was nonetheless embedded in this connection. In the 1970s and 1980s, there were a series of commitments made by the Labour Party to sexual reform, including the adoption of free and legal abortion on request as party policy in 1975 and 1977 and a comprehensive programme of gay and lesbian rights in 1985. But the road to these commitments was winding and the road from them continues to be uneven and sometimes circular. Between the 1910s and the 1970s, for example, despite a number of interventions, the party leadership consistently resisted the formal discussion of abortion and birth control as party policy. In 1925, the question of birth control was deemed 'not one which should be made a political Party issue'.[17] Half a century later and barely two years before the passing of both the 1967 Abortion Act and the National Health Service (Family Planning) Act, Labour's women's organization refused to circulate pamphlets advocating abortion law reform because it was not party policy.[18] Even after the conference commitment to gay rights in 1985, a senior party adviser worried that '[t]he gays and lesbians issue is costing us dear'.[19]

Several themes emerge from a study of the relationship between sexual politics and Labour politics which touch upon important questions in the political and social history of twentieth-century Britain, such as the relationship between feminism and socialist politics, the link between gender and political parties and ideology, and the space of politics in the twentieth century.[20] One of the

---

[16] On the contribution of the first to the family planning movement, see Audrey Leathard, *The Fight for Family Planning* (London: Macmillan, 1980).

[17] *Labour Party Conference Report [LPCR]* (1925), 44.

[18] Labour Party Archives, People's Museum, Manchester [LPA], National Labour Women's Advisory Committee [NLWAC]/M/71/12/65, NLWAC, Minutes, 2 December 1965.

[19] Colin Hughes and Patrick Wintour, *Labour Rebuilt: The New Model Party* (London: Fourth Estate, 1990), 19; see also Richard Heffernan and Mike Marqusee, *Defeat from the Jaws of Victory* (London: Verso, 1992), 170–1.

[20] For the larger European context of the relationship among socialism, social democracy, and feminism, see Helmut Gruber and Pamela Graves, (eds), *Women and Socialism/Socialism and Women* (New York: Berghahn, 1998); Geoff Eley, *Forging Democracy* (New York: Oxford University Press, 2002). On gender and Labour, see Pat Thane, 'Visions of Gender in the Making of the British Welfare State: The case of Women in the British Labour Party and Social Policy', in Gisela Bock and Pat Thane (eds), *Maternity and Gender Policies: Women and the Rise of the European Welfare States 1880s–1950s* (London: Routledge, 1991); Amy Black and Stephen Brooke, 'The Labour Party, Women and the Problem of Gender, 1951–66', *Journal of British Studies* 36 (1997), 419–52; Francis, 'Labour

most important of these concerns class and sexual politics. At critical points in the early twentieth century, the sexual politics of birth control and abortion advocacy was a form of working-class politics. What moved people to political agency on birth control and abortion was the consciousness that heterosexual experience was shaped by class position. When asking for legal abortion or greater access to contraceptive advice, working-class women recognized not only the particular material contours of working-class life (determined by poor housing, unstable employment patterns, and bad nutrition) but also the sense of difference between their sexual lives and the lives of middle-class women, for whom contraception was not only available but affordable, for whom the law on abortion was made more pliable with money and easier access to the medical profession. The class identity of working-class women was, in this way, as framed by sexuality as it was by the economy or education. Talking about reproduction was talking about class as much as it was talking about gender. Indeed, sex was a way of talking about class, a means of constituting class identity and drawing lines of class difference. Mike Savage has suggested that the alleviation of working-class economic insecurity lay at the root of formal and informal working-class politics.[21] This was also true of the demands for birth control and abortion. The pursuit of sexual politics in the 1920s and 1930s followed a familiar pattern in working-class politics, through the formation of grassroots, if transient, collective organizations, such as the EMWWA, or the use of existing working-class organizations such as the WCG, the TUC, and the Labour Party.

This underlines the relevance of class as a category in twentieth-century British politics. In 1990, Michael Freeden remarked that ideology was the 'stranger at the feast' of twentieth-century British history.[22] Twenty years later, it is class that has become the stranger at the feast, cast into the shadows by greater interest in cultural and imperial history. Despite much talk of the 'new political history', engaging with class still proves difficult for political historians. Recent work by Mike Savage, Selina Todd, and Matt Houlbrook has done a great deal to reopen our interrogation of class in important ways.[23] The present book argues that it can be through sexuality that we understand the place of class more fully and through class that sexuality can be understood more clearly. The history of sexual politics in the twentieth century is, until relatively recently—the 1970s—at least partially a narrative about the working classes. In this picture, an understanding of class was

and Gender'; Karen Hunt, 'Fractured Universality: The Language of British Socialism before the First World War', in John Belchem and Neville Kirk (eds), *Languages of Labour* (London: Ashgate, 1997).

[21] Mike Savage, *The Dynamics of Working-Class Politics: The Labour Movement in Preston 1880–1940* (Cambridge: Cambridge University Press, 1987), 15.

[22] Michael Freeden, 'The Stranger at the Feast: Ideology and Public Policy in Twentieth-Century Britain', *Twentieth Century British History* 1 (1990), 9–34.

[23] Selina Todd, 'Affluence, Class and Crown Street: Reinvestigating the Post-War Working Class', *Contemporary British History* 22 (2008), 501–18; Mike Savage, 'Affluence and Social Change in the Making of Technocratic Middle-Class Identities: Britain, 1939–55', *Contemporary British History* 22 (2008), 457–76; Mike Savage, *Identities and Social Change in Britain since 1940: The Politics of Method* (Oxford: Oxford University Press, 2010); Houlbrook, *Queer London*.

built from the experience of reproduction and shaped by language. Class was a dynamic category, but remained a point of reference in social identity and in political campaigns well into the late twentieth century.

If class was an animating force in sexual politics at least until the late 1960s, changing understandings of gender were also critical in shaping the political treatment of sexual questions. Between the 1910s and the 1960s, two gendered protagonists were particularly important to reproductive politics: the working-class mother and the breadwinner male. In the first half of the century, reproductive politics was a form of maternalist politics, aimed at empowering women in their roles as mothers, even if, ironically, this meant limiting that role through birth control. This was not an explicit argument for women's rights but rather an acknowledgement of the failure of the breadwinner male to sustain the family. Maternalism could be both an engine of radical, rather than reactionary, political and social change and a means of addressing the day-to-day needs of working-class people.[24] Pat Thane has suggested that the focus upon the home and motherhood in Labour women's politics was an attempt to 'provide the base for the liberation of women rather than their insuperable bondage'; this book explores in detail how that worked in sexual politics.[25] The women of the EMWWA spoke, for example, not of women simply as reproductive vessels, but rather as workers, as contributors to the household economy and as protectors of the home, in other words, in a variety of roles. Sexual autonomy, sexual control, and motherhood were not competing or contradictory qualities, but complementary ones. This served as the foundation of the EMWWA's argument for the legalization of abortion and challenged a more reductive view of femininity and motherhood. In a quiet way, it also revised the meanings of working-class motherhood, domesticity, and sexuality from within, rather than without the context of the working-class family. One of the underlying arguments of this book is that political change often emerged from within the terms of existing ideologies and structures; it was a consequence of the ambiguities and inadequacies of gender ideology and a testament to the distance between such ideology and experience, the unwinding and remaking of language about motherhood, gender, class, and sexuality.

In the struggle within socialism and within working-class movements over reproductive issues before the 1970s, Labour men and women found agency, collectively and as individuals, in debating the meaning of particular words or concepts such as 'motherhood'. In the 1920s, for instance, the campaign for wider access to birth control launched by the WBCG not only used the figure of the beleaguered working-class mother to win empathy and support for its cause, but its arguments also helped to produce a different kind of figure, an empowered mother-citizen, whose claim on politics was not simply about state allowances, but sexuality.

---

[24] See Jean Quataert, 'Socialisms, Feminisms, and Agency: A Long View', *Journal of Modern History* 73 (2001), 613.

[25] Pat Thane, 'The Women of the British Labour Party and Feminism, 1906–1945', in Harold L. Smith (ed.), *British Feminism in the Twentieth Century* (Amherst, MA: University of Massachusetts Press), 129.

The persistence of the relationship between class, maternity, and reproductive politics on the Left can be seen well into the 1970s and 1980s, when debates over the defence of the Abortion Act were often couched in the defence of the position of working-class women who would not have had the same access as middle-class women to reproductive control without the reforms of 1967. However, in the 1950s and 1960s, we can see the beginning of a change in the language guiding advocacy of birth control and abortion law reform. Increasingly, a new protagonist emerged, a more sexually autonomous woman, whose marital or family status was not fixed. This book argues that in the late twentieth century a different form of sexual politics developed, which had, at its heart, not class, the family, or marriage, but the individual. This also had an important effect on the development of gay and lesbian rights because the dominance of the family and maternity in the consideration of sexual issues left little discursive room for the consideration of gay and lesbian rights. This was not, however, a linear or smooth change; rather, it was uneven and sometimes partial, appearing only with great clarity in the late 1970s and 1980s.

In the 1970s, second wave socialist-feminists entirely rejected what they called the 'bourgeois family relationship'.[26] Instead, abortion and birth control were perceived as securing a liberated femininity detached from the family and motherhood. Access to legal and free abortion guaranteed individual sexual fulfilment. 'The fight for abortion', wrote three socialist-feminists in 1978, 'is primarily a fight for sexual freedom'; it afforded the 'right to express our sexuality freely'.[27] Class issues were not completely abandoned: one particular concern was working-class women's access to therapeutic abortion. But socialist-feminists in the 1970s did turn away from the idea that abortion could preserve the working-class family; instead, they looked to transform or reject the family by freeing up women's sexuality, again, through abortion. It was about the emancipation of women as individuals first. In the 1960s, Sheila Rowbotham has recalled, she was 'driven by a longing for a sexuality which was not about possession or being possessed, for forms of relating and loving I could hardly express or even imagine', to which abortion and birth control were critical.[28] In this way, a new kind of femininity was articulated through sexual politics, more clearly rooted in an argument for equal rights for women, unmoored from the context of motherhood and family.

Similar currents can be seen in the intersection between campaigns for homosexual equality on the Left. In the late nineteenth century, Edward Carpenter made homosexual emancipation a key to social and political transformation. But this vision paled in the first decades of the twentieth century. Even for the most advanced socialists, the cause of homosexual rights was a difficult language to speak. In the 1950s, a gradual route to reform was opened up by the Wolfenden Report. At the same time, Labour intellectuals accepted that homosexual law

---

[26] 'For a Socialist Position on Abortion', *Socialist Woman* (May–June 1973), 8.
[27] Angela Phillips, Dorothy Jones, and Pat Kahn, 'Abortion, Feminism and Sexuality—a Long, Hard Look at the NAC', *Socialist Woman* 6/3 (Spring 1978), 8.
[28] Sheila Rowbotham, *Promise of a Dream: Remembering the Sixties* (London: Penguin, 2000), 160.

reform might be one of the next steps towards a more progressive and civilized Britain. This was in no way homosexual emancipation. As Matt Houlbrook and others have suggested, the decriminalization of some aspects of homosexuality in 1967 depended upon the construction of a particular kind of respectable homosexual. But, again, there was an intersection between Labour politics and sexual reform in that this was in accord with a particular socialist vision of social change. Just as the working-class mother might be seen as a protagonist within a particular, familiar context, the respectable homosexual was situated within the ambit of acceptable social liberalism. In the 1970s and 1980s, this changed. Both women's liberation and gay liberation placed far greater emphasis on individual emancipation and sexual autonomy and were rooted in attacks upon the family and traditional sexual categorizations.

Highlighting this shift towards individual rights shaping debates on homosexuality and reproductive control in the 1970s and 1980s qualifies two particular ways of periodizing postwar Britain. In the first case, the present book argues that the growth of what has been called the permissive society lies well before the 1960s, less in terms of individual sexual freedom than in the way that the links between family, gender, and sexuality were being worked out in the 1940s and 1950s.[29] This was not a revolution from without, but from within. That being said, the full impact of changes in postwar sexual mores needs to be located in the 1970s and 1980s rather than only in the 1960s. The present book examines the roads to and from the epochal moment of 1967, but it argues that it is those roads that are perhaps ultimately more important than the moment itself. Secondly, it has been suggested that the immediate postwar period was characterized by a greater emphasis on the 'self'.[30] This book suggests a more uneven and delayed periodization to this change. In terms of the political treatment of sexual issues, this emphasis upon the self did not appear until relatively late, the 1970s and 1980s, largely through women's and gay liberation. Before that, categories such as class and family remained important reference points in sexual politics.

The challenges of the 1970s and 1980s were also about the nature of left-wing politics. Women's liberation and gay liberation also claimed new spaces and methods of Left activism, outside the more traditional precincts of more traditional lobbying organizations.[31] For the first time, for example, the street became a forum for sexual politics in Britain. In the late 1980s, particularly through experiments like Ken Livingstone's GLC, we can see a conflict between old and new styles of left-wing politics particularly over the issue of gay and lesbian rights. Thus, once again, sexual politics became a way of understanding socialist politics.

Ironically, the movements that placed greater emphasis upon a new form and space of Left politics, such as women's liberation and gay and lesbian rights,

---

[29] On this, see also Frank Mort, *Capital Affairs* (London: Yale University Press, 2010).

[30] See Anthony Giddens, *The Transformation of Intimacy* (Stanford: Stanford University Press, 1992); Becky Conekin, Frank Mort, and Chris Waters (eds), *Moments of Modernity* (London: Rivers Oram, 1999).

[31] See Eley, *Forging Democracy*.

ultimately found their way to the centre. Despite the exploration of new forms and spaces of politics, parliament remained the focal point of sexual politics in the late twentieth and early twenty-first centuries. This was largely because sexual politics continued to be shaped by parliamentary legislation, whether this was about the defence of the Abortion Act or the campaign against Section 28. The new politics needed the old politics. What was so interesting was the interplay between the two. And, ironically, if we look at gay and lesbian politics, the achievement of legislative reform towards equality depended not upon the leftward movement of the Labour Party but rather its rightward move in the shape of New Labour. It was the modernization of the Labour Party after 1987 that accommodated many of the precepts of gay and lesbian equality, largely because of the relationship between the idea of individual rights and the hope for a progressive response to Thatcherism. Thus, the achievement of legislative reform in the early twenty-first century was hardly the realization of utopia, but rather the transformation of the political centre. This was not without substance. In this, language was once again important. Concepts of 'family', 'parent', and 'marriage' all changed in the twenty-first century.

The story of sexual politics since the 1880s is, thus, in some ways a story about socialist and working-class politics, moving through discussions of utopia, the experience of working-class life, and community to ideas of individual rights. What remained constant was the importance of politics. Throughout this period, sexual change had to be achieved politically. Returning to Oakes, Roche, and Horsfall, we see not simply a sense of frustration, but an imperative, that, as Horsfall said, the individual conscience *had* to be expressed politically, or, for Oakes and Roche, the concerns of working-class women *had* to be articulated politically, in whatever form was possible. The personal was not simply political; it was *forced* to be political.

Before setting out the structure of the book, it is important to establish particular empirical frameworks. The first is demographic. In the twentieth century, the reproduction rate declined significantly. It reached its lowest point in the 1930s, moved up again to the levels of 1900 by the early 1960s, then again fell in a sharp fashion, so that by the 1970s, the reproduction rate in Britain was approaching the levels of the 1930s.[32] For contemporaries at the midpoint of the century, the most striking aspect of this change was the fall in working-class fertility. In 1949, the Royal Commission on Population argued that the working-class birth rate had declined from 3.94 children for all marriages made between 1900 and 1909 to 2.49 children for those who married between 1925 and 1929.[33] The Royal Commission also believed that the deliberate use of birth control was the cause of fertility decline. Men and women were achieving within the private sphere what they were asking for in the public sphere—the control of reproduction—even if, as Kate Fisher has recently argued, this was not always a rational or deliberate path.[34]

[32] See Cook, *The Long Sexual Revolution*, 15.

[33] Cmd. 7695, *Royal Commission on Population* (London: HMSO, July, 1949), 29, 34.

[34] See Fisher, *Birth Control and Marriage in Britain*.

It is also important to set out the legal and political framework shaping sexuality. Until 1967, the practice of abortion was governed by the 1861 Offences Against the Person Act (which made it illegal to procure an abortion under any circumstances), and the Infant Life (Preservation) Act of 1929, which allowed medically administered abortion 'for the purpose only of preserving the life of the mother', with the definition of 'life' usually excluding social or psychological considerations.[35] Between the 1930s and the 1960s, the practice of abortion was also affected by case law, in particular, *Rex v. Bourne* in 1938 which established that there might be non-physiological reasons accepted for a legal, therapeutic abortion. The legal and political framework guiding access to knowledge about birth control and birth control appliances (and later the Pill) is perhaps less spectacular than that of abortion, but no less important. In the late 1870s, the birth control advocates Annie Besant and Charles Bradlaugh had to fight in court to publish birth control information. This kind of case was less common as the twentieth century went on, but we should not forget that in 1923, just as birth control clinics were being established in urban areas in Britain, two socialists, Rose Witcop and Guy Aldred, were charged and found guilty of distributing what was considered an 'obscene' pamphlet, Margaret Sanger's *Family Limitation*.[36] More than thirty years later, the National Health Service (Family Planning) Act of 1967 encouraged local authorities to improve access to birth control information without reference to marital status and age; in 1974, the Department of Health and Social Services allowed doctors to prescribe the Pill to girls under 16.

Homosexuality remained illegal until 1967. Buggery had long been a capital offence, but in 1861 this was changed to a prison sentence. The 1885 Labouchère Amendment made other forms of homosexual activity illegal. Lesbianism was not illegal, despite an attempt in the 1920s, but, as shall be noted, the expression of lesbianism began to attract more legal attention in the interwar period. The legal ability to have sex was determined by age of consent laws, passed in 1885, then amended, most recently in 2003.

The present book is structured in three sections. After an introductory chapter discussing the origins of the relationship between sexual reform and socialism in the late nineteenth century, section 1 looks at the discussion of birth control and sexual emancipation between the two world wars. Chapter 2 examines the struggle over the issue of birth control information in the 1920s in the Labour Party; Chapter 3 explores utopian ideas of sexual and socialist reform through two writers, Dora Russell and Naomi Mitchison; Chapter 4 looks at the politics of abortion law reform in the 1930s, particularly as they touched upon the Labour Party and working-class women. Section 2 examines the different roads towards the major legislative reforms of 1967 on abortion, sexual offences, and family planning, all of which altered the law on reproductive control and homosexuality. Chapter 5 argues that on the Left and within the framework of working-class life, the 1940s and 1950s were critical decades in the rethinking of questions such as family,

---

[35] *The Infant Life (Preservation) Act* (19 and 20 George 5, c. 34), Section 1, Subsection 1.
[36] See *The Times*, 11 January and 10 February 1923.

femininity, and reproduction. Chapter 6 examines the Abortion Act, the Sexual Offences Act, and the Family Planning Act passed during the Labour government of 1966–70. The final section of the book is entitled 'Roads from 1967'. It argues that though there were disparate paths away from the reforms of that year, which suggested new ideologies and new forms of Left politics through women's liberation and gay liberation, the discussion of sexual reform was still bounded by the terms of the settlement in 1967 and tightly linked to the Labour Party. These chapters—on the defence of the Abortion Act and the gay and lesbian rights movement—also suggest that the focus of sexual politics nonetheless also changed substantially, from the family and class to the individual. As already suggested, the protagonists of these debates were new and unfamiliar: sexually liberated and autonomous men and women. The concluding chapter looks at the reforms enacted by the Labour governments of 1997–2010 and suggests that this programme was situated in a newer sense of individual rights.

1

Beginnings
Socialism and Sexual Reform, 1880s to 1920s

The relationship between socialism and sexual reform was mapped in important ways from the 1880s to the early 1920s by figures such as Edward Carpenter and Stella Browne and organizations such as the FWG and the WCG. The promotion of the sexual emancipation of women and homosexuals, a commitment to the amelioration of the position of the working-class woman and the working-class family, and the belief that the reform of sexuality was firmly linked to the reform of politics were important aspects of this interest. The present chapter explores these links as well as considering how the gendered development of the political Left in Britain, and, in particular, the fledgling Labour Party, disciplined the way sexual issues were approached by socialist and working-class organizations.

Socialism emerged in Britain in the early nineteenth century hand in hand with ideas of sexual reform. Robert Owen and his followers envisioned a utopia built upon sweeping social, economic, and political change, in which conflict would be replaced by cooperation, rapacious individualism by harmonious community, and inequity by equality. Love, including sexual love, was to be the lifeblood of this new world. As one Owenite proclaimed in 1845: 'the love of human kind at large finds its highest expression, and is ... brought to focus in the free and unthwarted union of individuals of different sexes'.[1]

The liberated and equal sexual union of individuals was to be a catalyst of social transformation: the world would be remade in the private sphere as much as in the marketplace and the workshop. Economies of sex were connected to economies of work, class oppression was related to sex oppression, and principles guiding economic and social life in the new world would also guide private life. Dismantling traditional marriage might give heterosexual men and women freedom and equality. These reforms would bring emancipation and fulfilment in both private and public worlds. For Owen, it promised a return to a 'natural' state uncorrupted by private property and capitalism.[2] Owenites promoted contraception as a means of separating reproduction from sexuality, thus giving women the same sexual freedom as men. The inheritors of this tradition in the mid-nineteenth century included the free love advocate James Hinton.[3]

---

[1] Taylor, *Eve and the New Jerusalem*, 44–5.   [2] See Taylor, *Eve and the New Jerusalem*, 41.
[3] For a discussion of Hinton, see Seth Koven, *Slumming* (Princeton: Princeton University Press, 2004).

But the apparently brilliant promise of this new sexual life failed to gain wide purchase among some of those it sought to liberate, notably working-class women, because, as Barbara Taylor has argued, it was blind to the particular social and economic context of working-class life in the early nineteenth century. In this we can see one of the tensions running through the relationship between sexuality and socialism over the last two centuries, between the utopian and the everyday, the transformative and the ameliorative. Whatever was imagined in Owenite thought, women's lack of reproductive control remained a fact of day-to-day material existence.[4] Arguments for birth control also met antipathy because they were associated with a punitive and constrictive Malthusianism directed at the working classes.

The resurgence of socialism in the late nineteenth century was accompanied by a renewed interest in the links between socialist reform and sexual reform. This must be seen within the context of a broader Victorian debate about sex and gender. The perception of male sexuality and male power was crucial. The Criminal Law Amendment Act of 1885, which, among other things, raised the age of consent for girls to sixteen, was the legislative result of campaigns against predatory male sexuality.[5] Male homosexuality also attracted considerable attention. Though the death penalty for buggery was dropped in 1861, it remained an offence punishable by a prison sentence. Laws against other kinds of homosexual acts were formalized in the 1885 Labouchère amendment.[6] With the prosecution of Ernest Boulton and Frederick Park, the investigation into male prostitution in Cleveland Street in 1889, and, most famously, the trial and conviction of Oscar Wilde in 1895, homosexuality became a publicly defined sexual deviance.[7]

The position of women also changed in this period. The enfranchisement of some working-class men in 1867 raised the question of female enfranchisement. Other legislation, such as the Matrimonial Causes Act and the Married Women's Property Acts, also provoked questions about women's position in the public sphere. The 'woman question' became an important social question, as well, symbolized by the noisy arrival of the 'New Woman', distinguished from her forebears by greater educational opportunities, independence, and autonomy.

The 'woman question' and the debate over male sexuality broke down the silences around sexual life. This was signalled by public events, such as the 'Maiden Tribute' campaign, the 1877 trial of Charles Bradlaugh and Annie Besant on grounds of obscenity for publishing a birth control tract, and the trial of Oscar Wilde in 1895. The subject of sex was also flattered by growing intellectual interest in the late nineteenth century. The writing of George Drysdale and James Hinton and the pioneering work of European sexologists like Magnus Hirschfeld circulated

---

[4] See Taylor, *Eve and the New Jerusalem*; Clark, *The Struggle for the Breeches*, Chapter 4.

[5] See Judith Walkowitz, *City of Dreadful Delight* (Chicago: University of Chicago Press, 1992).

[6] See H.G. Cocks, *Nameless Offences: Homosexual Desire in the Nineteenth Century* (London: I.B. Tauris, 2003).

[7] See Morris B. Kaplan, *Sodom on the Thames: Sex, Love and Scandal in Wilde Times* (Ithaca: Cornell University Press, 2005); Matt Cook, *London and the Culture of Homosexuality, 1885–1914* (Cambridge: Cambridge University Press, 2003).

among younger intellectuals interested in developing a 'science' of sex. One of these, Havelock Ellis, began to publish his monumental work, *Studies in the Psychology of Sex* before the First World War.

Looking back from the 1930s, Ellis noted, '[w]e were in those days eager young Socialists . . . and cheerfully faced the desirability of putting society on a new foundation at one stroke, whether or not of a revolutionary nature'.[8] For many late Victorian and Edwardian intellectuals and writers, an interest in understanding and reforming sex fell in step with a belief in socialism. There emerged at the end of the nineteenth century a younger generation in revolt against both the excesses of capitalism and the rigidity of bourgeois society.[9]

Looking at the relationship between socialism and sex at this time, it is clear that one of those intersections was a common language, animated by ideas of evolution, revolution and liberation. The socialist revival of the late nineteenth century was roughly clustered around three ideological strands: Marxism (particularly through the Social Democratic Federation (SDF)); gradualist Fabian socialism developed by Sidney Webb and others; and the ethical socialism represented by a variety of writers and organizations, from Robert Blatchford and William Morris to the Clarion Clubs and the Independent Labour Party (ILP). The discourse of science and evolution was particularly powerful in the ideology of the SDF and the Fabians. The 'scientific' socialists, whether Marxist or Fabian, considered that socialism was the ideology of either revolution or rational evolution. Evolution was a particularly important concept for Fabian socialists. Society was perceived as a comprehensible organism, capable of evolving through rational social reform initiated by the state. 'Evolution', wrote Sidney Webb in *Fabian Essays in Socialism* (1889), 'is the substitution of consciously regulated co-ordination among the units of each organism, for blind anarchic competition.'[10]

Fabians often spoke of the 'inevitability of gradualness', the confidence that socialism would triumph. The same confidence guided ethical socialism. Keir Hardie, the founder of the Independent Labour Party and a leading voice of ethical socialism, asserted that it was 'self-evident . . . that our present industrial system is nearing its end'.[11] The utopia following the demise of capitalism would be built upon equality, fellowship and the elevation of labour. Ethical socialism promised a new life and a new world, in which all aspects of human society and human relations would be revolutionized.[12] This had a material, even sensual, aspect. For William Morris, for example, the body was a vessel of social well-being. In an essay from 1888, he put 'a healthy body' as the first of socialism's aims. Expounding on

---

[8] Havelock Ellis, *Questions of Our Day* (London: Bodley Head, 1936), 63; quoted in Nottingham, *The Pursuit of Serenity*, 81.

[9] See Nottingham, *The Pursuit of Serenity*, 136.

[10] Sidney Webb, 'Historic', in George Bernard Shaw (ed.), *Fabian Essays in Socialism* (London: Walter Scott, 1889), 60.

[11] Quoted in Stephen Yeo, 'A New Life: The Religion of Socialism in Britain, 1883–1896', *History Workshop Journal* 4 (1977), 22.

[12] Yeo, 'A New Life', 17.

this, he wound together the sensual and the political, including in his vision of a socialist utopia the ability 'to enjoy the moving of one's limbs and exercising one's bodily powers . . . to rejoice in satisfying the due bodily appetites of a human animal without fear of degradation or sense of wrong-doing: yes, and therewithal to be well-formed, straight-limbed, strongly knit, expressive of countenance—to be, in a word, beautiful.'[13] There was, therefore, a clear link in ethical socialism between the regeneration of the body politic and the regeneration of the material body. The utopia of *News from Nowhere* (1890) was as evident in the beautiful faces and strong bodies of its inhabitants as in the physical pleasantness of their surroundings and the elegant, simple fairness of their social organization. The link between the body and utopian politics echoed earlier Owenite ideology. It also offered a framework for thinking about sexual reform. Both the cold light of science and the warm vision of utopia thus infused late nineteenth-century socialism.

This was also driven by the 'woman question'. Works such as August Bebel's *Woman Under Socialism* (1879) and Frederick Engels' *The Origin of the Family, Private Property and the State* (1884) considered the relationship between sex oppression and class oppression and the nature of the family. Socialist-feminists in the late nineteenth century saw socialism as a means of emancipating women. What was less clear was what such emancipation meant for women. Some saw socialism bringing a better deal within the framework of traditional domesticity. Leading male socialists such as Morris believed that in the socialist utopia, the 'natural' role of women in the home and as mothers would be elevated.[14] Maternalism was also central to the outlook of leading ILP women such as Katherine Bruce Glasier, Enid Stacy, and Margaret MacDonald, who believed in the importance of women's productive work while valorizing motherhood and the home.[15]

I

The work of three particular writers, Edward Carpenter, Karl Pearson, and Olive Schreiner, all of whom were self-professed socialists and intellectuals interested in exploring new ways of thinking about sexuality, illustrates the intersections and tensions among socialism and sexual emancipation in the late nineteenth century. All three linked the liberation of sexuality with a broader vision of socialist change. All saw sexuality as political and all three perceived that a key to political change lay in the radical redefinition of gender and sexuality. Schreiner wrote in 1911, 'on the path toward the higher development of sexual life on earth . . . it is perhaps woman . . . who is bound to lead the way and man to follow'.[16] For Carpenter, just as importantly, it was the emancipation of homosexuality that might be the

[13] William Morris, 'How We Live and How We Might Live', in *News From Nowhere and Selected Writings and Designs* (Harmondsworth: Penguin, 1986), 170–1.
[14] Morris, *News from Nowhere* in Penguin edition, 235.
[15] See Hannam and Hunt, *Socialist Women*, 68–9.
[16] Olive Schreiner, *Woman and Labor* (New York: Frederick Stokes, 1911), 21.

1.1 'Edward Carpenter', photograph by Alfred Mattison, unknown date, copyright National Portrait Gallery, London, x87106

foundation to political transformation; he suggested in *Homogenic Love* (1895), that homosexuality, or what he called 'comrade-union', could be the 'moving force in the body politic'.[17]

Born in 1844, Carpenter pursued an academic career at Cambridge before moving north to Sheffield and becoming involved in adult education and socialist politics. Carpenter worked within groups such as the Fellowship of the New Life, the SDF and the Socialist League, committed, as Sheila Rowbotham has suggested, both to the 'practical recasting of socialism' and a 'transformatory vision of the emancipation of body and spirit'.[18] Carpenter was a homosexual and, in the north, he pursued a series of relationships with working-class men, feeding his desire for 'non-possessive loving companionship'.[19] Carpenter was also interested in exploring the social, political, and intellectual dimensions of sexuality, encouraged by friendships with Havelock Ellis and J.A. Symonds. Where Carpenter may have

[17] Edward Carpenter, *Homogenic Love* (Privately printed, 1894), 47.
[18] Rowbotham, *Edward Carpenter*, 173.
[19] Rowbotham, *Edward Carpenter*, 133.

departed from the developing realm of sexology was in his mysticism and Romanticism influenced by Walt Whitman.[20] He also believed that socialism could be built through sexuality, a conviction he shared with Symonds, who thought that sexual relationships and, in particular, homosexual friendships 'could further "the right sort of Socialism"'.[21]

In 1893 and 1894, Carpenter wrote four pamphlets on sexuality: *Woman and Her Place in a Free Society; Marriage in a Free Society; Sex-love and its Place in a Free Society*; and *Homogenic Love and its Place in a Free Society*. The first three were brought together as *Love's Coming of Age* in 1896, which went through numerous editions by the early twentieth century. Central to the book was a celebration of the body, based upon a more open approach to sexuality. Carpenter wanted to liberate the body and sex from the shame in which both were cloaked. Sex, he argued, was but the 'allegory of love in the physical world', promising both pleasure and spiritual fulfilment.[22] Both could be related to a wider sense of community. The pleasure of the body was the foundation of a regenerated body politic: 'a healthy delight in and cultivation of the body and all its natural functions, and a determination to keep them pure and beautiful, open and sane and free, will have to become a recognized part of national life'.[23] Union was the 'prime object of sex', and sexual union was simply but profoundly a private manifestation of a public good, fellowship.[24] This link between sex and community was suggested in the various editions of his long, mystical prose poem, *Towards Democracy* (1883): 'Him I touch and her I touch, and you I touch . . . I who desired one give myself to all. I who would be the companion of one become the companion of all companions.'[25] The body was, in this way, a vehicle of political change.[26]

The fourth pamphlet Carpenter had written in 1893–4, *Homogenic Love*, had to be privately printed and was not published as part of *Love's Coming of Age*, because its subject matter was homosexuality. The political climate was inimical to this, given the Wilde trial and conviction in 1895. Placing homosexual love and desire in the context of a Classical inheritance allowed Carpenter to suggest, in a critique of heterosexual hegemony, that homosexual passion might offer a different and perhaps higher social function than heterosexual love and reproduction: 'the philosophical connections and ideas which transform our lives and those of society'.[27] Carpenter counterposed the 'quite necessary but comparatively material basis of matrimonial sex-intercourse and child-breeding' with the promise of 'social and mental activities of the most necessary kind' realized through homosexual association.[28] 'Comrade-love', as he called it, could only be ignored or repressed at the risk

---

[20] See Rowbotham, *Edward Carpenter*, 145, 153, 208.
[21] Rowbotham, *Edward Carpenter*, 187.
[22] Edward Carpenter, *Love's Coming of Age* (London: George Allen and Unwin, 1896, 1930), 27.
[23] Carpenter, *Love's Coming of Age*, 27.
[24] Carpenter, *Love's Coming of Age*, 28.
[25] Edward Carpenter, *Towards Democracy* (London: George Allen and Unwin, 1883), 74.
[26] See Weeks, *Sex, Politics and Society*, 171–5.
[27] Carpenter, *Homogenic Love*, 42–3.
[28] Carpenter, *Homogenic Love*, 45, 44.

of 'considerable danger or damage to the common-weal'.[29] Carpenter also believed that homosexuality might provide a foundation for a more robust democracy. Evoking Whitman's aspirations for democratic comradeship, Carpenter suggested that 'this attachment was already alive and working', existing 'dim and inchoate in the heart of the people' in the practice of homosexuality. Far from being a threat to the social order, homosexuality might actually be a glue of that order and a radical force for community:

> ...the homogenic passion ramifies widely through all modern society...while this passion has occasionally come into public notice through police reports, etc. in its grosser and cruder forms—its more sane and spiritual manifestations—though really a moving force in the body politic—have remained unrecognized.
>
> It is hardly needful in these days when social questions loom so large upon us to emphasise the importance of a bond which by the most passionate and lasting compulsion may draw members of the different classes together, and (as it often seems to do) none the less strongly because they are members of different classes. A moment's consideration must convince us that such a comradeship may, as Whitman says, have 'deepest relations to general politics'.[30]

A kind of socialist politics was being developed through homosexual sex; it was a 'moving force in the body politics' between classes. Homosexuality was a transformative current, the possible lifeblood of a new world. Carpenter's legacy to the development of socialist sex reform is immense and perhaps most notable in the way he created a particular kind of protagonist, the emancipated homosexual as an agent for social and sexual change.

It must also be acknowledged that Carpenter's view of sexuality between the classes did not exclude the sense that it would be the higher classes providing the leadership to a working-man lacking a 'powerful organizing faculty'.[31] Carla Hustak has argued that Carpenter's argument for a transformed sexual life was about realizing the 'potentiality of white bourgeois men'.[32] Though Carpenter also saw sexuality as a bridge between the sexes, there is something to the idea that discussing the emancipation of sex introduced an idea of class difference in the experience of sexuality, in other words, that sexuality was both universal and class-specific.

Karl Pearson was Professor of Applied Mathematics and Mechanics and the founder of the Men and Women's Club. His eclectic intellectual interests— Pearson might have suffered accusations of being a dilettante had he not also been 'humourless' and a 'lump of ice'—were unified by a passion for rational, scientific inquiry.[33] A committed socialist, he was also a devoted follower of Darwin and later an acolyte of Francis Galton, the prophet of eugenics in England.

---

[29] Carpenter, *Homogenic Love*, 43.
[30] Carpenter, *Homogenic Love*, 47–8.
[31] Carpenter, *Love's Coming of Age*, 33.
[32] Carla Hustak, 'Radical Intimacies: Sexual Ethics and the Transatlantic Politics of Love in the Sex Reform Movement, 1900–1930', unpublished PhD thesis, University of Toronto, 2010, 320.
[33] Walkowitz, *City of Dreadful Delight*, 137.

Pearson saw socialism as bringing a new morality. Socialists were to become 'preachers' of that new morality.[34] But this was not a religion of fire, brimstone, or a glowing new life. Socialism was, instead, a 'rational motive for conduct', rooted in the recognition of the dynamics of evolution.[35] Like religion, it demanded sacrifice, and, in particular, the sublimation of the individual to the demands of the social. Socialism represented the 'subjection of all individual action to the welfare of society' and 'reverence towards Society incorporated in the State'.[36] That state would enforce this new imperative in a planned programme of eugenics.

For Pearson, women and sex were critical issues for socialist action. He supported the emancipation of women, particularly through the establishment of female economic independence. This was not merely for the sake of individual freedom or autonomy, but so that women could contribute their labour to society. Pearson wanted to see the abolition of marriage and the lifting of moral prohibitions on sexual experimentation and freedom. This was not done in the spirit of celebration: Pearson's most explicit discussion of sexual pleasure came in a hearty, if confusing, comparison of intercourse to mountain-climbing with a friend.[37] On reproduction, Pearson's statist and eugenic views were clear. Maternity was about 'citizen-making'; it was a key 'social activity', and thus subject to state intervention.[38] No limits could be placed on the power of the state in shaping reproduction, with ordered, rational planning of reproduction to be a fixture of the new socialist morality.

Evolution allowed the marriage of sex and socialism in Pearson's work. Others shared this outlook. Havelock Ellis's interest in social hygiene similarly rested upon rationalized reproduction and motherhood.[39] Eugenics was, therefore, at the heart of some socialist discussions of reproduction, a kind of parallel to the application of scientific rationality in other spheres of socialism. Reproduction was also linked to the good of society. The socialist-feminist Jane Hume Clapperton remarked in her *Vision of the Future* (1904) that selective breeding was 'the master-spring to a rapid evolution of general happiness'.[40] The 'social', in this way, included reproduction. As Carolyn Burdett has stated, '[e]ugenics made procreative sexuality of the first order of importance for the successful nation of the twentieth century'.[41] This was a critical turning point, as it meant an argument for the inclusion of reproductive sexuality as an issue of the public sphere. In this way, socialists apprehended sex as

[34] Karl Pearson, 'Sex and Socialism', in *The Ethic of Freethought* (London: Adam and Charles Black, 1901), 412.

[35] Pearson, 'The Moral Basis of Socialism', in *The Ethic of Freethought*, 304; 'Sex and Socialism', 414.

[36] Pearson, 'Sex and Socialism', 412; 'The Moral Basis of Socialism', 305.

[37] Walkowitz, *City of Dreadful Delight*, 158.

[38] Pearson, 'The Woman Question' (1885), quoted in Angelique Richardson, *Love and Eugenics in the Late Nineteenth Century: Rational Reproduction and the New Woman* (Oxford: Oxford University Press, 2003), xii–xiv.

[39] See Nottingham, *The Pursuit of Serenity*, 183.

[40] Quoted in Richardson, *Love and Eugenics in the Late Nineteenth Century*, xiv–xv.

[41] Carolyn Burdett, 'The Hidden Romance of Sexual Science: Eugenics, the Nation and the Making of Modern Feminism', in Lucy Bland and Laura Doan (eds), *Sexology in Culture: Labelling Bodies and Desires* (Chicago: University of Chicago Press, 1998), 57.

reproduction, demanding state action, just as production did, in the construction of a new, regenerated society.

The South African Olive Schreiner made her name with the pioneering feminist novel *Story of An African Farm* (1883). She came to London in 1881 and soon fell in with progressive circles. She also fell in love with Pearson, an affection that went unrequited. Schreiner published *Woman and Labor* in 1911, a plea for the recognition of a productive role for women. This began with a meditation on sexuality. Schreiner reflected that contemporary discussions of sexuality were not indications of degeneracy or corruption but rather directions towards a new world, 'toward a higher appreciation of the sacredness of all sex relations, and a clearer perception of the sex relation between man and woman as the basis of human society, on whose integrity, beauty, and healthfulness depend the health and beauty of human life, as a whole.'[42] Schreiner viewed sex in both utopian and eugenic terms. Like Carpenter, Schreiner saw the sexual body as a vessel towards a new world and a new life, representing 'the essentially Good and Beautiful of human existence'.[43] She ventured, in a letter to Pearson, 'that in the future, human reproduction would be possible without sex. . . . Then the sexual systems might be used exclusively aesthetically for purposes of pleasure; for sympathy and union between human beings.'[44] Schreiner suggested that female emancipation and a more progressive view of sexuality were not merely virtues in themselves, but, more importantly, essential to the health and regeneration of society, nation and race.[45] Female 'parasitism'—the refusal to grant women a productive or active role in society— led to degeneracy.[46] In other words, sexuality was still to be sublimated to a higher purpose, that of society; women's sexuality was to be freed not only for its own sake, but for the sake of society. Schreiner's work represented a melding of the sexual and social utopianism of Carpenter and the scientific, statist approach of Pearson. She ended *Woman and Labor* with an evocation of a new sexual and social world: 'an Eden created by their own labor and made beautiful by their own fellowship . . . we see a new earth; but therein dwells love—the love of comrades and co-workers'.[47]

These arguments about the relationship between sex and political change were not, of course, shared by all on the Left in the late nineteenth century. Perhaps the broadest criticism, and one that was to reverberate through the twentieth century, was that sex was simply not the most pressing issue for socialists. Robert Blatchford, the founder of the *Clarion* newspaper and author of *Merrie England* (1894) stated: 'reform—or rather reorganization—of the sexual relations must *follow* the economic and industrial change . . . the time is not ripe for Socialists, as Socialists, to meddle

---

[42] Schreiner, *Woman and Labor*, 18–19.
[43] Schreiner, *Woman and Labor*, 21.
[44] Quoted in Lucy Bland, *Banishing the Beast* (London: I.B. Tauris, 1995, 2002), 21.
[45] See Burdett, 'The Hidden Romance of Sexual Science: Eugenics, the Nation and the Making of Modern Feminism'; Burdett, *Olive Schreiner and the Progress of Feminism: Evolution, Gender, Empire* (Houndmills: Palgrave Macmillan, 2001).
[46] Schreiner, *Woman and Labor*, 97.
[47] Schreiner, *Woman and Labor*, 298.

with the sexual question.' Blatchford also remarked that 'the whole subject is "nasty" to me' and there was, as well, a prudishness to some socialists' response.[48] Beatrice Webb lamented the promotion of free love in the novel *In the Days of the Comet* (1906) by H.G. Wells because she believed that man's evolution was dependent upon 'the subordination of his physical desires and appetites to the intellectual and spiritual side of his nature'.[49]

Discussions of sex also opened up divisions between sex reformers and feminists. As Lucy Bland and others have suggested, the relationship between sexual radicalism and Victorian feminism was highly ambivalent, particularly given that some feminist campaigns targeted the excesses of male sexuality and male privilege, leaving little room for female sexual pleasure or freedom. Even advocates of sexual reform such as Pearson inflamed feminist sensibilities. The Fabian Emma Brooke was appalled, for example, by Pearson's privileging of the state in reproduction, wanting instead 'a woman's choice', because, she argued, 'a woman's body is . . . not her own'. She also attacked Pearson's nonchalant attitude towards male sexuality. 'The truth is,' Brooke wrote, 'you men have murdered Love . . . you have killed the inspiration in the woman's heart by abuses of all kinds.'[50] This had a particular effect upon the question of contraception. Though feminist women wanted the right to voluntary, rather than involuntary, motherhood, they did not link this to a firm belief in contraception, which might facilitate male licentiousness and violence and was, besides, perceived as immoral. Feminist participation in the Malthusian League was less about sexual emancipation than about seeing eugenics as a vessel of female sexual control. Jane Hume Clapperton was a rare example of a woman who argued for birth control towards the end of obtaining sexual pleasure as well as the protection of women.[51]

New relationships between socialism and sex were also being lived as much as envisioned at the *fin de siècle*. Socialist men and women like Carpenter, Edward Aveling, and Eleanor Marx all tried to lead new kinds of sexual and romantic lives, whether this meant homosexual unions or 'free' heterosexual unions. Though homosexuality was discussed by Carpenter and J.A. Symonds, heterosexual marriage attracted more open examination by socialists in the late nineteenth century. The idea of 'free unions' or 'free love', separated from the traditional institution of marriage, appealed to some socialist women as a means of rejecting gender oppression and carving out a new landscape of female freedom within the context of equal love between men and women. Eleanor Marx famously lived in a 'free union' with Edward Aveling. An even more spectacular controversy exploded when a young SDF socialist, Edith Lanchester decided upon a 'free union' with a working-class man. Her family forcibly committed her to an asylum, until she was freed by legal

[48] Quoted in Tsuzuki, *Edward Carpenter*, 122; Rowbotham and Weeks, *Socialism and the New Life*, 116.
[49] Norman and Jeanne MacKenzie, *The Diary of Beatrice Webb*: Volume Three: *1905–24: 'The Power to Alter Things'* (London: Virago/LSE, 1984), 30 November 1906, 61.
[50] Bland, *Banishing the Beast*, 21, 29.
[51] See Bland, *Banishing the Beast*, 189, 211, 221.

action. As June Hannam and Karen Hunt suggest, this produced considerable discussion of marriage and free love within the socialist movement.[52] Though it led to demands that socialist parties like the SDF and the ILP consider the problem of marriage within their programmes, there was no unanimous view on 'free love' and 'free unions' within the ranks of socialist women. In other spheres of the socialist movement, such as anarchist socialism, there occurred a bracing rethinking of gender roles and sexuality.[53] But often it was left to fiction for socialist women to imagine new forms of heterosexuality removed from the older constraints of traditional marriage.[54]

II

Within the nascent movement for a parliamentary socialist or working-class party, there was much less support for sexual radicalism.[55] There were concerns, for example, that a commitment to 'free love' might strangle the parliamentary socialist movement at birth. In Glasgow before the First World War, 'free love' was an insult thrown at socialist candidates in local elections by those defending traditional domesticity.[56] If we look at the development of labour politics in the nineteenth and early twentieth centuries, it is clear that the gendered culture and organization of working-class politics and socialism in the late nineteenth century determined to some degree the political reception of ideas about sexuality. The figures of nineteenth-century working-class men and women cast long shadows across the twentieth century in this respect; indeed, the story of gender and sexuality within Labour politics in the twentieth century is a narrative about the changing understanding of those figures and the purchase they had on outlook, strategy and ideology.

The economic and political struggles of the working classes in the Victorian period set up a gender ideology that emphasized the identification between class and masculinity.[57] The male breadwinner wage, or family wage, became central to working-class political and economic action, even if that wage remained beyond the reach of most working-class families, a source of conflict and tension within

---

[52] See Hannam and Hunt, *Socialist Women.*

[53] See Matthew Thomas, 'Anarcho-Feminism in late Victorian and Edwardian Britain, 1880–1914', *International Review of Social History* 47 (2002), 1–31.

[54] See Chris Waters, 'New Women and Socialist-Feminist Fiction: The Novels of Isabella Ford and Katharine Bruce Glasier' and Ann Ardis, '"The Journey from Fantasy to Politics": The Representation of Socialism and Feminism in *Gloriana* and *The Image-Breakers*' in Angela Ingram and Daphne Patai (eds), *Rediscovering Forgotten Radicals: British Women Writers 1889–1939* (Chapel Hill: University of North Carolina Press, 1993).

[55] See Hannam and Hunt, *Socialist Women*, Chapter 3.

[56] See J.J. Smyth, *Labour in Glasgow 1896–1936: Socialism, Suffrage, Sectarianism* (East Linton: Tuckwell Press, 2000), 170–1.

[57] On work and women, see Deborah Valenze, *The First Industrial Woman* (New York: Oxford University Press, 1995); Sally Alexander, 'Women's Work in Nineteenth Century London: A Study of the Years 1820–60s', in *Becoming a Woman and Other Essays in Nineteenth and Twentieth Century Feminist History* (London: Virago, 1994).

marriage.[58] The quest for independence and respectability animated the working classes in the nineteenth century, both at the work place and in the sphere of politics. This was at once an epic public landscape of heroic male workers fighting employers and aristocrats to claim their rightful place in the nation and a restrained domestic interior with a dependent wife and children in the background. In late nineteenth-century politics, citizenship was assumed to be male citizenship.[59] This can also be seen in the outlook of early socialist and labour parties, with its emphasis upon the economic interests of male workers, such as the eight-hour day, the securing of the family wage and greater power for trade unions, and their self-representation, with manly independent workers at the centre of such portraits.[60] Reproduction and domestic labour were not recognized as labour. Whereas men could use the ideal of labour to fight for respectability in the public sphere, women could not do so on the same terms. Instead, women's entry into citizenship came through a very gendered route, that of motherhood. From the 1870s, an emerging social imperialism rooted in worries about national strength focused on mother-hood as the foundation of a strong nation.[61] Unsurprisingly, this interest was class-biased, with working-class mothers serving as the focal point of state and voluntary action.[62] Even if the assumptions were not to bring women into a new framework of social citizenship, this maternalist interest established 'women's public relation-ships to politics and the state, to community, workplace, and marketplace'.[63] Such

---

[58] Hilary Land, 'The Family Wage', *Feminist Review* 6 (1980), 55–77; Sally Alexander, 'Women, Class and Sexual Differences in the 1830s and 1840s: Some Reflections on the Writing of a Feminist History', *History Workshop Journal* 17 (1984), 123–49; Wally Seccombe, 'Patriarchy Stabilized: The Construction of the Male Breadwinner Norm in Nineteenth-Century Britain', *Social History* 11 (1986), 53–76; Sonya Rose, *Limited Livelihoods* (Berkeley: University of California Press, 1992), Chapters 5 and 6; Keith McClelland, 'Masculinity and the "Representative Artisan" in Britain, 1850–80', in Michael Roper and John Tosh (eds), *Manful Assertions* (London: Routledge, 1991); Ellen Ross, '"Fierce Questions and Taunts": Married Life in Working-class London, 1870–1914', *Feminist Studies* 8 (1992), 575–602; Ellen Ross, *Love and Toil: Motherhood in Outcast London 1870–1918* (New York: Oxford University Press, 1993).

[59] Jon Lawrence, *Speaking for the People* (Cambridge: Cambridge University Press, 1998); Anna Clark, 'Gender, Class and the Constitution: Franchise Reform in England, 1832–1928', in James Vernon (ed.), *Re-Reading the Constitution* (Cambridge: Cambridge University Press, 1996).

[60] Laura Ugolini, '"By All Means Let the Ladies Have a Chance": *The Workman's Times*, Independent Labour Representation and Women's Suffrage, 1891–4', in Angela V. John and Claire Eustance (eds), *The Men's Share* (London: Routledge, 1997).

[61] See Anna Davin, 'Imperialism and Motherhood', *History Workshop Journal* 5 (1978), 9–66; Gisela Bock and Pat Thane (eds), *Maternity and Gender Politics: Women and the Rise of European Welfare States 1880s–1950s* (London: Routledge, 1991); Seth Koven and Sonya Michel (eds), *Mothers of a New World: Maternalist Politics and the Origins of Welfare States* (London: Routledge, 1993).

[62] See Jane Lewis, *The Politics of Motherhood: Child and Maternal Welfare in England, 1900–39* (London: Croom Helm, 1980), Chapters 2 and 3; Caroline Rowan, '"Mothers, Vote Labour!" The State, the Labour Movement and Working-Class Mothers', in Rosalind Brunt and Caroline Rowan (eds), *Feminism, Culture and Politics* (London: Lawrence and Wishart, 1982); Carol Dyhouse, 'Working-Class Mothers and Infant Mortality in England, 1895–1914', *Journal of Social History* 12 (1978), 121–42; Jane Lewis, 'The Working-Class Wife and Mother and State Intervention, 1870–1918', in Jane Lewis (ed.), *Labour and Love: Women's Experience of Home and Family 1850–1940* (Oxford: Blackwell, 1986).

[63] Seth Koven and Sonya Michel, 'Womanly Duties: Maternalist Politics and the Origins of Welfare States in France, Germany, Great Britain and the United States, 1880–1920', *American Historical Review* 95 (1990), 1079; see also Susan Pedersen, 'Gender, Welfare, and Citizenship in Britain during the Great War', *American Historical Review* 95 (1990), 1004; Susan Pedersen, *Family,*

discussions of motherhood became central to new thinking on the links between birth control and socialism.

As we have already seen, women and sex figured importantly in the development of British socialism in the late nineteenth century. But, in terms of formulating a programme for political action, across the spectrum of ethical socialism, Fabianism, and SDF Marxism, British socialism largely addressed the needs of male workers through such policies as the right to work, unemployment relief, the minimum wage and eight-hour day, and legal protection for trade union rights. The ILP, founded in 1893, also centred its attention on the male worker. Ethical socialists such as Blatchford and Morris looked to the restoration of dignity to male workers; the utopias such writers presented had at their core very traditional gender stereotypes of manly artisans and maidenly women.[64] Keir Hardie was a notable advocate of women's economic and political rights, seeing the 'sex problem... [as] the Labour problem', but in this, as in many things, Hardie was exceptional.[65] The Labour Representation Committee founded at the turn of the century (which took the formal name of Labour Party in 1906) was inevitably a product of such a climate. Its singular purpose was to get more working men into Parliament and to 'promote legislation in the direct interest of labour'.[66]

There was a distinct socialist-feminist voice within the institutional framework of the British Left and working-class politics by the time of the founding of the Labour Party.[67] The Women's Industrial Council (WIC) (1894–1916); the WCG (1883–), and the Women's Labour League (WLL) (1906–18) enjoyed informal rather than formal associations with larger and male-dominated organizations such as the TUC, the Cooperative Society, and the Labour Party.[68] At the same time, they pursued a separate sphere of interest for female labour activists centring on the home and family. Just as lines of responsibility and role fell along gendered lines in working-class families, within the broader Labour movement, women and men were gathered into separate organizations and separate pursuits. This is not to dismiss these organizations. The WCG was a critical sphere of working-class women's political activism well into the twentieth century. It was also one seat of opposition to a male-only view of working-class politics, concentrating instead upon the outlook of its members, who were mostly married women. By the early

Dependence and the Origins of the Welfare State in Britain and France, 1914–45 (Cambridge: Cambridge University Press, 1993).

[64] David Howell, *British Workers and the Independent Labour Party 1888–1906* (Manchester: Manchester University Press, 1983), 354–6, 380–1.

[65] Quoted in Geoffrey Foote, *The Labour Party's Political Thought* (London: Croom Helm, 1985), 50.

[66] *Labour Representation Committee Founding Conference* (London: Labour Representation Committee, 1900).

[67] See Karen Hunt, *Equivocal Feminists: The Social Democratic Federation and the Woman Question 1884–1911* (Cambridge: Cambridge University Press, 1996); Sally Alexander, 'Fabian Socialism and the "Sex-Relation"', in *Becoming a Woman*; Hannam and Hunt, *Socialist Women*; Krista Cowman, 'Giving Them Something to Do: How the Early ILP Appealed to Women', in M. Walsh (ed.), *Working Out Gender: Perspectives from Labour History* (Aldershot: Ashgate, 1999), 119–34.

[68] Collette, *For Labour and For Women*, 75 ff.; Graves, *Labour Women*, 12–14.

1930s, the WCG had over 80,000 members.[69] That the principal organizational structure of British socialism was one that favoured the interests of the working man shaped the relationship between reproductive politics and socialist politics in the twentieth century. What provided an intersection between women's working-class politics and the politics of the wider Labour movement was motherhood, which also prepared the ground for the articulation of a particular brand of working-class sexual politics.

III

This discussion of motherhood occurred against the backdrop of a steady drop in the rate of reproduction in Britain from the 1870s to the 1930s.[70] There are multiple explanations for this change, but a key factor was the deliberate limitation of families through the spacing of births, abstinence from intercourse, and the use of contraceptive methods (coitus interruptus most commonly) and contraceptive appliances. The last included spermicides (used with a syringe or a sponge), diaphragms, and sheaths, sometimes available by post or from a chemist's. Until the late nineteenth century, contraceptive information tended to be in the hands of doctors. This monopoly on knowledge was broken by the publication and popular success of works such as Annie Besant's *The Law of Population* (1877) and H.A. Allbutt's *The Wife's Handbook* (1889). The Malthusian League, founded in 1876, helped distribute millions of pamphlets advocating family limitation and setting out the means to do so.[71]

There were class differences in the practice of contraception and fertility patterns in nineteenth-century Britain.[72] It is often thought that middle-class couples were the agents of contraceptive modernization, driven by either aspiration or a desire to preserve their living standards. Knowledge and appliances demanded money and access to medical expertise. Because of cost, as well as a lack of adequate privacy and knowledge, the use of contraceptive appliances was usually not an option for working-class women. Abstention, the 'safe' period, and abortion were usually what were left as birth control for working-class women. Abortion had long been an accepted practice within working-class life, often sustained by networks of female knowledge. There were a variety of methods, including the ingestion of herbs, drugs, chemicals, and pills bought from the chemist's or the herbalist's. There was a thriving, and, if not underground, at least discreet trade in abortifacient pills among patent medicine merchants. Less common was the use of instruments such as knitting needles. The threat to health and life was extremely high. Abortion was also illegal. Infanticide had been formally criminalized in 1803; in 1861, the

---

[69] See Gillian Scott, *Feminism and the Politics of Working Women: The Women's Cooperative Guild, 1880s to the Second World War* (London: UCL Press, 1998).
[70] See Cook, *The Long Sexual Revolution*, 15.
[71] See Weeks, *Sex, Politics and Society*, 46.
[72] See Simon Szreter, *Fertility, Class and Gender in Britain 1860–1940* (Cambridge: Cambridge University Press, 1996).

Offences Against the Person Act explicitly made the practice of procuring an abortion or performing an abortion a criminal act. But, as Patricia Knight suggests, abortion was common within working-class life and viewed with considerable tolerance.[73]

By 1914, it was widely assumed that there was a gap between middle-class and working-class fertility.[74] This perception dovetailed with concerns about the living conditions of the urban working-class and, in particular, working-class mothers and children. A eugenic fear of race suicide or national degeneration was a powerful aspect of this concern.[75] A movement for maternal and infant welfare centres gathered pace to address the condition of working-class families, without interfering with the labour market.

Around this time, two women's organizations affiliated with the Labour Party produced books that identified working-class women's inability to control their fertility as a major social problem. In 1913, Maud Pember Reeves published *Round About a Pound a Week* based upon research by the FWG on the household budgets of working-class families. In *Maternity: Letters from Working Women* (1915), Margaret Llewelyn Davies, the General Secretary of the WCG, presented 160 letters on the experience of motherhood from the wives of 'the better paid manual workers'.[76] Women's lack of control over reproduction was a recurring lament of both works. First of all, this placed women at the mercy of men's sexual demands, without even the power of an 'animal'.[77] Uncontrolled fertility also deepened the problem of working-class poverty. It was not only a drain on working-class men and women but also a 'handicap' on the state.[78] These works permitted a glimpse into the interiors of working-class lives in a variety of ways, from the household budget to sex. They also set out a new kind of political agenda, linking private lives to socialist action, less in terms of utopia than in terms of everyday life.

A different protagonist for political action emerged through *Maternity* and *Round About a Pound a Week*. Where working-class and socialist organizations had turned on the pivot of the working man, the work of the FWG and WCG women placed the working-class mother at the centre of the socialist imagination. This offered a critique, sometimes oblique, sometimes direct, of the predominance of the working man and the breadwinner ideology. *Round About a Pound a Week* laid bare the inadequacies of the breadwinner wage, demonstrating, in empirical terms, the near impossibility of maintaining a working-class family on male wages. More often than not, it was the bodies of mothers and children that paid the price for this inadequacy. Birth control was the implicit solution to this predicament.

---

[73] See Patricia Knight, 'Woman and Abortion in Victorian and Edwardian England', *History Workshop Journal* 4 (Autumn 1977), 56–69.

[74] Recent research suggests this was erroneous: see Szreter, *Fertility, Class and Gender*, 535.

[75] See Davin, 'Imperialism and Motherhood'; Ross, *Love and Toil*; Lewis, *The Politics of Motherhood*.

[76] Women's Cooperative Guild, *Maternity: Letters from Working-Women* (London: G. Bell and Sons, 1915), 3.

[77] WCG, *Maternity*, 27–8.

[78] Maud Pember Reeves, *Round About a Pound a Week* (London: Virago, 1913, 1999), 215.

'[W]omen dread nothing so much', Reeves wrote, 'as the conviction that there is to be still another baby with its inevitable consequences—more crowding, more illness, more worry, more work, and less food, less strength, less time to manage with.' Family limitation was implied as a cure to poverty. This also had imperialist or eugenic overtones. A 'masculine State', previously attentive only to the interests of 'male voters, and, until lately, chiefly those of the richer classes', had to feminize itself, facilitating better lives for mothers and children, not least because the alternative was the continued presence of men, women, and children who would become a 'handicap for the very State of which they are part'.[79] The solution was not the older, and more masculine, 'family wage', but rather economic independence for all women and state help in motherhood.[80]

If *Round About a Pound a Week* mapped the domestic economy of working-class women through the eyes of a middle-class socialist, *Maternity* allowed working-class women to express themselves. Margaret Llewelyn Davies, the editor of the collection, presented 160 letters, largely from the wives of 'the better paid manual workers', all on the experience of working-class motherhood. With a few exceptions, it was an unrelenting account of 'perpetual overwork, illness and suffering'.[81] This was an experience of the body. The collection also charted the heavy price paid in maternal mortality and morbidity and infant mortality. There was a direct connection in *Maternity* between the material experience of the body and the articulation of class consciousness, gender identity, and a nascent working-class feminism.

Husbands figured strongly in women's accounts of reproduction. A good husband was one who was supportive, helped out with the household labour, was physically strong and, perhaps most important, was stably employed and sexually restrained. Time after time, correspondents tied problems in maternity to the vicissitudes of the male employment market. Women paid for this uncertainty with their bodies. But sexual conflict was also critical. In several letters from the collection, women complained of sexual victimization by men. 'Fathers ought to control their bodies for the sake of the mother and child', one woman wrote, 'I could quote several instances where a mother's life has become intolerable through the husband's lack of control.'[82] One respondent wove together the language of sex and working-class politics: 'I had my fifth baby, and had also a miscarriage, and then I went on strike.' Others articulated a feminist position: ' . . . no amount of State help can help the suffering of mothers until men are taught many things in regard to the right use of the organs of reproduction, and until he realizes that the wife's body belongs to herself, and until the marriage relations takes a higher sense of morality and bare justice . . . the wife is still the inferior in the family to the husband. She is first without economic independence, and the law therefore gives

---

[79] Pember Reeves, *Round About a Pound a Week*, 153, 215.
[80] See Sally Alexander, 'Introduction', in *Round About a Pound a Week*, x–xv.
[81] WCG, *Maternity* 3.
[82] WCG, *Maternity*, 65–6.

the man, whether he be good or bad, a terrible power over her.' We can see here the working through of tensions between the complementarity of the sexes and conflict. What was also clear was a sense of class distinction and consciousness from the experience of reproduction. The introduction to *Maternity* pointed to the 'different conditions under which the middle-class and working-class woman becomes a mother'.[83] Differences in reproductive experience were reflections of class society and an argument for a sense of class consciousness. It was also, of course, an argument for socialist action. The authors of *Maternity* did not explicitly argue for state support for birth control, but it was acknowledged as a need to craft a 'human and humane life' of other things beyond 'poverty and work'.[84]

Just before the First World War, the birth control question was vented on the pages of *Labour Woman*, the publication of the WLL. Many of the same themes found in the work of the FWG and the WCG could be discerned in its columns, albeit with a more explicit discussion of the solution of birth control access. In July 1913, F.N. Harrison responded to comments by the Archbishop of York by arguing that working-class parents had to practise a kind of responsible family planning 'according to their economic position, whether their aim is to have a small family, born, tended, housed, clothed, fed, and educated as human beings have a right to be or a large family sharing penury as its portion and growing up to be feeble hewers of wood and drawers of water for the more fortunate members of the community'.[85] There was also a clear eugenic strain in what Harrison had to say. The article prompted some discussion, including a criticism of the use of birth control. Support for birth control included the suggestion that family planning had to be linked to male wages; even if those wages were, in fact, 'breadwinning' for the entire family, 'it would still be advisable and commendable to limit the family according to the strength and capacity of the mother and other circumstances, and that all women should have some knowledge of this matter'.[86]

The period before the First World War also saw increased interest in working-class sexuality from the Malthusian League. In 1913, it began to promote birth control information in the East End of London, circulating about 21,000 pamphlets by 1917 and planning to establish a birth control clinic.[87] New organizations also appeared at this time, which once again demonstrated the overlap between socialism and sexual reform. The most notable was the British Society for the Study of Sex Psychology, which was founded in July 1914. Its first president was Edward Carpenter and among its most active members was Stella Browne, who played a central role within the birth control campaign of the 1920s.

---

[83] WCG, *Maternity*, 4–5, 6.
[84] WCG, *Maternity*, 7–8, 15–16, 14–15.
[85] F.N. Harrison, 'Wanted! Understanding: A Word to the Archbishop of York', *Labour Woman* 1/3 (July 1913), 43.
[86] H. Jennie Baker, Letter to *Labour Woman* 1/6 (October 1913), 88.
[87] See Weeks, *Sex, Politics and Society*, 189.

IV

Stella Browne was both a critical contributor to the history of sexual reform in the twentieth century and a transitional figure between the intellectual ferment around sexuality and socialism in the late nineteenth and early twentieth centuries, the world of left-wing politics and the developments of the 1920s and 1930s.[88] She also brought together questions of sexual orientation and reproductive control within a socialist vision.

Browne was born in Halifax, Nova Scotia in 1880. In 1907, she became librarian at Morley College in London and made a niche for herself as a self-described 'Left Wing feminist'.[89] She read and translated German works of sexology, and Havelock Ellis was also an important influence. Before and during the First World War, Browne marked herself out as a campaigner on issues of sexuality. As a contributor to the journal *The Freewoman*, she debated the question of women's sexual abstinence with Kathlyn Oliver. She also became involved, through the Malthusian League, in distributing contraceptive information to working-class people in Southwark, South London.[90] Browne wrote two important essays, 'The Sexual Variety and Variability Among Women' (1915) and 'Women and Birth Control' (1917); the former argued that women's sexuality was unfixed, an important statement of the potential for bisexual and lesbian rights. In 1935, she published a pioneering essay on 'The Right to Abortion'. Throughout her life, Browne refused to compromise her commitment to birth control and sexual freedom. Even among other sexual radicals, Dora Russell remembered, Browne cut a distinctive figure: '[r]ather untidy, careless about her looks and appearance. Quite irrepressible at getting up and interrupting a meeting or asking questions.'[91]

Browne's belief in birth control and wider sexual and feminist reform was coloured by socialist and class politics. As already noted, she had worked in poor neighbourhoods of South London. She also admired the work of the WCG as being more 'boldly constructive' in its approach to the problems of working-class sexuality than the Eugenics Education Society.[92] There was, nonetheless, a tinge of eugenics in Browne's work; she said, for example, that women needed a right to abortion 'if they are to breed a race of greater powers and finer standards of value'.[93] But the counterweight to this was the emphasis Browne gave to autonomy, agency, and variety in women's sexual lives. Browne was a member of the Communist Party

---

[88] On Browne, see Rowbotham, *A New World For Women*; Hall, *The Life and Times of Stella Browne*.

[89] Quoted in Lesley Hall, 'The Next Generation: Stella Browne, the New Woman as Freewoman', in Angelique Richardson and Chris Willis (eds), *The New Woman in Fiction and in Fact: Fin-de-Siècle Feminisms* (London: Palgrave/University of London, Institute for English Studies, School of Advanced Study, 2001), 226.

[90] See Rowbotham, *A New World for Women*, 12.

[91] IISH, DRP, 345, Dora Russell to Madeleine Simms, 9 February 1968.

[92] F.W. Stella Browne, 'Women and Birth-Control', in Eden and Cedar Paul (eds), *Population and Birth-Control* (New York: The Critic and Guide Company, 1917), 251.

[93] F.W. Stella Browne, 'The Right To Abortion', in Rowbotham, *A New World For Women*, 110.

1.2 'Stella Browne, 1930s', unknown photographer and date, copyright Keith Hindell

of Great Britain (CPGB) between 1920 and 1923.[94] Within the CPGB, she argued that socialist change had to include the issue of birth control, not only because this was a question of paramount importance for working-class people, but because it was a necessary feminist reform: '[n]o economic changes would give equality or self-determination to any woman unable to choose or refuse motherhood'.[95] In this way, socialism, feminism, and sex reform were all tightly linked. But Browne soon realized that this vision could not be fulfilled within the CPGB. Frustrated with its refusal to back the birth control and sex reform issue, Browne left the party in 1923 and moved over to Labour.

Browne took the arguments made by Pearson, Schreiner, and other nineteenth-century writers and infused them with an unqualified feminism. She asserted that women should have the right to be mothers 'under tolerable conditions and with some reasonable probability of a tolerable existence for their children'. This implied a full programme of social, sexual, and political reform, including the right to birth control. Without such reform, no state had 'the faintest right to demand a single additional birth'.[96] Unlike a previous generation of socialists interested in sex reform, Browne stressed the strength and the heterogeneity of female sexuality:

[94] See Hall, *The Life and Times of Stella Browne*, 96–7, 102–3, 111.
[95] Quoted in Rowbotham, *A New World for Women*, 28.
[96] Browne, 'Women and Birth Control', 248, 250.

'[t]he sexual emotion in women is not...weaker than in men. But it has an enormously wider range of variation; and much greater diffusion, both in desire, and pleasure, all through women's organisms.'[97] Browne also emphasized the need for women to have choice, agency, and independence in their sexual lives. '[O]ur bodies are our own', she wrote in 1935 with reference to abortion.[98] Again, we might see such a comment as a link between an older tradition of feminism (that of social purity, protecting the female body from rampant male sexuality) and a later strand, one that advocated women's power to exercise complete autonomy over their bodies. It is unsurprising that the second wave feminist, Sheila Rowbotham, saw a progenitor in Browne. Writing during the First World War, Browne's interest in sexual reform was rooted in the assertion of women's freedom and rights. A woman was not 'a domestic utensil, but a citizen, a human being, and free in her motherhood and her love'. Securing rights and freedom depended upon the emancipation of women from the fear of pregnancy and allowing them to enjoy sexual pleasure: 'this is also the only line of freedom and a more varied and active life for women'. For this reason, birth control, including abortion, was an imperative demand. Browne also suggested that men were not reliable allies in the feminist cause. A 'masculine mythology' had long been complicit in 'suppressing and distorting all the facts of women's sexual and maternal emotions'; it had 'never been safe for women to trust to the gratitude and justice of groups of men'.[99]

Browne's work afforded a vision of how a new world was to be built through sex as much as through the economy and the state. In her argument for abortion, for example, she blurred the lines between sexual reform and political reform, suggesting that the two were as entwined as the bodies of lovers:

> It is also an argument for accuracy, sympathy, and candour in the study and treatment of sex, especially of the sexual sentiments and needs of women, and also for adequate housing, for economic justice, for international peace: stretching out from the bodies and bed of human lovers to all the dangers and dreams, hopes and achievements of the world today and the conquest of the future.[100]

Just as she believed that the achievement of socialism was coincident with women's rights, Browne thought that birth control and abortion were not isolated private issues, but linked to a different political and economic culture: 'The right to abortion is a key-point, going deep down to the roots of social philosophy and economic reality.'[101] Thus, in Browne's work, we can see how sexual liberation and birth control were the starting points in imagining the establishment of a completely transformed society.

---

[97] F.W. Stella Browne, 'The Sexual Variety and Variability Among Women and Their Bearing Upon Social Reconstruction', in Rowbotham, *A New World For Women*, 93. See also Lesley Hall, '"I Have Never Met the Normal Woman": Stella Browne and the Politics of Womanhood', *Women's History Review* 6 (1997), 157–82.

[98] F.W. Stella Browne, 'The Right to Abortion', in Rowbotham, *A New World For Women*, 114.

[99] Browne, 'Women and Birth Control', 248, 256, 250, 253, 256, footnote 9.

[100] Browne, 'The Right to Abortion', 119.

[101] Browne, 'The Right to Abortion', 116.

Between the 1880s and the 1920s, two strands had emerged in the relationship between socialism and sexuality. One boasted a vision of sex as a transformative force in the remaking of the world. The second concentrated on the amelioration of the position of the working-class mother. Both were linked by a sense that sexuality was not simply about the individual, but, more importantly, about larger communities and ways of belonging, whether to the family or society. There were structural and discursive constraints to these arguments. The first was the place of women within the nascent Labour Party. The second was the discursive context of working-class and socialist politics at this time, dominated by the figure of the breadwinner male. Other protagonists were appearing, the most important of which at this time was the working-class mother. Others, such as the sexually liberated woman or the homosexual man, existed and circulated within discussions of sexuality, but they had less purchase. In the period between the two world wars, the two axes of sexual politics on the Left—backstreets and utopias—continued to influence the way sexual reform developed.

PART 1

BACKSTREETS AND UTOPIAS
BETWEEN THE WARS

2

Clash

The Labour Party and Birth Control, 1923 to 1930

In her 1929 novel, *Clash*, the young Labour MP for Middlesbrough East, Ellen Wilkinson, recreated a 1920s' trade union meeting by having '[t]he inevitable mild middle-class lady g[iving] out leaflets on birth control' on the steps of the confer-ence hall.[1] From 1924 to 1930, the birth control question was a divisive fixture of many Labour conferences. During the 1924 conference of Labour women, for example, the writer and birth control activist Dora Russell was startled by the 'huge and terrifying' Labour Chief Woman Officer (CWO), Marion Phillips, bearing down on her, thundering '[s]ex should not be dragged into politics, you will split the Party from top to bottom'.[2] To this, Russell and many other Labour women paid little heed, duly dragging sex into politics. The birth control campaign became an attempt both to make reproductive control a socialist and working-class issue and to redress the gendered balance of Labour's structure and ideology. At the 1924 conference of Labour women, one delegate stated:

> . . . we are shirking our responsibility as a Party in not giving the lead to the women of the country, in not giving that word of hope and of life to the working-class woman which they are waiting to receive from someone. . . . In the abolition of poverty birth control is an essential factor.[3]

Before discussing this campaign in detail, it is important to set out a number of contexts that shaped it: the position of women after the First World War; the experience of unemployment; the place of women in the post-1918 Labour Party; and the decline of the breadwinner ideology.

I

The progress of women's rights ebbed and flowed between the wars. In the political realm, the enfranchisement of women in 1918 and 1928 encouraged mainstream political parties to court female voters in a variety of ways, but it did not funda-mentally change the course of British politics. An initial spate of women's

---

[1] Ellen Wilkinson, *Clash* (Nottingham: Trent, 1929, 2004), 15.
[2] Dora Russell, *The Tamarisk Tree* (London: Elek, 1975), 172.
[3] Labour Party, *Annual Conference of Labour Women* [*ACLW*] (1924), 96.

legislation in the 1920s, which led to significant reforms governing the professions and marriage, petered out after a decade and was followed by a period of retrenchment.[4] A place for women and the discussion of femininity and female rights had nonetheless been enshrined in the public sphere even if most parties saw women as problematic political subjects.[5]

There remained powerful undercurrents reshaping understandings of femininity, masculinity and sexuality between the wars. The most important affected women in their reproductive roles. The birth rate declined significantly between 1900 and 1940, from nearly thirty births per thousand in 1900 to just over ten by the early 1940s.[6] The early 1930s represented the bottom of this demographic trough. Birth control in working-class families was thought to be the single most important cause of this fall.[7] The 1920s and 1930s were also a period of moderate sexual liberalization.[8] This is perhaps best represented by the success of Marie Stopes's guide to sexuality, *Married Love*, first published in 1918. It became a bestseller, suggesting the importance of female sexual pleasure to companionate marriage. Stopes used her influence to establish a network of birth control clinics, particularly in working-class areas. By the late 1920s, some mainstream churches, such as the Church of England, had accepted the use of birth control within marriage. Sexual liberalization should not be exaggerated: it is clear that Britain remained sexually conservative before the 1940s.[9] But we must also acknowledge the visibility of sexuality in society and culture, not least in popular culture such as cinema and pictorial magazines.[10] Contemporaries certainly saw the period as one of sexual liberalization. The authors of the 1937 official report on Maternal Mortality and Morbidity noted that '[s]ince the Great War there has been a loosening of the conventions

---

[4] Such as the Sex Disqualification Act (1919); the Widows Act (1925); Matrimonial Causes Act (1925); the Guardianship of Infants Act (1924); New English Law of Property (1926); and the Law Reform (Married Women and Tortfeasors) Act (1935).

[5] See Jane Lewis, 'In Search of Real Equality: Women Between the Wars', in Frank Gloversmith (ed.), *Class, Culture and Social Change* (Brighton: Harvester, 1980). On politics, see David Jarvis, 'Mrs Maggs and Betty: The Conservative Appeal to Women Voters in the 1920s', *Twentieth Century British History* 5 (1994), 129–52; David Jarvis, 'The Conservative Party and the Politics of Gender, 1900–39', in Martin Francis and Ina Zweiniger-Bargielowska (eds), *The Conservatives and British Society* (Cardiff: University of Wales Press, 1996).

[6] See Richard Soloway, *Birth Control and the Population Question in England 1877–1930* (Chapel Hill, NC: University of North Carolina Press, 1982); Szreter, *Fertility, Class and Gender*; Cook, *The Long Sexual Revolution*.

[7] See Wally Seccombe, 'Starting to Stop: Working-Class Fertility Decline in Britain', *Past and Present* 126 (1990), 151–88 and Cmd. 7695, *Royal Commission on Population*, 34.

[8] See Lesley Hall and Roy Porter, *The Facts of Life: The Creation of Sexual Knowledge in Britain 1650–1950* (New Haven: Yale University Press, 1995), Chapters 9, 10, and 11; Hall, *Sex, Gender and Social Change in Britain Since 1880*, Chapters 6 and 7; Cate Haste, *Rules of Desire: Sex in Britain: World War One to the Present* (London: Pimlico, 1992), Chapter 4.

[9] Ross McKibbin, *Classes and Cultures: England, 1918–1951* (Oxford: Oxford University Press, 1998); Hall and Porter, *The Facts of Life*; Weeks, *Sex, Politics and Society*; Judy Giles, '"Playing Hard to Get": Working-class Women, Sexuality and Respectability in Britain, 1918–40', *Women's History Review* 1 (1992), 239–55.

[10] See Adrian Bingham, *Gender, Modernity and the Popular Press in Inter-war Britain* (Oxford: Oxford University Press, 2004); Marcia Landy, *British Genres: Cinema and Society 1930–1960* (Princeton, NJ: Princeton University Press, 1991).

which formerly governed the relations between the sexes, an extended use of contraceptive measures and a reputed increase in the practice of abortion'.[11]

We might also look elsewhere for changes in gender identity. In the sphere of hearth and home, Alison Light has argued that a 'conservative modernity' developed in gender relations between the wars. The reconstruction of the home and private life after the devastation of the First World War did not trap women, but rather placed the domestic and the ordinary at the heart of national life in Britain, establishing a powerful role for women.[12] The changing pattern of women's work outside the home was also important. There were moments of significant expansion—most notably during the two world wars. In particular sectors of the economy between the wars, industry swelled with female workers, many of them young, single women, but also an increasing number of married women. Single women overshadowed married women in participation rates, though between 1921 and 1951, there were considerable increases in the numbers of married women aged between 21 and 34 in the workforce.[13] Trade unions nonetheless remained resolutely male. At the trough of the depression in 1932 and 1933, with the numbers of female trade unionists remaining steady while male membership plummeted, the female percentage of the trade union movement was still under 20%.[14]

The pattern of increasing female employment stood in contrast to the experience of male employment between the wars. Between the beginning of the postwar slump in 1921 and the outbreak of the Second World War, no fewer than one million people were out of work in any given year. At the nadir of the depression in 1932, the unemployed comprised 23% of the manual labour force. If one could remain in work through the upheavals of the interwar depression, there was a discernible rise in living standards. By the 1930s, some working-class people and a growing stratum of the lower-middle classes participated in an expanding consumer society. But even with these important qualifications, unemployment between the wars tempered the rising working-class confidence and expectations coming out of the First World War. The desolation of Jarrow and the dull meanness of life on the dole were counterweights to the art deco splendour of the Hoover Factory on the Western Avenue and the gleam of the Bakelite radio sets adorning some working-class homes. Unemployment was gendered, affecting men more than women. Mining, a dominantly male industry since the 1840s, saw the number of insured employees drop from 1,346,900 in 1923 to 943,000 in 1939.[15] There was a comparable decline in other male sectors such as shipbuilding. Sally Alexander

---

[11] Cmd. 5422, Ministry of Health, *Report of an Investigation into Maternal Mortality* (London: HMSO, 1937), 117, 118.

[12] See Alison Light, *Forever England: Femininity, Literature and Conservatism Between the Wars* (London: Routledge, 1991).

[13] Figures are taken from the Department of Employment and Productivity, *British Labour Statistics: Historical Abstract 1886–1966* (London: HMSO, 1971) and Jane Lewis, *Women in England 1870–1950* (Brighton: Wheatsheaf, 1984), Chapter 4.

[14] See Elizabeth Roberts, *Women's Work 1840–1940* (London: Macmillan, 1988).

[15] *British Labour Statistics: Historical Abstract 1886–1914*, Table 111, 210–11.

has remarked that two images of the interwar working-class competed for attention in the 1920s and 1930s, one of the unemployed man eliciting pity, the other of the young working girl provoking scorn.[16] It is hardly surprising that a palpable sense of emasculation animated images of unemployment. Faced with the taunts of his sister, the unemployed hero of Walter Greenwood's famous proletarian novel *Love on the Dole* (1933) feels the shame of his 'miserable muscles', for example.[17] The loss of employment was linked to the loss of masculinity and self-respect. E. Wight Bakke's study of *The Unemployed Man* (1933) noted that every unemployed man felt 'the blow his self-confidence had suffered from the fact that the traditional head of the family was not able to perform his normal function'.[18]

Much of the Labour Party's unemployment policy before and after the fall of its second government of 1929–31 was aimed at restoring the position of the male worker. In part, this focused on raising benefit rates. After 1931, with the turn towards socialist planning and public works as a means of attacking unemployment, the point was to generate work through the nationalization of industry and financial institutions, planned investment, the redistribution of industry, and public works.

If the male worker suffered the shame of joblessness, it was the mother or wife who was perceived to bear the brunt of its poverty. Within working-class families, wives served as the managers of the family income. Maud Pember Reeves and the FWG had documented the difficulties of this role before the First World War, mapping the various strategies working-class women used to avoid poverty for their families. The answer to the question, '[h]ow does a working man's wife bring up a family on 20s a week?' was 'she does not', even in the families of skilled workers.[19] The question echoed more plaintively and urgently through the depression years. In 1941, Seebohm Rowntree estimated the poverty line to be below £2 13s a week for the necessities of life required by a family of four to five persons.[20] Though the average weekly wage for men during the 1920s and 1930s hovered around two or three pounds, unemployment benefit was much lower. At best, it was 33s a week for a family of four. As Elizabeth Roberts has shown, the exigencies of the 1930s intensified the pressure on working-class women to make ends meet. They responded to this in a variety of ways, using credit and pawnbrokers to bridge gaps in income, going out to work full-time, or pursuing part-time or casual work such as cleaning, midwifery, washing, or child-minding.[21]

---

[16] Sally Alexander, 'Becoming a Woman in the 1920s and 1930s', in *Becoming a Woman*, 203–24; on young women workers, see Selina Todd, *Young Women, Work and Family in England 1918–50* (Oxford: Oxford University Press, 2005); Miriam Glucksmann, *Women Assemble* (London: Routledge, 1990); Michael Savage, 'Trade Unionism, Sex Segregation and the State: Women's Employment in "New Industries" in Inter-War Britain', *Social History* 13 (1988), 209–28; Paul Thompson, 'Playing at Being Skilled Men: Factory Culture and Pride in Work Skills among Coventry Car Workers', *Social History* 13 (1988), 45–69.

[17] Walter Greenwood, *Love on the Dole* (Harmondsworth: Penguin, 1933, 1969), 17.

[18] E. Wight Bakke, *The Unemployed Man* (London: Nisbet, 1933), 70–1.

[19] Pember Reeves, *Round About a Pound a Week*, 21.

[20] Seebohm Rowntree, *Poverty and Progress* (London: Longmans, 1941).

[21] Elizabeth Roberts, *A Woman's Place* (Oxford: Blackwell, 1984), 136; Chapter 4; see also Sean O'Connell, *Credit and Community* (Oxford: Oxford University Press, 2009).

There were other costs to working-class women. At the dusk of the 1930s, Margery Spring Rice noted the damage to women's physical health such deprivation had caused and the 'intolerable burden' it placed on such women in other ways: '[the mother is] faced not only with the lack of sufficient income to buy for her family what is needed, but with the constant strain of uneasiness caused by the shadow of unemployment, with the fear of a reduction in an already insufficient wage, and with the fear of running into debt while endeavouring to meet such unvarying obligations as rent, hire-purchase, insurance, etc'.[22] George Orwell's *The Road to Wigan Pier* (1937) is striking for its valorization of male labour; his descriptions of the physical strength of miners might be seen as a counterweight to the images of the impotence of men in Wigan drifting in the hopeless tide of unemployment. But the author's own epiphany was actually triggered by the sight of a working-class housewife, vainly trying to salvage a respectable domesticity amid the ravages of poverty: '[a]t the back of one of the houses a young woman was kneeling on the stones, poking a stick up the leaden waste-pipe . . . [s]he had a round pale face, the usual exhausted face of the slum girl who is twenty-five and looks forty, thanks to miscarriages and drudgery; and it wore . . . the most desolate, hopeless expression I have ever seen.'[23]

The scar of unemployment thus disfigured the working-class family between the wars. Unemployment also distended gender ideology within this context. In particular, it undercut the male breadwinner ideal, throwing the weight of providing for the family on the already-stooped shoulders of wives and mothers. This did not destroy long-standing conceptions of gender ideology and identity, but it did inflame important tensions and contradictions within it. The material experience of unemployment and the undermining of the breadwinner ideology were crucial starting points for the discussion of birth control within the Labour Party in the 1920s.

The fate of this debate depended to some degree upon the particular structure and ideology of the party. The birth control debate coincided with a period in which Labour was not simply incorporating women for the first time in a formal way, but was, to a large degree, forming itself as a political party. The year 1918 witnessed both the partial enfranchisement of women and a new constitution for the Labour Party that included the creation of a separate women's organization and reserved places for women on the governing National Executive Committee (NEC). Individual female members of the party were offered women's sections to join within wards and larger borough constituencies. At the county and city level, there were advisory councils and regional organizations. Within Transport House, Marion Phillips became the party's CWO who, with the aid of two National Women Organizers, advised constituency organizations. The NEC also joined the Standing Joint Committee of Industrial Women's Organizations (SJCIWO), sending its four female members as representatives. The SJCIWO included union groups such as the Railway Women's Guild and the National

---

[22] Margery Spring Rice, *Working-Class Wives* (London: Virago, 1939, 1981), 190.
[23] George Orwell, *The Road to Wigan Pier* (Harmondsworth: Penguin, 1937, 1987), 18.

Union of Clerks as well as the Fabian Society and female representatives from the General Council of the TUC. In 1919, the SJCIWO was invited to act as an 'Advisory Committee on Women's Questions' to Labour.

The 1918 constitution thus created a new space for women within the party. This recognized women's formal place in the public sphere as economic and political actors, but also marked them as a discrete political category. It set in place important tensions in the relationship between the party and women throughout the entire century. Discursively and structurally, Labour was a gendered being. This had important consequences for the apprehension of sexual issues in a political framework.[24]

In immediate terms, the attempt to bring women into the party through constituency organizations and women's sections was successful. By 1922, female membership of the party was estimated to be nearly 100,000. Four years later, this stood at 250,000 with 1,656 women's sections across the country. These sections offered a rich associational life for women involved in socialist and working-class politics. They were crucial in canvassing at elections, organizing fund-raising and also providing a forum for the discussion of policy by Labour women.

It is, of course, impossible to generalize about the outlook and approach of all women working within the Labour sphere in the interwar period. The party contained a variety of kinds of Labour women, some more radical than others, some middle class and others working class, some more confident about calling themselves feminist. The focus of such activists before 1918 had been not only the suffrage, but also the conditions of life for working-class women. Work was certainly one, but far more important in the interwar period was the question of motherhood. Much of the argument within Labour politics in the 1920s and 1930s dwelt upon what motherhood represented and what purchase it had within the larger ambit of Labour politics. This was a crucial factor in arguments about birth control.

If the relationship between Labour women and feminism tended to favour action, making the particular place and experience of working-class women the starting point, whether there was a particular feminine approach to Labour politics and ideology in the period after the First World War and the relationship between this and class consciousness should also be discussed. At the point of female enfranchisement and the inclusion of women into the Labour Party, there was some consideration of the 'problem' of women in socialist policy. The contributors to *Women and the Labour Party* (1920) stressed the different spheres of women within a broad equality through essays on nurseries, homes, maternity, and domestic work. Labour women might therefore be represented as equal within the party, but the site from which their political action sprang was very much the home, not the workplace: they were equal, but different.[25] Throughout the 1920s, Labour's

---

[24] For general overviews of women in the interwar Labour party, see Graves, *Labour Women* and David Howell, *MacDonald's Party* (Oxford: Oxford University Press, 2002), Chapters 20 and 21.

[25] See Harold Smith, 'Sex vs. Class: British Feminists and the Labour Movement, 1919–29', *Historian* 48 (1984), 19–37; Graves, *Labour Women*; Francis, 'Labour and Gender'.

election manifestos consistently highlighted this division. The 1923 manifesto asserted that the party 'stands for equality between men and women: equal political and legal rights, equal rights and privileges in parenthood, equal pay for equal work'.[26] In the election of the following year, women were specifically singled out for the discussion of food taxes, education, widows' pensions, and housing.[27] In Labour ideology, male work in the public sphere continued to underpin ideas about citizenship. The main protagonists of *Labour and the Nation* (1928) were, for example, 'workers who initiate and organise and plan, or who execute and manipulate and construct; whether they labour in the mine, in the factory and on the farm, or in the laboratory of the scientist and the office of the administrator'.[28] Labour policy in the interwar period was dominated by measures to remedy the plight of the male worker in a period of high unemployment and the sharp curtailment of trade union power, a tendency that increased as the interwar period went on. Women may have had common cause with men, but their political subjectivity was different, constituted less by work than by the supporting roles they played as mothers and wives.[29]

Though Labour women rarely disputed the place of women in the party's ideology, they did try to reinterpret the meaning and importance of women's roles. This included the vigorous pursuit of policies such as family allowances and the establishment of maternity clinics. Labour women's official publications began with the home and motherhood. In 1929, the SJCIWO told electors that 'the care of mother and baby is one of the bases of a healthy community'. Labour's socialist values lay with the determination to achieve 'within the nation . . . the conditions which are necessary for a happy childhood' and to make 'of family life a harmony of well-being, material and spiritual'.[30] In these ways, the private sphere was politicized. What was less clear was how this might change socialist policy, if at all. Even the SJCIWO believed that the victory of socialism would be secured largely through the improvement of conditions and wages for male workers and the application of central economic planning and public ownership.[31] In other words, the emphasis on motherhood and a politicized private, female sphere did not dislodge the importance of the public, male sphere in the SJCIWO's vision.

The invaluable work by Pamela Graves in recovering the experiences of working-class activists within Labour politics makes clear the deeply ingrained sense of separate spheres in working-class lives.[32] Women identified with the home, men with the workplace. What women lacked was an organizational basis for this identification. These different sites produced different kinds of class formation, with the trade union being important for men and the home for women. This is

---

[26] Labour Party, *Labour's Appeal to the Nation* (London: Labour Party, 1923).
[27] Labour Party, *Labour's Appeal to the People* (London: Labour Party, 1924).
[28] Labour Party, *Labour and the Nation* (London: Labour Party, 1928), 5.
[29] See, for example, Mary MacArthur, 'The Women Trade Unionist Point of View', in Marion Phillips, *Women and the Labour Party* (London: Headley, 1920), 20, 28.
[30] SJCIWO, *Women and the General Election* (London: SJCIWO, 1929), 16, 28.
[31] See, for example, SJCIWO, *Labour Women Report on Socialism and Our Standard of Living*, 29.
[32] See Graves, *Labour Women*, Chapter 2.

crucial, of course, in the shaping of Labour women's concerns. There are similar conclusions offered in local studies of interwar Labour and female employment in the 'new' industries.[33]

If Labour ideology and structure tended to favour the idea of separate spheres, we can see, however, that another pillar of gender ideology—the emphasis on the male breadwinner—was being undermined in the 1920s. Policies such as birth control reflected, in part, a continuation of concerns about the health of working-class mothers and the stability of the working-class home. It was also a challenge to the primacy of the breadwinner ideology in socialist and working-class politics. Birth control was not the only policy debate to reflect this. The controversy over the issue of family allowances also highlighted fractures in Labour's gender ideology. As Graves has suggested, family allowances began a debate on 'ideas about gender roles that were deeply imbedded in working-class culture'.[34] The family allowance debate resounding through the Labour movement between 1926 and 1931 was a narrative with two main characters, the male breadwinner and the working-class mother, and a Greek chorus of working-class children in want, witnesses to the failure of male wages. Arguments for sex reform were, in part, also built upon an acknowledgement that the breadwinner ideology had failed. In its place stood a plaintive, if more assertive, working-class mother asking to be armed with tools to protect her family from economic distress, whether those tools were family allowances or effective birth control.

II

In advanced feminist and socialist circles, as shall be discussed in Chapter 3, birth control was linked with the full emancipation of women and utopian visions of free sexuality. But the birth control campaign of the 1920s was rooted in the plight of working-class motherhood. This picked up the threads of work done in *Round About a Pound a Week* and *Maternity* before and during the First World War. After 1918, unemployment and continuing poverty intensified the desire for contraceptive information among working-class women. Letters written in the 1920s by such women to the birth control advocate Marie Stopes bore poignant witness to the physical and economic strain of large families.[35] Even when birth control information was available, birth control methods often remained out of the economic reach of many working-class people. In 1935, it was estimated that a condom cost sixpence, while cervical caps, when they could be fitted, cost between three and

---

[33] See Savage, *The Dynamics of Working-Class Politics*, Chapters 3 and 7; Jane Mark-Lawson, Mike Savage, and Alan Warde, 'Gender and Local Politics: Struggles over Welfare Policies 1918–1939', in Linda Murgatroyd et alia (eds), *Localities, Class and Gender* (London: Pion, 1985); Glucksmann, *Women Assemble*, Chapters 2, 6, and 8.

[34] Graves, *Labour Women*, 108.

[35] See Ruth Hall (ed.), *Dear Dr Stopes: Sex in the 1920s* (London: Cox and Wyman, 1978), 17, 18, 19, 23.

seven shillings.[36] Given an average weekly income of anywhere between about three and four pounds a week during the interwar period, this was not an inconsiderable expense.[37] Kate Fisher has recently challenged the idea that lack of sexual knowledge was widespread among working people, emphasizing, in particular, men's sexual agency.[38] But women, whether for reasons of respectability or not, showed older patterns of sexual ignorance. In 1937, Elizabeth Oakes and Ivy Roche of the EMWWA testified to the 'amazing ignorance among women' regarding contraception.[39]

The birth control campaign of the 1920s was an attempt to address such conditions. Graves has argued that the treatment of birth control as an issue within the Labour movement in the 1920s was less about striking a blow for feminist independence than about extending the terms of what welfare meant within socialist ideology.[40] This brought out the tensions circling around the issue of women's place in the Labour Party. But, building on the work done by Graves, we can see a number of other currents in the birth control campaign. The first is the way the campaign evinced a particular kind of class-consciousness born of the experience of sex and reproduction. This was a gendered class-consciousness from a female perspective, as powerful in its sense of inequality and powerlessness as any. We can also see the birth control campaign as an example of the relationship between middle-class women and working-class politics. Finally, a particular kind of socialist language about sex was forged in the birth control campaign.

The immediate roots of the campaign lay in the establishment of birth control clinics in urban areas and the question of local government provision of contraceptive information. In 1921, two birth control clinics were opened in London, one by Stopes in Holloway, the other by the Malthusian League (soon to rename itself the New Generation League) on the Walworth Road south of the River Thames. Other clinics followed in Wolverhampton, Manchester, Cambridge, Glasgow, Birmingham, Nottingham, and Bristol. With support from local trade unions, Labour women founded a Glasgow clinic.[41] An early survey suggested that for the most part the clientele of such clinics were working-class women.[42] There was also an underground economy of information. The St Pancras Birth Control Education League, for example, gave out handwritten notices with information on contraception and the promise of the name of a 'Lady Doctor' who would fit Dutch caps and

---

[36] Joan Malleson, *The Principles of Contraception: A Handbook for the General Practitioner* (London: Gollancz, 1935), 155.

[37] See *British Labour Statistics: Historical Abstract 1886–1968.*

[38] Fisher, *Birth Control, Sex and Marriage in Britain.*

[39] TNA, MH 71/25, Oral Evidence to Interdepartmental Committee on Abortion of Mrs Ivy E. Roche and Mrs E. Oakes, East Midlands Working Women's Association, 12.

[40] Graves, *Labour Women*, 81.

[41] Rowbotham, *A New World For Women*, 48; see Peter Fryer, *The Birth Controllers* (London: Secker and Warburg, 1965).

[42] Norman E. Hines, 'English Birth Control Clinics', *Eugenics Review* 59/4 (1928), 159; Deborah Cohen, 'Private Lives in Public Spaces: Marie Stopes, the Mothers' Clinics and the Practice of Contraception', *History Workshop Journal* 35 (1993), 95–116.

provide pessaries and the names of other birth control organizations ready to 'teach the Dutch method'.[43]

The establishment of birth control clinics served only to underline what was perceived as a crisis of sexual ignorance. Lella Secor Florence was an American who founded a birth control clinic in Cambridge in the 1920s. In her book *Birth Control on Trial* (1930), she set out the struggles faced by working-class women in their sexual lives:

> Fear, shame, anxiety—the ever-haunting dread of another pregnancy; work, toil, pain, weariness; crying babies; washing, cooking, scrubbing; nursing the sick, carrying water; no rest, no relief, cut off, isolated; patient, suffering; denied all joy, all beauty—slaves if ever slaves there have been—can anyone deny the right of one of these women to rebel against this ever-increasing burden of unwanted children? Can anyone deny her need of some contraceptive which she can use despite all her work and weariness and on which she can absolutely rely?

In one particular example, Florence placed a 'thin and white and ghost-like' mother between 'lovely children, beautifully cared for' and a selfish and demanding husband who 'will not use the sheath'. Sex, in this picture, was viewed only with fear: '[t]he whole act, which ought to be a happy expression of their love for each other, becomes a strained and miserable business, more often than not resulting in quarrels, ill-temper and worry'.[44] Advocates of birth control information for working-class women saw this in terms of liberating such women from the past and placing them in the present:

> . . . we can free mothers entirely from the fear of unwanted pregnancies . . . [and] so conserve their health to a very large extent. We can free the sex life of these people from the unnatural and bad psychological restrictions that are at present happening. We can produce [a] state of happiness, stability and normality . . .[45]

The relationship between contraceptive knowledge, the public sphere, and state involvement was soon the subject of controversy. In 1918, the Maternity and Infant Welfare Act had helped establish a network of centrally funded, local-government-run clinics for the care of mothers and children. But such centres were not permitted to give out birth control information and so information about birth control and birth control clinics operated outside of local government. In December 1922, the Edmonton Maternity Committee in north London dismissed one of its health visitors, Nurse E.S. Daniels, for giving out the address of the birth control clinic in nearby Holloway. The Ministry of Health supported her dismissal on the basis that Maternity and Infant Welfare centres could only give birth control information to women who were already pregnant or nursing. The case attracted

---

[43] International Institute for Social History, Amsterdam [IISH], Dora Russell Papers [DRP], 404, St Pancras Birth Control League, handwritten notice [no date, 1926?].

[44] Lella Secor Florence, *Birth Control on Trial* (London: George Allen and Unwin, 1930), 51, 64–5, 104.

[45] Helena Wright, *Report of the Conference on the Giving of Information on Birth Control by Public Health Authorities* (London: privately published, 1930), 14.

attention from working-class and middle-class advocates of birth control.[46] A few months later, in early 1923, two socialists, Rose Witcop and Guy Aldred, were charged with obscenity for distributing a pamphlet by the American Margaret Sanger designed to educate working-class women about sex and contraception.[47] The case attracted considerable interest from a coterie of London intellectuals. One particularly interested spectator was Dora Russell, the young wife of the philosopher Bertrand Russell and a recent convert to Labour. The prosecution of Witcop and Aldred appalled her: 'I could not see why information which a middle-class woman could get from her doctor should be withheld from a poorer woman who might need it far more.'[48]

The New Generation League stepped in to help organize support for Daniels, Aldred, and Witcop in 1923. The League included figures such as Stella Browne, Dora Russell, and Janet Chance who helped spearhead birth control and abortion campaigning within the Labour Party over the next decade and a half. Labour MPs sympathetic to birth control included F.A. Broad, the Labour MP for Edmonton and Dorothy Jewson, the Labour MP for Norwich.[49] Some women, Stella Browne in particular, decided to make connections with the grass roots of Labour and working-class women's organizations. Browne advertised 'theory and practice talks' on birth control for 'Women's Guilds, Labour Parties and Co-operatives'.[50] For the most part, talks were given in London or its environs, in areas such as North Kensington, Battersea, Walworth, Fulham, Kennington, Paddington, Stoke Newington, and Basingstoke. But Browne also toured Wales, sponsored by local sections of the CPGB. According to Browne, the response was overwhelming: 'every foot of floor space was packed and women, mostly with babies clasped in their arms, stood five deep in rows behind the chairs'.[51] In part, Browne's speeches were about giving information on birth control. But the popularity of her talks among the South Wales miners also led her to believe that she was erasing 'the biased, superficial and time-serving assertion of the "antagonism" and "inherent conflict" between Marxian or any other Socialism and birth control'.[52] Browne attempted to promote a rational approach to birth control in a eugenicist way while gently promoting sexual liberation: '[s]ocialists should realize the beautiful and inspiring aspects of sex'.[53] She also emphasized the class aspects of the birth control question, underlining differences between the middle-class and working-class experience of reproduction. In Tredegar in January 1924, her tour of Wales this time sponsored by the local Labour Party, Browne told an audience of the 'underhand attempts...to suppress among the poor, the knowledge freely available to the wealthy'.[54] Her reports again noted

[46] Rowbotham, *A New World For Women*, 49; Graves, *Labour Women*, 85.
[47] Russell, *Tamarisk Tree*, 168.
[48] Russell, *Tamarisk Tree*, 169–70; see also *The Times*, 11 January and 10 February 1923.
[49] *New Generation* 3 (January 1924), 1.
[50] *New Generation* 2 (July 1923), 79.
[51] F.W. Stella Browne, 'Birth Control in Taff Vale', *New Generation* 2 (October 1923), 117.
[52] *New Generation* 2 (September 1923), 107.
[53] Browne, 'Birth Control in Taff Vale', 116–17.
[54] F.W. Stella Browne, 'My Tour in Monmouthshire', *New Generation* 3 (January 1924), 8–9; Rowbotham, *A New World For Women*, 51–3.

the support of working-class women, 'many of them with their breadwinners out of work'.[55]

This work coincided with the formation of the first Labour government in January 1924. In March 1924, Witcop, Russell, and a number of other socialist-feminists such as Frida Laski (wife of socialist intellectual and academic Harold Laski), Ruth Dalton (a local councillor in London and briefly MP for Bishop Auckland, while deputizing for her husband, Hugh Dalton), Leah L'Estrange Malone (the wife of the maverick politician Cecil L'Estrange Malone, the first Communist MP to sit in the House, later a convert to the ILP), and a young doctor in training, Joan Malleson, published an open letter in *Labour Woman* appealing to all party members 'who realise the need for [contraceptive] knowledge among the workers, to raise the matter for discussion at their branch meeting; to send resolutions to our Labour Minister of Health, and to the forthcoming Party Conferences, and to sign a petition that such information be given'.[56]

Other groups within the Labour orbit had already mobilized on the issue. In 1923, the WCG passed a resolution calling for all maternity and child welfare centres be able to give out contraceptive information, rather than referring women to private doctors. The editorial staff of *Labour Woman*, headed by Marion Phillips, responded with 'Birth Control: A Plea for Careful Consideration', warning readers of the 'moral considerations' around birth control that might undermine Labour's unity on 'an issue which is not a political one, but is in a very special sense a matter of private conviction'. This became the first line of defence against discussing birth control: 'we do plead that this subject of the relations of husband and wife should not be treated as a political issue at all'.[57]

The Labour women's conference of 1924 received a number of resolutions on birth control from local women's sections in London, the North of England, and Scotland, leading to a composite resolution on the agenda asking that birth control information be given freely to working mothers by state maternity and child welfare clinics. Maternity was the starting point for sex reform. Addressing the conference, Jenny Baker of Finchley, North London, said that 'for the good of maternity . . . or the good of the babies, it is necessary that some knowledge of this sort should be disseminated'. The disparity in experiences of sex and reproduction between middle-class and working-class women was stressed. This was perhaps partly a rhetorical strategy.[58] Dora Russell spoke, for example, of the women 'who visit Harley Street physicians' for sex knowledge: 'we say it is a crying shame that this advice should not be made available to the working mother who desires it'. This was not just a middle-class rhetorical strategy. Working-class speakers also drew out this sense of inequality and disempowerment: '[w]e feel as working women, the working women should have the right to say how many children they are able to

[55] Browne, 'My Tour in Monmouthshire', 9.
[56] *Labour Woman*, 12/3 (March 1924), 46.
[57] *Labour Woman*, 12/3 (March 1924), 34.
[58] See Stephen Brooke, 'Bodies, Sexuality and the "Modernization" of the British Working Classes', *International Labour and Working Class History* 69 (June 2006), 122–43.

have. . . . The wealthy woman says how many children she can have . . . we say that the working mother should be able to get the knowledge even though she has no money.' Mrs Lane, from the mining constituency of Houghton-le-Spring, Durham, talked of uncontrolled fertility being one of the 'great social problems . . . interlocked one with the other' that 'oppress us'. The 'us' was, of course, a class reference. In this way, talking about sex was also talking about class, forging a shared consciousness of class from sex.

The deep sense of inequality and disempowerment felt by working-class women in comparison with middle-class women made the private experience of sex a natural field for socialist action. One delegate wanted birth control recognized as a form of social welfare: '[i]n the abolition of poverty birth control is an essential factor'. This sought to make access to birth control information a part of socialist policy. There were few opposing voices from the floor. But the speakers on the podium shifted uneasily at the prospect of the resolution succeeding. The SJCIWO had insisted that there was too much conflict among medical experts about birth control. Instead, it recommended including birth control as part of a larger inquiry into maternity.[59] This was ignored by the conference delegates and the original resolution was carried by a large majority. Russell wrote to her husband just after the vote: 'all the delegates at the Conference seem to be mad to discuss the question. I'm afraid we haven't only lit a candle but started a blooming conflagration.'[60] In the months following, pro-birth control resolutions continued to be submitted to the national leadership of the women's sections.

Some activists had been stirred into action by the intransigence of the new Labour government. On 9 May 1924, four days before the women's conference, Russell and Leah L'Estrange Malone had organized a deputation to John Wheatley, the (Catholic) Minister of Health in the short-lived 1924 Labour government. Russell was accompanied by H.G. Wells, F.A. Broad, fellow Labour MPs H.G. Romeril and Sam March, and representatives from the Walworth centre, the East Finchley Labour women's section, and Battersea Borough Council. The deputation requested that in government-run organizations and institutes, birth control advice be given to married women. This proposal was placed within the context of maternity and class. Russell told John Wheatley that birth control would give 'working women access to knowledge which was readily available to people who can afford to pay for it'.[61] The memorandum submitted by the delegation to Wheatley featured the case of 'Mrs F'. At 34, she had had eighteen pregnancies. A 'careful and clean mother', she was nonetheless at her wits' end. She refused to have sex with her husband, encouraged him to have sex with other women, and had herself tried to procure an abortion on numerous occasions. The plight of 'Mrs F' was contrasted with the position of middle-class women able to consult doctors and use birth control. The delegation was careful to dodge accusations of immorality by

---

[59] *ACLW* (1924), 85.
[60] Bertrand Russell Archives, Hamilton, Canada [BRA], Dora Russell to Bertrand Russell, 13 May 1924.
[61] IISH, DRP, 402, WBCG Deputation to Minister of Health, 9 May 1924.

stressing that birth control should primarily be for married women with one or more children.[62] Wheatley demurred, saying that it was not within the authority of the Ministry to alter the policy on birth control access; this could only change through parliamentary legislation.[63] Russell remembered the deputation as getting a 'dreadful' reception, but succeeding 'as regards uniting different types of people and points of view and making people listen [to the] cause of working mothers'.[64] Following the women's conference, the SJCIWO also met with Wheatley on birth control. He reiterated his opposition to changing the policy 'without the express authority of Parliament' and doubted 'whether the working-classes were really united on the subject'.[65]

Russell later wrote that 'Mr Wheatley had stirred a hornets' nest: all through 1924 we buzzed and stung'.[66] *New Generation* accused Wheatley of betraying his class.[67] The minister's response served only to convince Russell and others that birth control was a political issue to be resolved through the Labour Party and the political sphere. Soon after, Dora Russell, Dorothy Jewson, Ernest and Dorothy Thurtle (Ernest was MP for Shoreditch in London, Dorothy the daughter of the leading Labour politician George Lansbury and a local councillor in Shoreditch), Leah L'Estrange Malone, and Frida Laski formed the WBCG with a number of delegates from the women's conference. Dorothy Jewson became President and Russell acted as Honorary Secretary between 1924 and 1928. The latter also drafted many of the group's statements. The WBCG was never a huge organization. Within a year, it had only 128 members, but enjoyed affiliations from about 19 Labour women's sections and WCGs.[68] Significantly, with the exception of Dorothy Jewson, no female Labour MPs associated themselves with the WBCG. The WBCG was dominated by a middle-class leadership and thus was less an organization that grew up from the working-class than one that sought to represent working-class people. That leadership also featured mostly married women and mothers, thus placing single women such as Jewson and Browne in a more ambiguous position.

The WBCG's aims were clearly class-based: '[t]o bring within the reach of working people the best and most scientific information on Birth Control'. This would be accomplished in two ways. The first was to work within the Labour movement '[t]o strengthen public opinion among workers as to the importance of Birth Control in any scheme of social progress'. Following this, the Ministry of

---

[62] IISH, DRP, 402, WBCG, Memorandum by Deputation to Ministry of Health, 9 May 1924 (London: WBCG, 1924), 3, 7.

[63] IISH, DRP, 402, WBCG, Deputation to Minister of Health, 9 May 1924. See also Russell, *Tamarisk Tree*, 171–2.

[64] BRA, 8.10, Dora Russell to Bertrand Russell, 10 May 1924.

[65] Modern Records Centre, University of Warwick [MRC], MSS 292/824/1, Memorandum, Meeting between John Wheatley and deputation from Standing Joint Committee of Industrial Women's Organizations, 31 July 1924.

[66] Russell, *Tamarisk Tree*, 174.

[67] *New Generation* 3 (September 1924), 97.

[68] IISH, DRP, 402, Russell, 'Report of the Founding and Work of the Workers Birth Control Group and the Attitude of the English Labour Party Towards Birth Control', no date [1925].

Health and Parliament had to 'recognise Birth Control as an essential part of Public Health work'.[69] The group sought to disassociate Labour birth control advocates from charges of Malthusianism, even if several of its members had roots in that movement and in eugenics. Birth control was not to be about middle-class people limiting the fertility of working-class people, but about working-class women having the power to make that choice themselves: 'the mothers ... should be the chief ones to decide when the children are born'.[70] Leah L'Estrange Malone told the Malthusian League that it 'was not our business to inculcate the duty of having small families on those who preferred large ones, but it was our business to see that those women who desired to limit their families should have every opportunity of doing so'.[71] The WBCG hoped that birth control would give working-class women 'knowledge, rights and economic help'.[72]

Its campaign offered a new kind of political protagonist. Its members may have represented working-class women as helpless victims in a struggle to maintain their struggle against poverty as a means of winning empathy, but the WBCG also portrayed women as citizens and, within the socialist struggle, as comrades. This was particularly clear in the post-suffrage era. In an appeal to male workers, the group evoked working women as new actors on the stage of socialist action: 'to-day and to-morrow they are your friends and comrades. They stand beside you to make laws and to create the workers' commonwealth'.[73] In this way, the WBCG used the issue of birth control to write a new kind of politicized class identity, based in sex and motherhood, but grounded, as well, in power and equality.

The WBCG distinguished itself from other birth control groups through its political character. Russell wrote: 'the Group was formed definitely as a political organisation seeking political action through its Party and the Trade Unions and Cooperative Guilds ... [t]he Group did not wish to work in antagonism to existing birth control organisations but distinguished itself from them in its political aims'.[74] In such a fashion, the WBCG played back the response of the Minister of Health:

> We have been told that the Public Health Service through the Maternity and Welfare Centres *will not be allowed to give Birth Control advice to working mothers ... without the express authority of Parliament* [emphasis in original]. That being so, this becomes a political question and we are bound to ask political people to help us.[75]

The WBCG rejected the narrow vision of the political promoted by Marion Phillips:

---

[69] IISH, DRP, 402, WBCG Membership Form, 1924.
[70] WBCG, *To Our Men Comrades* (London: WBCG, no date).
[71] *New Generation* 5 (December 1926), 124.
[72] IISH, DRP, 402, Russell, 'Report of the Founding and Work of the Workers Birth Control Group and the Attitude of the English Labour Party Towards Birth Control', no date [1925], 9.
[73] WBCG, *To Our Men Comrades*.
[74] IISH, DRP, 402, Russell, 'Report of the Founding and Work of the Workers Birth Control Group and the Attitude of the English Labour Party Towards Birth Control', no date [1925], 5.
[75] WBCG, *To Our Men Comrades*.

It is argued by many that birth control is not a political question. It is bound to be a political question in the sense in which the Labour Party and the Independent Labour Party and the Communist Party understand politics. You cannot deal with housing, education, agriculture, mothers' pensions without reference to this question. It is one of the first principles of the Labour outlook that politics is not a game of parties but deals with the vital questions in the life of the people.[76]

The WBCG was careful to work within a maternalist context. In part, this served as a counterweight to the potential controversy of birth control. As already noted, among its leadership, there were only two unmarried women, Stella Browne and Dorothy Jewson. As an MP and local councillor, Jewson took a particular risk in her advocacy of birth control. Concentrating on married women was a conscious decision. The 'control of [the WBCG's] policy was to be in the hands of men and women who had known the responsibility of parenthood'.[77]

In her account of the origins of the WBCG, Russell accorded mothers the greatest authority to speak about birth control: 'it is those who love children and care most satisfactorily for their own, who are the strongest and most eloquent advocates of birth control'.[78] But mothers, Russell claimed, had been 'somewhat neglected in the feminist fight of the last fifty years'. Now, they had to show 'some degree of pugnacious feminism' to win the battle for birth control. There were some hints of eugenics in this. Birth control was linked to the vision of a 'healthy and intelligent community', in which children would have 'space, air, good food, care and thorough education', there would be 'really happy homes', and, most importantly, mothers would be 'healthy' and allowed to be 'creative'.[79] But it was more clearly rooted in a changing view of femininity: '[t]he view that woman existed solely for procreation has passed out of our social outlook'.[80]

The strategy of the WBCG was to mobilize support for birth control from the bottom up, through the Labour women's sections. On behalf of the WBCG, Russell campaigned up and down the country, in constituency parties and women's sections, as the self-described 'enfant terrible' of the Labour movement.[81] In particular, she visited working-class districts in the North, Scotland, and Wales, stressing the importance of birth control as an issue and talking about sex as a problem. After a visit to Motherwell in 1925, she wrote:

People are *just ripe* for education about sex. . . . The women blush and are terrified when they hear me say things that they dare not say themselves. The strength of a

[76] IISH, DRP, 402, WBCG, Memorandum by Deputation to Ministry of Health, 9 May 1924 (London: WBCG, 1924), 9.

[77] IISH, DRP, 402, Russell, 'Report of the Founding and Work of the Workers Birth Control Group and the Attitude of the English Labour Party Towards Birth Control', no date [1925], 6.

[78] IISH, DRP, 402, Russell, 'Report of the Founding and Work of the Workers Birth Control Group and the Attitude of the English Labour Party Towards Birth Control', no date [1925], 6.

[79] WBCG, *To Our Men Comrades*.

[80] IISH, DRP, WBCG, Memorandum by Deputation to Ministry of Health, 9 May 1924 (London: WBCG, 1924), 12.

[81] BRA, 8.10, Dora Russell to Bertrand Russell, 27 March 1925.

taboo is a thing one scarcely realizes until one gets among people like these—Wives who would really sooner die than complain of intimate pains to their husbands.[82]

Russell might be forgiven some hyperbole for her claim, after a tour to the same area the previous year, that '[w]e have absolutely won the people. They talk of nothing else in the Foundry and Steel works!'[83] Of course, the ambiguous lines of class over the question of birth control are notable: Russell's self-portrayal underlined her middle-class authority, even as she tried to build a working-class politics of birth control.

The case for birth control was made not only in the vocabulary of class difference and maternal health, but also by appropriating the language of work, a language which, as already pointed out, coloured Labour thought about citizenship. The female body lay at the heart of these arguments; it was represented as a vessel of labour, albeit one of reproductive labour. The reproductive work of mothers was compared with the productive work of miners. In the mid-1920s, the miners comprised an emotive centre to labour politics, particularly because of the crisis of the coal industry. But the miner was also the physical embodiment of labour, a highly gendered symbol of working-class politics, whose body was tempered by hard, physical work.[84] Russell contrasted, for example, the attention given to male miners, their bodies, and their work with the inattention paid to the bodies and work of working-class mothers. She chastized the Labour Party for supporting 'the miners' right to seven hours only of his dangerous toil [while] they will stifle the voice of his wife whose hours are longer[,] whose toil is more dangerous than his'.[85] Danger was thus entwined with the reproductive work of the female body: the dangers of childbirth haunted the female body in its work as much as broken limbs and choking coal dust did for miners in their work. Just as the bodies of miners needed protection in their work, so too did those of mothers. Russell told the 1928 conference of Labour women: '[m]others had a trade union interest in this matter, which need[s] safeguarding by political action'.[86]

This was also an argument about rights and citizenship. Women claimed the protection of their bodies, through birth control, on the basis of their reproductive labour. Russell wrote in the ILP's publication, *New Leader*: 'we demand that the mother, like her economically occupied husband, shall be placed in a position of maximum freedom to determine under what conditions she will or will not perform her function'.[87] Citizenship had to include workers of hand, mind, and womb.

[82] BRA, 8.10, Dora Russell to Bertrand Russell, February 1925.

[83] BRA, 8.10, Dora Russell to Bertrand Russell, 18 March 1924.

[84] See for example, Orwell, *The Road to Wigan Pier*, 23. See also Eric D. Weitz, 'The Heroic Man and the Ever-Changing Woman: Gender and Politics in European Communism, 1917–1950', in Laura L. Frader and Sonya O. Rose (eds), *Gender and Class in Modern Europe* (Ithaca, NY: Cornell University Press, 1996).

[85] IISH, DRP, 405, untitled draft, no date [1926].

[86] *ACLW* (1928), 26.

[87] Dora Russell, 'Is Birth Control a Feminist Reform?', *The New Leader* (London), 2 October 1925.

Like other workers, women were united by their reproductive labour. These mother–citizen-workers were placed in the context of post-suffrage politics:

> We are equal citizens with men and claim the right to protection in our work—even, and more especially when it is child-bearing—that the men workers claim.... We mothers are claiming, like every other worker to-day, simply the right to decide our working conditions, hours, wages, [and] capacity to have and rear so and so many children, need of technical knowledge or instruction for State schools or clinics.[88]

Such arguments had the same reference points as more conventional socialist language in the 1920s (work and motherhood), but birth control would give women a new independence and autonomy within these contexts. Through birth control, a woman might be as independent in her reproductive work as a man was in his productive work. Women obtained a kind of property in reproductive labour through their bodies. Like property in labour for men, this gave life to a political ethos about rights and independence.

Russell and the WBCG thus constructed socialism from the material experience of the female body within the terms of an existing socialist language about work and motherhood. In some ways, appropriating the language of work was a means of identifying, rather than competing with Labour men. But arguing for an equivalency between productive and reproductive labour also positioned work in the unfamiliar sphere of the sexual and the reproductive, centring it upon the female body. Similarly, while not challenging motherhood as a primary identity for women, maternity was rewritten in radical ways. Women's claims upon citizenship as mothers were emphasized, but they were also portrayed as autonomous workers and citizens who claimed public and private rights over their bodies on their own terms. This evoked motherhood less as a natural or spiritual category, or one circumscribed by the family, than as a professional or functional category. On the birth control issue, Russell, for example, saw 'the rising of the Trade Union spirit among the mothers'.[89] There was, however, an important premise to all of these arguments: the male breadwinner had failed. The backdrop to much birth control advocacy was a familiar one in the 1920s, a landscape of economic devastation, where male jobs had been lost and union power rolled back. In 1924, for example, after touring South Wales, Stella Browne evoked the 'hideous poverty and misery... the hopelessness that has hardly lifted since the great betrayal of Black Friday'.[90] Even if the arguments of Russell and the WBCG worked within the terms of socialism and maternal feminism, they still challenged the meaning of work, the position of motherhood in socialist discourse, the breadwinner ideology, and, not least, the boundaries of what was considered political.

---

[88] IISH, DRP, 404, Dora Russell, 'What the Women Have to Say', no date [1926]; WBCG, Memorandum by Deputation to Minister of Health, 9 May 1924, 12.

[89] IISH, DRP, 403, Dora Russell to *Socialist Review*, undated [1926].

[90] Browne, 'My Tour in Monmouthshire', 9.

This was a new kind of socialism. But such arguments of course still evoked a particular kind of body and femininity. Women's labour remained primarily reproductive labour. Sexuality was about the need for protection, not pleasure. Birth control was the right of married mothers, not all women. The vista of femininity and sexuality in these arguments had limited horizons, bounded by a language of maternity and work. Given the conservatism of contemporary Labour politics, the urgency of the question of maternal mortality and morbidity, and the threatening shadow of unemployment falling over working-class communities in the 1920s, undoubtedly there were few other practical alternatives to this route. Russell, for one, understood the limitations and costs of such tactical compromises. After a meeting at a local Labour Party in Croydon in 1924, for example, she was challenged by a group of young supporters espousing a more radical vision of sexual emancipation: 'I said as a private person I agreed with them, but as a public propagandist it wasn't advisable to go so far.'[91] That same month, another sex radical confronted her:

> The girl... attacked me also for making our birth control campaign so respectable. Said we should have had *un*married women and 'made a gesture' for full distribution of information. I said I wasn't out to 'make a gesture' but to help women with stitched up insides and prolapsed wombs. The gulf between women who've had babies and women who haven't is immense... Obviously birth control means a completely new morality, but I really don't see the use to screaming that out when you can't even get people to take action on clear medical grounds.[92]

Russell's reference to the experience of motherhood and her insistence upon the physical threat of 'stitched up insides' and 'prolapsed wombs' is notable, teasing out the differences between female bodies as much as their similarities. But she conceded the point that there were limits to what could be said about the experience and possibilities of the female body within the context of the Labour Party and within the terms of the socialist language she and the WBCG had adopted. The very language used to promote a socialism of the female body foreclosed a more radical statement of sexual liberation and women's rights.

The Labour women's sections became the terrain on which the debate over birth control as a socialist issue was played out. Large majorities carried resolutions asking for the distribution of birth control information through local government at the women's conferences of 1925 and 1927; there was no conference in 1926 because of the General Strike. The issue enjoyed great support among local Labour women's sections and WCGs; in 1926, there were over fifty resolutions supporting birth control at the cancelled women's conference of that year.[93] That same year, the ILP also passed a resolution in favour of local government bodies disseminating birth control advice. In 1929, an ILP pamphlet stated that 'the enlightenment of women on measures of birth control was an essential part of the maternity work

[91] BRA, 8.10, Dora Russell to Bertrand Russell, 14 April 1924.
[92] BRA, 8.10, Dora Russell to Bertrand Russell, 28 April 1924.
[93] See Graves, *Labour Women*, 90–1.

done by the public health centres'.[94] Some opposition from the grass-roots membership did emerge. At the 1925 conference, for example, a Mrs Quinn from Leeds announced that '[w]orking mothers did not want instructions in impure and unchaste matters'. But her comments caused 'disorder' in the hall and only six other women voted against the birth control resolution.[95]

It is clear that birth control was seen as an issue not about morality or conscience or only of the private sphere, but one entrenched in a social welfare and class perspective and distinctly political. Dorothy Jewson told the 1926 Labour conference, '[i]t was a Party question . . . because the women of the Party had made it one'.[96] But it was exactly on the point of whether or how birth control was political that the Labour Party and the leadership of the women's sections expressed their disagreement. The latter had never supported birth control. Marion Phillips feared that birth control would divide the party and distract it from what she considered more important aims, unity first of all, but also other, less innovative, welfare programmes. The leadership of the Labour women's sections also rejected the notion that birth control was anything but a troublesome distraction for the party. In 1926, the editors of *Labour Woman* told their readers that the questions of birth control and access to contraceptive information were 'not party political in their nature'; they would only divide Labour and become a 'means for impeding the progress of the Party'.[97] In his interwar study of the young Labour Party, the German Egon Wertheimer reflected that this was the most significant faultline between European democratic socialism and the British Labour Party, the latter's discomfort with sexual questions, with Marion Phillips the most obvious exemplar of this attitude.[98]

The national party leadership was also unsympathetic to the question. First of all, the NEC made little distinction between promoting birth control and widening access to information about it. A major concern was the Catholic and religious vote, a constituency that the party was eager to gather into its fold as the Liberals fell apart.[99] Such fears should not be easily dismissed. In 1927, Glasgow was home to a bitter conflict on the local politics over birth control. The municipal Labour Party was split over the question whether the city's libraries should carry copies of Marie Stopes's publication, *Birth Control News*. Birth control became an issue at the municipal elections of the same year and though it may not have proved decisive, it was perceived as a factor in a weak showing for Labour candidates, with the Catholic vote actively mobilized on the issue.[100]

---

[94] ILP Leaflet No. 4, *What Women in the ILP Stand For* (September 1929).

[95] *ACLW* (1925), 125.

[96] *LPCR* (1926), 205.

[97] 'Birth Control and the Labour Party Executive', *Labour Women* 14/10 (October 1926), 151.

[98] See Egon Wertheimer, *Portrait of the Labour Party* (London: Putnam, 1939), 89–91, cited in Howell, *MacDonald's Party*, 347.

[99] Neil Riddell, 'The Catholic Church and the Labour Party, 1918–31', *Twentieth Century British History* 8 (1997), 179–82.

[100] See Smyth, *Labour in Glasgow 1896–1936*, 151, 184–7.

Related to this was the fear that sanctioning birth control distribution would diffuse the unity and clarity of the party at a critical moment. In the 1920s, Labour purged itself of a number of what the NEC considered deviant tendencies, the Communists not least.[101] The support for birth control might well be seen in this light as a burgeoning sex separatism that had to be quashed. Finally, there was the consistent rejection of the idea that birth control could be political. This was formally articulated in the 1925 NEC annual report: 'the subject of Birth Control is in its nature not one which should be made a political Party issue, but should remain a matter upon which members of the Party should be free to hold and promote their individual convictions'.[102]

The 1925 annual conference of the party saw the first open conflict between those within the women's sections supporting birth control and the party leadership. Jenny Baker, a WBCG member, moved a reference back of the section of the NEC's annual report dealing with birth control. She appealed to Labour men for support on the issue and argued that the birth control issue was clearly one of class inequity between 'working women' and the women who did not need the information so much and who had had it for many years, those who could afford to pay for it. But the NEC maintained its line, with Florence Harrison Bell remarking that '[p]ersonally, she deprecated making it a Party question, not because she was afraid, but because she had had the experience of a long and happy married life, and would deprecate any Party interfering in the intimate relationships between husbands and wives, fathers and mothers and children'.[103] The reference back was lost by a vote of 1,824,000 to 1,053,000, a vote which at least showed that the advocates of birth control within the party enjoyed a base of support beyond the constituency parties, most likely from the Miners Federation (MFGB).

There was much angry reaction to the 1925 decision. The marginalization of women's concerns was a recurring point. Dorothy Jewson wrote that it was 'no new thing for the women of the Labour Party to find questions of particular interest to themselves placed at the end of a long agenda'.[104] Dorothy Thurtle railed that the NEC 'only have use for women so long as they have no opinions of their own but are willing to do the donkey work of the Party'.[105] This led to strong criticisms of the constitutional structure of the party. On behalf of the WBCG, Russell asked: 'Why reserve seats for women at all [on the NEC], if they are not to represent the views of Labour women?'[106] The editors of *Labour Woman* responded by saying that the NEC had to represent the interests of the party 'as a whole', not the interests of women: '[s]ometimes they may not be the same'.[107]

---

[101] See Graves, *Labour Women*, 91; Stuart MacIntyre, *A Proletarian Science* (London: Lawrence and Wishart, 1980).

[102] *LPCR* (1925), 44.

[103] *LPCR* (1925), 191–2.

[104] Dorothy Jewson, 'The Labour Party Conference and Birth Control', *New Generation* 4 (November 1925), 127.

[105] Dorothy Thurtle, 'Mrs Thurtle's Protest', *New Generation* 5 (April 1926), 40.

[106] *Labour Women* 13/12 (December 1925), 206.

[107] *Labour Women* 13/12 (December 1925), 203.

For the most part, the political debates over access to birth control stayed within the sphere of Labour politics. But in February 1926, Ernest Thurtle introduced a bill in the Commons under the ten-minute rule to allow married women knowledge of birth control from local authorities, thus articulating directly the aims of the WBCG. Thurtle explicitly made this a question of social welfare, to 'remove one of the disabilities of poverty'. For Thurtle, it was also a case of obvious class inequality between upper- and middle-class women who could afford such knowledge and working-class women who could not. Thurtle focused on the condition of the working-class wife: '[t]here is no more tragic figure in our civilization than the over-burdened mother of a large family in the poor, over-crowded districts in this country'. In this case, he spoke partly in socialist and partly in Malthusian tones, believing that allowing 'working-class people to exercise a wise restriction in the size of their families would have an immediate ameliorative effect on the conditions of those workers'. But he also saw birth control as a consequence of gender equality, giving a woman the right to 'decide what the size of her family should be'. Another Labour MP, James Barr, a Presbyterian minister, spoke against the bill, saying it was a 'policy of despair', one that avoided the real question of politics, the unequal distribution of wealth in the country.[108] Thurtle's bill was lost by a vote of 167 to 81, with prominent Labour figures such as George Lansbury, F.W. Pethick-Lawrence, Philip Snowden, and Ellen Wilkinson voting for the motion.

The 1926 party conference saw pro- and anti-birth control forces coming into further conflict. The NEC held that the 1925 conference had decided the issue and, as a matter of principle, this meant that a three-year rule suspending discussion of the question could be invoked. Birth control supporters opposed this, referring back that portion of the NEC's report. It was a debate of considerable intensity. At one point, for example, a voice from the floor claimed that adopting birth control would 'smash the Labour Party'.[109] Dora Russell made an impassioned plea that the party consider the question:

> Let any of them imagine a section of the Party bringing a proposal to Conference which they considered vital to their life and health and being told by the Executive that they could not discuss it on a resolution because it could not be a party question, would it not make them wild? Well, the women were wild ... to the women it was as important as the seven-hours day was to the miners, and their opinion ought to have the same weight as the Miners' Federation had in their matters. Birth control was important to their health, leisure, and happiness.[110]

The party leader, Ramsay MacDonald, raised the spectre of neo-Malthusianism as a threat to the independence of the working-class family. He also argued that a commitment to birth control would cripple the party's electoral prospects. MacDonald instructed female supporters of the party that they might 'go on with their work ... if they wished, but not to try to dig ditches between the women and the

[108] *Parliamentary Debates* (Commons), 189, 9 February 1926, cs. 849, 851, 852.
[109] *LPCR* (1926), 206.
[110] *LPCR* (1926), 202.

rest of the Party'.[111] In the end, Russell and her allies were rewarded: the conference voted narrowly (1,656,000 to 1,620,000) to refer the matter back to the NEC's consideration, to be considered and discussed at the 1927 conference. Support came from the National Union of Railwaymen and the MFGB.[112] Graves has suggested that the MFGB supported the cause of birth control as an act of 'reciprocity' for women's support during the strike.[113] Russell also believed that the unions felt that the NEC had treated the women 'badly'.[114]

But the party conference the following year saw the miners in a much-weakened position, more eager to solicit the support of the wider party following the debacle of the General Strike. MacDonald also made a direct appeal to miners to keep faith with the leadership on the birth control issue, writing to the miner and Labour MP Stephen Walsh on the eve of the 1927 Labour conference:

> The Executive . . . is very anxious to keep the question of Birth Control absolutely outside the realm of party politics and an attempt is going to be made to defeat us on that and commit the party as a party, to a view on this subject. The people who wish to do this are reckoning upon the Miners' vote, and undoubtedly, if they get it, it will make the situation very uncertain. Nobody knows better than you what this would mean to the Party, and if the Federation is going to take on responsibility for this along with its other troubles—God help it![115]

After a deputation in favour of birth control from the women's conference met with the NEC, the latter decided to return to its 1925 decision. The debate at the 1927 conference rivalled the intensity of the previous year. Advocates of birth control continued to stress that the dissemination of contraceptive information was a legitimate measure of social reform. The ILP intellectual H.N. Brailsford remarked, for example: '[a]ll they were asking was that these poor working women should have effective liberty'.[116] An emotive moment came with the speech of a young mother and miner's wife from Chopwell, near Tyne and Wear:

> She had held her baby of a few months old, in her arms, as she listened, tragically intent, to the preceding speeches, but she took her place on the rostrum alone. She spoke as a young mother in a hurry, after fifteen years in industry. Working women demanded and believed that if the ban were raised, knowledge would help them, and in Conference after Conference, had demanded it. Was that not enough? Surely the miners would not turn the women down?[117]

[111] *LPCR* (1926), 206.

[112] Russell, *Tamarisk Tree*, 188; on women's support and the miners' lockout, see Hester Barron, *The 1926 Miners' Lockout* (Oxford: Oxford University Press, 2010), Chapter 3; Sue Bruley, 'Women', in John McIlroy, Alan Campbell, and Keith Gildart (eds), *Industrial Politics and the 1926 Miners' Lockout* (Cardiff: University of Wales Press, 2004); Sue Bruley, 'The Politics of Food: Gender, Family, Community and Collective Feeding in South Wales in the General Strike and Miners' Lockout, 1926', *Twentieth-Century British History* 18 (2007), 54–77.

[113] Graves, *Labour Women*, 95.

[114] BRA, 8.10, Dora Russell to Bertrand Russell, 13 October 1926.

[115] Quoted in Howell, *MacDonald's Party*, 354.

[116] *LPCR* (1927), 231.

[117] Browne, 'Labour Sandbags Birth Control', 124.

But the women were turned down. Representatives of two large unions, the Transport and General Workers and the General and Municipal Workers, voiced their opposition, as did Arthur Henderson. The reference back was lost by a majority of 2,610,000 votes. The reaction of Labour women to this defeat was, according to Stella Browne (admittedly not an unbiased witness), 'deep and widespread indignation and disgust...at their cowardly betrayal by the men's organizations'.[118]

But there was also a sense of exhaustion on the question and deference to the growing authority of the leadership. The issue came up again at the women's conference of 1928. With Arthur Henderson in attendance, Dora Russell spoke with obvious exasperation at the treatment of birth control by the rest of the party: 'she characterized the recommendations of the Executive as specious and evasive'.[119] Henderson once again articulated his fear that the question would be a divisive one within the party and with voters. What was striking about the debate, however, were the Labour women who came forward to deny the worth of birth control as a political issue. Mrs Bamber of the National Union of Distributive and Allied Workers argued that there were other social welfare issues of greater importance: '[w]e had no right to make this a Party question. At the moment we should concentrate on such vital questions as housing and unemployment, on which progress must be made before we could hope to secure the limitation of families.'[120] More surprisingly, given she had supported Thurtle's parliamentary initiative, Ellen Wilkinson dismissed the idea that it was a class issue: 'the issues between one class and another must be planks in our programme, but this was quite a different matter'.[121] Birth control died a close death at the 1928 women's conference, defeated by three votes. Why had opinion on the question changed? It is likely that the call of party unity, made so strongly by the party leadership, took root in the women's sections, particularly in the run-up to an election. Even the *New Generation* admitted that the election weighed heavily on the minds of women who were bitter towards the party.[122] Loyalty to the party may well have suppressed the desire to pursue the issue. It is striking, for example, that in the heart of mining country, the Durham Labour Women's Advisory Council and its women's sections never recorded a discussion of birth control in the 1920s, though this may have been a case of not formally noting such discussions.[123] This is not to deny the wide support of Labour women for the birth control issue, as was clear between 1924 and 1927, but the coming election and the wake of the General Strike may well have focused minds on unity, rather than division.

The struggle over birth control was the source of considerable disillusionment and anger for those involved with the WBCG. Russell had long been infuriated by

---

[118] 'Miss Browne's Meetings', *New Generation* 6 (December 1927), 136.
[119] *ACLW* (1928), 26.
[120] *ACLW* (1928), 27.
[121] *ACLW* (1928), 27.
[122] *New Generation* 6 (November 1927), 121.
[123] See Durham County Record Office, Durham [DCRO], D/X 1048/2: Durham Labour Women's Advisory Council minute book, 1 November 1923–21 August 1929.

Labour's intransigence, telling her husband in 1925, 'I hate the Labour Party and men are quite disgusting.'[124] Russell felt that the unions and figures such as Wilkinson had simply betrayed the cause and abandoned women: '[o]ur friends turned traitors'.[125] In 1928, she and Leah L'Estrange Malone put down a protest within the London Labour Party at 'the indifference shown at Blackpool by the Trade Union and other sections of the Labour Movement both to the women's decisions and to a subject which is vital to the health and happiness of women and children'. They were the only supporters of this resolution.[126]

Two years later, Ellen Wilkinson told Russell: 'there may be some news to tell you about the Ministry of Health and B.C. I am working at it underground. Of course I have to be frightfully careful about any publicity but there seems to be some movement.'[127] In 1929, a minority Labour government was returned to power. Arthur Greenwood became Minister of Health, with Susan Lawrence as his Parliamentary Secretary and Wilkinson as Lawrence's Parliamentary Private Secretary. In July 1930, the Ministry of Health quietly circulated Memorandum 153/ MCW allowing birth control information to be given through local authority clinics to married women if there seemed a threat to health from a further pregnancy. It is hard to believe that Memorandum 153/MCW was not, in part, a muted response to the birth control campaign, as well as to the pressure of local Medical Officers of Health sympathetic to that campaign and encouraged by the autonomy granted them by the 1929 Local Government Act. In March 1931, the WBCG dissolved itself, with some of its members helping form the National Birth Control Council, which eventually became the FPA.

There might have been satisfaction, but there was no sense of elation at this victory within the ranks of Labour women at this decision. This was because the debate on birth control information had revealed painful truths about the character of the Labour Party. Not least, it showed a sense of sex antagonism within the party. In the debates on birth control, both sides referred to a sense of separateness between men and women on the question. Women also complained that the party was not listening to them, or taking their needs seriously, which developed into a constitutional challenge over the role and relevance of the women's sections.[128]

The birth control controversy illustrated the difficulties of changing the gender balance of Labour ideology. Birth control was supported within Labour ranks not principally as a means of achieving equality or liberty for women. Instead, it was perceived as a crucial measure of social welfare and class reform at a time of economic depression. This did not make it dependent upon economic circumstances, but it did allow entry into socialist ideology. The NEC responded by saying that this was a 'specialist, non-Party' issue, one that could not be accommodated within socialist ideology as it was then conceived. This debate was partly about the

---

[124] BRA, 8.10, Dora Russell to Bertrand Russell, March 1925.
[125] BRA, 8.10, Dora Russell to Bertrand Russell, 6 October 1927.
[126] LMA, London Labour Party, Women's Advisory Committee, Minutes, 16 January 1928.
[127] IISH, DRP, 418, Ellen Wilkinson to Dora Russell, 26 May 1930.
[128] Graves, *Labour Women*, 110–14; see also Howell, *MacDonald's Party*, 344–6.

legitimacy of particular categories in Labour's socialism and outlook.[129] Issues such as unemployment and planning were seen as legitimate because they resided in the public sphere; those like birth control and abortion resided in the private sphere and thus had no political credibility. Birth control forcefully brought these tensions into play, because it was perceived as a specifically 'female' issue that involved sexuality. What this overlooked, first of all, was the way that birth control could be both private and public, about sex and class. The campaign for birth control foregrounded a specifically feminine claim on the categories of 'public' and 'class', but this found no recognized place in Labour's socialism.

But the campaign did see the production, through the birth control question, of new visions of femininity and politics. Though it was rooted, in part, in a Malthusian and eugenicist background, the WBCG moved out of this to make clear the link between the empowerment of women through birth control and political action. Its rhetoric certainly depended upon the portrayal of working-class women as victims of their bodies, but it also presented those same women as citizens with political rights. The lynchpin of such arguments was working-class motherhood. In this way maternalism was a powerful force. What is also clear is the way that sexuality, in this particular example, birth control, became a means of expressing class consciousness. It is true that we have fewer working-class voices than middle-class voices, but there is a sense of class difference between middle-class and working-class women being articulated by working women in Labour women's sections and WCGs, in South Wales and Glasgow as well as London. That class difference was accentuated by the middle-class leaders of the birth control movement; their arguments depended upon class difference. Class and reproductive politics on the Left were, therefore, inextricably wound together. The birth control campaign as it was waged by the WBCG found ways of talking politically about sexuality by the adoption of a socialist vocabulary. This not only changed the meaning of the political, it also reflected a politicized view of the private. These currents continued, albeit in a more submerged fashion, with the abortion issue in the 1930s.

[129] See Riley, *'Am I That Name?'*; Graves, *Labour Women*; Harold Smith, 'Sex vs. Class: British Feminists and the Labour Movement, 1919–29'; Pedersen, *Family, Dependence and the Origins of the Welfare State in Britain and France, 1914–45*. See also Thane, 'The Women of the British Labour Party and Feminism, 1906–45'; Gillian Scott, *Feminism and the Politics of Working Women*, Chapter 6.

3

Writing and Living New Worlds
Socialism, Sex, and Emotions

In the late nineteenth century and during and after the First World War, figures such as Olive Schreiner, Edward Carpenter, and Stella Browne had combined a belief in improving access to birth control with a more ambitious faith in the utopian possibilities of sexual liberation for men and women. Both ideas rested within a socialist outlook, reflecting, sometimes imperfectly, socialism's embrace of both material amelioration and the achievement of a new kind of society based upon principles of equality, freedom, and fellowship. The birth control campaign of the 1920s was an exercise in the politics of sexual reform as social reform, concerned with the material aspects of working-class lives. However important this was, there was little in it to suggest more radical vistas of sexuality as a path towards a fundamental change in human life and social being.

But a number of the women associated with the birth control movement and the campaign to legalize abortion described in the next chapter did explore such vistas, not simply in their writing, but also in their lives. Dora Russell and Naomi Mitchison were two such women, socialists and sex reformers who tried, and sometimes failed, to imagine and lead new lives, combining political activism with sexual freedom in the interwar period.

Russell and Mitchison set out what could not be discussed through the birth control movement of the 1920s, a politics of sexual liberation and pleasure within a context of sexual reform and socialist politics. This work was both innovative and radical, a rethinking of the possibilities and breadth of politics and socialism and an imagining of how political the personal might be. Most striking was their belief that emotions, as much as sexual bodies, had to be remade in the establishment of a new society and new relations between men and women.[1] This chapter uses their work to think about the continuity of utopian ideas about sexuality in the twentieth century.

The work of writers such as Russell and Mitchison is not easy to accommodate into histories of sexuality. It perhaps fits with what Virginia Nicolson has called 'experiments in living' of the Bloomsbury set, but this denudes the work and the lives of their political meaning.[2] It was not as obviously influenced by sexology,

---

[1] On this theme, see also Hustak, 'Radical Intimacies', Chapter 2.
[2] See, for example, Virginia Nicolson, *Among the Bohemians: Experiments in Living, 1900–39* (London: Penguin, 2003).

medicine, or psychology as that of other writers. Nor is it easy to place within socialist developments of the interwar years, being out of step with an increasing emphasis upon planning and the economy. It did not claim great influence in either the spheres of sexual reform or socialism. But despite the ideological and intellectual idiosyncrasies of Russell's and Mitchison's writing, we can, nonetheless, discern the inheritance of earlier utopian sex reformers and socialists like Carpenter and Browne. In turn, Russell and Mitchison also created a legacy for women's liberation in the 1970s. The exceptional, peculiar qualities of Russell's and Mitchison's writing must of course be respected, situated as they were in a particular feminist context of the interwar period and coloured with a fierce sense of the modern emerging from the 1920s and 1930s. A particularly interesting thread was the belief that sex offered an experience of personal transcendence that could permeate society, in other words that physical, personal transcendence could become social and political transcendence. In the discussion of Edward Carpenter and Stella Browne in Chapter 1, a similar theme was noted, captured, for example, in Carpenter's desire to move from being the 'companion of one' to 'the companion of all companions' or Browne's description of the chiliastic possibilities offered by sexual freedom, imagining 'economic justice and international peace . . . stretching out from the bodies and beds of human lovers'.[3] The same fiery hope could be seen in Dora Russell's desire to 'build a trade union of lovers . . . to conquer the world'.[4] What is interesting about the work was how it was situated, not in a sense of the self, in other words in a personal or individual sexual liberation, but rather in a sense of relationships and communities, whether as lovers, spouses or members of families.

The chapter offers an examination of the writing and lives of Dora Russell and Naomi Mitchison in the 1920s and 1930s. This focus is needed in part to give detailed consideration to their arguments about sexual liberation, but also to use biography to illustrate a series of broader tensions within this work, not least between the imagining of sexual reform and the living of it. In many ways, the work and lives of Russell and Mitchison formed an attempt to see individual emancipation and the transformation of society as limitless in their possibilities. But we must also understand the ways that the very attempt to imagine and live a new world of socialism and sexual freedom, to open up the private and public world, contradictorily revealed limitations, exclusions, and compromises.

The most obvious problem was creating such a world in everyday life. The personal did not always bear the weight of the political. Towards the end of her life, Naomi Mitchison suggested that her own marriage was an attempt to break down the boundaries between private and public, born of a 'hope for a new kind of world, for something different, happier, more honest, for a new relationship between people who had been cut off from one another by money, power and class structure . . . I tried to begin the change with personal relations.'[5] But fifty years

---

[3] Carpenter, *Towards Democracy*, 74; Browne, 'The Right To Abortion', 119.

[4] Dora Russell, *Hypatia, or Woman and Knowledge* (London: Kegan Paul, 1925), 39.

[5] Naomi Mitchison, 'Preface' to Dorothy Sheridan (ed.), *Among You Taking Notes: The Wartime Diary of Naomi Mitchison 1939–45* (Oxford: Oxford University Press, 1986), pp. 12–13.

earlier, she had been somewhat more careful. In 1930, Mitchison remarked that the 'sexual life of people in general and particularly perhaps of married people' was, like all ordinary life, 'a compromise between what we need and what is allowed us by modern conditions'.[6] There remained a considerable distance between the fulfilment imagined in the writing of figures like Mitchison and Russell and the lives they were able to lead.

We might also note other kinds of limitations in the work of these women. One was about what Stella Browne might have called the variability of sexual identity. For Russell and Mitchison, sexual liberation and social change was largely, though not completely, associated with heterosexuality; there were exceptions to this that will be discussed below. As Jeffrey Weeks has pointed out, thought on homosexuality and same-sex rights remained underdeveloped on the Left after the 1920s.[7] The work of Russell and Mitchison did little to change that. When they discussed sexual freedom and emancipation as an engine of social change, it was largely with reference to marriage and heterosexuality. This is not entirely true of Mitchison's historical fiction, as Lesley Hall has pointed out, and her discussions of adolescence did deal with homosexuality.[8] But it was not a dominant theme of the writing she explicitly dedicated to sexual questions, undoubtedly a testament to the difficulties of writing explicitly about homosexuality. As suggested in Chapter 1, Stella Browne may have been exceptional in her treatment of same-sex sexuality.

This is not, however, to efface the very important changes occurring in the conception and perception of homosexual identity for men and women in the interwar period. This was, for example, a critical time for the development of lesbian identity in Britain.[9] The libel trial launched by Maud Allen in 1918, the attempt to criminalize lesbian activity in 1921, the growth of a lesbian subculture in London and, most importantly, the suppression of Radclyffe Hall's lesbian novel, *The Well of Loneliness*, in 1928 brought lesbianism into the public sphere. The interwar period was also important for the development of homosexual culture. Homosexuality remained an important focus both of sex reform discussion—through the forum of the World League of Sex Reform, for example—and in the unfolding field of psychology.[10] What, however, male and female homosexuality lacked in this period was, to a large degree, a political purchase or vision in the way that had been seen with Edward Carpenter. There are exceptions to this, as will be

---

[6] Naomi Mitchison, *Comments on Birth Control* (London: Faber and Faber/Criterion Miscellany, No. 12, 1930), 5.

[7] Jeffrey Weeks, *Coming Out: Homosexual Politics in Britain, from the Nineteenth Century to the Present* (London: Quartet, 1977), 147.

[8] See Lesley Hall, *Naomi Mitchison: A Profile of Her Life and Work* (London: Aqueduct Press Conversation Pieces, 2007).

[9] See Doan, *Fashioning Sapphism*; Laura Doan, '"Acts of Female Indecency": Sexology's Intervention in Legislating Lesbianism', in Bland and Doan (eds), *Sexology in Culture*; Alison Oram, '"Sex is An Accident": Feminism, Science and the Radical Sexual Theory of *Urania*, 1915–40', in Bland and Doan (eds), *Sexology in Culture*; Rebecca Jennings, *A Lesbian History of Britain* (Oxford: Greenwood, 2007), *Chapter 8*.

[10] See, for example, Chris Waters, 'Havelock Ellis, Sigmund Freud and the State: Discourses of Homosexual Identity in Interwar Britain', in Bland and Doan (eds), *Sexology in Culture*.

noted in a short discussion of Alec Craig and Sylvia Townsend Warner, but a clearer politics of homosexual and lesbian equality waited until the 1950s and 1960s. Thus, to concentrate upon what Russell and Mitchison had to say largely in terms of heterosexuality is not to ignore developments in homosexuality, but to suggest that they were of a different political colouring.

Russell and Mitchison's attempt to articulate a utopian socialism of the sexual body, a rallying-point for the future, universal development of human society was, ironically, also exclusive in terms of class. Russell and Mitchison acknowledged, sometimes implicitly and sometimes explicitly, that sexual utopianism and sexual freedom were yet more examples of the privileges of the upper middle classes. This serves as an illustration of the bifurcated nature of sexual politics in the twentieth century. Sexual reform was, in the first place, about birth control as a means of sustaining the working-class family. But for middle-class socialist-feminist writers, birth control and abortion were also the first steps towards the transformation of gender roles, the family, and, indeed, society. Through their writings and lives, figures like Russell and Mitchison tried to forge a particular kind of modern, female, and middle-class subjectivity. They consciously steeped their arguments for sexual and social reform in the idea of the modern. Such ideas often used, however regretfully, working-class sexuality as a counterpoint to modern sexuality.

A final, but predictable, irony was that the very attempt to talk about sexuality in a political context largely marginalized the writers as political figures. Both Russell and Mitchison tried, and failed, to become Labour MPs. Russell contested Chelsea in 1923 and Mitchison the Scottish Universities in 1935. Russell was heavily involved in her local London Labour Party (though went with the ILP in the 1930s) and Mitchison ended up as a local councillor in Scotland. Russell's and Mitchison's interest in the private sphere, in sexuality, and in birth control left them on the fringes of Labour politics. Indeed, they would not have been able to write on sexuality if they had been mainstream political figures in the interwar period. Despite their marginalization as political figures, there remains much of political interest in the work of Russell and Mitchison. Not least, we might see their writing as a rare example of how the utopian tradition of socialist sexual politics was kept alive in the mid-twentieth century, a link between the late nineteenth century and the late twentieth century.

This chapter is structured around separate discussions of Russell and Mitchison. It then briefly examines the relationship of this work to thought on sexual emancipation and homosexuality and the emerging medical and psychological literature on sex. The chapter concludes with a discussion of the emotional culture envisioned in their work and the demands of living sexually radical lives.

I

Dora Russell was the product of a fairly conventional, middle-class Edwardian childhood. At Cambridge, she experienced a feminist and radical awakening that guided her personal and political outlook. After university, Russell led a bohemian

3.1 'Dora Russell, 1920s', unknown photographer, copyright Collection International Institute of Social History, Amsterdam

life, furnished with fleeting 'amourettes'.[11] One of these romances was with the philosopher Bertrand Russell. Their affair soon became a serious relationship and after Dora became pregnant with their first child in 1921, they married. Any fears Dora had that marriage would compromise her freedom were soon eclipsed by the conviction that her partnership with Bertrand promised not merely personal contentment, but world-historical change. The Russells' marriage would be an experiment in a new morality, in which sexual freedom and commitment would be combined.[12] Dora felt the pull of sexual freedom no less than Bertrand, a situation further complicated by the impotence he experienced in his sexual relations with

---

[11] BRA, 8.9, Dora Black to Bertrand Russell, 20 July 1919.
[12] See Russell, *The Tamarisk Tree*, Chapter 8; Bertrand Russell, *Marriage and Morals* (London: Allen and Unwin, 1929).

Dora after 1924.[13] Motherhood also tempered Dora's experience of sexual freedom and romantic travails in the 1920s and 1930s. She had four children between 1921 and 1932, two with Bertrand and two with an American journalist, Griffin Barry. She and Russell divorced in 1935.[14]

The publication of *Hypatia* in 1925 and *The Right to Be Happy* two years later afforded Russell a more expansive canvas for talking about the radical possibilities of birth control than her work with the WBCG. The books established Russell as an authority on sexuality, the family, and feminism outside the Labour Party and beyond the shores of Britain.[15] She was invited on tours of America and enjoyed odd pockets of transatlantic influence: in 1930s Montreal, for example, *The Right to Be Happy* became a bible for free-thinking bohemians.[16] Closer to home, Dora influenced Bertrand's interest in questions of morality and the private sphere, leading to the publication of his *Marriage and Morals* in 1929.

Hypatia and *The Right to Be Happy* joined a larger postwar sex reform literature promoting what has been called the 'new eroticism', the 'reconfiguration' of heterosexuality and 'mutuality'.[17] Russell's work might be distinguished from other examples of this literature by its lack of a sexological, scientific, medical, or instructional approach to sex.[18] Rather, her books are grounded in philosophy, literature, socialism, and feminism. Given her involvement in the Labour Party and the WBCG, it may not be surprising that they also showed a deep interest in politics and questions of class. Amid allusions to classical myth and literature, French hedonism, and Eastern philosophy, for example, Russell mused that 'the feminism of working mothers might bring a new and powerful contribution to our work'.[19]

The emancipation of female sexuality was the underlying theme of both works. The liberation of the female body in the enjoyment of sexual pleasure was a recurring theme in this ode, affording the progress of women towards equality and freedom. '[T]he body is no mere box to hold the mind', Russell wrote in *Hypatia*, 'but a temple of delight and ecstasy: a temple to hold the future if we will. To me the important task of modern feminism is to accept and proclaim sex.'[20]

---

[13] See Ray Monk, *Bertrand Russell: The Ghost of Madness 1921–1970* (London: Jonathan Cape, 2000), 50–1, 91–2. See also Nicholas Griffin (ed.), *The Selected Letters of Bertrand Russell: The Public Years 1914–70* (London: Routledge, 2001).

[14] See Russell, *Tamarisk Tree*; Harriet Ward, *A Man of Small Importance* (Debenham, Suffolk: Dormouse Books, 2003).

[15] *Spectator* (London), 12 December 1927.

[16] Molly Ungar, 'The Last Ulysseans: Culture and Modernism in Montréal, 1930–9', unpublished PhD thesis, York University, Toronto, 2003. Bertrand nonetheless suggested, as their marriage was breaking up, that Dora's fame had something to do with his reputation: '[i]t is obvious what you gained by being my wife'. BRA, 8.9, Bertrand Russell to Dora Russell, 4 March 1933.

[17] Lesley Hall, 'Impotent Ghosts from No Man's Land, Flappers' Boyfriends, or Crypto-Patriarchs? Men, Sex and Social Change in 1920s Britain', *Social History* 31 (1996), 61; Lesley Hall, 'Feminist Reconfigurations of Heterosexuality in the 1920s', in Bland and Doan (eds), *Sexology in Culture*; Marcus Collins, *Modern Love* (London: Atlantic, 2003), 41.

[18] See Cook, *The Long Sexual Revolution*, Part 2.

[19] Russell, *Hypatia*, 61.

[20] Russell, *Hypatia*, 24–5.

Russell's emphasis upon the body and sexuality was an attempt to define a consciously modern femininity. Judith Walkowitz has spoken of the 'self-pleasuring, embodied and expressive female self' that was articulated through 'fantasies of escape and pleasure'; Russell's work was an example of this, an exercise in modern female subjectivity.[21] Sexuality was an important aspect of Russell's construction of modern femininity: 'especially during the years of war, young women took the last step towards feminine emancipation by admitting to themselves and their lovers the mutual nature of sex-love between man and woman. . . . It is the experience of modern women that sex is an instinctive need to them as it is to men.'[22] Like other 'new' feminists, Russell rejected the coyness of a previous generation of feminists who had 'dared not cry out that women had bodies'.[23] For Russell, this was part of a feminist struggle. Women's oppression was founded upon the reduction of female sexuality to reproduction: '[w]hen one of the sexes acquires a dominant position it seems invariably to attempt to compel the other to lead a life conditioned entirely by the functions of sex and parenthood'.[24] This put a 'mask between [woman] and reality'.[25] Against men who 'tried to persuade women that their part in sex is pregnancy and childbirth', Russell stressed women's physical pleasure in sex; against the 'old iron cage of monogamy', she asserted that women were 'polyandrous'; against a singular view of female sexuality, she stated that '[t]he plain truth is that there are as many types of lover among women of all classes as among men'.[26] '[M]ale repression' and the 'morals of convention and superstition' stood in the way of feminist advance. Men had to accept women's right to sexual pleasure and freedom (while not using 'free love as a means to getting their socks darned cheaply').[27]

But Russell also saw the emancipation of sex and the liberation of the female body not only as the necessary destruction of a patriarchal order, but as part of building a new harmony between men and women. It was a means of getting beyond a 'ceaseless sex war'.[28] Men and women had to be freed from the power relations and exploitation that had formerly governed sex. Once this happened, and a new heterosexuality was established, a modern, democratic family would follow. These private reforms would make 'for the economic evolution of our society out of capitalism into socialism'.[29] The citizens of Russell's ideal society were sexually active men and women finding physical and spiritual fulfilment with one another

---

[21] Judith Walkowitz, 'The "Vision of Salome": Cosmopolitanism and Erotic Dancing in Central London, 1880–1918', *American Historical Review* 108 (2003), 340.

[22] Russell, *Hypatia*, 32–3, 41.

[23] Russell, *Hypatia*, 21. On Edwardian feminism and sexuality, see Lucy Bland, *Banishing the Beast* (London: Penguin, 1995); Margaret Jackson, *The Real Facts of Life: Feminism and the Politics of Sexuality c. 1850–1940* (London: Taylor and Francis, 1994). On post-1918 feminism and sexuality, see Hall, 'Feminist Reconfigurations of Heterosexuality in the 1920s'.

[24] Dora Russell, *The Right to Be Happy* (London: Routledge, 1927), 138.

[25] Russell, *The Right to Be Happy*, 148.

[26] Russell, *The Right to Be Happy*, 186; Russell, *Hypatia*, 33.

[27] Russell, *The Right to Be Happy*, 155.

[28] Dora Russell, *In Defence of Children* (London: Hamish Hamilton, 1932), 82.

[29] Dora Russell, 'The Economic Significance of the Modern Family', *Science and Society* 11/2 (February–May 1937), 63.

on equal terms. '[S]ex-love' was both 'the most intense instinctive pleasure known to men and women' and a means of achieving 'physical sympathy . . . intimate union . . . [and] exquisite harmony' between two people.[30] This was, she told the 1929 congress of the WLSR, 'a morality directed to human happiness'.[31]

In her writing, Russell made a conscious attempt to articulate the physical pleasure of bodies having sex and the transcendence that such sensuality might offer men and women. She used the genre of romance—the intense and sometimes hyperbolical idealization of heterosexual relations—to represent sex. Through romance, Russell could capture the erotic tension and physical pleasure of sex. An example from *Hypatia* illustrates her writing in this respect: '[m]en and women are not creatures of clay, nor disembodied spirits; but things of fire intertwining in understanding, torrents leaping to join in a cascade of mutual ecstasy'.[32] The dual end-points of this romance were thus the material experience of mutual orgasm and the transcendent sense of fulfilment with another person. The differences between the sexes would be erased in a moment of sensual pleasure. Romance provided a means of expressing the sexual pleasure of the body to Russell's readers in a familiar narrative form. Heightened rhetorical and romantic flourishes ('things of fire intertwining in understanding', 'torrents leaping to join in a cascade of mutual ecstasy') were attempts to represent the physical pleasures of foreplay, intercourse, and orgasm in language outside the sexological, physiological, or pornographic.

Russell's use of romance in this respect is intriguing. We can trace a number of connections between it and other literary work of the 1920s. Russell's evocation of sexual ecstasy has echoes, for example, in the novels of D.H. Lawrence.[33] Her romantic and erotic idealization of heterosexuality also resonates with Marie Stopes's odes to the 'celestial intoxication' of sex and the work of popular writers such as Elinor Glyn.[34] But it might also be linked to other traditions of women's writing in the modernist period. Recent criticism has shown how women writers have used romance to represent female sexuality and the body in potentially radical ways.[35] Work on female modernism has also suggested that women artists and writers took traditional forms and narrative structures, like romance, to express a peculiarly female perspective on modernity.[36] We might take one example from the 1920s to illustrate this. In the novel *Dusty Answer* (1927), Rosamond Lehmann adopted a traditional genre of women's writing, the romance novel, and infused it

---

[30] Russell, *The Right to Be Happy*, 128, 132.
[31] IISH, DRP, 407, Welcome speech to Sex Reform Congress, London, September 1929.
[32] Russell, *Hypatia*, 80; Russell, *The Right to Be Happy*, 155.
[33] See Carol Dix, *D.H. Lawrence and Women* (London: Macmillan, 1980), Chapter 6.
[34] Marie Stopes, *Married Love* (London: A.C. Fifield, 1918), 26.
[35] See Tania Modleski, *Loving With A Vengeance: Mass-Produced Fantasies for Women* (New York: Methuen, 1982); Rita Felski, *The Gender of Modernity* (Cambridge, Mass.: Harvard University Press, 1995), 129–31.
[36] See Janet Wolff, 'The Invisible Flâneuse: Women and the Literature of Modernity' and 'Feminism and Modernism', in her *Feminine Sentences* (Berkeley: University of California Press, 1990); Alison Light, *Forever England: Femininity, Literature and Conservatism Between the Wars* (London: Routledge, 1991); Billie Melman, *Women and the Popular Imagination in the Twenties: Flappers and Nymphs* (London: St Martin's Press, 1988).

with subversive evocations of powerful female sexuality and sharp criticisms of English masculinity.[37] Lehmann used romance as a means of representing modern women's claim to sexual pleasure. In her work, romance becomes a way of framing new views of the female body and sexual pleasure.[38] The protagonist of *Dusty Answer*, Judith Earle, is a modern woman expressing her sexuality in a changed postwar landscape. This is signalled by a sensual self-consciousness about her own body: '[s]he took off her few clothes and stepped in, dipping rapidly; and the water slipped over her breasts, round her shoulders, covering all her body. . . . The water was in love with her body.'[39] Judith embarks upon a failed romantic quest to find sexual and spiritual fulfilment. We can see in Judith the embodiment of a modern and sexualized femininity, the same kind of femininity explored in the pages of *Hypatia* and *The Right to Be Happy*. Though they worked in disparate literary spheres, both Lehmann and Russell used the form of romance as the means of imagining this new femininity.

A consistent theme running through Russell's work was the conviction that sex was a political issue. '[T]he sex problem', she wrote in *Hypatia*, 'is as fundamental in politics as the class war, and more fundamental than foreign trade and imperial expansion.'[40] She wrote, for example, that if the transcendence of the sex act could spread through a divided society and world: '[s]uch an experience alone, widespread, would be worth ten million platforms blaring pacificism'.[41] For Russell, political change was rooted in sexuality in a number of different ways. She made clear links, first of all, between sexual pleasure, heterosexual romance, and political utopianism. Indeed, the first step on the road to utopia began with the skin, nerves, and flesh of men and women. Russell believed that a radically reformed public world would be built upon the sexually emancipated body:

> Let those men and women who know, who enjoy, and who are unafraid, open the prison gates for the rest of mankind. Let them teach and live, conquer public opinion, show that they can do better than those that traffic in the old wares of superstition and of hate. These feed upon destruction and despair, but they shall flourish on security and peace. Let such men and women build a human society in the image of human beings, vivid, warm, and quick with animal life, intricate and lovely in thought and emotion. Let this society have the natural grace and agility of an uncorseted body whose form springs from the play of living muscles, whose deftness and sure purpose arise from thought and action closely intertwined. . . . Such a society, like the human beings that composed it, would be at home in the world, not fearing change but perpetually developing in suppleness and wisdom, perpetually devising new forms and new sources of delight.[42]

---

[37] See Judy Simons, *Rosamond Lehmann* (London: St Martin's Press, 1988).

[38] Nicola Humble, *The Feminine Highbrow Novel, 1920s to 1980s: Class, Domesticity and Bohemianism* (Oxford: Oxford University Press, 2001), 202–3; Sydney Janet Kaplan, *Feminine Consciousness in the Modern British Novel* (Urbana: University of Illinois Press, 1975), 115, 177.

[39] Rosamond Lehmann, *Dusty Answer* (Harmondsworth: Penguin, 1927, 1986), 48.

[40] Russell, *Hypatia*, 4.

[41] Russell, *The Right to Be Happy*, 131–2.

[42] Russell, *The Right to Be Happy*, 294–5.

The sexually liberated body became the cipher for the good society: 'uncorseted', emerging from the 'play of living muscles', bringing together 'thought and action', 'quick with animal life', seeking 'delight'. In a phrase that linked socialist language to sex reform, Russell called for a 'trade union of lovers . . . to conquer the world'.[43] A public utopia would arise from private utopias between men and women. Private narratives of sex and romance would lead to public narratives of social peace, freedom and equality. In this way, political desire was not only equated with sexual desire, but flowed from that desire. Revolutionizing the context of childbirth with the emancipation of sexuality would also lead to a political utopia, as she suggested in 1925: '[Sex love] is the expression of the intimate love and comradeship of two human creatures who will use it by mutual consent, when time and circumstances seem good to them, to create the children of their dreams . . . the life of the child under modern industrialism may become not only possible—which it is not now—but glorious, and human society be shaped to meet our boldest dreams.'[44] Sexuality was thus not marginal to politics, but rather its centre.

This approach placed Russell's work amid the currents of sexual utopianism circulating in nineteenth- and twentieth-century socialism. Sexuality became a way of talking about a socialist utopia. Anarchist feminists and figures as disparate as Walt Whitman and the Soviet feminist Aleksandra Kollontai (whom Russell had met in 1919 and venerated the rest of her life) all envisaged, in different ways, the remaking of men, women, and society through sexuality.[45] Though it is unlikely that Russell was familiar with the tradition of Owenite socialism, there are similarities between the erotic libertarianism of that tradition and her work. Both were informed by a dual vision of political and sexual reform, infused by what Sally Alexander has called the 'flow of sensuality'.[46] Another obvious parallel is Edward Carpenter.

Weaving heterosexual desire and fantasy into the vision of a transformed political world represented a challenge to a traditional view of politics limited to the public sphere. And again, the body was central to Russell's argument, a way of linking private and public spheres. But we must also observe that the language chosen to articulate this vision also produced particular kinds of bodies. These were heterosexual romances and bodies producing heterosexual utopias. Unlike Stella Browne, Russell did not discuss the potential variability of female sexuality or discuss

---

[43] Russell, *Hypatia*, 39.

[44] IISH, DRP, 403: Untitled draft, no date [1925].

[45] See Matthew Thomas, 'Anarcho-Feminism in late Victorian and Edwardian Britain, 1880–1914', *International Review of Social History* 47 (2002), 1–31; Bryan K. Garman, '"Heroic Spiritual Grandfather": Whitman, Sexuality and the American Left, 1890–1940', *American Quarterly* 52 (2000), 90–126; Marie Marmo Mullaney, 'Sexual Politics in the Career and Legend of Louise Michel', *Signs* 15 (1990), 300–22; Beatrice Brodsky Farnsworth, 'Bolshevism, the Woman Question, and Aleksandra Kollontai', *American Historical Review* 81 (1976), 292–316; Jay Bergman, 'The Idea of Individual Liberalism in Bolshevik Visions of the New Soviet Man', *European History Quarterly* 27 (1997), 57–92. For Russell's view of Kollontai, see Dora Russell, 'A Great Revolutionary Leader', *New Society* (London), 28 February 1980.

[46] Alexander, 'Women, Class and Sexual Differences in the 1830s and 1840s: Some Reflections on the Writing of a Feminist History', 143. See also Taylor, *Eve and the New Jerusalem*, 42–8.

same-sex sexuality.[47] Even if sexual, romantic, or parental relationships might be transient, rather than permanent, Russell implied that the sexual emancipation of women would be realized through heterosexuality and, in part, through men. Relying upon tropes of romance and utopianism fixed the expression of female sexuality in heterosexuality. In her own life, Russell showed little, if any, interest in the issue of homosexuality. Indeed, it is possible that she denied, or at least ignored, the homosexuality of one of her lovers of the late 1930s. This is not, at the same time, to endorse the charge made by Sheila Jeffreys and Margaret Jackson that interwar feminists uncritically accepted a patriarchal structure.[48] Russell stressed the need to reform men and, tempered by her own scepticism about monogamy, argued that women should explore a variety of relationships beyond marriage. But the language Russell chose in order to argue for the politicization of sex may have narrowed its possibilities.[49]

The radiance of Russell's imagining of a sexual and political utopia did not blind her to the question of class. Russell made clear to the readers of *Hypatia* and *The Right to Be Happy* that the material experiences of sexual pleasure and motherhood were shaped by class position. Class was written on the body. For the middle classes, '[t]he lack of sexual freedom is a terrible burden, but the remedy ultimately lies in their own hands'.[50] For working-class women, the body and sexuality were potential threats to security and life. In contrast to the vision of romance and fantasy used to convey sexual pleasure, Russell deployed a dystopian narrative about sexual danger, even disaster, to represent the sexuality of working-class women:

> ... [t]he life of the working woman who intends maternity is becoming well-nigh impossible, and she knows it.... The mother works till the last moment, has a difficult confinement and inadequate attention, and gets up too soon.... Then it goes on, baby after baby up to ten and eleven, always in one room and no more money coming in.[51]

This was premised on a critical view of working-class women of previous generations who 'used to breed like animals, dumbly caring for their offspring as best they could'.[52] It was also based on a particular view of working-class masculinity, a restatement of the critical view found in early twentieth-century accounts such as *Maternity* and the Victorian views of someone like Frances Power Cobbe.[53]

---

[47] On Browne, see Hall, '"I Have Never Met the Normal Woman": Stella Browne and the Politics of Womanhood'.

[48] Sheila Jeffreys, *The Spinster and Her Enemies: Feminism and Sexuality, 1880–1930* (Boston: Pandora, 1985); Jackson, *The Real Facts of Life*.

[49] On a similar theme in the history of gay life in the twentieth century, see Houlbrook, *Queer London*.

[50] Russell, *Hypatia*, 58.

[51] Russell, *Hypatia*, 61, 62–3.

[52] Russell, *In Defence of Children*, 64.

[53] See, for example, Susan Hamilton, 'Making History with Frances Power Cobbe: Victorian Feminism, Domestic Violence, and the Language of Imperialism', *Victorian Studies* 43 (2001), 437–60.

Russell again used the body as a metaphor in terms of class. She evoked class inequality by stressing the difference between working-class and middle-class bodies: 'Contrast the working woman of forty or fifty, with her shapeless body, her bad artificial teeth, her inaptitude for athletic movement, with the upper-class mother who, at forty, nowadays may be as sprightly as her adolescent sons and daughters.'[54] Any politics of the female body had to be one concerned with addressing the difference between the material experiences of middle- and working-class bodies. Thus, even the road to sexual liberation revealed class difference and turned back, in a way, to the question of birth control as a means of eliminating such inequalities. But it also demonstrated that even the imagining of a sexual utopia involved evoking class difference.

In the early 1930s, Russell's energies were increasingly sapped by the demands of running her experimental school, Beacon Hill, and by her crumbling marriage and relationship with Griffin Barry. She and Bertrand finally divorced, on the worst possible terms, in 1935. From that point on, Russell's voice as a socialist sex reformer was muted, overwhelmed as she was by the vicissitudes of her private life and economic situation.[55]

II

Born in 1897, Naomi Haldane was the only daughter of a distinguished family of science—her father was a noted scientist and her brother, J.B.S. Haldane, became a famous science writer. At the age of 18, she married Dick Mitchison. Obtaining a copy of Stopes's *Married Love* helped both enjoy sex, but it is also clear that sex between husband and wife remained unfulfilling. Each sought what Naomi called 'something better' with other people and both began to take lovers.[56] This was done with mutual consent and the Mitchisons' marriage, if unorthodox, was strong and enduring. In many respects, Dick and Naomi managed free love in the context of a long-term relationship better than many of their contemporaries.

Like Dora, Mitchison combined her belief in sexual freedom with maternity. She had seven children, all with Dick Mitchison. Two things facilitated blending maternity and sexual experimentation. The first was household help. The second was birth control. In her memoirs, Naomi detailed the method she used: a Dutch cap and pessaries. Birth control was also an issue with which Naomi became involved politically. Through her close friend (and Dick's lover), Margery Spring Rice, she helped out at the North Kensington Women's Clinic, doing interviews with working-class women, raising funds and even acting as a test subject for birth control methods. She also helped organize an important conference on birth

[54] Russell, *In Defence of Children*, 77. On this wider issue, see Brooke, 'Bodies, Sexuality and the "Modernization" of the British Working Classes'.
[55] See Russell, *Tamarisk Tree*.
[56] Naomi Mitchison, *You May Well Ask* (London: Gollancz, 1979), 70; see also Hall, *Naomi Mitchison*; Jill Benton, *Naomi Mitchison: A Biography* (London: Pandora, 1992), 60.

3.2 'Naomi Mitchison, 1925', photograph by *Evening Standard*, copyright Hulton Archive/Getty Images 3068951 (RM)

control in London in the early 1930s and, like Russell, contributed to the discussions of the WLSR.

In the 1920s and 1930s, Mitchison secured critical and commercial success with a series of historical novels. Mitchison's novels, set in the ancient world, were notable for their strong and often sexually autonomous female characters. Moiro in *Cloud Cuckoo Land* (1925) and Der Erif in *The Corn King and the Spring Queen* (1931) are women of beauty and intelligence; Der Erif was also invested with magical powers and a profound connection to the natural world. Mitchison used fictional characters from the ancient world to represent modern concerns with femininity.

Mitchison's political beliefs developed slowly. She was an instinctive feminist and began to write on feminist issues, particularly birth control, in the late 1920s. Her relationship with socialism was more ambivalent. The General Strike failed, for example, to stir her. But as she and her husband moved into the orbit of the Labour writers G.D.H. Cole and Margaret Cole, socialism became the Mitchisons' political faith. Dick Mitchison was adopted as the Labour candidate for King's Norton (Birmingham) in 1931 and 1935 and was elected as MP for Kettering in 1945, eventually being made a Labour peer in 1964. As already noted, Naomi herself was the unsuccessful Labour candidate for the Scottish Universities in 1935 and ended up as a local councillor in Scotland in the 1950s.

Mitchison offered a reflection upon sex in her 1930 pamphlet, *Comments on Birth Control*. This was remarkable in taking on both the mundane aspects of sex and its transcendent qualities. And, consistent with someone who listed her recreation as 'hitting back' in *Who's Who*, Mitchison could also be drily funny about sex.[57] 'Adequate love-making is hard for tired people', she wrote; 'under modern conditions, many people might find it worked better to keep their deep love-making only for the holidays.'[58] At another point, Mitchison reflected archly upon the seed of sexual disappointment always ready to flower into life thanks to the burdensome planning demanded by female contraception: 'if the woman makes her own preparations, she has the feeling that they must not be wasted. Bang goes sixpence, or whatever the sum is in wear and tear of pessary, quinine, moral pride and so on. She may, not unreasonably, feel hurt if her man turns over and goes to sleep with no more than a kiss.'[59]

Mitchison desired 'a general clearing-up of our love life'.[60] In particular, she wanted to confront the dilemma of modern sex: '. . . there is something profoundly wrong with the sexual life of people in general, and particularly perhaps of married people, in our present urban civilization'.[61] Like Russell, Mitchison saw the potential for complementarity between men and women through sex. In ideal circumstances, 'men and women should attain such a complete intimacy, such barrier-breaking union' in sex.[62] Sex was, she recalled, the most powerful of a number of 'new channels of communication to other lives'.[63] Sex was perceived as transcendent, in this case dissolving the boundaries of individual being. But breaking down barriers between individual men and women was but one of the possibilities offered by sexual intimacy. As with Stella Browne and Russell, Mitchison also thought that sex could lead to the remaking of society. Her starting point for this was, perhaps, an unlikely one. In *Comments on Birth Control* she reflected upon the sexual lives of 'primitive islanders' of the Pacific.[64] Of course, in the 1920s, primitivism was a consistent touchstone of modernism. But Mitchison took such enthusiasm one step further. In primitive societies, she argued, people were able to control their bodies and enjoy 'complete sexual licence' before marriage without pregnancy, and thus without offending social mores.[65] This led her to even more ambitious speculation:

[57] *Who's Who* (London: Adam and Charles Black, 1934).
[58] Naomi Mitchison, *Comments on Birth Control* (London: Criterion Miscellany No. 12/Faber and Faber, 1930), 21, 22.
[59] Mitchison, *Comments on Birth Control*, 17–18.
[60] Mitchison, *Comments on Birth Control*, 31.
[61] Mitchison, *Comments on Birth Control*, 5.
[62] Mitchison, *Comments on Birth Control*, 7; Bertrand Russell also based some of his arguments upon this work; see Russell, *Marriage and Morals*, 19–24.
[63] Naomi Mitchison, *All Change Here* (London: Bodley Head, 1975), 141.
[64] Mitchison, *Comments on Birth Control*, 26.
[65] Mitchison, *Comments on Birth Control*, 26.

Now my interpretation of this . . . is that these islanders are among the few people in the world who are still in a primitive community of which the persons are not separated out into individuals. That is to say they are all more or less in communion with one another, so that impulses and ideas of a kind travel through them as through a single body. . . . It is against the good and the will of the Trobriand community that women should have children before they are adult and settled into their place as adult women. And the women realize this good and this will, not with their minds, but so deeply with their bodies that they cannot go against it unless some outside force (a missionary, for instance) comes to pull them away from their community and break the continuity between them and the rest of the tribe.[66]

Mitchison suggested that the members of primitive communities were so at one with one another, so immersed in a sense of communality, that this actually shaped reproduction: women would not get pregnant from sex before marriage because the community would not allow it. And so here there is a kind of reversal of the equation between the public and the private. The public shaped the private; the pull of community was like the moon, affecting the tides of the body right down to reproduction. Sex allowed the transcendence of individual being and in doing so had a social as well as sensual value. In contrast, according to Mitchison, Western and Northern societies—'civilization'—had seen that deep sense of community crumble into an alienating individualism.[67] But sex might put this fractured state back together. Socialist utopianism and sex reform thus again went hand in hand. For Mitchison, sexual reform provided a potential foundation for a real revolution in human development: 'a community of a new kind, becoming again conscious of one another and of their own central will and good and unity'.[68]

This 'magic' could begin in the English home through a combination of the stability and commitment of long-term relationships and the excitement of sexual experimentation. Mitchison's work combined high-flying utopianism with an unsentimental assessment of married life. Mitchison very much believed in long relationships. But monogamy was also the enemy of passion and lust: '[v]ery few normal couples with their own jobs and their own intellectual interests, keep up a devouring passion for one another all their lives'.[69] More than Russell or even Stella Browne, Mitchison gave some thought to not only the intense fires of passion, but the mellower embers of settled love. Sex in the latter phase was sometimes portrayed by Mitchison as bleak, more about a lack of options than ardour: ' . . . there is . . . the mere desire for any bit of he or she flesh . . . because they are living in the same house, sleeping most likely in the same bed, because it is very complicated practically and emotionally to do anything . . . the couple still go on'.[70] To make up a kind of sexual deficit, Mitchison argued for reconciling marital fidelity and extramarital sex; the belief in the 'certainty' of long-term partnership

---

[66] Mitchison, *Comments on Birth Control*, 26–7.
[67] Mitchison, *Comments on Birth Control*, 27.
[68] Mitchison, *Comments on Birth Control*, 27.
[69] Mitchison, *Comments on Birth Control*, 27.
[70] Mitchison, *Comments on Birth Control*, 14–15.

was not 'incompatible' with either partner 'being in love, with a more or less sexual passion, with someone else'.[71]

Mitchison also reflected upon the mechanics of sex and its emotional and physical pleasures. The sheer clumsiness of female contraception using pessaries and quinine, as well as the awkwardness and potential unreliability of Dutch caps and sheaths, were, for Mitchison, impediments to a fulfilling sexual experience. This is not to say that she was ambivalent about the need for birth control. For women and families, particularly working-class families, life was 'unbearable' without contraception.[72] In this context, Mitchison was concerned about the inadequacy of current birth control (and male competence) in facilitating female orgasm: ' . . . so lamentably often the woman's sexual experience is anyway incomplete. An astonishingly large proportion of women of all classes have never experienced the final and satisfying crisis, this partly through our fantastic religious and social education, and partly through the incompetence of their husbands.'[73]

But, as in Russell's work, there was a class divide here. Though she was an activist for working-class birth control, Mitchison was most interested in the difficulties of sexuality for middle-class people: 'what one cannot help wondering is, how well the same methods work on rather different circumstances and people, who had not the same preliminary miseries to contend with, and who can afford the luxury of considering at length the finer shades of their own emotions and ideas'.[74] Similarly, heterosexuality was taken for granted as the framework of sexual revolution for men and women. Unlike Stella Browne, Mitchison assumed a certain fixedness of female and male sexuality (even when she herself had had same-sex experiences). As with Russell, the opening up of a vision of sexual emancipation was not without its exclusions and closures.

III

Before turning to the question of emotions in the work of Russell and Mitchison, it is worth thinking about their connections to other currents in interwar sex reform. Both women certainly had links to that wider movement. The first was through birth control. As we have seen, Russell was one of the leaders of the WBCG. For her part, as already mentioned, Mitchison became involved in birth control at a local level in London and helped organize a major conference on the question in 1931. Both Russell and Mitchison contributed to wider discussions of sexual questions, through the WLSR, a pan-European organization with a small English chapter. The high point of the English WLSR came in 1929 when it hosted the League's annual congress, an event co-organized by the Australian doctor, sex reformer, and educationalist Norman Haire and Dora Russell. The WLSR was committed, as

---

[71] Mitchison, *Comments on Birth Control*, 15–16.
[72] Mitchison, *Comments on Birth Control*, 9.
[73] Mitchison, *Comments on Birth Control*, 24.
[74] Mitchison, *Comments on Birth Control*, 10.

were Russell and Mitchison, to the conscious liberation and modernization of sexual ethics.

In other ways, however, there are few clear connections between Russell's and Mitchison's writing and other writing on sex in the 1920s. As already suggested, there was more politics, feminism and romance than science or sexology in their work. The kinds of themes highlighted by Cook in her study of sex manuals are to be found only to a small degree in the writing of Russell and Mitchison.[75] As Ivan Crozier has pointed out, even the collaboration of Haire and Russell in the 1929 WLSR in fact highlighted many of the differences of approach between sex reformers like Haire and writers like Russell and Mitchison. Russell, Mitchison, and Stella Browne all gave papers at the congress, but Haire felt that the overt feminism of their contributions compromised the scientific or medical advancement of sex reform. At the end of the congress, he and Russell amicably went their separate ways. The reason Haire raised for this was instructive: he suggested that Russell was, first and foremost, a 'political revolutionary' rather than a sex radical. Her approach to the question was framed in the context of something with which he was uncomfortable, the idea of political transformation.[76]

Homosexuality did not figure highly in the writings of Russell and Mitchison. In part, this is because their work centred upon revolutionizing femininity and heterosexuality. In part, it was consonant with a larger neglect of homosexuality by left-wing thinkers. But we might also see that there were intellectual dissonances between what Mitchison and Russell were doing and how ideas of homosexuality were developing between the wars. Neither Russell nor Mitchison showed much obvious interest or background in either sexology or Freudian psychoanalysis. Russell, for her part, was sometimes dismissive of Freudianism. But this occurred at a time when thought on homosexuality was being constructed from two sometimes competing intellectual strands, the work of Havelock Ellis and that of Sigmund Freud.[77] So, in an important way, connections could not be made between the kinds of arguments for sexual and political reform offered by Russell and Mitchison and those emerging in other areas of sexual reform. This can partly be attributed to the dominance of a traditional gender ideology in thinking about sex and the feminist emphasis that Russell and Mitchison placed upon improving the position of women. What this resulted in was a political and sexual radicalism sensitive to one aspect of sexual behaviour, but blind to another.

Where we might see a connection between homosexuality and politics is in the realm of literature. A younger generation of poets in the 1930s famously flirted with Marxism. At least in the case of W.H. Auden, this was sometimes connected to the homoeroticization of the working-class man.[78] Stephen Spender similarly explored

[75] Cook, *The Long Sexual Revolution*, Part 2.

[76] Ivan Crozier, '"All the World's a Stage": Dora Russell, Norman Haire, and the 1929 London World League for Sexual Reform Congress', *Journal of the History of Sexuality* 12 (2003), 35.

[77] See Chris Waters, 'Havelock Ellis, Sigmund Freud and the State: Discourses of Homosexual Identity in Interwar Britain', in Bland and Doan (eds), *Sexology in Culture*.

[78] See, for example, Marsha Bryant, 'Auden and the Homoerotics of the 1930s Documentary', *Mosaic* 30 (1997), 69–91.

homosexuality in an explicitly political context, shaped variously by the rise of fascism, the Great Depression, and an engagement with Marx and Freud; as Richard R. Bozorth suggests, writers like Auden, Spender, and Christopher Isherwood 'saw the "new country"' as one of sexual liberation.[79] The lesbian poets and lovers Sylvia Townsend Warner and Valentine Ackland joined the Party in 1934 and believed that the emancipation of homosexuals was part of the political revolution to which they aspired.[80] Townsend Warner is particularly interesting in this regard. Her 1936 novel, *Summer Will Show*, told the story of a 'parallel political and sexual awakening', a lesbian love story against the background of the 1848 revolutions; in its last scene, having witnessed the apparent death of her female lover, the main character opens the pages of the newly published *Communist Manifesto*.[81] The literary efforts of Townsend Warner and the Auden Group did not, however, shape the politics of the Left. There were specific political impediments to this. As Lucy Robinson has suggested, the revolutionary quality of Marxism did not always extend to sexual revolution, and, in particular, was often inimical to arguments for even the tolerance of homosexuality, which was seen as a bourgeois deviation.[82]

In these ways, Russell and Mitchison's writing reflected some currents in sex reform work of the interwar periods and not others. It was, of course, linked to the modernization of society. At the same time, it shared a relative blindness to the liberation of homosexuality. Its political nature and its lack of roots in either sexology or psychoanalysis meant that Mitchison's and Russell's writing rested in something of a *cul de sac*. Where, however, their work departed in a fascinating way was on the question of emotions.

IV

In 1980, Dora Russell remarked to the novelist Doris Lessing, 'I am sorry that nowadays marriages—or should I say sex partnerships—last such short times—people lose a great deal in not having such relationships.'[83] At first glance, this comment might simply seem to reflect a generational difference. Russell was, by then, in her eighties, and her reaction to some elements of the sexual revolution of

[79]   Richard R. Bozorth, '"But Who Would Get It?" Auden and the Codes of Poetry and Desire', *ELH* 62 (1995), 711.

[80]   On Ackland, see Frances Bingham, 'Labours of Love', *The Guardian* (London), 20 May 2006; on Sylvia Townsend Warner, see Heather Love, *Feeling Backward: Love and the Politics of Queer History* (Cambridge: Harvard University Press, 2007); Jane Garrity, *Step Daughters of England* (Manchester: Manchester University Press, 2003); Claire Harman (ed.), *The Diaries of Sylvia Townsend Warner* (London: Chatto and Windus, 1994).

[81]   Kristin Ewins, 'The Question of Socialist Writing and Sylvia Townsend Warner in the Thirties', *Literature Compass* 53 (2008), 663; see also Terry Castle, 'Sylvia Townsend Warner and the Counterplot of Lesbian Fiction', *Textual Practice* 4 (1990), 213–35; Sylvia Townsend Warner, *Summer Will Show* (New York: NYRB, 1936, reprinted 2009).

[82]   See Robinson, *Gay Men and the Left*, Chapter 1.

[83]   IISH, DRP, 64, Dora Russell to Doris Lessing, 31 March 1980.

the 1960s had been mildly disapproving, despite her commitment to sexual freedom and women's rights. In 1965, for example, she had written, '[o]f late I have been much struck by the frequent assumption that marriage and parenthood are a sort of trap, the virtual end of a woman . . . as a freely developing individual. Surely to fall in love, to have children, should represent a new and wonderful stage in the unfolding of human personality; it is tragic to envelop this with a sense of resentment and unwilling personal sacrifice.'[84] Similarly, when Mitchison spoke of her open marriage, she pointedly remarked that her sexual adventures almost always happened in the context of love.[85]

But this difference of opinion was not merely an example of one cohort of radicals raising their eyebrows at another, or the late blooming of social conservatism in both women. Instead, it speaks to an element of the work of sex reformers and feminists that is sometimes forgotten: the emotional context of sexual emancipation.[86] Sexual liberation was not, for Russell and Mitchison, only about the liberation of bodies. It was also about the establishment of a new emotional culture that would complement, and indeed help construct, a new political culture. Writers like Russell and Mitchison (and others in Britain, like the novelist Ethel Mannin, Ellen Wilkinson in *Clash*, Janet Chance's *Cost of English Morals* of 1931 and *Romance of Reality* of 1934, and the Fabian Margaret Cole's *Marriage: Past and Present* of 1938) devoted considerable space in their work to questions of love, as much as questions of sex and equality; indeed, love, sex, and equality were all tightly linked.[87] Thinking about emotions widened out the landscape of sexual and socialist politics by mapping the myriad possibilities and demands of the new world. If there was to be a transformation of bodies and politics, was there also to be a transformation of emotions? Writers like Mitchison and Russell believed that the structure of feeling and emotion—whether love, jealousy, or desire—would have to be both harnessed and changed to bring a new world of equality and freedom into being.

By stressing the centrality of the emotions to sexual and political change, Mitchison and Russell tried to extend the meaning of socialism as well. The 1920s and 1930s witnessed an increasingly technocratic and bloodless Fabianism dominating mainstream socialism in Britain. This road to the socialist commonwealth was paved with central economic planning and nationalization of industry, so-called 'practical socialism'.[88] What was lost was the sense that society and human character could experience a wider transformation. An earlier tradition of ethical

---

[84] Dora Russell, 'The Eclipse of Woman', *Anarchy* 56 (October 1965), 292.

[85] See, for example, Naomi Mitchison, *You May Well Ask* (London: Gollancz, 1979), 70.

[86] Claire Langhamer suggests, for example, that love is often left out of the history of sexuality. See Langhamer, 'Love and Courtship in Mid-Twentieth-Century England', *Historical Journal* 50 (2007), 173–96; a notable exception is Suzanne Raitt, 'Sex, Love and the Homosexual Body in Early Sexology', in Bland and Doan (eds), *Sexology in Culture*.

[87] On Ethel Mannin, see Judy Greenway, '"Together We Will Make a New World": Sexual and Political Utopianism', in Gert Hekma (ed.), *Past and Present of Radical Sexual Politics* (Amsterdam: Mosse Foundation, 2004).

[88] On this, see Elizabeth Durbin, *New Jerusalems* (London: Routledge and Kegan Paul, 1985); Stephen Brooke, *Labour's War* (Oxford: Oxford University Press, 1992).

and utopian socialism had contained this possibility. It was also evoked in the work of Russell and Mitchison. Linking sex and emotions with political change allowed, in particular, a vision of ecstasy and transcendence to have a place in socialist and radical ideology. At its essence, the new world would be built upon the transcendent power of love—beginning with the sexual passion between lovers and the familial love between parents and children, love that would spread through society, dissolving social difference and conflict. This idea of ecstasy and transcendence was critical to earlier socialists and radicals such as Carpenter and Whitman and can also be seen, more recently, in the work of intellectuals and feminists such as Georges Bataille and Luce Irigiray.[89]

Finally, it is through a discussion of the emotions that we can see socialist feminists thinking about the costs and demands of sexual, social, and political change. Transformation asked most of the emotions. Russell and Mitchison were not, in this regard, unreserved in their advocacy of sexual freedom. First of all, they gave consideration to the costs of sexual freedom on the emotions of individuals. There was, secondly, an irony to how they saw the relationship between sexual freedom and emotion. The free expression of sexuality depended, in large part, upon the rational restraint of emotions—jealousy and possessiveness most notably—rather than their free expression.

The cultural history of emotion has stressed the social role of emotions, whether, in the words of Joanna Bourke, in the way emotions 'mediate between the individual and the social', or, through the work of Niklas Luhmann and Norbert Elias, in the way modern society is founded on, respectively, the nurturing of intimate personal relations and emotional restraint.[90] Barbara Rosenwein has also emphasized this social aspect to emotions, pointing to the formation of shifting emotional communities across time.[91]

Russell's and Mitchison's work illustrated all of these points; they were interested in constructing a new emotional community, which would itself provide a new basis for modern society, a kind of emotional citizenship, based upon a balance of emotional expression and restraint.[92] A central thread to Mitchison's and Russell's late-twentieth-century memoirs was that their open marriages comprised a conscious attempt to embrace modernity and create a new world from the bedroom out. This was consistent with their writing in the 1920s and 1930s. In their lives and writing, Mitchison and Russell were, in Marshall Berman's terms, 'subjects' of modernity, attempting to live and promote 'freedom, dignity, beauty, joy,

---

[89] See Amy Hollywood, *Sensible Ecstasy: Mysticism, Sexual Difference and the Demands of History* (Chicago: University of Chicago Press, 2002).

[90] Joanna Bourke, 'Fear and Anxiety: Writing About Emotion in Modern History', *History Workshop Journal* 55 (2003), 113; Niklas Luhmann, *Love As Passion: The Codification of Intimacy* translated by Jeremy Gaines and Doris L. James (Stanford: Stanford University Press, 1998); Norbert Elias, *The Civilising Process* trans. by Edmund Jepthcott (Oxford: Blackwell, 1994).

[91] Barbara H. Rosenwein, 'Worrying About Emotions in History', *American Historical Review* 107 (2002), 821–45.

[92] On a different aspect of this, see Martin Francis, 'Tears, Tantrums and Bared Teeth: The Emotional Economy of Three Conservative Prime Ministers, 1951–64', *Journal of British Studies* 41 (2002), 354–87.

solidarity'.[93] This would be accomplished by a conscious reinvention of what it meant to be women in the 1920s and, more broadly, by advocating the reinvention of men and women through sexuality and emotions. For her part, Russell fervently believed that society was on the edge of fundamental change, wrought through the body and the emotions:

> ...there has never been a time in human history when men and women, both free creatures, have been free to love without the coarseness or triviality engendered by ignorant superstition.[94]

Love, as much as sex, was the foundation of the good society. The point of sexual emancipation was, in part, to free love from constraint or oppression; 'love', Russell wrote, 'can only be liberated by checks to power'.[95] Sexual pleasure was good, in its own right, but it was best experienced in the context of love, whether this was sexual passion, 'comradely love' (used in a different meaning from Carpenter), or even the 'kindness, friendliness' of a long relationship. Indeed, both Russell and Mitchison could sound quite traditional on this point. Mitchison was, for example, arch in her judgement of American mores:

> ...I am inclined to think also that it is possible to overdo the business of casual affairs, as practised for instance... by many of the American young. It seems to show a certain poverty of imagination to have to plunge at once into the final expression of emotion. No wonder they write so little good poetry.[96]

In his *Marriage and Morals* (1929), Bertrand Russell, though generally less political than his wife, made a similar connection between love and politics. Sexual instinct, he wrote, was not unhealthy, but it was incomplete without the 'deep intimacy and intense companionship of happy mutual love', which was 'the best thing that life has to give'. It had, as well, social aspects, because without the experience of such love 'men and women cannot attain their full stature, and cannot feel towards the rest of the world that kind of generous warmth without which their social activities are pretty sure to be harmful'.[97]

Writing about love also meant writing about parenting and families. As already argued, Mitchison and Russell were maternal feminists as well as sex radicals. This position is captured in Russell's statement that '[w]oman loves sex and loves children'.[98] Mitchison similarly remarked that 'intelligent and truly feminist women want two things: they want to live as women, to have masses of children by the men they love... and they want to do their own work, whatever that is'.[99] Though both believed that there should be 'voluntary' parenthood and that sex

---

[93] Marshall Berman, 'The Signs in the Street: A Response to Perry Anderson', *New Left Review* 145 (1985), 115, 123.

[94] Russell, *The Right to Be Happy*, 259–60

[95] Russell, *In Defence of Children*, 125.

[96] Mitchison, *Comments on Birth Control*, 11.

[97] Russell, *Marriage and Morals*, 123.

[98] Russell, *The Right to Be Happy*, 145.

[99] Mitchison, *Comments on Birth Control*, 25.

should be for pleasure as much as reproduction, and both were individualists, these positions did not displace a belief in the family. Creating children and creating families were not weights on sexual emancipation, but, rather, complements to it. Indeed, familial and parental love were perceived, with sex, as amongst the driving forces of a new society. Russell suggested, for example, that there was 'nothing more likely to transform society than that men and women should love one another without stint or fear, and unashamedly yield to the physical tenderness they feel for each other and their children. Let these emotions rather than glory, grandeur, virtue, or riches enlist their intelligence in private and public life.'[100]

For many of these writers, the reform of the private world could not be separated from the public world; indeed, the values of public and private worlds seeped into one another. Of men and women's relationship, for example, Mitchison remarked, 'there must be no social ownership, no patriarchy . . . I cannot see how it is going to be done without some form of equalitarian society'.[101] In a similar vein, the Fabian Margaret Cole (also a good friend of Naomi Mitchison and reputedly a lover of Dick Mitchison) was speaking of society as much as marriage when she questioned the possibility of progress for women without public and private change: '[c]an equal partnership, equal development of personality, be attained under a system of inequality?'[102] Russell saw 'the trend of the modern family towards equal rights and responsibilities and freedom' as 'one of the forces tending to replace the old economic order by a new, more democratic one'. This even had an economic consequence: '[b]ecause of its egalitarianism, the modern family is the breeding ground of a democratic sentiment which seeks expression not only politically, but industrially . . . such homes become models for industrial democracy'.[103] Emotion therefore was something that linked private and public worlds; affect collapsed the boundaries between the intimate and the political.

Love—whether physical or emotional—was thus perceived as the catalyst of a new society. This has echoes in work from other centuries and other writers.[104] As a political ethos, it remains, of course, somewhat vague, but has the advantage (at least for socialist ideology) of marrying everyday life to an idea of a utopian commonwealth, even if we mean a commonwealth of emotions as much as property. And, in the 1930s, there was one mainstream (and male) socialist writer who similarly argued that 'emotional education' was a foundation for a politics of democratic socialism.[105]

---

[100] Russell, *The Right to Be Happy*, 259.

[101] Naomi Mitchison, *Home and a Changing Civilization* (London: John Lane/Bodley Head, 1934), 153.

[102] Margaret Cole, *Marriage: Past and Present* (London: J.M. Dent, 1938), 288.

[103] Dora Russell, 'The Economic Significance of the Modern Family', *Science and Society* 1/2 (February–May 1937), 56, 60.

[104] See, for example, Réné Scherer, 'Fourier's Rally of Love', in Hekma (ed.), *Past and Present of Radical Sexual Politics* 15; Luce Irigiray, *I Love To You* (New York: Routledge, 1996); Luce Irigiray, *Democracy Begins Between Two* (New York: Routledge, 2000).

[105] See Evan Durbin, *The Politics of Democratic Socialism* (London: Routledge and Kegan Paul, 1940); see also Stephen Brooke, 'Evan Durbin: Reassessing a Labour "Revisionist"', *Twentieth-Century British History* 7 (1996), 27–52.

There was another connection to modernity here. It is certainly true that sex reformers like Russell and Mitchison wanted a radical reform of gender roles and ideology. But they did not necessarily suggest eviscerating traditional forms of human association, like companionate marriage or the family. This suggests the ambiguous qualities of modernity, at least in Britain, at once evoking the new and seeking some sense of stability in existing structures. Richard Sennett has suggested that one end-point of modernity's trajectory is narcissism, an over-emphasis on the individual at the expense of society.[106] In Mitchison and Russell, there is certainly a sense of the importance of individual expression and fulfilment, but this is connected to a sense of the social, building up a community through sex and a new emotional and political culture, between lovers, within families, and, finally, between citizens.

Russell and Mitchison saw sex and emotions as the motors of a new society. In this way, both would be harnessed to create a new society. It is also important to consider how emotions had to be controlled. This was particularly true because of the emphasis on free sexual expression. How was that reconcilable with long-term love? Both Mitchison and Russell accepted that in long-term relationships, the passion and excitement of sex was lost between two people. As has already been shown, Mitchison recognized that monogamy took a heavy toll on a healthy sense of lust. How then to maintain healthy sexual lives and committed emotional lives? For Mitchison and Russell, sexual freedom was one answer; 'being in love, with a more or less sexual passion, with someone else' was, according to Mitchison, 'compatible' with marriage.[107]

But to explore this world of sexual freedom and love, emotions would have to be managed. Jealousy and possessiveness were, of course, the most obvious problems. Russell realized (from her experience) that sexual freedom often left relationships on a knife-edge: '[i]f one ceases to act in the generous spirit of modern morality, the other perforce must abandon that position also; deep resentment ensues, with the break-up of the home, as well as humiliating battles over the children'.[108] A fellow WBCG veteran and later founder of the ALRA, Janet Chance similarly wrote about the rationalization of emotions and sex. '[W]hat we have to achieve', she argued, 'is a harmony of our various selves', but it was not sexual instinct or emotion that could reliably bring such harmony; rather, it was 'realistic thought'.[109] For the Fabian Margaret Cole, the key was loyalty. Extramarital passions were, she said, a likely product of modern marriage, creating considerable emotional damage. But modern marriage had to develop a 'loyalty which can take [extramarital affairs] in its stride'.[110] Others felt that jealousy was not for moderns. The author of *Sex and Revolution* (1934), Alec Craig argued that '[t]he modernist recognizes the existence

---

[106] See Richard Sennett, *Fall of Public Man* (New York: Norton, 1992).
[107] Mitchison, *Comments on Birth Control*, 15–16; see also Bertrand Russell, *Marriage and Morals*, 142.
[108] Russell, *In Defence of Children*, 131.
[109] Janet Chance, *The Romance of Reality* (London: George Allen and Unwin, 1934), 63.
[110] Margaret Cole, *Marriage: Past and Present* (London: J.M. Dent, 1938), 297.

of jealousy, but regards it as a deplorable rather than a laudable thing'.[111] For Russell, the management of emotions centred upon the separation of sexual from parental relationships. Once children were in the picture, Russell seemed to argue, sexual freedom had to be restrained, at least temporarily: '[l]et men and women have as much sexual freedom as they desire, provided they will realize that the deliberate creation of children is a thing apart, involving probably a long period of mutual partnership, or the greatest possible care in bestowing and providing for the children'.[112] She also believed that marriage as it existed simply nurtured the wrong emotions—in particular, male possessiveness. Marriage had to be changed in order to facilitate a different emotional culture.

In such ways, there was a recognition that, for all the talk of free sexual expression, there also had to be a rational management of the emotions to facilitate this. In other words, the emotional economy that would accompany sexual freedom and socialism was marked by restraint as much as by freedom. It is not altogether fanciful to suggest that just as mainstream socialists stressed the rational planning of an economy of production and distribution, socialists like Russell and Mitchison suggested the application of rationality to a new emotional economy. This was not entirely about repression, but restraint in order to facilitate greater sexual expression.

Russell and Mitchison were also attentive to the ambiguities of sexual freedom. This sense of ambiguity was rooted in experience, a point best illustrated in the first place by art rather than life. In 1935, Mitchison ventured into fiction with a contemporary setting. *We Have Been Warned* was a critical and commercial failure. Mitchison later remarked ruefully that it was 'my first modern book, and plenty of trouble it caused me'.[113] The novel's descriptions of free love, sex, abortion, and contraception, explicit for the time, earned its rejection by both Mitchison's usual publisher, Jonathan Cape, and the radical publisher, Victor Gollancz, who feared it would damage the socialist cause. The novel was eventually published by Constable to poor reviews and public indifference. But it is, as one of Mitchison's biographers notes, both an unfortunate novel and 'extremely interesting'.[114]

In it Mitchison wrestles with the ambiguities of both socialism and sexual freedom for women. 'What does a socialist woman do?' is the question that haunts the novel's protagonist, Dione Galton. In many ways, Dione exemplifies modern femininity, poised between a number of worlds. She believes in sexual freedom, women's independence, and progressive causes such as birth control and the Soviet Union. But she also harbours doubts. She longs to feel an unequivocal commitment to socialism and the cause of the working classes, but she knows that she is ambivalent about both. Canvassing on his behalf among working-class people in 'Sallington' (the novel's fictional stand-in for Birmingham), she reflects, 'I am a foreigner here, I don't belong'.[115]

[111] Alec Craig, *Sex and Revolution* (London: George Allen, 1934), 71–2.
[112] Russell, *The Right to Be Happy*, 188.
[113] Naomi Mitchison, *Saltire Self Portraits* (Edinburgh: Saltire Society, 1986), 1.
[114] Jenni Calder, *The Nine Lives of Naomi Mitchison* (London: Virago, 1997), 122.
[115] Naomi Mitchison, *We Have Been Warned* (London: Constable, 1935), 62.

Sexual freedom also troubles Dione. She moves within circles that encourage the free discussion of sex and liberated sexual behaviour. Her sister-in-law runs a birth control clinic in London and her husband dispenses blandishments to read Havelock Ellis along with tutorials on the woollen trade to his Oxford undergraduates. Dione herself uses contraceptives and encourages her husband to have an affair with a young Soviet woman. But her own exploration of sexuality is marked by hesitant steps. Dione thinks of giving herself sexually to a Communist virgin as a means of helping him overcome his repressions. This is unsuccessful, the virgin in question having already been relieved of his repressions by some no-nonsense Soviet women. A few months later, again at the hands of a Communist, Dione suffers a near rape.

At no point, therefore, does she actually have a satisfying extramarital affair, in contrast to her husband. This disquiets Dione. The novel also signals some ambivalence about contraceptives. Dione is disgusted by the 'foul, horrifying touch' of a condom, while her husband talks of the 'beastly contraceptives' used by Dione.[116] Though a supporter of abortion and someone who considers having one for an unwanted fifth pregnancy, Dione is shocked after witnessing an abortion performed without anaesthesia while on a tour of the Soviet Union. All of these things suggest Mitchison's qualified approach to sexual freedom, at once supporting it while discerning its costs and ambiguities. In one passage, Mitchison has Dione thinking about the connection between sex and socialism. When asked by the Communist virgin why she might have sex with him, Dione believes that it is as much an act of public politics as personal desire:

'We are both of us Socialists, we love all mankind, and so we love one another' . . . . She thought, I must give him the truth and said low: 'Mustn't Socialist people be kind to one another? Mustn't we share everything? It's wrong, isn't it . . . to be one thing in politics and another in living? I'm trying now to live the same way that I think.'[117]

Being a socialist woman is identified with being sexually free, even if both socialism and sexual freedom are attended by ambiguities and challenges. It was a position that demanded a political, sexual, and emotional commitment.

The landscape of utopia was not, therefore, without its unevenness and ambiguities. Of course, there is no direct relationship between life and writing, but, it is worth thinking about Mitchison's and Russell's emotional lives between the wars not least because, as Michael Roper has suggested, emotions can allow a glimpse into the sometimes ragged fit between experience and representation.[118] In this respect, we have to acknowledge the complexity of Mitchison's and Russell's emotional lives. It could be said that, for Mitchison, the attempt to reconcile sexual freedom and marriage was a successful experiment. But Mitchison did not celebrate it as such without qualification. She suggested in her memoirs that she took a lover only after her husband was 'looking elsewhere' and that she was not 'casually

---

[116] Mitchison, *We Have Been Warned*, 412, 145.
[117] Mitchison, *We Have Been Warned*, 239–40.
[118] Michael Roper, 'Slipping Out of View: Subjectivity and Emotion in Gender History', *History Workshop Journal* 59 (2005), 57–72.

promiscuous' so that she could preserve 'a good relationship with [her] spouse [and] children'.[119] Such considerations did not, she reflected in her essay on birth control, prevent 'plenty of emotional crossing and double crossing'.[120] As for her lovers, confusion and regret were as apparent as joy and pleasure. At one point, for example, she was in love with both her estranged male lover and his wife. Speaking of such affairs in her memoirs, she remarked that she recalled the 'pain almost more clearly than the delight'.[121]

Pain was undoubtedly the price of sexual freedom and experiment for Dora Russell. Even with all the confident talk about setting an example of modern marriage, it is clear that the Russells' marriage was riven with the emotional cost of sexual freedom. Bertrand in particular was jealous of his wife's lovers, even when he was having affairs himself. For him, a line was crossed when Dora had, in his words, 'any man's children'.[122] Dora's reaction had been growing confusion at her husband's attitude. The marriage finally broke apart in the early 1930s, after Dora had two children by Griffin Barry and Bertrand entered into a long-term affair. They divorced acrimoniously in 1935. By the end of the marriage, she was furious, telling H.G. Wells that it was all down to 'patriarchal possessiveness'.[123] The power relations that Russell hoped would be assuaged through love eventually overwhelmed that love. By the late 1930s, Russell had withdrawn from the wider public stage, in an attempt to save Beacon Hill, her school. By the end of the 1930s, Mitchison was mostly based in Scotland. Both Mitchison and Russell seemed deflated by the failures of the 1930s. Borrowing from Yeats, Russell entitled her chapter on the 1930s 'Things Fall Apart'. For her part, Mitchison wrote that it was 'a bore being ahead of your time'.[124]

The 1940s and 1950s were not entirely dead periods for socialist feminism and sex reform, as shall be suggested in Chapter 5, but the millenarian possibilities enunciated in the 1920s and 1930s did not reappear until the late 1960s. At that point, the relationship between sexual and political reform was restated, by hippies, the New Left, and, not least, the women's liberation and gay liberation movements; Wilhem Reich remarked in 1968, for example, that '[n]o sexual revolution is possible without social revolution'.[125] 'Make Love Not War' was a more famous adage, of course. In Britain of the 1960s, second wave feminists like Sheila Rowbotham were 'driven by a longing for a sexuality which was not about possession or being possessed, for forms of relating and loving I could hardly express or even imagine'.[126]

---

[119] Mitchison, *You May Well Ask*, 70–1.
[120] Mitchison, *Comments on Birth Control*, 17.
[121] Mitchison, *You May Well Ask*, 70.
[122] BRA, 8.9, Bertrand Russell to Dora Russell, 4 March 1933.
[123] IISH, DRP, 9, Dora Russell to H.G. Wells, 9 July [no year: late 1930s?].
[124] Mitchison, *Among You Taking Notes*.
[125] Quoted in Dagmar Herzog, *Sex After Fascism: Memory and Morality in Twentieth Century Germany* (Princeton: Princeton University Press, 2005), 155.
[126] Sheila Rowbotham, *Promise of a Dream: Remembering the Sixties* (London: Penguin, 2000), 160.0

This was a path already explored by writers and activists like Russell and Mitchison some forty years before. Russell and Mitchison had argued for a new sexual and emotional culture as the basis of a new society, but, at the same time, had shown both the glittering promise and the hard demands of a politics of the personal. For them, sex, emotions, and politics were bound together by a belief in the transcendent power of love, even if lived experience was a reminder of the everyday costs of that love.

4

Abortion and Working-Class Politics in the 1930s

In 1931, the second Labour government fell in the face of a deepening economic crisis. The party emerged from the wreckage of government and a disastrous election determined to rebuild through an explicitly socialist policy.[1] The tools in this programme would be the control of industry through public ownership and central planning of investment and distribution. Against this background, the Labour women's sections in the 1930s were notably quiet compared with the 1920s. Various factors account for this. The unwavering intransigence of the NEC on issues such as family allowances and birth control undoubtedly blunted the enthusiasm of any activists willing to pursue these issues further. That the Labour government allowed local authorities to distribute birth control also realized one element of the WBCG campaign, even if it did not feel like a victory, and the WBCG formally disbanded in March 1931, its work taken up by the National Birth Control Association. Finally, the very scale of the crises of the 1930s, both at home and abroad, may have also helped derail campaigns which could be perceived as narrowly based in women's interests.[2]

But the questions that had inspired women's action on birth control in the 1920s did not go away in the 1930s. Some, indeed, may have intensified. At the beginning of the decade, unemployment was at its worst. Statements from the SJCIWO continued to emphasize that: '[t]he effect of wage reductions, of the cuts in unemployment pay, and the cutting down of relief work though bearing directly upon the man, are ultimately shouldered by the wife'.[3] Even after the nadir of the depression had passed and economic recovery began to bring prosperity in the south-east, London, and Midlands, there may have been a great desire to protect this by finding new sources of working-class income and security beyond the breadwinner wage. Part-time work for women was an especially important trend. According to the SJCIWO, such work was attractive because of working-class women's 'desire for a higher standard of living'.[4] This aspiration may also have

---

[1] See Ben Pimlott, *Labour and the Left in the 1930s* (London: Unwin Hyman, 1977); Durbin, *New Jerusalems*; Brooke, *Labour's War*, Chapter 1.

[2] Graves, *Labour Women*, 199.

[3] SJCIWO, *Reports on How Women Fare Under Reactionary Government and Tariffs and the Housewife* (London: Labour Party, 1932), 7.

[4] SJCIWO, *Women in Industry* (London: Labour Party, 1935), 12.

translated into changing reproductive behaviour. The early 1930s also witnessed the birth rate hit a low point.

There was also continuing attention to the problem of maternal mortality and morbidity. Infant mortality had steadily declined through the first quarter of the twentieth century. But until the introduction of sulphonamide drugs in the late 1930s, maternal mortality remained at approximately five deaths in every thousand births, a figure which rose slightly between 1923 and 1936.[5] This elicited much concern from women's groups and the government. The Ministry of Health commissioned two inquiries into the problem in 1932 and 1937. The problem of maternal mortality encouraged various groups to explore the idea of a national maternity service. Having pushed for improvements to maternity and child services throughout the interwar period, the TUC collaborated with the British Medical Association (BMA) in formally proposing a national maternity service.[6] In 1939, the Labour Party came out with a major report proposing the establishment of a national maternity service that would provide comprehensive ante- and post-natal clinics and home helps for pregnant women.[7]

But even with this attention to the problems of maternity, birth control remained off the agenda. There were certainly sections of the Labour movement that continued to discuss the question well after its apparent demise in 1928. The WCG, for example, thought, in 1929, that it would 'get information as to the methods of birth control used' by its members.[8] The WCG congress of 1930 supported the teaching of 'sex hygiene' to adolescents.[9] In 1938, the conference held by the New Fabian Research Bureau (NFRB) on the health services agreed that '[b]irth control advice was necessary for economic and health reasons'.[10] But there was still little to compare with the intense campaigning of the WBCG, with one exception: abortion law reform.

In the birth control campaign of the 1920s, abortion issue had divided the WBCG. Stella Browne wanted its inclusion, but Dora Russell worried that 'talk of abortion was hindering our campaign'.[11] In the 1930s, with the question of the distribution of contraceptive information at least partly resolved, socialist-feminists and working-class women interested in the problem of birth control and family planning increasingly turned to abortion as the next issue on their agenda. They used many of the same arguments deployed in the 1920s to push the idea of abortion as a question of class politics and social welfare. Many of the same themes accompanying birth control in the 1920s—the articulation of a class consciousness

[5] See Lewis, *The Politics of Motherhood*, Chapters 4 and 5.

[6] See, for example, MRC, MSS 292/824/1, TUC General Council, Summarised Report of Deputation to Ministry of Health, 27 February 1930.

[7] See MRC, MSS 292/842/2, LG 128, Labour Party, 'A National Maternity Service', June 1939.

[8] Brynmor Jones Library, Hull [BJL], Women's Cooperative Guild Papers [WCG], DCW 1/9, Central Committee minutes, 23 January 1929.

[9] BJL, WCG, DCW 2/11, Annual Congress (1930–1), 21.

[10] BJL, Socialist Medical Association Papers [SMA], DSM 4/1, New Fabian Research Bureau, Conference on the Health Services, Maidstone, 22 and 23 October 1938, 13.

[11] IISH, DRP, 345, Dora Russell to Keith Hindell, 10 November 1972.

through a question of sexuality and the reshaping of maternity—can also be seen in the abortion law reform campaign of the 1930s.

As already suggested, the practice of abortion in Britain in the twentieth century was governed by the 1861 Offences Against the Person Act and the 1929 Infant Life (Preservation) Act. The usual means of a safe, therapeutic abortion was curettage. By the 1930s, there were those within the medical and legal professions who were frustrated at either the injustice or the ambiguity of the existing abortion law. Despite the provisions of the 1929 Infant Life (Preservation) Act, doctors were only too aware, as the medical journal *The Lancet* stated, that 'the present state of the law renders a doctor liable to indictment'.[12] Though many of the convictions for abortion involved those outside the medical profession, doctors who performed abortions also faced the prospect of prosecution: in 1936, for example, a female doctor was sentenced to three years' imprisonment for performing five abortions.[13] There was also considerable disquiet in legal circles. Some wanted to see the criteria justifying abortion widened to include social or economic reasons. In 1931, while finding a woman guilty of procuring an abortion and causing the death of another woman, Justice McCardie famously attacked the state of the abortion law: 'I cannot think it is right that a woman should be forced to bear a child against her will.'[14]

What McCardie and others also recognized was that there was a class divide in access to therapeutic abortion. Middle-class women were more likely to be able to obtain therapeutic abortion through private health care under the terms of the 1929 Act, by getting a medical practitioner to attest to a potential 'threat' to life. In more ambiguous circumstances, it was easier for middle-class women to afford the high fees required for a therapeutic abortion. It is important not to exaggerate the safety or availability of therapeutic abortions for middle-class women, but they remained more accessible to them than to many working-class women. This did not mean that abortion was, however, uncommon. Compared to other forms of contraception, access to non-medical abortions was relatively easy within working-class communities. But it remained an extremely dangerous practice. Working-class women relied upon abortifacient pills (such as Beecham's pills and Penny Royal Bitter Apple) available through chemists, herbalists, or the post, the insertion of implements such as crochet hooks and knitting needles, or folk remedies such as slippery elm bark.[15] At best, such methods were ineffective. At worst, they were fatal. Between 1926 and 1934, the mortality rates as a result of unsafe abortion amounted to about 14% of all puerperal deaths.

Despite the physical risk of abortion and its potential for criminal prosecution, working-class women saw abortion as an effective and economical means of family

---

[12] 'The Law of Abortion', *The Lancet* (London), 13 June 1936.
[13] *The Times*, 1 July 1936.
[14] *The Times*, 19 December 1931.
[15] H.J. Drew Smythe, 'Indications for the Induction of Premature Labour', *British Medical Journal* (London), 13 June 1931, 1018–20; Margaret Salmond, 'Induction of Abortion', *The Lancet*, 4 April 1931, 745–7.

limitation.[16] The reasons for abortion were invariably economic ones. The Midwives Institute testified in 1937 that '[t]he predominant cause...was financial anxiety...economic security would make abortion an unknown thing'.[17] An inability to control fertility was the motivation behind most of the cases of abortion in a 1938 study of Derby. These were, for the most part, married women who had already had four children and who 'considered they had "done their share"'.[18] Abortion was often related to the lack of other kinds of effective contraception. 'If birth control information were made available to working-class mothers,' remarked another study in 1930, 'the main cause of the prevailing high rate of abortion would be removed, and maternal health would be greatly improved in consequence.'[19] Kate Fisher has shown that, for the most part, working-class women saw abortion outside of a moral context and simply as a means of birth control.[20]

In the interwar period, concerns about maternal mortality and morbidity highlighted the threats to health of unsafe abortions. The second report on maternal mortality in 1937 noted illegal and unsafe abortions as a significant cause of puerperal mortality. Though the statistics were understandably sketchy, it suggested that the number of abortions had risen between 1926 and 1934. This finding led directly to the establishment in 1937 of an interdepartmental committee on abortion by the Home Office and the Ministry of Health. As we shall see, this committee became an important forum for the airing of views on abortion.

Advocating legalized abortion remained a frontier few women's groups wished to cross in the 1930s. The WCG did pass a resolution favouring legal abortion in 1934. This emerged both from concern about maternal mortality and with an attempt to be progressive about 'modern conditions and ideas...making of abortion a legal operation that can be carried out under the same conditions as any other surgical operation'. Significantly, this produced only one letter of dissent among its membership.[21] In 1932, there was a public meeting on abortion organized by Norman Haire, Stella Browne, Dora Russell, and Janet Chance,

---

[16] Patricia Knight, 'Women and Abortion in Victorian and Edwardian England', *History Workshop Journal* 4 (Autumn 1977), 56–69; Angus McLaren, *Birth Control in Nineteenth-Century England* (London: Croom Helm, 1978), 215–53. See also Barbara Brookes, 'Women and Reproduction c. 1860–1919', in Lewis (ed.), *Labour and Love*; Joanna Bourke, *Working-Class Cultures in Britain 1890–1960* (London: Routledge, 1994), Chapter 2; Elizabeth Roberts, *Women and Families* (Oxford: Blackwell, 1995), Chapters 4 and 5; Melanie Tebbutt, *Women's Talk: A Social History of Gossip in Working-Class Neighbourhoods, 1880–1960* (Aldershot: Scolar, 1995), 75, 88; Sally Alexander, 'The Mysteries and Secrets of Women's Bodies: Sexual Knowledge in the First Half of the Century', in Mica Nava and Alan O'Shea (eds), *Modern Times* (London: Routledge, 1996).

[17] TNA, MH 71/22, Memorandum of Midwives Institute, no date [1937].

[18] R.G. Cooke, 'An Analysis of 350 Cases of Abortion', *British Medical Journal*, 14 May 1938, 1045–7.

[19] Edith How-Martyn and Mary Breed, *The Birth Control Movement in England* (London: John Bale, Sons and Davidson, 1930), 18–19.

[20] See Kate Fisher, '"Didn't Stop to Think, I Just Didn't Want Another One": The Culture of Abortion in Interwar South Wales', in Franz X. Eder, Lesley Hall, and Gert Hekma (eds), *Sexual Cultures in Europe: Themes in Sexuality* (Manchester: Manchester University Press, 1999).

[21] BJL, WCG, DCW 1/10, Central Committee minutes, 7 and 8 May 1934. See also WCG *Annual Congress Report* of that year.

through the WLSR British Section, at the London School of Hygiene. The National Council of Women (NCW) also supported legal and safe abortion as did the National Council for Equal Citizenship, but other groups saw the question as untouchable. Alice Jenkins, one of the most important abortion campaigners of the twentieth century, noted that some mainstream feminist organizations, like the National Citizens' Association, literally met questions about abortion with silence.[22] When the reform of the abortion laws was discussed, usually the focus was on the criteria for a therapeutic abortion. Most advocates of abortion law reform wanted, in varying degrees, the definition of 'threat to life' to be expanded, so that it included psychological or social and economic reasons. This was a way of allowing a woman to decide upon a termination depending upon the particular conditions of her life.

What was happening in other countries also influenced British thinking on abortion. In Germany, the Left had mobilized behind an attempt to lift the prohibitions on abortion.[23] Scandinavia, a region of continuing interest for socialists between the wars and after, saw Sweden legalize abortion in 1938 on a variety of grounds with Denmark following in 1939. The Soviet Union had famously legalized abortion in 1920, only to criminalize it again in 1936. But British socialists travelling to Russia before 1936 invariably made a Soviet abortion ward one of their tourist stops. The Fabian Margaret Cole noted, with some approval, the rationality of abortion policy in the Soviet Union; abortions had to be carried out in state hospitals or clinics, the fees charged were negligible or non-existent, and women convalescing from abortions were paid a wage.[24]

There were two moments in the 1930s when abortion was brought into public discussion in Britain. One was the 1938 trial of the distinguished gynaecologist Aleck Bourne. The establishment of the official Interdepartmental Committee on Abortion in 1937 was another. The 1930s also saw the foundation of a pressure group that went on to play a crucial role in the eventual reform of the abortion law in 1967, the ALRA. This chapter examines the Bourne case and the Interdepartmental Committee largely through the work of the ALRA. It also discusses the EMWWA, which, as already noted in the Introduction, was formed by working-class Labour women in response to the Interdepartmental Committee.

The work of the ALRA and the EMWWA picked up themes set out in the 1920s. First of all, we can see the power of maternalism in arguments for abortion law reform. The exhausted mother was still at the heart of arguments for reproductive control. But the EMWWA also offered a more nuanced view of working-class motherhood, which was placed in the context of the decline in importance of the breadwinner male and the rise of a more complex figure at the heart of

---

[22] See Alice Jenkins, *Law for the Rich* (London: Gollancz, 1960), 23.

[23] See Atina Grossman, *Reforming Sex: The German Movement for Birth Control and Abortion Reform 1920–1950* (New York: Oxford University Press, 1995).

[24] Margaret Cole, 'Women and Children', in Margaret Cole (ed.), *Twelve Studies in Soviet Russia* (London: Gollancz, 1933), 183–4; see also Sidney and Beatrice Webb, *Soviet Communism: A New Civilisation?* (New York: Scribner, 1936), Volume 2; Fannina W. Halle, *Woman in Soviet Russia*, trans. Margaret M. Green (London: Routledge, 1933).

working-class family life, a mother who worked, who wished to be a mother but have the right to reject motherhood, whose desire still remained the building up of the family's standard of living, whether this was through work or reproductive control. Looking at both the ALRA and the EMWWA also affords a sense of how interwoven class and gender consciousness were around the birth control issue. The EMWWA articulated a clear sense of working-class identity against what they perceived as a very different reproductive experience of middle-class women. The ALRA was led by middle-class women; their advocacy of birth control tended to be on behalf of working-class women. Their own identity as middle-class women was bound up in part with the ability to represent women whose reproductive experience was not their own, as well as being able to have access to politicians, the civil service, and the medical and legal profession. Finally, we can see an undeniable if ambiguous relationship between abortion politics and Labour politics.

I

In 1935, Joan Malleson, a doctor with a surgery in London's prestigious Harley Street, called an informal meeting on abortion with Janet Chance, Stella Browne, and Alice Jenkins.[25] All had been involved in the WBCG. Browne had long been an advocate of legal abortion. Malleson and Chance had established a birth control clinic in Ealing in 1933.[26] Early in 1936, joined at a small café off Piccadilly by other socialist-feminists and veterans of the WBCG campaign such as Frida Laski and Bertha Lorsignol, they formed the ALRA.[27] For over thirty years, the ALRA was the principal locus of the pro-abortion movement in Britain, playing a critical role in the campaign for the 1967 Act.

Chance and Jenkins were the driving forces behind the ALRA. Chance was able to fund the organization from her own private wealth, while Jenkins looked after the organization and was a boundless source of energy as a lobbyist and speaker. Thirty years after the ALRA's establishment, Russell offered portraits of the two women: 'Alice Jenkins [was] a slender, rather frail but determined and devoted person. . . . [Janet Chance] was a robust looking "country" woman . . . [she] was fresh, good looking, clear cut strong face, very useful person because she was so eminently "respectable".'[28] In her later years, Jenkins tended to favour a practical and pragmatic route to abortion law reform. But earlier in her life, she espoused more radical hopes, expressing, in 1929, her 'belief in the need for some revision of the accepted morality of our generation' characterized by 'a healthier, happier, and decidedly holier atmosphere on this great subject of Sex and its Relation to Life

---

[25] This followed the publication of a letter by Malleson on abortion; see *New Statesman and Nation* (London), 10 February 1934.

[26] Madeleine Simms, 'Conscript Parenthood: The Problem of Secret Abortion', *Women's Choice: A Magazine of Reproductive Rights*, 2/1 (Spring 1994), 8–9.

[27] On the formation of the ALRA, see Jenkins, *Law for the Rich*, 46–61.

[28] IISH, DRP, 345, Dora Russell to Madeleine Simms, 9 February 1968.

4.1 'Alice Jenkins', unknown date, unknown photographer, Wellcome Library, London, L0019514, copyright Abortion Choice

abundant'.[29] In 1933, in her home borough of Ealing (where she was also a founder of the Anti-Litter League), Jenkins mobilized a meeting protesting a speech by the Catholic writer G.K. Chesterton. Jenkins was the daughter of a single mother and had three children with her common law partner.[30] Janet Chance shared a similar outlook to Jenkins. Chance had been involved in the Malthusian League, later joined the WBCG and participated in a sex education centre for working-class people in Westbourne Grove in London. She also wrote three books in the 1930s that set out her vision of sexual reform, beginning with *The Cost of English Morals* (1931).[31] She saw the modern world as 'sexually insane', instead longing for a

[29] IISH, DRP, 7, Alice Jenkins to Dora Russell, 10 November 1929.
[30] On Jenkins, see Stephen Brooke, 'Jenkins, Alice (1886–1967), *Oxford Dictionary of National Biography*, Oxford University Press, May 2006, online edn Jan 2008 [http://oxforddnb.com, accessed 19 August 2010].
[31] On Chance, see Stephen Brooke, 'Chance, Janet (1886–1953), *Oxford Dictionary of National Biography*, Oxford University Press, May 2006, online edn Jan 2008 [http://oxforddnb.com, accessed 19 August 2010].

4.2 'Janet Chance', unknown date, unknown photographer, Wellcome Library, London, L0019510, copyright Abortion Choice

civilization that kept the 'fire of sex clear and alive'.[32] Chance stressed the physical pleasure of sex, its 'naked freedom' as part of the possibility of 'physical health, physical fitness and physical beauty' in a new world.[33] These women thus brought to the question of abortion some of the conceptions shaping the discussion of sexuality in previous periods, notably a belief in the emancipatory and transformative aspects of sex discussed in the previous chapter. But when they came to discuss the reform of abortion laws in a practical sense, what they focused upon was something quite different, the conditions of working-class motherhood.

The ALRA's first conference was held in May 1936. Continuities with the outlook of the WBCG were apparent. Speakers separated abortion from any eugenicist, Malthusian, or natalist concerns; it was an issue that had to be considered 'quite apart from the subject of the decline of population'. But maternity continued to be a touchstone. Russell talked of 'creative motherhood' and women whose principal concern was not their own welfare, but the welfare of their families.

---

[32] Janet Chance, *The Romance of Reality* (London: George Allen and Unwin, 1934), 70, 68.
[33] Chance, *The Romance of Reality*, 90; see also Janet Chance, *Intellectual Crime* (London: Noel Douglas, 1933).

Only one speaker, Stella Browne, explicitly represented abortion as the path towards sexual liberation. For her, the ban on abortion was 'a sexual taboo, it is the terror that women should experiment and enjoy freely, without punishment'. What linked the two approaches was a language of rights and choice. Russell spoke of abortion as a 'right of woman'. Joan Malleson insisted that the choice for motherhood or for abortion '*must rest with the woman herself*'.[34] The ALRA's aims were, first of all, to foster discussion of abortion, and, with a reform of the law in mind, to encourage the introduction of 'social and economic reasons' as well as factors of mental or physical health, as justification for a therapeutic, legal abortion. An abortion would be legal in consultation with a medical practitioner, but, ultimately, it would be the decision of the woman herself.[35]

The ALRA was not a mass organization. It was led by middle-class women. Some, like Malleson, were professionals. Others were married women who dedicated considerable time to voluntary activities. There was some overlap in membership with other organizations dedicated to sex reform, such as the British Sexological Society and the Eugenics Education Society. Its board of honorary vice-presidents and its Medico-Legal Council were filled with members of the establishment, from the Conservative MPs Robert Boothby and Arnold Wilson to writers such as H.G. Wells and Julian Huxley to academics like Glanville Williams, reader in English Law at Cambridge. Discussing sex in the interwar period may not have been *outré*, but, as already suggested, abortion was not regarded as an easy issue for public discussion. A group like the ALRA had, therefore, to be concerned about gaining legitimacy and respectability. The first way it did so was by girding itself in the armour of the reputations of the great and good. With the exception of the ageing Lothario H.G. Wells, none of its vice-presidents, council members or advisers could be termed sex radicals. The legitimacy of the ALRA was thus secured in its association with a respectable establishment. The spaces which the ALRA chose to pursue its aim of legal abortion were consciously circumscribed in the 1930s. There was no attempt to convert the general public, even if newspapers like the *Daily Mirror, News Chronicle*, and *Reynolds News* were sympathetic. Instead, conversion efforts were focused on the medical and legal professions in the hope that medical practice and case law could be influenced.

The ALRA was formally non-partisan and always insisted it was non-political. But, like the WBCG, the ALRA linked its fortunes with the Labour Party. There were non-Labour politicians involved with the ALRA, as already noted, but the ALRA never worked with the Conservative or Liberal parties in the way it did with the Labour movement, including the WCG, Labour Party women's sections, and publications such as *Tribune* and *New Statesman*. In 1936, for example, it approached a number of women's sections about sending speakers and information on the question.[36] One of its early aims was persuading 'six "key" women' in the

[34] IISH, DRP, 344, ALRA Conference 1936, 15 May 1936, 9, 20, 28.
[35] See Jenkins, *Law for the Rich*, Appendix 3, 92.
[36] See, for example, LMA, ACC 2417/H/2, London Labour Party, Women's Advisory Committee, 7 September 1936; LMA, ACC 2417/H/30/1, West Middlesex Labour Women's Advisory Council, Minutes, 10 July 1936.

Labour Party and Cooperative Society to sponsor a resolution at a Labour women's conference.[37] Malleson and others attempted to promote the cause within circles more directly connected to the party leadership. In 1938, for example, the NFRB debated abortion as part of a conference on the health services.[38] Much of the ALRA's local or provincial activity was conducted in affiliation with or even through Labour women's sections.[39] By the outbreak of war in 1939, sixty-nine groups had affiliated to the ALRA, mostly Labour women's sections and WCGs. The ALRA's class composition is more difficult to ascertain. The leadership was clearly metropolitan and middle-class. But the ALRA was committed to recruiting working-class people to its cause. The existence of a 'penny' membership, which numbered 734 by 1939, suggests some working-class participation. It distributed handbills reading: 'DO YOU WANT THE ABORTION LAWS CHANGED? If you do JOIN US and we can tell the Minister of Health that thousands of working mothers and fathers say—YES!'[40] The ALRA also achieved respectability by the kind of working-class women it reached. As members of Labour women's sections and WCGs, such women were, for the most part, older, married, and respectable. They were as much anchors of respectability for the ALRA as its medico-legal council.

The ALRA's chosen political home may have been within the Labour Party's latticework of socialist, feminist, and working women's organizations, but the possibility of securing a place for its aspirations within Labour's politics of course remained very slight. The Labour Party (including its women's sections) remained officially hostile to the consideration of abortion law reform.[41] In 1935, the annual conference of Labour women only discussed abortion in the context of mental illness during a pregnancy; the same year, the SJCIWO refused to deal with the issue.[42] Two years later, with a government inquiry into the matter in the offing, the SJCIWO staved off discussion of the matter.[43] *Labour Woman*'s coverage of the official report on Maternal Mortality did not even mention abortion. The Socialist Medical Association (SMA), an affiliated organization of Labour medical practitioners, never discussed the issue in the 1930s. Nonetheless, the maternal mortality reports of 1932 and 1937 and the severity of the depression in the early years of the decade kept up interest in the problem of abortion, particularly as it affected working-class women.

---

[37] CMA, SA/ALR/1/2/1, ALRA, Minutes, 11 January 1937, 15 March 1937, 20 February 1938, 28 April 1938.

[38] BJL, SMA, DSM 4/1, New Fabian Research Bureau, Conference on the Health Services, 22 and 23 October 1938.

[39] See CMA, SA/ALR/1/3/2–3, ALRA, Annual Reports, 1937–8, 1938–9.

[40] IISH, DRP, 368, ALRA Handbill, no date [1938?].

[41] See, for example, National Conference of Labour Women, *Reports on Maternal Mortality and the Maternity Services and Women in Industry* (London: Labour Party, 1935).

[42] See *ACLW* (1935); LPA, Standing Joint Committee of Women's Industrial Organizations, Minutes, 14 March 1935.

[43] See responses in LMA, ACC 2417/H/2, London Labour Party, Women's Advisory Committee 13 October 1937, Minutes, 8 November 1937, 4 January 1938.

Within the ALRA, there were various ways of arguing for legal abortion. Stella Browne was the most vocal advocate of abortion as an 'absolute right' for women to achieve both sexual liberation and personal emancipation.[44] As Sheila Rowbotham has noted, in this regard, Browne was a link between the sex reformers of the early twentieth century and second-wave feminists.[45] 'Abortion must be the key to a new world for women', Browne wrote in 1935. She believed that the public emancipation of women in such areas as politics and the economy demanded and was dependent upon their emancipation in the private sphere of sexual and reproductive practice: 'freedom of choice and deliberate intention are necessary for [women] in their sexual relations and their maternity, if they are to make anything of their status and opportunities'. Towards this end, Browne advocated abortion as an 'absolute right' spanning public and private realms.[46] This was what Browne termed 'intimate liberation'. Browne believed that a woman should be able to receive an abortion, on request, 'up to the viability of her child', ideally in the first three months of pregnancy.[47]

But other ALRA members avoided making any link between abortion and sexual liberation. Their arguments resonated more strongly with those made in the 1920s for access to birth control. Abortion was perceived, first of all, as a measure of social welfare for working-class mothers. Once again, class and maternity were all-important. Some arguments for abortion buried claims for sexual emancipation. Janet Chance appropriated, for example, the language of sexual propriety in order to make an argument for legal abortion: '[t]his Association deplores irresponsible behaviour with its consequences in shallow experience, illegitimacy and venereal disease, and it holds that one of the first ways of promoting responsible sexual behaviour of fine and enduring quality is to make marriage more tolerable'.[48] It was not a preoccupation with sex that produced abortion but the strains of working-class domesticity: '[t]he women who ask for abortion are not obsessed: the large majority are working-class women who for good reason consider the birth of a child at a given time a threat to the welfare of the home, a burden too heavy for their own strengths or their husband's earnings, and a disaster for the children already born'.[49] The key to making this situation more tolerable was not the rejection of sexuality, but the reconciliation of conjugal sexuality with the protection of the health of working-class wives and the economic position of working-class households. Legalizing abortion on social or economic grounds would effect this reconciliation. ALRA members often made the point that the reconciliation between conjugal sexuality and domesticity was already enjoyed by women of the middle and upper classes. One contrasted 'women who have money' with the 'women who still appear in the press cuttings' in the legal treatment of abortion; another argued

---

[44] Browne, 'The Right to Abortion', 113.
[45] See Rowbotham, *A New World For Women*, Section 4.
[46] Browne, 'The Right to Abortion', 113–14.
[47] Browne, 'The Right to Abortion', 117.
[48] Janet Chance, *The Case for the Reform of the Abortion Laws* (London: ALRA, 1936), 13.
[49] Chance, *The Case for the Reform of the Abortion Laws*, 11.

that 'abortion was given to wealthy women every day in Harley-street [*sic*] and that knowledge and service should be available to all classes'.[50] As with the birth control campaign of the 1920s, therefore, the politics of class and maternalism were the starting points for abortion advocacy.

Arguing for abortion on grounds of class and maternalism did not disable a feminist case for the advancement of women's rights. This emerged from the articulation of motherhood as a form of citizenship deserving recognition. In 1936, after Stalin had outlawed abortion in the Soviet Union, Janet Chance and Alice Jenkins pointed out the civic virtues and rationality of mothers in Russia and Britain, emphasizing '[t]he devotion of the working woman to her family in both countries under conditions of personal sacrifice'.[51] Jenkins and Chance wanted an acknowledgement of mothers as rational citizens, due public rights and obligations to protect the private sphere. Sometimes this was suffused by a condescending view of working-class mothers, but it remained an argument for public citizenship through maternalism: '[t]hey are our fellow citizens, ignorant no doubt of much, but as fit as others are, in many cases far fitter, to judge whether in the interests of the race or the home, another birth is a benefit or a crime'.[52] In this context, the ALRA often used the term 'voluntary' or 'responsible' parenthood. Arguments for reform of the abortion law also contained an argument for a woman's inalienable right over her body in the sphere of reproduction. It would be the woman's decision to exercise this right: '[t]he facts of abortion . . . make it primarily a woman's question. . . . The woman for these reasons claims that, should there be a diversity of opinion in any particular case, she should have the casting vote.'[53] The ALRA's language of abortion reform thus placed arguments for individual rights and female citizenship within a framework of maternalist and class concerns, an approach also seen in the 1920s over birth control. What emerged from this framework was an argument that both spoke to the lived experience of women as mothers, and, at the same time, suggested a radical view of maternity, one that highlighted independence, not dependence, and control rather than powerlessness.

II

In the 1930s, the ALRA relied upon educative efforts within the Labour movement and women's organizations. It also sought sympathizers from those within the medical and legal professions frustrated with the existing abortion law. An opportunity to challenge the law came in 1938. In April, a soldier raped a 14-year-old girl in the West End of London. The girl became pregnant. Her parents took her to Joan Malleson, who contacted Aleck Bourne. Aleck Bourne was one of Britain's

---

[50] Margot Edgecombe, 'Marital Difficulties and Abortion Law Reform', in ALRA, *Backstreet Surgery* (London: ALRA, 1939), 15; Janet Chance, quoted in *Liverpool Daily Post* (Liverpool), 3 December 1936.

[51] *New Statesman*, 17 October 1936.

[52] Chance, *The Case for the Reform of the Abortion Laws*, 11.

[53] Chance, *The Case for the Reform of the Abortion Laws*, 12.

leading gynaecologists, the consulting obstetrical surgeon at St Mary's Hospital in London, and, between 1938 and 1939, the President of the Obstetrical and Gynaecological Section of the Royal Society of Medicine. He was also a known supporter of birth control advice, particularly for working-class women.[54] Hoping to test the existing laws, Malleson requested that Bourne perform an abortion on the girl: 'Many people hold the view that the best means of correcting the abortion law is to let the medical profession extend the grounds in suitable cases until the law becomes obsolete as far as practice goes.'[55] Bourne agreed. He also made clear that he would write to the Attorney General and 'invit[e] him to take action'.[56] The abortion was performed on 14 June 1938. Bourne was charged soon afterwards.

The Bourne trial became a public spectacle about abortion. That the National Government's Attorney General, Sir Donald Somervell, personally prosecuted the case underscored the gravity of this spectacle. Bourne entered a plea of 'not guilty', arguing that he performed the abortion to save her life from 'mental collapse' rather than physical danger.[57] Somervell adhered to the letter of the 1929 Infant Life (Preservation) Act, rejecting any psychological basis for legal abortion. Crucial to Bourne's defence was his belief that the girl was 'normal' and 'moral'; she did not have what he called a 'prostitute mind', proved to him by her 'complete breakdown' during a gynaecological examination.[58] Other witnesses, such as Joan Malleson, similarly stressed the girl's morality and respectability; in her original letter to Bourne, read before the court, Malleson had remarked that 'the girl's parents are so respectable that they do not know the address of any abortionist'.[59]

Bourne was acquitted. Superficially, the outcome seemed to offer a 'wide and liberal view of the meaning of "preservation of the life of the mother"', one which included social or psychological reasons.[60] But ALRA activists realized the limited scope of the victory, criticizing those 'who think that, especially after the Bourne case, all is well'.[61] In 1938, the organization stated that the decision was 'not enough': 'abortion should be legal for economic reasons as well as health reasons'.[62] The social context of class remained paramount in the organization's mind.

The Bourne case brought attention to the ambiguities of abortion law and it did help doctors trying to extend the legal criteria in which they performed abortions. But it did so under exceptional circumstances and with arguments that had very little reference to the central concerns of abortion reformers in the 1930s. The Bourne case came to trial because a prominent middle-class, male doctor had made a public spectacle of the case of a 'respectable' (and thus probably middle-class)

---

[54] See his comments in Norman Haire (ed.), *Some More Medical Views of Birth Control* (London: Unwin, 1928), 88.

[55] *The Times*, 19 July 1938.

[56] *The Times*, 19 July 1938.

[57] *The Times*, 20 July 1938.

[58] *Law Reports: 1 King's Bench* (1939), Central Criminal Court, *Rex v. Bourne*, 18 July 1938, 688–9.

[59] *The Times*, 19 July 1938.

[60] *The Times*, 20 July 1939.

[61] Edgecombe, 'Marital Difficulties and Abortion Law Reform', 15.

[62] ALRA, *The Bourne Case and After* (London: ALRA, 1938).

young girl. The abortion had been performed safely, within the precincts of a major hospital. Bourne's professionalism had been continually emphasized. This was the framework of middle-class access to abortion, whether in its environment, its actors, or even in the network of contacts between a girl, her parents, a Harley Street doctor and a leading gynaecologist. It was a network unavailable to working-class women. It should also be remarked that the Bourne trial tended to legitimate, rather than challenge, dominant views of femininity, particularly as they related to sexual mores. The central character in the trial was a girl, rather than a woman. She was a victim of rape. Most importantly, she was deemed 'moral' and 'normal', which meant not sexually active. Female sexuality was associated, indeed, with the 'prostitute class' of women. Finally, it is important to note that during the Bourne trial it was two upper-middle-class, professional men of high social standing—Bourne and Justice McNaghten—who judged femininity and drew its boundaries.

III

The Bourne case coincided with government interest in abortion. After the concerns expressed in the 1937 report on maternal mortality, the Home Office and the Ministry of Health established an Interdepartmental Committee on Abortion. The Committee was chaired by Sir Norman Birkett, a barrister and, briefly, a Liberal MP. Its membership included leading members of the medical and legal professions. Dorothy Thurtle, the daughter of former Labour leader George Lansbury and a local Labour politician in Shoreditch as well as a veteran of the WBCG and a founding member of the ALRA, was included on the committee. She was the only member openly sympathetic to the cause of abortion law reform. The Committee met for two years, receiving written and oral evidence from a variety of groups such as the ALRA, the Joint Council of Midwifery, the BMA, and the National Council for Equal Citizenship. It published its final report in 1939. The Majority Report of the Committee acknowledged that 'economic and financial reasons' were the leading causes of abortion and admitted that 'the law relating to abortion is freely disregarded among women of all types and classes', but rejected the legalization of abortion for 'social, economic and personal reasons'. Nonetheless, it did allow that there might be clarification of legal abortion in cases where threat to the mother could be demonstrated, along the lines of the Bourne judgement.[63]

Though the Labour Party did not participate in the inquiry, there were requests made by local women's sections to present evidence to the Committee. In December 1937, for example, the West Bermondsey women's section asked the London Labour Party Women's Advisory Committee to secure a seat on the Committee, 'supporting the view that working-class opinion should be given direct recognition'.[64] These requests went nowhere. But Labour women did participate. This was

---

[63] TNA, MH 71/30, Ministry of Health and Home Office, Report of the Interdepartmental Committee on Abortion, 1939, Majority Report, Conclusions, paras. 6, 14.
[64] LMA, ACC 2417/H/8, Nineteenth Annual Conference, 11 December 1937.

not only through the contributions of socialist-feminists involved in groups such as the ALRA but with the activity of explicitly working-class women's organizations such as the EMWWA, the only working-class group to present evidence to the Committee.

The Committee's work underscored the centrality of class in the consideration of abortion. The working-class woman, with her double burden as wage-earner and mother, was the common subject of concern among all parties in these deliberations. This was, in part, a discussion between middle-class participants about the working classes. In its testimony, the ALRA delegation, which included Janet Chance, Joan Malleson, and Stella Browne, emphasized illegal and unsafe abortions as principally a problem of working-class women: '[t]he safer abortion is always done by the medical profession, and the unsafer is occasionally done by themselves, but rarely in the middle and upper classes of society'.[65] In particular, it was tied to the maintenance of living standards among the working classes during the depression: '[t]he reason most often given for desiring abortion is the maintenance of an adequate standard of life for the family as a whole; whether this be judged financially, or in terms of health, house room, ambition in education, or general well-being'.[66] It was, therefore, a question of social welfare. It was also a question of inequality. In the words of Janet Chance, 'the working woman needs this relief more than her sisters'.[67]

The link between abortion and class was also apparent in empirical evidence presented to the Committee by people involved in health care. Dr Violet Russell, the Assistant Medical Officer for the London Borough of Kensington, conducted a survey of 500 women in the spring and summer of 1937.[68] Russell had not concerned herself with the problem of abortions or attitudes towards sexuality in the richer areas of the borough. Instead, she concentrated on its northern half, where there were cramped accommodations and a low average weekly income, to 'ascertain the attitude of the working-class parents in Kensington towards childbirth and the bringing-up of children'.[69] Based on a survey of a thousand of its members, the Midwives Institute similarly noted the relationship between economic deprivation and illegal abortion, stating that '[a]bortionists will flourish in any industrial area where financial and housing conditions are so bad'.[70]

---

[65] TNA, MH 71/21, Interdepartmental Committee on Abortion, Oral Evidence of Abortion Law Reform Association representatives (J. Chance, S. Browne, J. Malleson, and G. Thesiger), 13 October 1937.

[66] TNA, MH 71/21, Interdepartmental Committee on Abortion, Abortion Law Reform Association, Memorandum, AC Paper, No. 13.

[67] TNA, MH 71/21, Interdepartmental Committee on Abortion, Oral Evidence of Abortion Law Reform Association representatives (J. Chance, S. Browne, J. Malleson, and G. Thesiger), 13 October 1937.

[68] As Lara Marks has recently shown, birth control was a particularly strong issue in Kensington; see her *Metropolitan Maternity: Maternal and Infant Welfare Services in Early Twentieth Century London* (Amsterdam: Editions Rodopi B.V., 1996), 148–50.

[69] TNA, MH 71/21, Interdepartmental Committee on Abortion, Violet Russell, 'Report of an investigation into the question of contraception and abortion', 1937, 1.

[70] TNA, MH 71/22, Memorandum of Midwives Institute, no date [1937].

Concerns about modern femininity (particularly with respect to motherhood) and sexual morality ran through the Committee's deliberations. Most of its members were pessimistic and often alarmist in this regard. Some felt that legal abortion would merely contribute to an existing welter of sin, increasing 'the number of people who were having promiscuous intercourse'. They were especially concerned that the modern age had brought with it an antagonism to motherhood: 'the fashion of having children has gone out'. At points, this anxiety strained credibility. The EMWWA's representatives were asked, for example, 'Would there be any children?' if abortion were legalized. At least one Committee member seemed surprised to hear that '[t]here are women who want to have families and babies, and all the rest of it?'[71]

Given the gravity of this point with the Committee, it is not surprising that advocates of abortion emphasized women's morality and commitment to mother-hood, especially that of working-class women. Single women were, for example, rarely mentioned in this regard. Violet Russell stated that her control group of 500 working-class women were 'respectable young citizens of the working-class', with-out the usual stigmata of working-class immorality: '[m]ost of the women were clean and careful with their dress and there was very little evidence of drunkenness'. Russell explicitly addressed the question of moral decay among working-class women:

> . . . there is no deterioration in the character of the young working-class woman of the present day, who possesses all the devotion and affection for her husband and her children which was shown by her predecessors. What is now developed in these young parents, which was often absent in the past, is a sense of responsibility for the future of their children shown by the frequently repeated phrase that 'it is not fair to bring children into the world in poverty'.

In this context, Russell assured the Committee that '[t]he maternal instinct is strong'.[72] Working-class women continued to be good mothers and good citizens: their use of abortion did not detract from these qualities.

Maternalism also ran through the ALRA's evidence to the Committee. The ALRA stressed that illegal abortion was not the choice of selfish, irrational, and promiscuous women, but that of 'parents who loyally serve the best interests of the family, as they see them'.[73] Janet Chance held that 'voluntary parenthood' was the 'considered judgement of serious citizens', not the symptom of an immoral society.[74] But the ALRA also saw the question in terms of feminist progress. The right of choice for which the ALRA argued was not only couched in terms of

---

[71] TNA, MH 71/25, Interdepartmental Committee on Abortion, Oral Evidence of East Midlands Working Women's Association representatives (I. Roche and E. Oakes).

[72] TNA, MH 71/21, Interdepartmental Committee on Abortion, Violet Russell, 'Report of An Investigation into the Question of Contraception and Abortion', 1937, 2, 6.

[73] TNA, MH 71/21, Abortion Law Reform Association, Memorandum, AC Paper, No. 13.

[74] TNA, MH 71/21, Interdepartmental Committee on Abortion, Oral Evidence of Abortion Law Reform Association representatives (J. Chance, S. Browne, J. Malleson, and G. Thesiger), 13 October 1937.

membership as citizens within the public sphere, but carried with it an argument for female autonomy in both public and private spheres. Asked by the chairman of the inquiry, '[I]s the motive force acting behind the Association' to reduce maternal morbidity, or is it an extension of women's rights?', Joan Malleson responded, '[p]erhaps we might say it is some of both'.[75] Stella Browne gave evidence both with the ALRA and as an individual. In both contexts, she stressed her belief in abortion as part of extending 'the rights and happiness of women...I aim at making life more bearable and more interesting and better and bigger for the majority of women.'[76] In her evidence as an individual, she went further. Abortion was an integral aspect of a woman's 'right to love', to explore sexual pleasure: 'I do not think that to refrain from sexual intercourse out of fear...is in any way a virtue.'[77]

IV

In 1937, the women's section of the East Midlands Regional Organization of the Labour Party, centred mostly in Derby and Nottingham, had requested that the party represent its interest to the Interdepartmental Committee. Because Labour refused to discuss abortion at its annual conference, this request was turned down. But Oakes and Roche told the committee, '[t]he women of the East Midlands were so anxious that evidence of conditions here should be in your hands', 'this non-political Association was formed out of the political body', and thus was born the EMWWA.[78]

In the East Midlands, according to the EMWWA, the male breadwinner had disappeared. His place had largely been taken by women: 'in our part of the Midlands it is safe to say that 75 per cent of the wage-earners are women and juveniles... in many cases, the women are the sole wage-earners'.[79] In the 1920s and 1930s, the collieries of the East Midlands, a primary employer of men, witnessed a significant downturn. Short-time working became the norm, with the consequence that many men were unable to maintain their families on their working wage, to their great shame, as one colliery journal noted: 'Big strong men cried like babies for sheer want and frustration.' In Donisthorpe, south Derbyshire,

[75] TNA, MH 71/21, Interdepartmental Committee on Abortion, Oral Evidence of Abortion Law Reform Association representatives (J. Chance, S. Browne, J. Malleson, and G. Thesiger), 13 October 1937.
[76] TNA, MH 71/21, Evidence of Abortion Law Reform Association representatives (J. Chance, S. Browne, J. Malleson, and G. Thesiger), 13 October 1937.
[77] See TNA, MH 71/23, Interdepartmental Committee on Abortion, Oral Evidence of Stella Browne, no date [1937].
[78] TNA, MH 71/23, Interdepartmental Committee on Abortion, East Midlands Working Women's Association, Memorandum, 16 November 1937; resolutions in favour of abortion law reform were also received from a number of Women's Sections of local Labour parties and chapters of the Women's Cooperative Guild.
[79] TNA, MH 71/25, Oral Evidence to Interdepartmental Committee on Abortion of Mrs Ivy E. Roche and Mrs E. Oakes, East Midlands Working Women's Association, 1.

men were only earning about £1 a week from two and a half shifts.[80] It thus became women's responsibility to support the family, before and after marriage.[81] In the East Midlands, there was less evidence of 'new' industries employing women and young workers, but there were older industries such as hosiery and lace-making that employed large numbers of women, as did singular concerns such as the Players' cigarette factory in Nottingham.

Women's economic responsibility for the family was the main factor motivating abortions: '[t]he women feel that so long as their wages are necessary for keeping the home going, a pregnancy would be a disaster and an abortion is resorted to'. For the sake of their families, 'they dare not be out of work'.[82] In the absence of effective and accessible birth control, such 'economic pressure' made abortion imperative. The EMWWA felt justified in making one of its criteria for legal abortion 'where the woman was a wage-earner'. Their argument for abortion thus evolved out of what was perceived as the collapse of one kind of gender economy and the rise of another. In this, of course, women took on the role of breadwinner. The state was perceived not to have stepped into that role, not, at least, through the punitive Means Test. As one of the EWMMA representatives argued to the Committee: 'under the Means Test under which so many of our people live, you are allowed 2s. for each child . . . [a] mother may feel that 2s. is not enough to justify another child'.[83]

Abortion was common in the East Midlands. Oakes had been a midwife from the 'corner of a little tiny colliery village'. Between 1925 and 1934, she had met 122 women who had, among them, 227 miscarriages; '[t]here are not many accidental miscarriages in those figures', Oakes asserted.[84] Some of these abortions had been done with knitting needles, but the vast majority were done with the use of drugs like quinine and red lead or herbs, provided by local chemists or herbalists. Oakes and Roche also knew of women who had gone to Nottingham to get abortions done. The principal concern Oakes and Roche had was of the threat to women's health from dangerous drugs. The enemies in this were certainly chemists and herbalists. If abortion could be provided safely by doctors, then women would not go to the chemists and herbalists 'for the appalling things they go for to-day'. In the area Oakes and Roche represented, access to birth control was difficult. There was no municipal maternity or infant welfare clinic, only a voluntary clinic in Nottingham where a doctor attended every other week. Birth control devices were 'out of the monetary scope of the working classes'. Ideally, the EMWWA wanted to

---

[80] See Colin P. Griffin, '"Three Days Down the Pit and Three Days' Play": Underemployment in the East Midland Coalfields between the Wars', *International Review of Social History* 38 (1993), 330.

[81] See Todd, *Young Women, Work, and Family in England 1918–1950*, 61–2.

[82] TNA, MH 71/23, East Midlands Working Women's Association, Memorandum to Interdepartmental Committee on Abortion, 16 November 1937; MH 71/25, Oral Evidence to Interdepartmental Committee on Abortion of Mrs Ivy E. Roche and Mrs E. Oakes, East Midlands Working Women's Association, 1.

[83] TNA, MH 71/25, Oral Evidence to Interdepartmental Committee on Abortion of Mrs Ivy E. Roche and Mrs E. Oakes, East Midlands Working Women's Association, 2, 7.

[84] TNA, MH 71/25, Oral Evidence to Interdepartmental Committee on Abortion of Mrs Ivy E. Roche and Mrs E. Oakes, East Midlands Working Women's Association, 4.

see more municipal clinics and better provision of birth control. But they also believed that women should be able to go to a doctor, request an abortion, pay a reasonable fee, and have the abortion done safely. The Association asked that abortion be legalized not only in cases of rape, incest, or criminal assault, but on social or economic grounds: 'where [the] mother is a wage earner and/or another child would be a burden'.[85]

Oakes and Roche were, in their own way, as insistent as Stella Browne that women should have an 'absolute right' to abortion.[86] During their testimony to the Interdepartmental Committee, Roche and Oakes were continually pressed to answer whether a range of social provisions (such as better unemployment insurance, family allowances or the establishment of crèches at the workplace) or better economic conditions might stave off demands for abortion. Though they acknowledged that such measures and conditions would certainly help, Roche and Oakes still maintained that working-class women needed access to safe and legal abortion. This determination shone through a tense exchange between Birkett and Roche:

> Q. What it really comes to is this: that the woman can go to a doctor and say: 'Please give me an abortion'? That is really what it comes to, if she is to be the judge. There is to be no appeal from it. It is universal, legalised abortion. That is what Mrs Roche is advocating?
> A. Yes.
> Q. If the mother is to be the judge of the economic circumstances, it really means that you have complete universal, legalised abortion, does it not?
> A. Well, what I want is this—
> Q. Is that so? Is that really the point of view which you desire to put?
> A. May I answer it in this way?
> Q. You must certainly answer in any way you like; but the question is capable of an answer Yes or No. That is really your point of view, I take it, is it not?
> A. Then may I say Yes? . . .
> Q. That is perfectly logical and perfectly right: but what you are really saying is this, is it not: I do advocate universal, legalised abortion, because the existing situation is very much worse in its evils than legalised abortion would bring about?
> A. Yes, I think that is so.[87]

The same determination ran through Oakes and Roche's belief that it was the woman, and the woman alone, who should decide whether she should get an abortion. Roche and Oakes also insisted that as a choice, abortion had to be left solely in the hands of individual women, not those of the state, the medical profession, or even husbands. 'The person who actually bears the burden', they said, 'should have the last say.' This was particularly true of 'social' or 'economic' abortions. Only the woman affected, Roche stated, could be the judge of 'economic

---

[85] TNA, MH 71/25, Interdepartmental Committee on Abortion, Oral Evidence of East Midlands Working Women's Association representatives (I. Roche and E. Oakes), 1.

[86] Browne, 'The Right to Abortion', 113.

[87] TNA, MH 71/25, Interdepartmental Committee on Abortion, Oral Evidence of East Midlands Working Women's Association representatives (I. Roche and E. Oakes), 11–12.

circumstances'; if she saw those economic circumstances put at risk by the birth of another child, she had a right to an abortion: 'if a woman goes and asks for it on economic grounds, then it does seem to me that she should have it'. This was particularly important, of course, with respect to the medical profession and husbands. Of the latter, Oakes and Roche argued that most men 'would agree' to an abortion 'if there was no money coming in except the money his wife brought, plus the money he may get them from the Means Test'. Any man who would disagree with his wife was 'not worth considering'.[88]

But the representatives of the EMWWA similarly emphasized that they were defending, rather than challenging, motherhood and domesticity. 'Women in the main are just as anxious to have children as ever they were', Roche and Oakes stated, but unemployment and poverty had made multiple pregnancies an untenable economic prospect for working-class women: 'they are frightened of the present insecurity of their position'.[89]

The EMWWA offered a much more nuanced view of working-class femininity than many middle-class abortion or birth control advocates. Its arguments for legal abortion were made in terms that viewed women in a variety of roles: as workers, for example, as head of the domestic household, or as agents within the welfare system. These working-class women stressed the complexity of the female body and their desire for agency to reconcile its various roles in a modern society and economy. One particular point was about age. The EMWWA was concerned about the social stigma attached to unmarried mothers, not least because it limited the freedom and autonomy of the young woman if she was compelled into marriage: 'marriages of this sort are very dreadful—it is horrible to be forced to marry just because they are going to have an unwanted child'. It also advocated sex education within schools 'long before the school-leaving age'.[90] What is also striking is how a sexual politics based upon material experience was offered by the EMWWA. This was largely about class, about the articulation of a particular class-based experience, and it was this class experience that led to a particular kind of political agency. But articulating arguments for legal abortion also involved emphasizing a new kind of gender politics that envisaged wives and mothers within a traditional context empowered with sexual choice and autonomy, a development of some themes first seen in the 1920s.

V

The Interdepartmental Committee submitted its final report in 1939. The majority of the Committee suggested that the law should allow therapeutic termination if pregnancy would endanger life and health. But this was not an argument for

---

[88] TNA, MH 71/25, Interdepartmental Committee on Abortion, Oral Evidence of East Midlands Working Women's Association representatives (I. Roche and E. Oakes) 6–7.
[89] TNA, MH 71/25, Interdepartmental Committee on Abortion, Oral Evidence of East Midlands Working Women's Association representatives (I. Roche and E. Oakes).
[90] TNA, MH 71/25, Interdepartmental Committee on Abortion, Oral Evidence of East Midlands Working Women's Association representatives (I. Roche and E. Oakes).

the radical revision of the abortion laws. The Committee made clear that it believed that 'the induction of abortion is, on ethical, social and medical grounds essentially an undesirable operation, justifiable only in exceptional circumstances, and the Committee is strongly opposed to any broad relaxation of the law designed to make social, economic, and personal reasons a justification for the operation'. This was grounded in the belief that legal abortion would destroy the 'religious and ethical teaching and . . . fundamental principles on which society is based'.[91] Abortion would encourage sexual liberalization, proving 'an added temptation to loose and immoral conduct[;] . . . [t]here would . . . almost inevitably be a tendency for promiscuous sexual intercourse to be more common' in a period during which 'a loosening of the bonds of sexual morality . . . [and] . . . a tendency for the gratification of sexual desires by unmarried persons' had already occurred.[92] For the Committee, this consideration of 'the effect upon public morals' was rooted in the complexity of modern femininity and the threat this posed to traditional gender ideology:

> A marked change has . . . occurred in family life. Women have entered into competition with men in numerous spheres of activity. The wife is not infrequently the principal, and sometimes the sole, wage-earner in the family. . . . Changed social circumstances may have made the problem more acute. Many avenues of employment are open to the single woman, and the child may be, or may be thought to be, a hindrance to her progress in the career she has chosen.[93]

The evidence provided by abortion reformers had done little to suggest that abortion was undermining 'fundamental principles' such as motherhood and community. Their argument was, of course, the opposite. Working-class women were not entering into 'competition' with men so much as having to find ways of compensating for male unemployment towards the end of preserving the working-class family. But the report ignored this evidence and presented instead an alarmist vision of a society on the edge of a sexual abyss.

Dorothy Thurtle submitted a minority report. She noted the support for legal abortion among women's organizations like the WCG and the NCW. In particular, she emphasized the authority of working-class and women's voices on this issue: 'I do not accept the view expressed in some quarters that these women are ignorant and uninstructed in this matter. On the contrary, from one important aspect, they are better instructed than any, because they are or represent the victims of the existing order of affairs.'[94] Thurtle took a maternalist line, arguing that abortion

---

[91] TNA, MH 71/30, Ministry of Health and Home Office, Report of the Interdepartmental Committee on Abortion, 1939, para. 230.
[92] TNA, MH 71/30, Ministry of Health and Home Office, Report of the Interdepartmental Committee on Abortion, 1939, paras. 235, 301.
[93] TNA, MH 71/30, Ministry of Health and Home Office, Report of the Interdepartmental Committee on Abortion, 1939, paras. 225, 275.
[94] TNA, MH 71/30, Ministry of Health and Home Office, Report of the Interdepartmental Committee on Abortion, 1939, para. 251.

should be legal for women with high fertility rates or who had already had four children.

The Second World War interrupted further discussion of abortion. There were some signs, however small, that opinion was changing on abortion within the Labour movement. In April 1939, the NFRB Health Services Subcommittee and Social Services made an oblique recommendation to abortion in the wake of the Bourne case: 'local authorities should be obliged to make the provision for birth control which is now permitted them, and ... it should be made clear that the phrase "injurious to health" covers potential injury not only to specific disease but to the general weakness that results from too frequent pregnancies and an over-burdened home life'.[95] In this way, however quietly, the idea of birth control and abortion as social welfare was accepted.

Abortion politics in the 1930s saw the restatement and development of some of the links between sex reform and Labour politics in the 1920s. Though a non-party organization, the ALRA clearly embedded its single-issue politics partly within the network of Labour women's organizations. In part because of the direct inheritance of its WBCG members, it also took up much of the same discourse seen in the birth control campaign of the 1920s. Most importantly, the abortion campaign saw the continuation of a class-based advocacy of reproductive rights. The working-class mother remained the pivot of this advocacy. Against the failure of the breadwinner ethos to sustain the working-class family, abortion was to be the means of protecting that family and saving the health of the working-class mother. As was suggested above, groups like the ALRA and Labour organizations like the EMWWA thus saw abortion as a form of social and maternalist welfare. But this was not a conservative maternalism. Central to abortion advocacy was, first of all, the belief that it was an individual woman's decision that had to be respected. At the same time, as already argued, abortion advocacy depended, especially in the testimony of the EMWWA, on the belief that the breadwinner ideology had failed in practice. Indeed, what we see through abortion is an attempt by working-class women and their middle-class allies to make up the distance between lived experience and the ideology of maternalism. Out of this, there emerged, again particularly through the testimony of the EMWWA, a vision of femininity that was both rooted in domesticity and motherhood and disruptive of those contexts, stressing women as wage-earners, as sexual beings, and, not least, as desiring power within the private and public spheres. Just as with the politics of birth control in the 1920s, the politics of abortion was a class politics. Working-class women clearly felt a class difference between their sexual experience and their experience of the abortion law between the wars and that of their middle-class counterparts. From the perspective of middle-class activists, stressing class difference remained as important in terms of abortion as it had been with birth control.

---

[95] BJL, SMA, DSM 4/1, Fabian Society, Health Services Sub-Committee and Social Services Committee, 'The Maternity and Child Welfare Services', 13 April 1939.

PART 2

ROADS TO 1967

5

A 'Silent', 'Modern' Revolution?

The Family, Femininity, and Reproductive Politics in the 1940s and 1950s

The sharp edge lent to sexual issues between the wars by the threat of economic insecurity and the hopeful vision of utopian social change dulled in the 1940s and 1950s. Utopian visions retreated almost entirely from socialist or feminist thought. War, reconstruction, and affluence wore away the fear of economic insecurity, especially for working-class people. In the political sphere, socialist thought was dominated by the agenda of postwar Labour governments inevitably more concerned with the public monuments of economic planning and social welfare than the transformation of the private sphere. Where in the 1920s and 1930s feminism had provided one spur for political action on sexual issues, the 1940s and the 1950s have sometimes been perceived as a 'political feminist hiatus'.[1]

Despite this, there were quiet, but substantial, shifts in the relationship between some sexual issues and Labour politics in the 1940s and 1950s. Understanding this demands a broad examination of the changing context of gender, sexuality, and family life in the 1940s and 1950s, particularly with relationship to the working classes. As well, it is important to think about the progress of birth control issues such as abortion in the postwar era. Both affected the reception of issues like birth control and abortion within Labour and working-class politics in the 1940s and 1950s and into the 1960s.

The present chapter explores the 1940s and 1950s and concentrates on the relationship between ideas of the family and reproductive control. Three questions are of particular interest. The first is what could be called the normalization of birth control in Labour politics in the 1940s and 1950s. In the 1920s and 1930s, even the discussion of birth control, let alone its implementation as party policy, was controversial in the eyes of the party's leaders and the leaders of the women's sections. In the 1940s and 1950s, birth control was accepted, almost blandly, as a normal part of family life. This seeped into policy assumptions. The evidence given to the Royal Commission on Population by two mainstream Labour women's organizations, the Standing Joint Committee of Working Women's Organizations (SJCWWO), the successor to the SJCIWO, and the FWG, shows that many of the arguments that were radical in the 1920s had become conventional wisdom by the

---

[1] Sheila Rowbotham, *Woman's Consciousness, Man's World* (Harmondsworth: Penguin, 1973), 12.

1940s. This did not lead to an immediate change in party policy, but it did signal a
very different set of assumptions about motherhood, family, and femininity.

The campaign for abortion law reform also witnessed a significant change in the
immediate postwar period. The ALRA was in the doldrums in the 1940s, still given
some life by its connections to a liberal elite and working-class women's organizations, but making no headway in changing the law. In the 1950s, the group
switched its focus to Westminster, seeking direct political change with the help
of a small group of mostly Labour MPs. This shifted the arc of abortion politics,
linking it more clearly to a parliamentary fate.

The chapter concludes with a broad discussion of the changing context of
femininity, women's lives and working-class life in the 1940s and 1950s, arguing
that this showed both continuity with the 1920s and 1930s and, at the same time,
provided the basis for a departure in thinking about the political context of birth
control. This section examines, in particular, the way that reconstruction and
affluence changed working-class gender roles and family life. Though there were
significant changes in the 1940s and 1950s, there were also important continuities.
Class remained a major aspect of sexual politics on the Left. Sexual politics
continued to be at its most effective and even radical, in many ways, when it was
about the terms of working-class domesticity and motherhood. But the 1940s and
1950s also marked the gradual loosening of the ties between sexual politics and
motherhood and the family. In the two decades following the war, we can see the
emergence of new ideas and experiences of femininity, not least within the working
classes. One of the critical changes was the increasing female participation in the
workforce that made working-class femininity more complex. Women were no
longer simply understood as mothers, but as citizens, consumers, and workers.
Appreciating this is crucial to an understanding of the longer story of the place of
sexual issues within Labour and working-class politics.

There are two questions of periodization that this chapter also qualifies. The first
is about the genealogy of the 'permissive' society of the 1960s. This chapter
suggests that the journey towards the permissive society of the 1960s and the
legal changes of 1967 was already gathering pace in the 1940s and 1950s. It has
also been argued that the postwar era witnessed a much greater emphasis on the
self.[2] Before the Second World War, arguments for sexual reform, whether in
terms of birth control or sexual orientation, were often tied to the protection of
existing collectivities (such as the family or the home), dependent upon women in
a particular context, motherhood, or, even in their utopian form, in a vision of new
kinds of community or companionship. In the 1940s and 1960s, there emerged a
more individualistic sense of the self and an emphasis upon the rights and
expression of that self. This book argues that this was not a linear, comprehensive,
or immediate change; it was, instead, partial, tentative, and uneven. There were
hints of this modernity in the 1940s and 1950s, but older reference points, such as
class and family, remained strong in this period. In the articulation of sexual

---

[2] See Conekin, Mort, and Waters (eds), 'Introduction', *Moments of Modernity*, 1–21.

politics, whether in terms of sexual expression, orientation or reproductive control, the emphasis upon self and individual rather than the family became more apparent in the 1970s and 1980s.

I

The Second World War highlighted the ambiguities around femininity, sexuality, and citizenship.[3] Wartime mobilization left women poised between public and private spheres and between productive and reproductive roles. Women were at once expected to contribute to the war effort through public work (particularly after the conscription of women beginning in 1941) and to maintain the traditional role of motherhood. War work also raised questions about gender equality.[4] Female sexuality was also a site of tension. Its expression was perceived as an important way of sustaining a sense of distinction between the sexes at a point when that distinction was blurred in other ways, but too much sexuality was perceived as disruptive.[5]

Political discourse reflected these ambiguous currents in varying degrees of celebration, perplexity, and concern. On the far Left, the CPGB asked '. . . can a woman be a wife, mother, worker, and active citizen at the same time?'[6] On the right, Conservative women recognized that though women still regarded 'the home as the centre of their well-being, they no longer regarded it as their boundary'.[7] Such sentiments were also apparent in the Labour movement. In 1943, for example, the WCG published a pamphlet entitled *Woman of Tomorrow*, which spoke of a 'new awareness by modern women of their rights and responsibilities in communal affairs' and the centrality of women to the public sphere: '[t]he woman of to-morrow, educated, independent, with her intimate knowledge of the primary necessities of existence, will make a vital contribution towards future democratic development'. Women had achieved this standing 'in the face of masculine prejudice and considerable opposition'. But if this transition in women's lives was celebrated by the WCG, it still recognized that traditional femininity was under threat. The 'independence' of younger women might descend into chaos with the 'serious absence of uplifting home influence'.[8] Even as the WCG praised 'modern' women, it wanted to place them within the framework of traditional domesticity.

[3] For this see Sonya Rose, *Which People's War?* (Oxford: Oxford University Press, 2003), 73–92, 107–50; Antonia Lant, *Blackout* (Princeton: Princeton University Press, 1991); Gillian Swanson, '"So Much Money and So Little to Spend It On": Morale, Consumption and Sexuality', in Christine Gledhill and Gillian Swanson (eds), *Nationalizing Femininity* (Manchester: Manchester University Press, 1996).

[4] See Penny Summerfield, *Women Workers During the Second World War* (London: Routledge, 1989).

[5] See Rose, *Which People's War*; Lant, *Blackout*; Gledhill and Swanson, *Nationalizing Femininity*.

[6] Communist Party, *Woman's Place?* (London: Communist Party, 1944), 15.

[7] Conservative Women's Reform Group, *When Peace Comes* (London: Conservative Women's Reform Group, 1944), 7.

[8] Women's Cooperative Guild, *Woman of Tomorrow* (Manchester: Woman's Cooperative Guild, 1943), 3, 2, 4, 9.

The war also brought to the surface anxieties about the future of family life in Britain, whether threatened by the dislocation of bombing, absent husbands, or female independence.[9] For the most part, family life in fact remained relatively stable. Compared with the pre-war period, there was an increase in the number of divorces after 1945, but this subsided somewhat in the 1950s, to rise again in the 1960s.[10] Like divorce, illegitimacy spiked in the mid-1940s, before falling back in the 1950s, only to move upwards again in the 1960s and 1970s.[11] The state of the family, marriage, and reproduction nonetheless remained a focus of concern for government, an anxiety that can be charted, as Jeffrey Weeks has pointed out, in the steady series of inquiries and royal commissions on aspects of family life, child care, and marriage, from the 1946 Curtis Report on children and the Royal Commission on Population of 1949, through to the royal commissions of the 1950s on divorce law reform, homosexuality, and prostitution.[12]

Worries about the future of the family inevitably involved the perception of marriage.[13] Marriage, it was believed, needed shoring up against the disruption of war. There was a particular desire to keep women happy within marriage and this led to a shift in views of sexuality.[14] In the 1940s and 1950s, government, voluntary groups, and some churches encouraged the promotion of female sexual pleasure as a central component of a successful and stable marriage.[15] Marriage manuals instructed husbands and wives in sexual techniques designed to bring mutual satisfaction.[16] Female sexual pleasure was critical to this literature.[17] The female orgasm became, according to Eustace Chesser, a contemporary observer of sexual mores, 'an important indication of successful sexual union' and thus a litmus test of marital happiness.[18] Its absence was seen as a cause of marital discord.[19] Chesser talked of the female orgasm as both a right and an obligation, not unlike the vote:

[9] See Sonya Rose, 'Sex, Citizenship and the Nation in World War II Britain', *American Historical Review* 103 (1998), 1147–76; Marilyn Lake, 'Female desires: The Meaning of World War 2', *Australian Historical Studies* 21/95 (October 1990), 267–84.

[10] See *Social Trends* (London: HMSO, 1971), Table 14, 57.

[11] See Jane Lewis and John Welshman, 'The Issue of Never-Married Motherhood in Britain, 1920–70', *Social History of Medicine* 10 (1997), 401–18; *Social Trends*, Table 13, 56.

[12] Weeks, *Sex, Politics and Society*, 236.

[13] See Claire Langhamer, 'Adultery in Post-War England', *History Workshop Journal* 62 (2006), 86–115; Pat Thane, 'Family Life and "Normality" in Postwar British Culture', in Richard Bessel and Dirk Schumann (eds), *Life After Death* (Cambridge: Cambridge University Press, 2003).

[14] See Louise Tracey, 'Reconstituting the Family: Education for Parenthood and Maternity and Child Welfare, 1945–60', in Lawrence Black et alia (eds), *Consensus or Coercion? The State, The People and Social Cohesion in Post-War Britain* (Cheltenham: New Clarion Press, 2001).

[15] See Gillian Swanson, '"So Much Money and So Little to Spend it On": Morale, Consumption and Sexuality'.

[16] See Cook, *The Long Sexual Revolution*; Weeks, *Sex, Politics and Society*; Birmingham Feminist History Group, 'Feminism as Femininity in the 1950s', *Feminist Review* 3 (1979), 48–65.

[17] See Hall, *Sex, Gender and Social Change in Britain since 1880*, 136.

[18] Eustace Chesser, *The Sexual, Marital and Family Relationships of the Englishwoman* (London: Hutchinson, 1956), 421.

[19] See, for example, Joan Malleson writing as 'Dr Joan Graham' aka 'Medica', *Any Wife or Any Husband* (London: Heinemann, 1951, 1955), 30.

The essential point to bear in mind is that the wife requires satisfaction equally with the husband. That is the 'love right' of every married woman. Every wife ought to take steps to secure it. Every husband ought to ensure that his wife secures it.[20]

The 1949 'Little Kinsey' survey of sexual attitudes by Mass-Observation (M-O) suggested that there remained a 'close correlation' between 'sexual satisfaction, and satisfaction with marriage in its entirety'.[21] Female sexual pleasure was thus increasingly accepted as a foundation of stable marriage in the postwar period. Chesser's major sex survey of 1956 stressed, for example, the importance of sexual satisfaction to a modern marriage, associating it with other 'modern' developments such as 'the growth of sexual knowledge and education, and the emancipation of women'.[22] The marriage guidance movement took sex instruction as one of the pillars of training young Britons for companionate marriage.[23]

The birth rate also attracted attention in the 1940s and 1950s. In his famous blueprint for postwar reconstruction, William Beveridge was blunt about the primacy of women's reproductive responsibilities: 'mothers will have vital work to do in ensuring the adequate continuance of the British race and British ideals in the world'.[24] But despite this natalist anxiety, the birth rate of the 1940s and 1950s in fact saw an increase from the 1930s. Between 1936 and 1940, there was an average of 14.7 births per 100,000 of population. In the 1950s, this rose to 15.85 and, in the early 1960s, to 18.1. But it was also clear that government and other agencies were willing to accept a lower birth rate and even to encourage family planning. The Royal Commission on Population of 1944–9 lamented the weakness in Britain's birth rate, but nonetheless accepted that the main cause of this was deliberate family limitation and that this had to be accepted.[25] The establishment of the National Health Service in 1948 afforded the FPA a number of financial resources directly or indirectly from the state.[26] From 61 family planning clinics just before the war, there were 400 by 1963. There was also greater acceptance of contraception within marriage from, for example, the Church of England.

To contemporary observers of the birth rate, one of the most striking changes was the apparent agency exercised by working-class men and women in limiting family size. This was particularly clear among working-class women in their twenties and thirties. Those emerging into adulthood in the 1930s and 1940s were armed with higher expectations of marriage, family life, and living standards

---

[20] Eustace Chesser, *Marriage and Freedom* (London: Rich and Cowan Medical Publications, 1946), 55.

[21] Leonard England, 'A British Sex Survey', *International Journal of Sexology* 2 (February 1950), 152.

[22] Chesser, *The Sexual, Marital and Family Relationships of the English Woman*, 421.

[23] Jane Lewis, 'Public Institution and Private Relationship: Marriage and Marriage Guidance, 1920–1968', *Twentieth Century British History* 1 (1990), 233–63.

[24] Cmd. 6404, *Social Insurance and Allied Services: Report by Sir William Beveridge* (London: HMSO, 1942), para. 531; see also Denise Riley, *War in the Nursery* (London: Virago, 1985).

[25] See Cmd. 7695, *Royal Commission on Population*, 29, 34; see also Pat Thane, 'Population Politics in Post-War British Culture', in Conekin, Mort, and Waters (eds), *Moments of Modernity*.

[26] Weeks, *Sex, Politics and Society*, 234.

and were determined to avoid large families.[27] Of course, this was a shift that may have begun in the 1930s, but it resonated most powerfully through texts of the 1940s. In this regard, agency was more clearly identified with women, rather than men, or at least women were noted by social observers as more vocal in their desire for smaller families. In 1947, a survey of *The Population of Britain* noted: '"[n]ot like my mum" was the usual phrase among young mothers of [the 1930s] who were so often warned by their own mothers not to expose themselves to the fate the latter themselves suffered when unemployment caught them with a largish family'.[28] In their 1951 study of 400 urban working-class people, Eliot Slater and Moya Wood-side remarked, '[p]eople do not want large families and large families are firmly associated in their minds with poverty, hardship and the lowering of standards'.[29] A year later, Ferdynand Zweig argued that working women shared a determination to practise birth control. Younger women particularly felt 'the need to mark their disagreement with the past, with the bad experience of their childhood'.[30] By the 1940s, the average number of children in working-class families had dropped from roughly four to two.[31]

Of course, this was not a sexual revolution. Though M-O could speak of a 'virtual absence of a moral code of sexual behaviour in society today' in 1945, four years later it asserted that there was still a prevalent feeling that 'sex for its own sake is wrong'.[32] Respectability remained particularly important within communities of working-class women.[33]

That this was more noticed in the 1940s than perhaps it had been in the 1930s may say something about a changing political context and a shift in the way of understanding the working classes. It occurred at a point when wartime and postwar governments were consciously managing the public sphere of economy and welfare. An analogy might be ventured here between postwar economic planning and family planning. The latter was to be as rational and controlled as the former. M-O spoke of a family 'deliberately conceived by intelligent citizens

---

[27] See Mass-Observation, *Britain and Her Birthrate* (London: John Murray, 1945), 54–62. See also Sally Alexander, 'Becoming a Woman in the 1920s and 1930s' and 'Memory, Generation and History: Two Women's Lives in the Inter-War years', in *Becoming a Woman and Other Essays in 19th and 20th Century Feminist History*; Marks, *Metropolitan Maternity: Maternal and Infant Welfare Services in Early Twentieth Century London*.

[28] Eva M. Hubback, *The Population of Britain* (Harmondsworth: Penguin, 1947), 57.

[29] Eliot Slater and Maya Woodside, *Patterns of Marriage: A Study of Marriage Relationships in the Urban Working Classes* (London: Cassell, 1951), 151.

[30] Ferdynand Zweig, *Women's Life and Labour* (London: Gollancz, 1952), 66.

[31] See Richard Soloway, *Birth Control and the Population Question in England 1877–1930* (Chapel Hill: University of North Carolina Press, 1982); Seccombe, 'Starting to Stop: Working-class Fertility Decline in Britain'; *Royal Commission on Population*; M. Bone, *Family Planning Services in England and Wales* (London: Macmillan, 1973).

[32] Mass-Observation Online (Marlborough: Adam Matthew Publications, 2001), FR2205: Sex, Morality and the Birthrate, February 1945; 3110: 'General Attitudes to Sex', April 1949, 20.

[33] Penny Summerfield and Nicole Crockett, '"You Weren't Taught That with the Welding": Lessons in Sexuality in the Second World War', *Women's History Review* 1 (1992), 435–54; for the persistence of this, see, for example, Geoffrey Gorer, *Sex and Marriage in England Today* (London: Nelson, 1971).

with modern outlooks and modern interests'.[34] In the mid-1950s, a member of the FPA's executive ventured that Labour women 'who believe in planning for the whole nation' would also be interested in family planning.[35] Thus, a working-class sexuality once perceived as chaotic, uncontrolled, and potentially dangerous both for working-class people and the nation was now represented as increasingly within the fabric of a managed and modern nation.[36]

II

To state there were no substantial changes in Labour's approach to questions of gender and sexuality in the 1940s and 1950s in response to these developments is not to say that there were no changes at all. There were subdued, though important, shifts in ideas about gender and the private sphere within Labour politics in the 1940s and 1950s that prepared the ground for some of the reforms of the 1960s. These developments went some way to normalizing the arguments about birth control and abortion in the 1920s and 1930s and to some degree also reflected changes in views of gender and sexuality in the 1940s and 1950s.

It is worth thinking about the Labour Party of the 1940s and 1950s and women's place within that party. The broad view of Labour in the immediate postwar period suggests a party finding it difficult to adapt to social change. The first six years after the war were, of course, years of power. The party concentrated less on new directions than on the realization of the programmes laid down in the 1930s. Once in opposition in 1951, Labour struggled, suffering intra-party division and electoral frustration. A key question here has been the party's apparent inability to adjust to economic and class change: the prosperity of the 1950s and the new social forces that this generated, such as youth culture and affluence, baffled Labour.[37]

It is perhaps not surprising, given this, to find that Labour showed little innovation with respect to areas such as sexuality or gender. But gender could not have been invisible to the party in the postwar period as there was a significant gender gap between the main parties between 1951 and 1964.[38] Labour seemed

---

[34] Mass-Observation, *Britain and Her Birthrate*, 227.

[35] Lady Tewson in *Labour Woman*, 44/1 (1956), 30.

[36] See Brooke, 'Bodies, Sexuality and the "Modernization" of the British Working Classes', 122–43.

[37] See James Cronin, 'Politics, Class Structure and the Enduring Weakness of British Social Democracy', *Journal of British Studies* 16 (1982–3), 124–42; Nick Tiratsoo, 'Popular Politics, Affluence and the Labour Party in the 1950s', in Lewis Johnman, Tony Gorst, and W. Scott Lucas (eds), *Contemporary British History 1931–61* (London: Scolar, 1991); S. Brooke, 'Labour and the "Nation" after 1945', in Jon Lawrence and Miles Taylor (eds), *Party, State and Society* (Aldershot: Scolar, 1997), 153–75; Lawrence Black, *The Political Culture of the Left in Affluent Britain, 1951–64: Old Labour, New Britain* (London: Palgrave, 2003), 36–7 in particular; Catherine Ellis, 'Ideas, Policy and Ideology: The British Labour Party in Opposition, 1951–9', unpublished DPhil thesis, University of Oxford, 1997.

[38] See Nicky Hart, 'Gender and the Rise and Fall of Class Politics', *New Left Review* 175 (May–June 1989), 19–47. On the period between 1945 and 1951, see Ina Zweiniger-Bargielowska,

unable or unwilling to do anything about this gender gap, in stark contrast to its reaction to the youth vote.[39] This was deepened by the relationship of the women's sections to the rest of the party during this period. In the 1920s, the impetus for sexual reforms like birth control had largely emerged from the women's sections of the party. This commitment also led to an interest in changing the power balance of the larger party. This did not occur in the 1940s and 1950s. There are a number of explanations for this. First of all, there were debilitating structural and discursive limitations on women's place and the treatment of their issues within the postwar Labour Party.[40] Women were certainly appreciated as supporters, if not agents of change, particularly at election time; indeed, the negative proof of this came just before the 1959 defeat, with the unpleasant shock that fully 34% of trade unionists' wives were undecided.[41] For their part, Labour women's sections were vibrant but complaisant in the 1940s and 1950s. They still constituted an impressive political network; in 1964–5, for example, there were 1,665 active women's sections, 206 women's constituency committees, and 71 women's advisory councils. Many sections were centres of lively activity, mixing both social life and political discussion, what one section called 'a good cup of tea and an exchange of ideas'.[42] But such activity did not translate into the kind of vitality that had spurred the discussion of birth control and other contentious issues in the 1920s. The women's sections had also begun a slow numerical decline. Even in an area like Durham, where the annual Miners' Gala was matched by a Women's Gala, there were signs of weakness: membership in the women's sections dropped from 4,728 in 1951 to 2,764 in 1969. The London Labour Party Women's Advisory Council that had been so active in the 1920s and early 1930s struggled in the 1950s. A particular problem was attracting younger women. Much of the membership of the women's sections comprised married, and usually older, women. A younger cohort was notable by its absence. As early as 1948, the otherwise healthy West Bermondsey women's sections observed that this was a difficulty.[43]

But despite this background, we can still see some assertion of innovative views of family life and femininity that revolved to some degree around the question of birth control. The first springboard for such perspectives was the population question.

In 1944, concern about a declining birth rate led to the establishment of a Royal Commission on Population. Two groups within the sphere of Labour politics were

---

'Rationing, Austerity and the Conservative Party Recovery after 1945', *Historical Journal* 37 (1994), 173–98; James Hinton, '"The Tale of Sammy Spree": Gender and the Secret Dynamics of 1940s British Corporatism', *History Workshop Journal* 58 (2004), 86–109.

[39] Ina Zweiniger-Bargielowska, 'Explaining the Gender Gap: The Conservative Party and the Women's Vote, 1945–64', in Martin Francis and Ina Zweiniger-Bargielowska (eds), *The Conservatives and British Society, 1880–1980* (Cardiff: University of Wales Press, 1996).

[40] See Black and Brooke, 'The Labour Party, Women and the Problem of Gender'.

[41] LPA, General Elections Sub-Committee, GE.E/Sub. 1, 'General Election Issues', 19 September 1959.

[42] LMA, ACC 2417/H/36/11, South Lewisham Central Women's Section, *The Socialist* (West Lewisham Labour Party), July/August 1963.

[43] LMA, ACC 2417/E/3/4, Annual Report, West Bermondsey Labour Party, 1947–8.

involved in the submission of evidence to the Royal Commission on Population, the SJCWWO and the FWG. The SJCWWO was, of course, within the inner circle of trade union and Labour Party women's organizations. The FWG had more of an unofficial status. Each represented different sides of Labour and socialist women's spheres. The SJCWWO was more working class, the FWG more middle class.

Giving evidence to the Royal Commission required both groups to talk about sexuality. Given its leaders' desire for silence on the matter in the 1920s, it is surprising that the SJCWWO grasped this nettle unblinkingly, basing its evidence for the Royal Commission on 'the extent of the practice of contraception [and] motives for family limitation' among its members (though, unfortunately, the means of obtaining this information remains obscure). The starting point for the SJCWWO's evidence was that 'birth-control is almost universally practised' among married couples. Though the SJCWWO suggested that the decision to limit fertility involved 'the deepest emotions and the most intimate personal relationships', it firmly linked that private decision with the public sphere. The experience of interwar unemployment had become, for example, 'part of the mental climate . . . [helping] to undermine confidence in the future', something that ordinary people exercised agency against in the private sphere. The higher standard of living enjoyed by more and more working-class people in the late 1930s and early 1940s encouraged people to protect what economic security they had obtained. The SJCWWO argued that the decision to limit families was, in fact, an attempt to improve family life: '[m]ost parents consciously desire and definitely plan to give their children a good start in life, and it is easier to do this for a small than for a large family'.[44] The arguments of a mainstream Labour organization like the SJCWWO in the 1940s thus echoed, if in a gentle way, those made by the WBCG and the ALRA in the 1920s and 1930s. The SJCWWO's evidence is also interesting for its construction of gender. Motherhood continued to be a crucial aspect of femininity, but the SJCWWO argued that it had to be given greater respect and support. Not least, motherhood had to be recognized as legitimate work 'contributing jointly and equally to the welfare and maintenance of the family', as much as the wages of the breadwinner male. But femininity was not solely defined by maternity. The SJCWWO made clear that women had an equal right to work outside the home, or to have the reconciliation of productive and reproductive roles facilitated by welfare legislation: 'a married woman should be entirely free to choose whether to devote herself to home and family or to enter employment outside the home'.[45] Thus, the SJCWWO disclosed consciously modern views of sexuality and gender, in which birth control was an accepted practice in the lives of modern women and their families.

[44] Standing Joint Committee of Working Women's Organizations [SJCWWO], *Reports on Population Problems and Postwar Organization of Private Domestic Employment* (London: SJCWWO, 1945), 3, para. 1, 4, para. 9, 4, para. 10, 5, para. 17, 4, para. 11, para. 13.
[45] SJCWWO, *Reports on Population Problems and Postwar Organization of Domestic Employment*, 12, para. 52, 11, para. 50.

We can see the same strands in the FWG's submission. At first glance, its evidence seemed steeped in a pro-natalist view, declaring 'the problem . . . is how to make people bring more children into the world than they do now'. A sluggish birth rate was linked to 'a declining standard of life; a hardening of the political arteries; a reduction in military power; a diminished influence in world affairs; a less adventurous and less vital social life'. But such pro-natalism was matched by a clear commitment to birth control as a matter of public policy. The FWG argued that 'an enlightened policy demands that the State should ensure that contraceptive knowledge is generally available to all who desire or need it (whether married or unmarried) . . . the only rational basis for a sound population policy is to ensure a state of affairs in which every child will be desired at the time of conception'. This reflected, of course, many of the policies espoused in the 1920s and 1930s. Like the SJCWWO, the FWG stressed the public aspects of private sexuality. In the 1920s and 1930s, the Depression moved from the work place and the labour exchange to the bedroom, inciting a 'spirit of defeatism and pessimism about the economic future of Britain which undoubtedly acted as a deterrent to parenthood'.[46] This gloom would only be dispelled by linking private measures such as birth control to public measures such as the maintenance of full employment, the establishment of comprehensive social services and the provision of cash benefits and tax rebates for would-be parents.

The FWG also related birth control to changes in femininity and the position of women. In this, it offered quite radical visions of femininity, masculinity, and family life. If the decline in the birth rate was located partly in the experience of interwar unemployment, it also involved new views of women's rights and roles of sexuality. The FWG made an explicit connection between feminist change, the modernization of sexual mores, and the transformation of femininity. While stating that 'a mother's first duty is to her children and her home', the Fabians welcomed the way birth control might reconcile different roles for women between private and public spheres. This included the 'fuller degree of self-expression as human beings' afforded modern women, their ability to take a 'full share in the duties and responsibilities of citizenship', and the possibility that birth control might promote companionability within marriage. Work was another example: 'women as workers are almost as necessary as women as mothers'. Clearly, there remained tensions between a conservative view of women as primarily, or most importantly, mothers, and women in new roles. But the Fabians opted for a 'revolutionary attitude': 'women must be free to choose whether to exercise only one or other of their functions or both together, without incurring any social criticism or hostility of [*sic*] they elect the much harder task of combining maternity with outside work'. This was 'a new set of values which will allow women to take their proper place in society, as mothers, workers, and citizens'. Masculinity and the boundaries of the breadwinner ideal also had to be transformed. In particular, childrearing had to

---

[46] London School of Economics Archives, London [LSE], Fabian Society Papers [FSP], K35/4, 'Evidence Submitted to the Royal Commission on Population by the Population Committee of the Fabian Society', June 1945, paras. 4, 193, 15.

become a 'joint, co-operative undertaking...not to be discharged by the father merely by his earning all the income'. The family had to be reinvented. Rounding out this vision was a belief in the liberalization of contraceptive knowledge. Importantly, the Fabians believed that this had to be accessible to both men and women, married and unmarried.[47]

The Fabian women believed that the birth rate could only be improved through the encouragement of a new context for motherhood and family life. This was a new kind of natalism: '[o]ur objective should be to ensure that more children will be born solely because their parents want them to be brought into the world'.[48] This context reflected interlocking spheres of social reform, the revision of gender roles, and sexual liberalization. Again, reform occurred within the terms of an existing ideology rather than without, but the contradictions and tensions within femininity and the pressures of class experience meant embracing more radical measures.

These views had resonances in the wider Labour movement. Herbert Morrison was rare among the Labour leadership in talking about women's issues. In a speech made in 1943, he noted that the falling birth rate reflected social action by working-class women: '[a]lthough our housewives have not become revolutionaries or set about political agitation, many of them have found their own means of avoiding the worst consequences of poverty. They have discovered that the more children the less there is to go round.'[49] Even the advent of a Labour government committed to welfare reform did not alleviate the belief in family planning as legitimate social action. In 1945, at the Labour women's conference, one delegate noted, regarding population policy, that '[w]ith a Labour Government in power, better housing, education and so forth would be obtained, but [I do] not believe that in any circumstances the woman of to-day would be willing to have a large family'.[50] Edith Summerskill, then MP for Fulham West, agreed, saying that the falling birth rate represented a 'silent revolt'.[51] By the late 1940s, Labour's *Notes for Speakers* could note: '[i]n a working-class home children meant poverty'.[52]

There were other issues that afforded Labour women's organizations the opportunity to talk about sexuality, if in an oblique way. Companionate marriage was one. The WCG cannot be said to be always sexually adventurous, inveighing, for example, against 'the exploitation of sex in Television programmes' and wanting the medium to 'show the results of venereal diseases, to prove the outcome of folly'.[53] But in many other ways, the WCG showed a progressive outlook on sexuality. It accepted the problem of population decline, but insisted,

[47] LSE, FSP, K35/4, 'Evidence Submitted to the Royal Commission on Population by the Population Committee of the Fabian Society', June 1945, paras. 69, 71–3, 95, 105, 108, 106–7, 109, 108.

[48] LSE, FSP, K35/4, 'Evidence Submitted to the Royal Commission on Population by the Population Committee of the Fabian Society', June 1945, para. 15.

[49] *Labour Woman*, 31/7 (July 1943), 71.

[50] *ACLW* (1945), 44.

[51] *ACLW* (1945), 45.

[52] Labour Party, *Speakers' Handbook 1949–50* (London: Labour Party, 1950), 325.

[53] BJL, WCG, DCW 2/29, Annual Congress, 1964, 37.

in a mild eugenicism, that quality was better than quantity.[54] Though it favoured heterosexual marriage, the WCG also supported homosexual law reform. In the late 1940s and 1950s, the WCG displayed a modern view of heterosexuality through its support for the marriage guidance movement. It welcomed the expansion of sexual instruction for married couples. 'Marriage and the home are the true foundation of civilization', a WCG document stated in 1950, 'and cannot be abolished without the destruction of society.' The key to saving it was reform in the public sphere (such as better economic and social conditions) and reform in the private sphere. In particular, building up sexually satisfactory partnerships was critical. This demanded expert advice and instruction, including information about birth control: 'there is still a very great deal of ignorance on the means whereby families may be limited, and a couple who live in constant fear of an unwanted pregnancy cannot have an harmonious sex life'. The WCG thus brought together two ideas of the 1920s and 1930s, sexual control and sexual pleasure. It wanted to see the promotion of those issues through WCG branches. This may have been within the context of marriage and domesticity, but it was also the articulation of a progressive position on sexuality as common sense:

> The marriages of the future must grow out of individual love, social security and intelligent thought. Happy marriages do not just come. They have to be thought about and worked for. This means we must concern ourselves with the sex education of our people and the Marriage Guidance Panel is the appropriate answer.[55]

There was also support for marriage guidance from the women's sections of the Labour Party to dispel the 'ignorance of facts, particularly on the physical aspect' of marriage, though Labour women baulked at state grants for marriage guidance panels, especially when faced with demands from other resources such as housing.[56] On behalf of the FPA, Lady Tewson told the readers of *Labour Woman* that young marrieds were able to 'start off on the right foot' armed with information about birth control in particular and sex in general, while other couples had 'been made happy by advice on the planning and spacing of children'.[57] Though *Labour Woman* was not much of a forum for the discussion of sexual questions in the 1950s, one of its regular columnists, Alma Birk, consistently promoted a mildly liberal attitude towards sex. In 1958, for example, reviewing pamphlets from the National Marriage Guidance Council, Birk complained that there seemed to be a prevailing view that 'women should not expect to get any pleasure out of sex, or alternatively there is something not quite decent about it if they do'.[58] The WCG became a strong supporter of sex instruction in schools and the provision of contraceptives through the National Health Service in the postwar period (even if

---

[54] BJL, WCG, DCW 5/20, Notes for Speakers, 'Improved Conditions for the Housewife', (1944, revised 1945).
[55] BJL, WCG, DCW 5/45, Speakers' Notes, 'Marriage Guidance', 1950, 2, 4.
[56] *ACLW* (1948), 22.
[57] *Labour Woman* 44/1 (1956), 20.
[58] *Labour Woman* 46/5 (1958), 63.

they were unhappy about the less than elegant possibility that contraceptives could be obtained from slot machines).[59]

What is striking here is that neither the SJCWWO, the FWG, nor the WCG could be described as hotbeds of radical feminism. Yet each quietly but firmly offered views of femininity, gender, and sexuality that were innovative, progressive, and attempted to describe rather than prescribe or constrain a consciously modern position of women. Nor was generation much of a factor here, at least in a disabling way. None of the three organizations was dominated or led by younger women—in fact, the SJCWWO and the WCG were representative of groups who were having a hard time attracting younger members. Of course, we must not exaggerate the sexual radicalism of the groups: the WCG, for example, staunchly opposed the Sodom of contraceptives from slot machines and the Gomorrah of sex on television, as much as it promoted the New Jerusalem of birth control, marriage guidance, and sex instruction. And, not unimportantly, the protagonist of these reflections was the married, rather than single, woman.

There was also a clear sense in the party of a generational sea-change. Partly in an attempt to widen the age demographic of its women's sections, the magazine *Labour Woman* ran a series of portraits of 'The Younger Generation'. The women in this series were all under 30, sometimes single, sometimes married, sometimes with children. What was common among several of them, however, was the way that the poverty and struggle of the interwar years was read through children and families. Nell Comrie, an infant school teacher, talked of the contrast between the 'clean, happy, healthy faces' of her charges in 1948 and what she remembered as a child in the 1930s: 'under-nourished, ricket-suffering children—product of the inter-war years of depression'. M.E. Gundy and Eleanor Taylor both gained their socialist convictions in miners' homes, not from their fathers primarily, but from the struggles of their mothers; Taylor remarked, 'I felt a sense of injustice that these struggles and sacrifices had to be made.'[60] As in the 1920s and 1930s, a political and class consciousness emerged from the experience and perception of reproduction. In other ways, social change was read through women's bodies and appearance. In 1945, Jennie Lee strikingly described the new woman Labour had to attract:

> I kept looking at a very pretty young woman who was sitting opposite me in the bus. . . . She was a working girl, that was plain enough, but she was a working girl of a type that has got to be carefully considered. In fact, she is part of the modern revolution, and a very important part. She has ideas about herself, about her clothes, about her young man, about the kind of home she hopes one day to run. It is something more than a roof over her head that she expects to have.
>
> What comes next for that pretty young woman and the others like her, and for the older women who are heartsick of the unnecessary drudgery of the home?
> This is who Labour has to speak to.[61]

[59] See BJL, WCG, DCW 2/17: Annual Congress, 1950 (Sixty-eighth), 33; DCW 2/24: Annual Congress, 1957 (Seventy-fifth), 45.

[60] *Labour Woman* 36/2 (February 1948), 40; 36/3 (March 1948), 54; 36/4 (April 1948), 76.

[61] Jennie Lee, 'Five Years of Opportunity', *Labour Woman* 33/8 (September 1945), 168.

In different ways, two other Labour MPs of this era, Eirene White and Somerville
Hastings, spoke of the older generation of working-class woman that had passed.
The former noted that 'excessive' and 'badly-spaced child bearing' had weakened
the position of working-class mothers, while the latter argued that the 'new look'
brought to Britain by the Labour government was not merely a shell, but the actual
reforming of working-class women's bodies from the 1930s: 'in those days women
of the wage-earning classes looked old both in comparison with their menfolk and
equally with their better-off sisters. But how different are things to-day, thanks to
the Labour Government.'[62] What was thus being emphasized was a new kind of
working-class woman, who had forcibly moved beyond the plight of her mother's
and grandmother's generation. In different ways, therefore, the 1940s and 1950s
witnessed important developments in the political perception of sexuality, the
family and gender within the Labour movement, even if this did not translate
into concrete policy.

III

If we turn to what had been perceived as the most difficult aspect of reproductive
politics, abortion law reform, we can also see the 1940s and 1950s as decades of
transition. These were not easy years for abortion law reform. The postwar era
showed the limits of abortion as a political issue and the limits of pressure group
politics. But it was an important period for the ALRA, when its central strategy for
achieving reform shifted, moving towards enacting a new law in parliament, rather
than influencing case law. In the late 1930s, the ALRA had reaped the benefits of a
high-profile trial and a government inquiry. Whether in the columns of the press or
the corridors of power, abortion became a question of lively debate. The Second
World War interrupted the progress of the issue. Discussing the termination of
pregnancy in a period of civilian and combatant casualties was, undoubtedly,
difficult even if the war created more of a market for abortions, given the strains
put on conjugal life by separation. War also made the work of a voluntary pressure
group physically difficult. Alice Jenkins recounted picking her way through debris-
strewn London streets in the middle of bombing raids in order to give talks on
abortion.

In 1944, the ALRA began to dust itself off. Jenkins used the increasing interest in
postwar reconstruction to talk about the place of abortion in the reform of women's
lives. A parliamentary supporter, the Labour peer Lord Listowel also offered to raise
abortion in the context of postwar reform.[63] The interest in postwar population
policy was also considered to be a way of talking about abortion and the ALRA
thought seriously about giving evidence, as the FWG and the SJCWWO did, to

---

[62]   Eirene White, 'The Neglected Child and His Family', *Labour Woman* 36/7 (July 1948), 178;
Somerville Hastings, 'Labour's "New Look"', *Labour Woman* 37/4 (April 1949), 77.
[63]   CMA, SA/ALR/A.17/1/4, Janet Chance Papers, Lord Listowel to Janet Chance, 1 May 1943.

the Royal Commission on Population, though it decided not to in the end. But the wartime concern about population decline was also a matter of concern for the ALRA. The hero of the 1938 legal case, Aleck Bourne, believed that the problem of falling birth rates was 'so serious' as to make discussion of abortion prejudicial and he resigned from the organization in 1945.[64]

After the Second World War, the ALRA was able to take up its efforts to realize 'the right of the individual to decide on parenthood' with greater facility.[65] As already discussed, the ALRA emerged from a markedly socialist-feminist background in the 1930s and worked through the grass-roots women's organizations of the Labour movement. But Alice Jenkins insisted that she was 'strictly *non-party*'.[66] Her own history of the ALRA stressed not connections with the Labour Party or working-class movement, but rather its relationship to non-party women's organizations such as the NCW and the National Women's Citizens Association. It is, of course, important to acknowledge the ALRA's non-party qualities. But it is also striking how strong the relationship between the organization and the Labour movement was in the 1940s and 1950s. This did not, of course, occur in a formal way. At no point in the 1940s and 1950s did the national Labour Party ever entertain the prospect of abortion law reform. Between the end of the war and 1961, there were no articles in *Labour Woman* on abortion. Only one resolution in favour of abortion law reform was submitted to the Labour Women's Conference in the same period. Just after the war, the North West Camberwell Women's Section proposed a resolution to legalize abortion by a medical practitioner 'when this procedure appears to be medically or socially desirable, either in her own interest or in that of the community'.[67] This did not make it to discussion at the 1946 conference. Indeed, abortion was not discussed at a Labour women's conference until 1961. Perhaps more surprisingly even the Socialist Medical Association refused to support abortion and did not discuss the question at any time in the 1950s or the early 1960s.[68]

But grass-roots elements of the Labour movement were some of the strongest pillars of the ALRA in the 1940s and 1950s. By 1947, thirty local women's sections and Women's Cooperative Guilds had affiliated to the ALRA.[69] The East Ham South Women's Section is a particular example. In the late 1940s, there was a consistent and sympathetic relationship between the ALRA and East Ham. In 1944, for example, the ALRA wrote to East Ham encouraging them to discuss the Royal Commission on Population and, further, to nominate possible delegates 'to represent working-class mothers on the Committee'. This was followed up with a

---

[64] See CMA, SA/ALR/A.17/1/13, 20, Janet Chance Papers, Aleck Bourne to Janet Chance, 28 September 1943, 6 December 1943 and 23 August 1945.

[65] CMA, SA/ALR/A.1/1, ALRA Minute Books, 10 October 1945. The phrase is that of Janet Chance.

[66] CMA, SA/ALR/A.3/6/34, Alice Jenkins to Kathleen Child, 13 May 1957.

[67] *ACLW, Resolutions for Annual Conference* (1946), 66.

[68] See CMA, SA/ALR/A.3/4/84, Audrey Jupp (General Secretary, SMA) to Jenkins, 22 November 1955. See also BJL, SMA, DSM 4/3: Circulars and minutes, 1950–8.

[69] CMA, SA/ALR/A.1/1, ALRA Report, 17 October 1947.

visit by Alice Jenkins, who talked generally about birth control and concluded with another suggestion that the section write to Transport House in order 'to send a delegate to sit on the "Royal Commission" in order to get an opportunity for the Workers Class [*sic*] to have a better deal in relation to "motherhood"'. The section circulated a copy of Jenkins's book *Motherhood*. After the war, the association between the two organizations continued, with the women's section affiliating to the ALRA, circulating its pamphlets, and sending delegates to the ALRA's meeting. In 1947, there was a large meeting, again addressed by Alice Jenkins. Throughout, East Ham South provided support and a sympathetic audience.[70] A continuity we can see between the 1930s and 1940s is the link between working-class Labour activism and abortion law reform, even if this remained on the margins of Labour politics.

There were other examples of such institutional and grass-roots support. In 1948, the WCG passed a resolution supporting the reform of the abortion law at its annual conference. The resolution demanded the legalization of abortion in circumstances that were 'medically desirable, either in her own interest, or in the interest of the community'.[71] At annual meetings of the ALRA in 1954 and 1955, there were delegates from fifteen WCGs and representatives from Labour women's sections.[72] There is no evidence from its files of any approaches made to, or received from, the Conservative and Liberal parties. Even in the early 1960s, the organizations on the ALRA's circulation list were all Labour ones: the SMA, the League of Labour Lawyers, and, of course, the Labour women's sections and the WCG.[73] Thus, it is possible to argue that though non-political, the ALRA remained loosely affiliated with the Left. Late in the 1950s, even Alice Jenkins seemed to suggest that the core of support for abortion law reform lay with 'all these intelligent working-class women' of the WCGs and the Labour women's sections: '[i]t looks as though the "working women" of this country will have to concentrate on this reform, for I fear the upper income groups won't'.[74]

Of course, the ALRA also had connections outside such political circles. In 1957, with the Mothers' Union dissenting, the NCW passed a resolution similar to one adopted in 1938, reaffirming support for 'legalisation of abortion under adequate safeguards'.[75] The BMA also expressed support for abortion law reform in 1953. But, again, there was not a sweeping consensus on the question—the National Marriage Guidance Council would not extend its support for better birth control advice to the question of abortion: 'we are not without a lively sympathy for your

[70] LMA, ACC 2417/H/35, East Ham South Women's Section, Minute Books, 25 January 1944, 29 February 1944, 22 January 1946, 11 November 1947.
[71] BJL, WCG, DCW 2/15, Women's Cooperative Guild, Annual Conference Report, 1948–9 (Sixty-sixth Conference), 33.
[72] See CMA, SA/ALR/A.1/2/2, Annual Meeting, 29 September 1954; Annual Meeting, 26 October 1955.
[73] CMA, SA/ALR/A.1/3/21, Annual report, 1963–4.
[74] CMA, SA/ALR/A.3/6/34, Alice Jenkins to Kathleen Child, 8 May 1957; SA/ALR/A.3/6/34, Alice Jenkins to Kathleen Child, 13 May 1957.
[75] CMA, SA/ALR/A.3/6/34, National Council of Women, Annual Conference, October 1957, Resolutions Adopted.

objects but at the same time we would not like to make it possible for instance, for the press to suggest that we are advocating easier abortion as a means to happy marriage'.[76] The ALRA also continued its tradition of recruiting its visible leadership—the members of its Medico-Legal council and its vice-presidents—from the ranks of the (almost exclusively middle-class) great and good. One of the most important figures in this regard was Glanville Williams, a noted legal expert who, in 1958, published *The Sanctity of Life and the Criminal Law*, which explored a number of moral questions in the prism of the existing law. Williams remained with the ALRA into the 1960s and drafted many of its parliamentary bills.

Another continuity was the centrality of class to the advocacy of abortion reform. In 1940, Thurtle expanded the arguments she had made in the minority report of the Interdepartmental Committee into a small book, *Abortion: Right or Wrong?* In this, Thurtle portrayed abortion first and foremost as a question of class difference:

> There is no doubt at all that for many years operations have been performed on wealthy women for reasons of slight ill-health, and even for quite frivolous reasons. No working woman would have been able to secure the same treatment for similar reasons.

Again, this may have been as much a rhetorical device as anything, but it was an effective one. In the circumstances of 'such glaring inequalities in treatment between those women who can afford to pay for an illegal abortion carried out by a skilled surgeon and the average woman, dependent on her own efforts or those of an unskilled amateur', 'social justice' demanded 'equal facilities and treatment'.[77] But it was also striking that Thurtle tried to normalize sexual activity and pleasure (albeit within marriage). This was placed in the context of a liberal modernity that, in the 1940s, excluded working-class people:

> Modern women are learning that their sex life is as important to them as to their husbands, and is not something about which to be furtive or ashamed. They know, further, that it need not be synonymous with child-bearing, and in consequence many married lives are enriched, and are fuller than those of earlier generations. Knowledge of modern scientific methods of birth control has made a significant contribution to marital happiness and mutual understanding. There are still too many women, however, who are unable to protect themselves against unwanted pregnancies, and who consequently feel bitterly at times towards their husbands. These are the women, frequently ill-nourished, exhausted and sick, who carry the burden that their wealthier sisters refuse to carry.[78]

Without equal access to contraception and safe abortion, working-class women were, therefore, consigned to a dark age of sexual danger and anxiety. The exclusion of working-class women from an increasingly liberal age of sexual modernity was restated in the 1947 ALRA pamphlet *Back-Street Surgery*. Margot Edgecombe underlined the threat to marriage of sexual unhappiness, not least the fear of an

---

[76] CMA, SA/ALR/A.3/4/30, A.J. Bryshaw (General Secretary, National Marriage Guidance Council) to Alice Jenkins, 29 April 1955.
[77] Dorothy Thurtle, *Abortion: Right or Wrong?* (London: T. Werner Laurie, 1940), 20, 22, 27.
[78] Thurtle, *Abortion: Right or Wrong?*, 32.

unwanted pregnancy, while Janet Chance again emphasized that the abortion question was about unequal access between women of different classes. In this, family life was paramount. Working-class women were not thinking of themselves, but their existing children, when they sought out abortions. They were being good mothers and responsible citizens in refusing motherhood: '... no responsible woman will wait for any golden future to find the life she wants for her children to-day. No; she would take steps to limit her family and show herself in so doing no criminal but a responsible mother and a praiseworthy citizen, if the law allowed her.'[79] There was a clear argument for greater female power with respect to the law, even if it was in relationship to both the medical profession and marriage:

> Who is best fitted to decide whether the pay-packet can stand another mouth to feed? The men who wrote down this law in 1861? The lawyers at the Old Bailey who wouldn't know the family if they met it in the street? The doctor who gives a few hours of his whole life to the consideration of the household? What nonsense! The father and mother in serious consultation with a doctor should have a say in managing their own pay-packet and the size of the family it will best support.[80]

In the 1930s, legal cases had provided mobilizing moments for the cause of abortion law reform, first with Justice McCardie's summation in 1931, then with the Bourne case of 1938. In the 1940s and 1950s there were two that underlined the continuing ambiguity of the law. The Bergmann–Ferguson case of April 1948 saw the acquittal of a female obstetrician and a female psychologist, on the grounds that a doctor could assess the physical or mental cost of pregnancy and, in good faith, perform a termination if such circumstances demanded it, a strengthening of the Bourne judgment. Where Bergmann–Ferguson departed from the Bourne judgment was the manner in which the women featured in the later case were more complex and varied than the rape victim of the Bourne trial. Some of these women were clearly older, becoming pregnant as a result of consensual sexual relationships, or a married woman concerned about the economic effects of a pregnancy. That abortion was a problem of all women, class and age notwithstanding, became an increasingly prominent theme in abortion advocacy in the 1960s. A later abortion trial confirmed the conclusions of the Bergmann–Ferguson trial, this time through a guilty verdict. In 1958, Louis Newton was found guilty of an illegal operation and manslaughter as a result of an illegal operation, after he performed an abortion on a single woman. In this case, the Crown successfully proved that Newton had not performed the abortion in good faith with regard to the woman's mental or physical health, suggesting that it was for remuneration.[81] In the wake of the Bergmann–Ferguson and Newton trials, medical practitioners could still feel that the law on abortion was unclear and that they could be liable to prosecution in ambiguous circumstances.

[79] Janet Chance, 'Back-Street Surgery', in Maud Ryan, Margot Edgecombe, and Janet Chance, *Back-Street Surgery* (Freefolk, Hale, Fordingbridge, Hants: Abortion Law Reform Association, 1947), 14.
[80] Chance, 'Back-Street Surgery', 17.
[81] *British Medical Journal*, 24 May 1958, 1277.

For a time, the ALRA remained committed to its previous strategy with the aim of influencing case law rather than introducing a new statute.[82] But early in the 1950s, it changed its thinking. The catalyst in the matter was Douglas Houghton, a Labour MP and the husband of Vera Houghton, who was the Secretary of the International Committee on Planned Parenthood and who had become involved with the ALRA in the late 1940s. Houghton sat for a Yorkshire riding and was also a member of the TUC's General Council. In November 1952, he told Alice Jenkins that 'the Labour Party have asked for subjects for Private Member's Bills and that he intended to suggest Abortion Law Reform'.[83] The ALRA quickly organized a meeting with Labour MPs early in 1953 and presented the case for a bill 'to either make statutory Bourne and Bergmann–Ferguson cases, for the "physical or mental health" of the women, or when "it appears medically or socially desirable either in her own interest or in that of the community that she shall not give birth to a child"'.[84] Ultimately, it was left to Joseph Reeves, the MP for Greenwich and an NEC member at the time, to present a bill drafted by Glanville Williams. Its intent was to allow only therapeutic abortions, and to clarify the law to allow medical practitioners to perform terminations 'in the interest of the mother's health and for the prevention of injury to her body'.[85] Only a few Labour MPs attended the ALRA meeting and it was a small band of mostly Labour MPs who ended up supporting the bill, which was talked out on 27 February 1953.[86] Nonetheless, Janet Chance felt that the commitment to a parliamentary strategy had reinvigorated the cause, noting to Alice Jenkins, 'I feel we have made a very definite move forward. . . . And have much to be thankful for . . . found good friends: Houghton (especially).'[87]

The Reeves bill was perhaps not the most auspicious beginning to a parliamentary campaign that culminated in the 1967 Act, but it was a beginning. After that, there was a bill put to the House of Lords in 1954 by Lord Amultree, once a National Labour peer.[88] For the first time, ALRA gained influential parliamentary connections. Houghton emerged as a consistent supporter of abortion law reform, joined in this by Kenneth Robinson. Robinson had been a physician before winning St Pancras North in 1949. He enjoyed some standing in the Parliamentary Labour Party as Opposition Whip and later served as shadow spokesman on health. In 1955, the ALRA tried to assess its support at parliament, and particularly within the Labour Party. Kenneth Robinson warned that there were many difficulties 'chief being the obscurantist attitudes of many MPs which was very strong. Prejudice, ignorance, and fear were formidable obstacles.' What was striking was

[82] CMA, SA/ALR/A.3/1/8, ALRA Private Conference, 23 March 1949.
[83] CMA, SA/ALR/A.17/6/5, Janet Chance Papers, Alice Jenkins to Janet Chance, 7 November 1952.
[84] CMA, SA/ALR/A.17/12/3, 'Statement [MPs' meeting]', 1952.
[85] *Parliamentary Debates* (Commons), 27 February 1953, c. 2506.
[86] See CMA, SA/ALR/A.3/2/18, Abortion Bill meeting, 24 February 1953. The only Conservative to support the bill was Robert Boothby.
[87] CMA, SA/ALR/A.3/2/3, Janet Chance to Alice Jenkins, no date [1953].
[88] See *Parliamentary Debates* (Lords), 26 January 1954, c. 411.

that the support in parliament did not, for the most part, come from female MPs. Both Robinson and Houghton were sceptical about relying upon female MPs to support abortion reform; the former said 'only a few' were interested, the latter counselled the ALRA that it was 'not wise to concentrate on women MPs'.[89] Indeed, of the twenty-seven female Labour MPs sitting in the House between 1945 and 1964, only a handful ever expressed support or interest in the question. Freda Corbet had supported the Reeves Bill in 1953. A high-profile female MP, the Bevanite Barbara Castle was non-committal on the issue, saying that she would give an abortion bill 'sympathetic consideration', but was too busy to do anything else. Eirene White had committed herself to marriage and divorce reform and would support abortion law reform, but would not sponsor a bill.[90] Only Lena Jeger became involved with the ALRA, taking on the position of vice-president in 1958; her involvement is discussed later in this chapter. The reluctance of female MPs to engage with the abortion issue in the 1950s is perhaps surprising. But many female MPs shied away from issues that might over-identify them by their gender. Barbara Castle remarked at one point, for example, that 'I always thought of myself as an MP, not as a woman MP.'[91] Few female Labour MPs were willing to accept the feminist label. But this did not prevent considerable action on issues to improve the social and economic position of women. The most obvious is equal pay, but there were others, such as divorce law and the protection of prostitutes. Often, these questions were pursued with the bipartisan support of female Conservative MPs. So it was not that female MPs were completely unwilling in the 1940s and 1950s to work for women's issues, rather that abortion was perceived as either too unpleasant or too controversial to be accepted as such an issue. Male MPs like Houghton and Robinson were perhaps more able, because of their sex, to support and promote abortion law reform.

The 1940s and 1950s also lacked a radical, feminist spokeswoman for abortion. No Stella Browne or Dora Russell emerged to make the case for abortion as a question of rights, whether in terms of class or gender. Indeed, there was little if any talk of 'demands' at all in the question, in contrast to the WBCG's advocacy of birth control in the 1920s. Published at the beginning of a new period but very much the product of work in the 1940s and 1950s, *Law for the Rich* (1960) by Alice Jenkins reflected many of the long-standing themes of abortion advocacy, but eschewed a radical or feminist position. It emphasized that abortion law reform was most of all about strengthening the position of the 'respectable mother', in other words helping women in a specific context, rather than as individuals. Reforming abortion was guided by a commitment to 'responsible' sexual behaviour and strengthening the position of the 'respectable mother' within heterosexual marriage: '[c]onscientious mothers are disturbed by the possibility that reformed law may lead to immorality . . . one must remember that the principal beneficiary under

---

[89] CMA, SA/ALR/A.3/4/77, Public meeting after Annual Meeting of ALRA, 26 November 1955.
[90] CMA, SA/ALR/A.3/4/64, Barbara Castle to Alice Jenkins, 20 June 1955; SA/ALR/A.3/4/65, Eirene White to Alice Jenkins, 21 June 1955.
[91] Quoted in Melanie Phillips, *The Divided House: Women at Westminster* (London: Sidgwick and Jackson, 1980), 160.

new law would be the decent mother of a family who has as many children as she can cope with'.[92] Though advocates like Jenkins avoided strict sexual codes and proscription, they did not depart, in public writing about abortion, from promoting an ethos of sexual restraint, especially for a younger generation: 'self-restraint and self-discipline are conducive to lasting happiness and contentment'.[93] Thus, the argument for abortion even into the 1960s rested upon women in a particular context—motherhood and family—and upon the restraint of the sexual self; restraint did not mean no expression of sexuality, but it meant the expression of it within particular contexts. There was no advocate such as Stella Browne (who died in 1957) to connect abortion with female emancipation or a more radical sexual politics of the body. What did remain clear were the class elements to abortion advocacy in the 1950s. The very title of Jenkins's *Law for the Rich* conveyed this, of course, as did the acknowledged support from working-class women's organizations.

IV

In the 1920s and 1930s, discussions of birth control had involved particular kinds of female protagonists, in particular the modern, enlightened, and largely middle-class woman and the beleaguered working-class mother. Discussions of birth control had also centred upon particular ideas of family life and domesticity. There were certainly continuities between such ideas and those developing in the 1940s and 1950s, but there were also particular social and economic conditions in the postwar period that helped shape a new sense of femininity and the home. This was especially important in terms of working-class life. Changing understandings of femininity and domesticity afforded a different purchase for birth control and abortion advocacy in the 1950s and 1960s.

The 1940s and, in particular, the 1950s have, as Claire Langhamer has pointed out, often been bathed in the warm light of 'a comfortable, consumer-bound and increasingly privatized domestic lifestyle accessible to all'.[94] Particular kinds of men and women took their place in this private *mise-en-scène*—breadwinner men who nonetheless helped with the garden and the children, and women for whom motherhood and consumerism were the main duties. It was a scene that damped down potential disruption or non-conformity. For this reason, the 1960s might be perceived as a rebellion against the 1950s. But, as Langhamer argues, this is a misleading picture. First of all, the home-centred discourse of the 1950s was only partly a new thing; it also represented the realization of aspirations rooted in the 1930s.[95] Secondly, the home was not necessarily immune to change or a refuge

---

[92] Alice Jenkins, *Law for the Rich* (London: Gollancz, 1960), 40, 41.
[93] Jenkins, *Law for the Rich*, 41–2.
[94] Claire Langhamer, 'The Meanings of Home in Postwar Britain', *Journal of Contemporary History* 40 (2005), 341.
[95] See Langhamer, 'The Meanings of Home in Postwar Britain'.

from emotional or sexual instability. Lesley Hall has rightly remarked that the 1950s were, for men and women, 'a period of instability rather than unthinking smug conventionality'.[96]

There were, for example, new vistas open to women in the 1950s that challenged any idea of stability or conventionality. Two examples—work and education— illustrate this point. In 1956, Alva Myrdal and Viola Klein published *Women's Two Roles*, which argued that women did not have to choose between reproductive and productive roles, but rather could reconcile the two in modern society: '[n]o longer need women forgo the pleasures of one sphere in order to enjoy the satisfactions of the other'.[97] Myrdal and Klein's work rested on the stated belief that women's two roles were afforded by the phases of women's lives—work followed by motherhood followed by the possibility of a return to work—and the unstated assumption that, whatever the life-stage, reproduction could be planned and controlled. This served as a riposte to the psychological literature by John Bowlby and Donald Winnicott that emphasized the importance of undistracted motherhood to child development. There were, therefore, different visions of domesticity in the 1950s that did not exclude productive roles for women. Similarly, changes in education also afforded a broader canvas for women's lives. The 1944 Education Act formalized universal access to secondary education for all children and in 1945 the state abolished fees in 'maintained' schools, thereby opening up many grammar school places. The effect upon girls' education and mobility is complex. It is clear that the curriculum continued to favour traditional domestic training for girls, against the more academic and technical education offered boys. The numbers of young women going into post-secondary education and post-graduate, professional education also remained small in comparison to young men. Before the late 1960s, for example, the proportion of men to women in higher education was four to one and in something like the law, forty to one.[98] But such constraints have to be put against the sense that some women felt looking back on the 1950s that the reformed education system laid down an avenue towards a new life, whether that life was away from the home or from a particular class. In 1985, for example, Valerie Walkerdine spoke of being a young working-class girl in the 1950s on the brink of a new life thanks to the education system: 'in the fifties . . . I felt set up, set up to want, to want to be different, special'. This was, as Walkerdine went on to argue, double-edged, carrying with it the threat of both 'doubt and uncertainty' and the promise that women like her would change society: '[y]ou should never have educated us, the ordinary girls of the fifties, for we are dangerous'.[99]

---

[96] Hall, *Sex, Gender and Social Change in Britain since 1880*, 166; Langhamer, 'Adultery in Postwar England'.

[97] Alva Myrdal and Viola Klein, *Women's Two Roles: Home and Work* (London: Routledge and Kegan Paul, 1956, second edition 1968), xvi.

[98] Dolly Smith Wilson, 'Gender: Change and Continuity', in Paul Addison and Harriet Jones (eds), *A Companion to Contemporary Britain 1939–2000* (Oxford: Blackwell, 2005), 253.

[99] Valerie Walkerdine, 'Dreams for an Ordinary Childhood', in Liz Heron (ed.), *Truth, Dare or Promise: Girls Growing Up in the Fifties* (London: Virago, 1985), 63–4, 74, 76.

Looking even briefly at the idea of women's work and the experience of education, it is therefore clear that gender identity (at least in terms of femininity) was not a site of stability, but rather of flux. What both work and education suggested was that the critical sphere of women's lives would not be simply the home or the workplace, but the road between. In simple terms, the complexity of female subjectivity was increasingly acknowledged and the pattern of women's lives more complicated. And, of course, in that, birth control played an important role and arguments for birth control were a reflection of that change. In the 1920s and 1930s, birth control was often perceived as a way of protecting the home. By the 1950s, we might see that it was becoming a way to keep open the path between the home and the beckoning public sphere, not simply a means of protecting the home but a way to express the individual feminine self.

Particular attention must also be paid to the relationship between working-class identity and gender in the 1950s. One starting point is economic change. The economic context of the postwar period was, of course, a stark contrast from the 1920s and 1930s. In 1931, at the nadir of the Depression, there were 2,630,000 registered unemployed in Britain. Twenty years later, there were 253,000, a tenfold fall. There was also, of course, a quantitative change in the earning power of working-class people in the postwar period. Between 1950 and 1960, real earnings rose by about a fifth. In this way, we might see the restoration of the breadwinner ideal, but the reality is more complex. Working-class living standards were also bolstered by state action, through food subsidies and welfare provision. But the growing importance of female work, and, in particular, the productive contribution of married women workers must also be acknowledged. The most significant shift was an increase in the number of married women doing part-time work.[100] Elizabeth Roberts has suggested that this was a 'truly transitional phase' in the history of women's work, even if the generally high wage levels in the 1950s and 1960s meant that women's wages tended to be used for the 'extras' in working-class life, rather than the staples.[101] The trade union movement initially spoke of this work as 'profitable relaxation' or 'a pleasant break from the lonely monotony of household duties'.[102] But it soon marked it as 'a silent revolution in industrial, economic and family life' and 'an essential and integral part of the economic life of the nation'.[103]

This was the economic background to the era of affluence, a period of prosperity and growing consumer power on the part of working-class people. Many accounts suggested that affluence changed both the working class and the idea of class in Britain. Richard Hoggart began his pioneering study of working-class culture, *The*

[100] See S. Brooke, 'Gender and Working-Class Identity in Britain during the 1950s', *Journal of Social History* 34 (Summer 2001), 773–95; Dolly Smith Wilson, 'A New Look at the Affluent Worker: The Good Working Mother in Post-War Britain', *Twentieth Century British History* 17 (2006), 206–29.
[101] Elizabeth Roberts, *Women and Families* (Oxford: Blackwell, 1995), 140, 139.
[102] 'They Enjoy Evenings at the Factory', *Labour: The TUC Magazine* 1/8 (April 1951), 266.
[103] 'Housewives Who Leave Home—Every Day', *Labour: The TUC Magazine* 6/2 (February 1957), 33; 'More Women Go Out to Work', *Labour: The TUC Magazine* 2/5 (January 1952), 140.

Uses of Literacy (1957), with the reflection: '[i]t is often said that there are no working classes in England now, that a "bloodless revolution" has taken place which has so reduced social differences that already most of us inhabit an almost flat plain, the plain of the lower middle- to middle-classes'.[104] In the 1950s and early 1960s, numerous surveys of British society spoke of a 'new fluidity' in class structure, a smoothing away of the previously sharp edges of class division and a blurring of class identity.[105] Critical to this was the belief that a new working class had emerged. Sociologists and political scientists began to speak of the 'embourgeoisement' of the British working classes, effected by welfare, full employment, and consumerism. Recent historical work by Selina Todd has rightly questioned the veracity of the effect upon class of affluence, but it remained an important discourse, a means of understanding and reorganizing class in the 1950s and 1960s.[106]

Gender, sexuality, and family limitation are often-neglected aspects of this change. In the considerable contemporary literature on the postwar working classes, working-class women were often the cipher for the representation of a modernized working class; their ability to control reproduction was a crucial part of their symbolic importance. This emphasized the break between the pre-war working classes and their postwar counterparts. Young housewives, often part-time workers, 'who have themselves come from large families, but intend to keep their own family small' became staple characters in books on the new working classes.[107] A study of women workers in Bermondsey noted the growing norm for working-class women of 'smaller families, better health, and an increased expectation of life'. Birth control had freed women from the unending demands of maternity and given them 'a second chance of employment in their thirties and forties'.[108] Ferdynand Zweig similarly linked birth control, rationality, and planning in the new woman worker: 'she believes in planning the proper size of the family and the proper timing of its growth, considering its advantages and disadvantages linked with the economic situation'.[109] In the language of these studies, sexual chaos had apparently been replaced by sexual control. The female body and sexuality came to symbolize, and indeed be a causative factor in the creation of, the new stability, security, and prosperity of the postwar working class, just as the female body and sexuality had symbolized working-class deprivation before 1939.[110] Michael Young and Peter

[104] Richard Hoggart, *The Uses of Literacy* (Harmondsworth: Penguin, 1957, 1958), 3.
[105] Rita Hinden, 'The Lessons for Labour', in Mark Abrams, Richard Rose, and Rita Hinden, *Must Labour Lose?* (Harmondsworth: Penguin, 1960), 119. See also Michael Young, *The Rise of the Meritocracy* (Harmondsworth: Penguin, 1958); Ferdynand Zweig, *The Worker in an Affluent Society* (London: Heinemann, 1961).
[106] Selina Todd, 'Affluence, Class and Crown Street: Reinvestigating the Postwar Working Class', *Contemporary British History* 22 (2008), 501–18.
[107] Mark W. Hodges and Cyril S. Smith, 'The Sheffield Estate', in Department of Social Science, University of Liverpool, *Neighbourhood and Community: An Enquiry into Social Relationships on Housing Estates in Liverpool and Sheffield* (Liverpool: University Press of Liverpool, 1954), 87–8.
[108] Social Science Department, London School of Economics, *Woman, Wife and Worker* (London: HMSO, 1960), 6.
[109] Zweig, *Women's Life and Labour*, 56.
[110] See Brooke, 'Bodies, Sexuality and the "Modernization" of the British Working classes'.

Willmott noted this connection in one of their studies of the London working classes: '[f]ewer children, longer lives, more space in the home, less arduous work— these are some of the changes which have profoundly influenced the local community'.[111] At the same time, the rhetoric used widely in the 1930s to describe much working-class sexuality was, by the 1950s, more specifically used to describe 'problem' families, rather than an entire class.[112]

The representation of women's bodies was crucial to this literature. In the 1930s, it was the beleaguered working-class mother, condemned to poverty through her husband's inability to control the public sphere of work and her inability to control the private sphere of reproduction, who fuelled the campaigns of the WBCG and the ALRA. But in the late 1940s and 1950s, a very different working-class woman seemed to have emerged. Perhaps the best example of the perceived change in working-class women's bodies and sexuality from the interwar to the postwar period can be seen in the work of someone who witnessed both periods, Lella Secor Florence. By 1956, Florence was working with a family planning clinic in Birmingham. She noted the perceptible and physical transformation in the largely working-class clientele of the Birmingham clinic: '[o]lder clinic workers... recall the poor, bedraggled and dispirited mothers of large families who registered in the early days, and notice how few of these appear today in comparison with the well-dressed and more self-confident type of woman'. This change was due in large part, Florence argued, to the work of the clinic among working-class families: '[f]amilies have been kept smaller and the progressive deterioration characteristic of over-large families has been increasingly avoided'.[113] Again, this change was read through the body. Working-class women were represented as achieving the modern control over their bodies that middle-class women had achieved in the 1930s. The narrowing of the difference between working-class and middle-class reproduction was noted by Ronald Fletcher in his 1962 survey of the British family: 'there is not now such a great degree of difference between the family of the middle-classes and the family of the wage-earning classes as there was during the nineteenth century'.[114]

These accounts also argued that affluence had reshaped working-class masculinity. The new working class was often constructed as featuring a new working man. With full employment, comprehensive welfare provision, and increasing rates of female participation in the workforce, the working man's role in securing the stability of the home now lay as much in companionability as in the breadwinner wage. In some accounts, this was cast in the mould of a female sexuality that needed to be satisfied and contained within marriage: 'if the relationship is very good, the wife becomes domesticated; if, on the other hand, the relationship is not very

---

[111] Michael Young and Peter Willmott, *Family and Kinship in East London* (Harmondsworth: Penguin, 1957, 1962), 24–5.

[112] See Geoffrey Field, 'Perspectives on the Working-Class Family in Wartime Britain', *International Labour and Working-Class History* 39 (1990), 3–28; Pat Starkey, 'The Feckless Mother: Women, Poverty and Social Workers in Wartime and Post-War England', *Women's History Review* 8 (2000), 539–57.

[113] Lella Secor Florence, *Progress Report on Birth Control* (London: Heinemann, 1956), 41.

[114] Ronald Fletcher, *The Family and Marriage* (Harmondsworth: Penguin, 1962), 127, 128.

satisfactory, she seeks companionship outside in order to find relief from her isolation and loneliness'.[115] In their studies of East London and new working-class suburbs, Michael Young and Peter Willmott claimed that '[i]n place of the traditional working-class husband, as mean with his money as he was callous in sex, forcing a trail of unwanted babies upon his wife, has come the man who wheels the pram on Saturday mornings'.[116] This marked, they asserted, a 'new kind of companionship between man and woman'.[117] By the late 1960s, Young and Willmott were hailing the appearance of what they called the 'symmetrical family' with less segregation between the roles of men and women.[118] Others saw the same shift. Pearl Jepthcott and her investigators from the London School of Economics argued that among the working families of Bermondsey wives were helped by 'co-operative husbands'.[119] What is striking is how the new working-class man was identified with a new companionability between men and women within marriage, including sexual companionship aided by birth control. This was equated with wider social and political change in class identity. Ferdynand Zweig made a strong connection between a working man who 'seeks his pleasures and comforts at home more than ever' and a wider transformation of working-class identity.[120] He concluded that '[t]he intensity of both class consciousness and class sub-consciousness seems to be on the decline'.[121]

New women, new men, and a new sexuality thus occupied the domestic interior of working-class life in the pages of sociological literature on the postwar working classes. The other side to this was that an older, more distinctive, more problematic working class, one that was hard to accommodate to the trend of modernization and 'embourgoisement', was also read as having a more distinctive, more problematic, and unmodernized sexuality. This was often situated in the North. *Coal is Our Life* (1956) chronicled a Yorkshire mining community in which class lines still seemed raw. It was also a community in which sexuality was a point of tension between men and women: 'sexual relations are apparently rarely satisfactory to both partners . . . women complained of their husband's selfishness in not considering the woman's complete satisfaction. The widespread practice of withdrawal as a measure of birth control can only detract from the likelihood of female orgasm.'[122] Madeleine Kerr's *The People of Ship Street* (1958) also looked at an older working-class community, this time in Liverpool. There the picture seemed as unchanged in terms of sexuality as it did in terms of class identity and the economy. Ship Street

---

[115] Zweig, *The Worker in an Affluent Society*, 173.

[116] Peter Willmott and Michael Young, *Family and Class in a London Suburb* (London: New English Library, 1960, 1967), 24.

[117] Young and Willmott, *Family and Kinship in East London*, 30.

[118] Michael Young and Peter Willmott, *The Symmetrical Family* (London: Routledge and Kegan Paul, 1973).

[119] Pearl Jepthcott, with Nancy Seear and J.H. Smith, *Married Women Working* (London: George Allen and Unwin, 1962), 91.

[120] Ferdynand Zweig, *The Worker in an Affluent Society*, 207.

[121] Zweig, *Worker in an Affluent Society*, 135.

[122] Norman Dennis, Fernando Henriques, and Clifford Slaughter, *Coal is Our Life* (London: Tavistock, 1956, 1969), 228, 230.

was a community immune to modernization, replete with large families, uncontrolled fertility, and comments such as 'If I have any more I'll put me head in the
gas oven or throw meself in the canal'.[123] An older sense of class was represented by
an older sense of sexuality.

The language of affluence and the representation of the postwar working classes
rested as much in representations of gender and sexuality as they did in economics
and community. Birth control was central to this representation. In the 1950s, the
female working-class body became associated with reproductive control and sexual
pleasure, a clear contrast to the representation of that body in the 1920s and 1930s.
It had achieved the qualities that the middle-class female body and middle-class
sexuality had enjoyed in the interwar period. In some contexts, female sexuality was
connected to a positive transformation of the working classes, a kind of sexual
'embourgeoisement' to accompany the economic and political 'embourgeoisement'
of the 1950s. Such constructions made it much more difficult to talk in authorita-
tive terms about the kind of working-class mother that had lain behind birth
control and abortion advocacy in the 1920s and 1930s, unable to control her
fertility and laden with a raft of children. But, in a way, even if the economic
context had changed, there was no less need for birth control. In the 1920s and
1930s, the protection of the home involved protecting it against poverty. In the
1950s, sustaining the prosperity and security of the home enjoyed with welfare and
affluence still had to be guarded with the use of birth control. Birth control would
keep the working classes within the sphere of modernization. Birth control was also
central to the protection of a new protagonist of postwar society, the working
woman; in this way, reproductive control was moving from one understanding of
class rooted in the family to another understanding of class rooted in the individual.
This shift was partial and uneven, but it did presage a later movement in the
political discussion of reproductive control.

But we have to remember that the studies of the 'new' working class were
constructions of class, based upon some empirical evidence, but also impressionistic
and indicative of a particular idea of working-class identity. We should also stress, as
Hera Cook's work has suggested, that contraception for most women remained
problematic until the advent of the Pill, introduced in the early 1960s, but not in
widespread use until the 1970s. Thus, there remained a tense distance between
the ideal of a controlled and secure domestic space and perhaps the reality of
continuing uncertainty over birth control.

One episode at the end of the period under study illustrates this. In the winter of
1958, Lena Jeger, the Labour MP for Holborn and St Pancras, wrote a series of
articles on abortion for the *Woman's Sunday Mirror*, a left-leaning tabloid. Jeger had
spent some of her parliamentary time in the months previous pressing the Conservative government to provide statistics on abortion, such as how many women had
been granted sick leave due to abortion (6,000 between June 1954 and June 1955)
and how many people were imprisoned under the Offences Against the Person Act

[123] Madeleine Kerr, *The People of Ship Street* (London: Routledge and Kegan Paul, 1958), 84.

(16 men and 21 women). In her articles for the *Woman's Sunday Mirror*, Jeger contrasted the dichotomy between the criminality of abortions and the women who sought them: 'The abortion laws concern the women of this country, and the men who love them, at the very heart of their lives. We all know women, law-abiding citizens who, with no sense of crime will "try everything" to end an unwanted pregnancy.' Jeger also took up the long-standing class argument about abortion, that middle-class people with enough money could secure a safe and legal abortion easily enough, while working-class people had to make do with unsafe and illegal abortions in the backstreets:

> Can anyone honestly say that the present system is 'moral' when it enables any promiscuous girl with not less than £150 to procure a professional, safe operation, while a struggling, middle-aged mother must carry her burden of weariness and sickness because she has never seen £150 and never will?[124]

In a later article, Jeger restated this class angle, but also emphasized the need for women's autonomy in the decision to have an abortion: '[m]any wives need help of other kinds—better housing, more understanding from their husbands, family-planning advice. But when doctors say a wife needs an abortion, then the Law should allow it.'[125] The response to Jeger's articles was very strong and she published some of the letters. But it was a letter she did not publish that is of considerable interest. It was received from a woman living in Newton Aycliffe in County Durham:

> I am writing on behalf of a large number of housewives on this new housing estate. A few months ago you were conducting a campaign for making abortion legal and we have waited in vain for something to be done about it. It would seem the <u>men</u> concerned have fallen asleep again over it. We want abortion made legal (with no ties) and we want it now. I am going to send you a list of names and addresses of housewives here whose lives are just an agony of wondering if they are pregnant again, there is no happiness in any of these homes for these women and so it means the men can't be happy either. I myself have three young kiddies and can never afford to buy anything new for myself, and I live in constant fear of having any more children. Another friend has five kiddies under the age of six and since the last one's birth she has refused to let her husband touch her. This does not make for married happiness. One other friend has three kiddies and is very cold towards her husband, he in turn has turned to drink and bad temper. Yet another woman with three kiddies who swears she will commit suicide if she ever finds herself pregnant again. I could go on but I am sure you have some idea just how unhappy we all are. We can't get to see whoever it is we should see about all this (yet) so we are appointing you as our spokeswoman and to advise us as to what we have to do. We don't want to wait any longer and we don't want 'promises' we want action. Maybe you could point out that the world is over-crowded as it is, also that there are no jobs and no homes for a great many people so why keep on having too many children.

---

[124] Lena Jeger, 'A Woman MP Denounces an "Unfair, Cruel, Man-Made" Law', *Woman's Sunday Mirror* (London), 19 January 1958.
[125] Lena Jeger, The Day I Tried to Kill My Husband', *Woman's Sunday Mirror*, 2 March 1958.

Apart from the reference to the new housing estate, this letter could have been written in the 1930s. The writer included herself among those who 'will take *anything* if I am ever pregnant again'. Her own husband had used condoms that had failed. She noted that the majority of women ended up practising withdrawal, which was 'bad for nerves' and sexually unsatisfying. Sexual pleasure was a point she returned to, talking about the need to have an anxiety-free sex life for the good of both men and women: 'A sexually satisfied man is a happy man, as it takes a woman to satisfy him sexually the answer is obvious, make the woman happy and free from worry, and there will be no more cold wives.'[126] What was also notable about the letter was the community formed out of desperation for reliable birth control. The desire for abortion in the 1950s was, in some ways, as or more pressing than the 1920s and 1930s, in part because of long-standing reasons, such as the fear of poverty and joblessness, but also because to lack reproductive control or suffer deprivation because of large families seemed so far from the ideal of affluence and a managed family. There has been some recent work on the 'rediscovery of poverty' charted by Richard Titmuss and other social scientists in the late 1950s, but we might also comment that, in the case of birth control, alongside portraits of a new working class, buoyed by small family size and economic security, and representations of a new working-class and perhaps middle-class femininity more autonomous than in the past, there persisted older continuities that continued to fuel campaigns for birth control and abortion.

Before the dawn of the 1960s, there occurred significant changes in the way gender and some sexual questions were framed within the context of Labour politics and working-class life. As suggested at the beginning of this chapter, these changes did not have a consistent dynamic, nor did they evince a complete or consistent topography, but they do suggest that, if not a 'sexual' revolution, then at least, to use the description of Jennie Lee and the TUC, a 'modern', 'silent' transformation was taking place. The year 1967 has come to represent the end of one phase of sexual politics and the beginning of another. It is important to remember that the road to that point was a long one, stretching back to the 1920s and 1930s, but with crucial junctures and turns in the 1940s and 1950s.

---

[126] LSE, Lena Jeger Papers, Isabel Surgeoner to Jeger, no date [1959].

6

Labour and the 'Liberal Hour', 1956–67

Abortion, Family Planning, and Homosexual Law Reform

In 1956, in his influential work *The Future of Socialism*, Anthony Crosland, a 'revisionist' seeking to reorient the direction of Labour's ideology, raised the prospect of making Britain a more 'civilized' country through the reform of the abortion, homosexuality, and marriage laws.[1] Three years later, Roy Jenkins, a fellow revisionist, similarly argued that an important and new avenue of democratic socialist policy should be what he called the 'civilization' of Britain, involving the party in 'many subjects which are normally regarded as outside the scope of party politics' including the abolition of the death penalty, the decriminalization of homosexuality in private, and the reform of the abortion laws.[2] By 1966, Jenkins was Home Secretary and openly encouraging Members of Parliament to pursue reforms in such areas.[3]

The following year, 1967, was a kind of *annus mirabilis* of sexual reform. Parliament decriminalized homosexual acts as long as these were in private and involved persons over the age of 21. It also passed David Steel's Abortion bill, allowing women to have, if not abortion on demand, at least more secure access to legal, therapeutic operations. The Labour government also formally empowered the National Health Service to provide contraceptive advice to all women regardless of their marital status and age after the passage of the National Health Service (Family Planning) Act. All three acts were the result of private members' bills (two by Labour MPs, Leo Abse and Edwin Brooks, one by a Liberal MP, David Steel), but they enjoyed unprecedented support from the Labour government, both in terms of drafting help and the granting of parliamentary time.

There was a sense at the time that these reforms were both a beginning and an end. They seemed to confirm the birth of a progressive society, in which 'civilization' was based upon sexual liberalism. The Abortion Act and the decriminalization of homosexuality became shorthand for the ascendancy of the 'permissive' society, the relaxation of public and private mores in the 1960s. Indeed, they often serve as both symbols and causes of the permissive society, facilitating the transformation of a drab and repressed society to 'swinging London', a kind of non-stop sexual festival in Britain that drew a different class of tourist to Carnaby Street, performances of

---

[1] C.A.R. Crosland, *The Future of Socialism* (London: Jonathan Cape, 1956), 357, 355.
[2] Roy Jenkins, *The Labour Case* (Harmondsworth: Penguin, 1959), 135.
[3] CMA, SA/ALRA/5/1/34/262, D.F. Pollock to Douglas Houghton, 13 June 1966.

the nude musical 'Oh! Calcutta!', gay clubs, and legal abortions. The Abortion Act also quickly became a cipher for the progress of women within the permissive society. At the end of 1968, for example, a script for the BBC's external service programme asked, rhetorically, whether England was a 'Paradise for Women' and concluded that with the achievement of legal abortion and steps towards equal pay, 'by and large, the battle for the equality of women has been won'.[4] Given the moderate degree of reform achieved with the decriminalization of homosexuality and abortion, this reputation is ironic.

Indeed, as shall be argued in this chapter and in the next section, the law reforms of 1967 introduced a number of questions about the relationship between sexuality (whether in terms of reproductive control or sexual orientation) and politics, as much as they resolved long-standing issues. These were, at best, utilitarian reforms that left open or provoked questions of class, gender, sexual equality, individual rights, and agency. In terms of abortion, the 1967 reform raised the issue of choice and access. With respect to homosexuality, the 1967 Act helped formalize a fundamental question of human rights and equality. The roads from 1967 were, as the next section will argue, about the uneven resolution of these questions.

Even if this was a beginning, we still have to recognize the 'ending' represented by the 1967 reforms. In December of that year, Dora Russell, now living in Cornwall, caught the spirit of this, when she described the National Health Service (Family Planning) Act as the final realization of the aims of the WBCG: '[w]e started the agitation which only now after forty three years has brought success—the demand that birth control advice should be an integral part of maternity care and available at maternity clinics under the Health services for all women who asked for such advice'.[5] In terms of homosexual and abortion law reform, the 1967 acts were realized through a particular kind of link between pressure groups and political parties, symbolized by the Homosexual Law Reform Society (HLRS) and the ALRA, following years of struggle. After 1967, this respectable path to political change was taken less and less. The space of abortion and gay activism also changed after 1967, from the centre of power to its fringes. There was a certain poignancy in the fact that Alice Jenkins, the long-time crusader for the ALRA, died on Christmas Day 1967, just after the Abortion Act for which she had fought so passionately was accorded Royal Assent.

Given the difficulties that questions of sex reform like birth control, abortion, and homosexuality had faced even a decade before 1967, it is important to ask why legislative action occurred in the 1960s, and why it occurred under a Labour government, which afforded the private members' bills critical parliamentary time without which they would not have passed.

An obvious starting point might be what has been called the advent of a 'permissive' society in the 1960s. In the literature on the 1960s, the extent of 'permissiveness' is the subject of much debate. Arthur Marwick saw the period representing a true cultural revolution, with 'a general sexual liberation, entailing

---

[4] CMA, SA/ALR/A.11/1/161, script for 'A Paradise for Women', 30 December 1968.
[5] IISH, DRP, 345, Russell to Madeleine Simms, 9 February 1968.

striking changes in public and private morals and . . . a new frankness, openness, and indeed honesty in personal relations and modes of expression'.[6] More recent accounts have emphasized the limits of change, describing it as 'often halting, fragmentary and bitterly contested', happening more at the level of a London-based elite than throughout society.[7] As this chapter and the next will suggest, these differences were important. It was not simply that acceptance of a liberal or progressive agenda was more obvious in London; it was more obvious in different parts of London than in others. As Chapter 9 shall show, Bermondsey was a more conservative place than Soho or Bloomsbury even in the 1980s. The northern Labour heartlands were not necessarily as hospitable to permissive ideas as north London; this is not to say that they were necessarily sexually conservative, but that it is an uneven landscape.

We might also think about the chronology and causes of 'permissiveness'. In the 1960s, contingent change intersected with longer-term developments rooted in the 1950s. More broadly, we have to see that the changes of the 1960s were not simply a loosening of the strictures of the conservative 1950s or a rebellion against the 1950s, but were also a consequence of trends in the 1950s or, indeed, the unwinding of that decade's ambiguities.

Four developments are particularly important. The first was in Labour ideology. The rise of 'revisionism' within the Labour Party as a response to ideological challenges in other areas also opened up a space for the consideration of moral issues such as abortion and homosexual law reform within the context of socialist action. To some extent, this might also be seen in the work of the 'New Left' in the late 1950s and early 1960s. Secondly, the 'rediscovery' of poverty in the late 1950s and early 1960s underlined the way in which some members of society, such as unmarried mothers and problem families, fell outside the world of plenty offered by the welfare state and the managed economy. This legitimated discussion of birth control and abortion as ways by which such social problems could be mitigated. Thirdly, just as the rediscovery of poverty suggested particular points of inadequacy in terms of social access and equality, high-profile criminal cases and, in particular, the Wolfenden Report on homosexuality and prostitution illustrated the limitations of the postwar political settlement in addressing individual liberty. This did much to establish it as a legitimate area of political action. Finally, and not least importantly, from the 1950s on, sexual issues were discussed with much greater openness within popular culture and the media. The former was particularly notable in this respect. Indeed, it is possible that kitchen sink drama and issue films were as important as something like the Wolfenden Report in establishing a space for the discussion of sexual questions. By the mid-1960s, because of all of these factors, the existing laws on abortion and homosexuality laws looked like they needed to be reformed to sustain the image of a modern society. This chapter examines each of these factors, then turns, in discrete discussions, to the reform of

---

[6] Arthur Marwick, *The Sixties* (Oxford: Oxford University Press, 1998), 18.
[7] Dominic Sandbrook, *White Heat* (London: Little, Brown, 2006), 191.

the abortion and homosexuality laws and the Family Planning Act of 1967. It begins with a discussion of Labour revisionism.

I

As already noted, the three major reforms of sexuality were passed under a Labour government, even if one—the Abortion Act—was the initiative of a Liberal MP. Both the Abortion Act and the Sexual Offences Act were helped by the work of avowedly non-partisan pressure groups and lobbyists. But the Labour government and, in particular, the Labour Home Secretary Roy Jenkins played a critical role in the passage of all three bills by affording them parliamentary time, an advantage enjoyed by few other private members' bills. This accorded with a sense that, ideologically and culturally, a younger generation within the Labour Party and government viewed reforms like abortion and homosexuality as part of a progressive agenda. The roots of this important change in attitude lie in the 1950s, in the attempts by so-called 'revisionists' to redraw Labour's socialism. This is a point first made by Jeffrey Weeks in his general history of sexual reform in Britain, but it is worth revisiting in detail.[8]

The end of the second Attlee government in 1951 marked, for some, the completion of one phase of Labour's socialism. Harold Wilson, who took the party leadership in 1963 and became Prime Minister in 1964, remarked that the end of the Attlee government also represented 'the end ... of a generation's policy-making'.[9] Electoral failure in three successive general elections in 1951, 1955, and 1959 made the process of rethinking socialist policy-making all the more urgent for a new generation. Sexuality was never explicitly discussed within the party in the 1950s and 1960s, but we might look to the debates over the revision of Labour policy and ideology as a possible context for thinking about a shifting landscape of political thought on sexuality and gender.

In much of the writing on ideology and policy in the 1950s, great stress was placed on the need to redraw the boundaries of Labour's socialism. If ideological discussions in the 1930s and 1940s had been dominated by questions of economic power, there was a new concern in the 1950s about personal freedom and mapping new frontiers of equality. The Home Policy Committee noted in 1955: '[t]hat classical socialist beliefs provide for an infinite extension of State activity does not alter the fact that formidable problems have already arisen ... [a] reconciliation of liberty with equality now requires the recognition that individual rights are at issue to an extent that embarrasses a Socialist Party'.[10] Some policy-makers and intellectuals showed an increasing interest in protecting individual liberty. In an essay on nationalization, for example, the party leader Hugh Gaitskell remarked that the

---

[8] Weeks, *Sex, Politics and Society*, 254–6.
[9] Harold Wilson, 'Let Us Face the Future', *Fabian Journal* 15 (March 1955), 3.
[10] LPA, National Executive Committee [NEC], Home Policy Committee, Re. 15, 'The Individual and Society', December 1955, 6.

ultimate goal of the party should be the protection of the individual, affording 'equal opportunity for the pursuit of happiness, however people decide they can best achieve this ... [w]hat the state should do is provide the framework, the opportunities through which people have the best chance of finding happiness for themselves'.[11] The 1956 party statement *Personal Freedom* argued that the promotion of such liberty was the responsibility of the state, which had to provide 'conditions in which all can enjoy full equality of opportunity and full social status' while ensuring that 'no one's standard of living need fall below the highest level the community can afford'.[12] The interest in individual liberty linked to equality was a long-standing feature of Left-liberal thought, of course: what had changed was the sphere of action. If economic equality had largely been accomplished in the public sphere with full employment and the welfare state, a new frontier of liberty and equality potentially lay in the private sphere.

The image of the party and its associations were also the focus of discussion. Right-wing Labour thinkers wanted to pare down the party's long-standing identification with the working classes. A journal associated with the revisionist cause, *Socialist Commentary*, asserted that socialism's 'basic appeal is not to class, but to conscience and community'.[13] After the electoral defeat of 1959, Anthony Crosland argued that the party had to reform itself along the lines of modern society; this meant tackling the relationship between class and party: '[w]e manifestly need to change the image of the Labour Party: in terms of issues, attitudes, and the underlying class identification'.[14] The Home Policy Committee concluded in 1962 that the party had to identify itself with progress and modernity, rather than class: 'we have somehow to get a new look more in keeping with contemporary conditions—brighter; more optimistic; more cheerful; more courageous in denouncing wrongful behaviour within the family as well as outside of it; a stronger passion for individual liberty'.[15] Thus, there was a conscious attempt to break with older representations of community symbolized by 'class' (and, indeed, even 'family') and create, in their place, newer representations of community based upon the private sphere, individual rights or in terms of an equality removed from class.

This interest in individual liberty, equality, progress, and modernity may have opened up a door to both the private sphere and questions such as sexual reform. Certainly, the 'revisionist' strain in Labour thinking in the 1950s evinced a much more sympathetic consideration of moral and sexual questions. Figures such as Crosland, Douglas Jay, and Roy Jenkins combined a sceptical attitude towards older socialist ends and means with a desire to open up socialism to new avenues of reform. Thinking about the reforms of the 1960s, Jeffrey Weeks has rightly spoken

[11] Hugh Gaitskell, *Socialism and Nationalisation* (London: Fabian Pamphlet No. 300, July 1956), 2.
[12] LPA, NEC, Home Policy Committee, Re. 60, 'Personal Freedom', May 1956.
[13] 'Equality with Quality', *Socialist Commentary* 19/5 (July 1955), 199–200.
[14] C.A.R. Crosland, *Can Labour Win?* (London: Fabian Pamphlet No. 324, May 1960), 14.
[15] LPA, RD 270, Home Policy Committee, 'Non-Manual Workers and the Labour Party', May 1962.

of the 'fit' between what he calls the 'moral reformism' of the revisionists and legislative achievements such as abortion law reform and the decriminalization of homosexuality.[16]

Anthony Crosland's work is a good example of this. Early in the 1950s, Crosland ventured a critique of an older Fabian tradition, represented by Sidney and Beatrice Webb, one 'of total indifference to art and beauty and freedom and radical individualism, a traditional of unnatural morality and priggish Puritanism'.[17] At the same time, he argued that, with capitalism transformed by the reforms of the postwar Labour governments, British socialists had to explore new frontiers.[18] The two points came together in a desire, articulated most famously in *The Future of Socialism*, to move beyond a bloodlessly economistic programme towards policy and ideology that would 'make Britain a more colourful and civilized country to live in'.[19] This would be a new horizon for Labour to journey towards:

> As our traditional objectives are gradually fulfilled, and society becomes more social-democratic with the passing of the old injustices, we shall turn our attention increasingly to other, and in the long run more important spheres—of personal freedom, happiness, and cultural endeavour: the cultivation of leisure, beauty, grace, gaiety, excitement, and of all the proper pursuits, whether elevated, vulgar or eccentric, which contribute to the varied fabric of a full private and family life.

Crosland rejected the dourness of Labour's previous identity: 'now we surely need a different set of values . . . a greater emphasis on private life, on freedom and dissent, on culture, beauty, leisure, and even frivolity. Total abstinence and a good filing-system are not now the right sign-posts to the socialist Utopia.' He believed the first step was to concentrate on lifting 'socially-imposed restrictions on the individual's private life and liberty'. This meant a range of social reform measures, including abortion law reform:

> . . . the divorce laws, licensing laws, prehistoric (and flagrantly unfair) abortion laws, obsolete penalties for sexual abnormality, the illiterate censorship of books and plays, and remaining restrictions on the equal rights of women. Most of these are intolerable, and should be highly offensive to socialists, in whose blood there should always run a trace of the anarchist and the libertarian, and not too much of the prig and the prude.[20]

As already noted, another revisionist, Roy Jenkins, made similar arguments for the 'civilization' of Britain.[21]

---

[16] Weeks, *Sex, Politics and Society*, 265–6.

[17] Quoted in Catherine Ellis, 'Total Abstinence and a Good Filing-System? Anthony Crosland and the Affluent Society', in Lawrence Black and Hugh Pemberton (eds), *An Affluent Society? Britain's Post-war 'Golden Age' Revisited* (London: Ashgate, 2004), 69.

[18] See C.A.R. Crosland, 'The Transition from Socialism', in R.H.S. Crossman (ed.), *New Fabian Essays* (London: Turnstile, 1952).

[19] C.A.R. Crosland, *The Future of Socialism*, 357.

[20] Crosland, *Future of Socialism*, 353, 357, 355. Crosland had also supported abortion law reform early in the fifties; see Ellis, 'Total Abstinence and a Good Filing-System', 69.

[21] Roy Jenkins, *The Labour Case* (Harmondsworth: Penguin, 1959), 135.

In such ways, sexual issues found a place within revisionist thought. This was a significant shift, paving the way for the acceptance of such reforms in the 1960s when revisionists like Crosland and, in particular, Jenkins, occupied Cabinet office and when a younger generation sharing their views filled the Labour benches in the House. But it should also be noted that issues like abortion and homosexual law reform were not necessarily considered 'specifically socialist or non-socialist' issues by revisionists like Crosland; rather they were issues that 'may be highly significant for welfare, freedom, and social justice, even though not assimilable into the old socialist-capitalist categories'.[22] They considered that the provenance of abortion and homosexuality was not socialism, but a kind of moral progressivism or liberalism. But the shift rendered abortion law reform comprehensible as political reform, rather than unthinkable, as it had been in previous decades.

Another Left tradition emerged in the late 1950s outside the Labour Party. This was the much-vaunted New Left, with writers such as Raphael Samuel, Perry Anderson, and Edward Thompson gathered round the *Universities and Left Review*, which became the *New Left Review*. The New Left did not explicitly address questions of sexuality or gender until the mid-1960s (most notably with Juliet Mitchell's epochal essay, 'The Longest Revolution'), but, as Lucy Robinson and others have suggested, the New Left's interest in questions of culture and youth opened them up to more unfamiliar spaces of politicization, such as culture and leisure, which eventually did provide a jumping-off point for the politics of the personal, whether we think of women's or gay liberation.[23] In the work of some thinkers outside the Labour Party, we can see parallels with Labour revisionism in a desire both to find a new way of thinking about socialist politics outside the economy and, as with earlier utopian socialist radicals, to make socialism about the remaking of people and society. Edward Thompson, for example, while complaining that a regrettable aspect of the 'apathetic decade' was that people were seeking 'private solutions to public evils', nonetheless acknowledged that socialism had to be about producing 'human nature' rather than only 'organizing production'.[24] Another contributor to the same collection aspired to a 'moral revolution' through socialism.[25] The intensity of such visions permeated social movements such as the CND and, as the memoirs of later radicals suggested, helped bring to life the sexual and gender radicalism underlying women's liberation and gay liberation.[26]

---

[22] Crosland, *Future of Socialism*, 354.

[23] Robinson, *Gay Men and the Left*, 28–30.

[24] E.P. Thompson, 'At the Point of Decay', in E.P. Thompson et alia (eds), *Out of Apathy* (London: New Left Review/Stevens and Sons, 1960), 5; E.P. Thompson, 'Outside the Whale', in Thompson (ed.), *Out of Apathy*, 185.

[25] Kenneth Alexander, 'Power at the Base', in Thompson et alia (eds), *Out of Apathy*, 266.

[26] See, for example, Sheila Rowbotham, 'The Women's Movement and Organizing for Socialism', in Sheila Rowbotham, Lynne Segal and Hilary Wainwright, *Beyond the Fragments: Feminism and the Making of Socialism* (London: Merlin, 1979), 21.

II

Sexual reform in the 1960s depended, in no small part, on the exposure of the existing law on abortion and homosexuality, and the general approach to sexual mores, as inadequate. A number of factors influenced this, such as the persistence of poverty, the highlighting of problems with the existing laws on homosexuality and abortion in the 1950s and 1960s, and the representation of these issues in popular culture.

In the 1920s and 1930s, arguments for contraception and abortion law reform had rested, in part, on an understanding of the link between family size and working-class poverty. In the 1950s, the picture was more confused. On the one hand, it seemed that welfare and full employment had removed the main causes of working-class poverty. At the same time, it was believed that working-class family size had been controlled. The last point was belied by evidence such as the letter to Lena Jeger discussed at the end of the previous chapter. But the 1950s also produced new ideas of poverty that continued to underpin arguments for widening contraceptive access, particularly when we look at the passing of the National Health Service (Family Planning) Act in 1967. This was the so-called 'rediscovery of poverty'. In some ways, it marked a continuous line with the increasing focus on problem families. But social scientists such as Brian Abel-Smith and Peter Townsend were keen to explode the idea that welfare and affluence had eliminated poverty. In an influential essay of 1962, Townsend argued against the 'almost dazed euphoria' of his colleagues in the social sciences to show that poverty persisted in the affluent society; three years later, he and Abel-Smith showed that the proportion of people living at the level of poverty had increased between 1954 and 1960.[27] Particular groups had been left exposed by the general improvement brought by the welfare state.[28] Two were of particular interest: children and what are now termed lone mothers or single-parent families. The Child Poverty Action Group was among the most important organizations emerging in response to the 'rediscovery' of poverty to lobby for improvements to the welfare state.[29] Other works focused on the poverty found in single-parent families.[30] Famously, the broadcast of Ken Loach's television play *Cathy Come Home* in 1966 underlined the

---

[27] Peter Townsend, 'The Meaning of Poverty', *British Journal of Sociology* 13 (1962), 211; Brian Abel-Smith and Peter Townsend, *The Poor and the Poorest* (London: G. Bell, 1965).

[28] See John Macnicol, 'From "Problem Family" to "Underclass", 1945–95', in Helen Fawcett and Rodney Lowe (eds), *Welfare Policy in Britain: The Road From 1945* (London: Macmillan/ICBH, 1999).

[29] See Maria Meyer-Kelly, 'The Rise of Pressure Groups in Britain 1965–75: Single Issue Causes and Their Effects', in Maria Meyer-Kelly and Michael Kandiah (eds), *'The Poor Get Poorer Under Labour': The Validity and Effects of CPAG's Campaign in 1970* (London: ICBH Witness Seminar, 18 February 2000); Tanya Evans, 'Stopping the Poor Getting Poorer: The Establishment and Professionalisation of the Poverty NGOs, 1945–1995', in Nick Crowson, Matthew Hilton, and James McKay (eds), *NGOs in Contemporary Britain: Non-State Actors in Society and Politics Since 1945* (Houndmills: Palgrave/Macmillan, 2009).

[30] See, for example, Margaret Wynn, *Fatherless Families* (London: Michael Joseph, 1964); Dennis Marsden, *Mothers Alone: Poverty and the Fatherless Family* (London: Allen Lane/Penguin, 1969).

persistence of poverty and deprivation in the brave new world of the welfare state and the managed economy. The mother and the size of the family remained a focus of reformers' concerns. Thus, contraception remained a live welfare issue in the era of affluence.

If poverty persisted as a factor in thinking about sexuality, homosexual law reform appeared a more novel cause in the 1950s. Early in the twentieth century, as discussed in previous chapters, homosexual reform was at the forefront of discussion by sex reformers on the Left, such as Edward Carpenter. But, as Jeffrey Weeks points out, the association between socialism and homosexual reform weakened between the 1920s and the 1950s. In Chapter 4, this was discussed in relation to the work of Dora Russell, Naomi Mitchison, and Alec Craig. The advent of Labour government in 1945 unsurprisingly changed little. As Home Secretary, Herbert Morrison was as enthusiastic in using the law to prosecute homosexuality as any previous holder of that office. In the 1950s, as we have seen, Labour revisionists did include homosexual law reform as part of what they saw as a programme to modernize and civilize Britain. But one problem, at least compared with the abortion campaign, was that homosexual law reform had little class purchase. Marxists tended to view the question as a bourgeois deviation that would somehow disappear with socialism. Working-class Labourites similarly viewed it as a middle-class or aristocratic vice. As Lucy Robinson has made clear, there were conflicting styles of homosexuality for Labour politicians. No homosexual Labour politician was, of course, out, at this point, but Tom Driberg at least was able to enjoy a certain notoriety as a homosexual that did not apparently dent his political standing, not that this was ever particularly high. By contrast, George Brinham, the Chair of the NEC between 1959 and 1960, suffered a much more depressing fate. Brinham was a trade unionist MP who was well in the closet when he was murdered by a casual pick-up in 1962: his killer was acquitted on the grounds of mitigating circumstances.[31]

This analysis might be broadened further. Despite ongoing connections between radical sex reform and socialism in the twentieth century, homosexual law reform had much shallower roots on the British Left than reproductive politics. Of course, there was good reason for this, as Brinham's sad fate showed: homosexuality was still firmly a mark of shame in a way that even an unwanted pregnancy was not. To be a male or female advocate of homosexual law reform was more difficult than being an advocate of abortion because abortion at least resulted from a normative, heterosexual context. But there is something more here. The enduring connection between socialist politics and reproductive politics rested on a particular subject embodying the need for reform: the working-class mother. Sex could be talked about because of this unifying figure. Of course, this limited what could be said about sex. Another protoganist of sexual discourse—the liberated, modern woman—had much less resonance in mainstream socialist culture, as Chapter 4 has suggested. Homosexual law reform was still more difficult. Before the 1950s,

---

[31] Robinson, *Gay Men and the Left*, Chapter 1.

the subject of homosexual law reform was still being developed, largely through the law and psychology. If advocates of birth control and legal abortion could effectively make a case based upon sexual difference (in other words, using motherhood as a starting point), this was not possible in the case of homosexuality. Indeed, as Houlbrook points out, the defiant celebration of sexual difference by Lady Austin's Camp Boys was far too disreputable even for other queer men.[32] What developed through the 1930s and later was a homosexual politics far more likely to have political purchase, featuring, as its central protagonist, a respectable and restrained subject who pursued his desires in private. Another point here is perhaps obvious: unlike women, homosexuals were not seen as political subjects. They were not workers to be organized, not voters to be won, not taxpayers to be appeased. They could not be conceived in political discourse, nor could they yet figure in political calculation.

The 1950s were a critical period for homosexual law reform. At the beginning of the decade, the spy scare involving Guy Burgess raised the spectre of a red and man-loving conspiracy against the democratic state. In other ways, however, the contra-dictions in the way that homosexuality was treated under the law and by society began to show. The Montagu–Wildeblood trial of 1954 illustrated the ambiguities of the law and highlighted the tragic position in which the law put 'respectable' men like Peter Wildeblood, the diplomatic correspondent for the *Daily Mail*, who saw his own homosexuality as 'essentially a personal problem, which only becomes a matter of public concern when the law makes it so'.[33] As Chris Waters has pointed out, Wildeblood did much to forge a modern and respectable homosexual identity.[34]

Partly as a result of the Montagu–Wildeblood trial, the Conservative govern-ment established a committee under Lord Wolfenden to inquire into two problems of public and private sexuality, the law on prostitution and the law on homosexu-ality.[35] Its report, published in 1957, steered a delicate course between the espousal of sexual libertarianism and the continuation of controls on private behaviour, recommending that private homosexual behaviour be decriminalized between persons 21 years of age or over, but public homosexual behaviour discouraged.[36] The Report also mapped out a particular kind of political response to sexual questions, defusing the controversy of such issues by ceding authority to profes-sionals and experts, rather than campaigners.[37] The Conservative government declined to act on the question, but it did kick-start a campaign for the revision of the existing laws. Not least, Wolfenden focused attention on the liberties of men

[32] Houlbrook, *Queer London*, Chapter 10.

[33] Peter Wildeblood, *Against the Law* (Harmondsworth: Penguin, 1955, 1957), 8.

[34] Chris Waters, 'Disorders of the Mind, Disorders of the Body Social: Peter Wildeblood and the Making of the Modern Homosexual', in Conekin, Mort, and Waters (eds), *Moments of Modernity*.

[35] See Geraldine Bedell, 'Coming Out of the Dark Ages', *The Observer* (London), 24 June 2007 for information on Wolfenden.

[36] See Weeks, *Sex, Politics and Society*, 239 ff.

[37] Frank Mort, 'Mapping Sexual London: The Wolfenden Committee on Homosexual Offences and Prostitution, 1954–7', *New Formations* 37 (1999), 92–113.

who were otherwise law-abiding; like the rediscovery of poverty, this was a kind of dark area in the otherwise bright and progressive welfare society.

There is little question, as Houlbrook has argued, that Wolfenden's reform agenda 'embodied a respectable, yet highly exclusive, "homosexual" subject' and was based upon 'the rejection of public manifestations of sexual difference'.[38] This was, however, the only likely way that rights for homosexuals would come about. It is striking that though revisionists such as Crosland might talk of anarchy and libertarianism, they did not go beyond thinking about homosexuality as a 'sexual abnormality' of men who were victims of an 'obsolete' law.[39] Rationality and control were, as Martin Francis has pointed out, also strands of revisionist culture within the Labour Party of the 1950s.[40] In this way, arguing for changing the law on homosexuality was less about arguing for the free expression of sexuality than the ability to live as a homosexual of a particular kind and within a specific context. One of the arguments that could be made about the relationship between homosexuality and socialism is that it is about a relationship between the sexual self and the body politic; in this respect, the homosexual self could only find a partial or highly defined place even in a sympathetic discourse.

Popular culture, in the form of film, fiction, radio and television, also opened up a space for the discussion of sexual questions in a way that had not been apparent before the mid- to late 1950s. In film, this was the golden age of 'social realism', with hard-hitting films like *Saturday Night and Sunday Morning* (1958) and *Room at the Top* (1959) dealing with the contours and tensions of class society in an age of affluence. In fiction and drama, the 'angry young men' of John Wain, John Osborne, and Alan Sillitoe similarly took on British society in a less polite and more open way. Such works afforded a public consideration of abortion.

It was as a mirror (albeit a distorted one) to the working classes that such literature was so striking in the 1950s. The rhythms and stories of working-class life took centre stage in the British imagination in a way not seen before. Working-class rebels like Arthur Seaton, Colin Smith, and Joe Lampton were the new anti-heroes. What distinguished such characters was a social defiance born of class society and a sinuous and often aggressive sexuality. Social realism was as much marked by its openness towards sexuality as towards class, with its working-class characters getting laid as much as paid in the affluent society. But a recurring theme in such works was the threat of pregnancy—one of the things the angry young men were angry about was the constraints thrown around their sexual libertinism by enforced domesticity and the new and disturbing stereotypes of working-class femininity.[41] And thus, as Dave Ellis has remarked, abortion was, in social realist film and fiction, 'an essential part of the genre'.[42] In many films and novels, there

---

[38] Houlbrook, *Queer London*, 262, 263.

[39] Crosland, *Future of Socialism*, 355.

[40] Martin Francis, 'The Labour Party: Modernisation and the Politics of Restraint', in Conekin, Mort, and Waters (eds), *Moments of Modernity*.

[41] See Brooke, 'Gender and Working-Class Identity in Britain during the 1950s', 788.

[42] Dave Ellis, '"Swinging Realism": The Strange Case of *To Sir With Love* and *Up the Junction*', *EnterText* 2.1 (2001), 70.

was a requisite abortion scene. In the novel *Saturday Night and Sunday Morning* (1958), for example, Arthur Seaton keeps his older, married lover company at the 'ceremony of "bringing it off"' with gin and a hot bath; the film version set the abortion scene off-screen, but still alluded to it.[43] In *Alfie* (1966), the account of a working-class Lothario, there is again an abortion scene.

'Social realism' also dealt with women's experience of abortion and pregnancy in a more open fashion than before. Three major such works (all of which became feature films)—the play *A Taste of Honey* (1959) by Shelagh Delaney and the novels *A Kind of Loving* (1960) by Stan Barstow and *The L-Shaped Room* (1960) by Lynne Reid Banks—featured main characters facing an unwanted pregnancy. To some degree, this was portrayed either as a consequence of working-class life or as the route of downward mobility. In *The L-Shaped Room*, an educated, middle-class woman 'falls' from the graces of respectable society as a consequence of her 'modern' sexual behaviour; along the way, she is introduced to the margins of British society— prostitutes, homosexuals, Afro-Caribbean immigrants, Jews, and lesbians. Nell Dunn's remarkable *Up the Junction* (1963), a kind of fictional social investigation of working-class women's lives in Battersea, portrayed abortion as something so normal in working-class life that one character's father 'went up the chemist and tried to get a stick of something they used before the war'.[44] But abortion was also represented as something illegal, often futile, and sometimes fatal. Indeed, the representation of it in fiction and film was consistent with images of sordid, backstreet operations, a kind of dark, Dickensian afterlife in modern Britain.

Film, fiction, and drama of the late 1950s and early 1960s thus gave higher visibility to the problem of unwanted pregnancy and, in particular, the issue of illegal abortion. But these works should also be perceived as foregrounding a new and modern form of female sexuality. To be sure, traditional stereotypes existed, but what we see pushing through these films are female characters who were not simply asexual wives and mothers. They were more sexual, less dependent upon men (whether that independence was forced upon them or not) or at least less attached to men, and more independent of family. This does not mean that women were liberated—far from it. What it did was deepen the already-existing tensions about women's roles. This construction of female subjectivity demanded the ability to reconcile roles and manage sexuality. There now was an expectation that women should be able to do this in order to be modern. This means that it was less about class, but it is connected with class: as in the 1920s and 1930s, there was an opposition between modern and working class. Abortion became a means of managing sexual modernity, albeit one that was hedged either by danger (in the backstreets) or exploitation (in the examination room).

Homosexual men figured in social realist works, notably as supporting characters in *The L-Shaped Room* and *A Taste of Honey*. But with the exception of 'issue' films such as *The Leatherboys* (1964) and most importantly *Victim* (1961), homosexuality did not take centre stage in the way unwanted pregnancy did in British film.

---

[43] Alan Sillitoe, *Saturday Night and Sunday Morning* (London: Paladin, 1958, 1990), 85.
[44] Nell Dunn, *Up the Junction* (Washington: Counterpoint, 1963, 2000), 47.

Nonetheless, a film like *Victim* did take the liberal-progressive line on homosexuality: that it was an outmoded problem that needed to be dealt with in a modern society to alleviate the position of the homosexual.[45]

In these various ways, we might see that the progress towards the reform of the laws on abortion and homosexuality and the Family Planning Act of 1967 were less rooted in a suddenly appearing permissive climate than in changes rooted in the 1950s and, not least, the opening up of a particular ideological space for the consideration of sexual questions. The chapter will now turn to a detailed examination of the three reforms of 1967.

III

In the spring of 1966, the ALRA newsletter referred to abortion as a 'fashionable' cause.[46] Momentum was building towards the reform of the abortion laws and liberal opinion marshalled behind this campaign. Television and radio programmes, smart magazines, and the broadsheet press all bestowed attention on a question that had once been clouded by shame. In the late 1950s and early 1960s, abortion was also granted higher visibility from the media. In November 1960, BBC's *Panorama* televised a programme on abortion. In 1965, BBC and ATV ran programmes dealing with abortion; '*Dr Finlay's Casebook*', the popular medical drama, featured an episode about illegal abortion. Marje Proops, a leading columnist for the *Daily Mirror*, announced her support for law reform in 1964, arguing that there was 'a law for the rich and a law for the poor . . . the present abortion laws are laws which favour the well-heeled'.[47]

The practice of abortion also received greater public attention through researched studies of its practice, most notably Moya Woodside's study of jailed female abortionists and *The Observer* journalist Paul Ferris's book-length examination, *The Nameless* (1966). Woodside mapped the often hidden world of backstreet abortions, while Ferris looked behind the respectable façade of the 'West End legal' to find waiting rooms filled with 'pretty, dressed-up, well-scented women . . . looking stonily into space' from whom doctors earned between £50,000 and £100,000 a year.[48] These studies offered portraits of two nations of abortion. One was found in dark alleyways and dingy rooms, stories which often ended in a hospital ward or a police cell. The second was a superficially brighter world, with abortions done above the law, by respected professionals behind the polished doors and brass plates of Harley Street. The difference between these nations inevitably involved money: between £5 for a backstreet abortion and £100 for a 'West End legal'. But motive and morality were reversed in these worlds. Woodside's interviewees—about forty

---

[45] See Andy Medhurst, '*Victim*: Text as Context', *Screen* 25 (1984), 22–35. I am grateful to Lucy Robinson for this reference.

[46] CMA, SA/ALR/A.11/3/12, ALRA, Newsletter 14 (Spring 1966).

[47] *Daily Mirror* (London), 26 November 1964.

[48] Paul Ferris, *The Nameless: Abortion in Britain Today* (London: Hutchinson, 1966), 112.

women in prisons in London and Manchester—were mostly older and married; most were housewives; most were working class. Perhaps idealistically, Woodside played down the financial motivation for performing abortions. Instead, her interviewees provided abortion out of gender and class solidarity. Indeed, because of this, the abortionists felt little sense of wrong-doing, even while in jail: 'I knew it was against the law, but I didn't feel it was wrong... I'm not ashamed of what I've done, even though it's against the law. It's human nature, and women have to help each other.'[49] Most were convinced of the 'injustice' of class differences between rich and poor in access to abortion. Most also felt what Woodside termed 'feminist views', whether this meant believing that abortion should be a 'right' for women or feeling that 'women have to help one another' in the face of men's power and irresponsibility: '[m]en made the laws; men got girls into trouble; men ill-treated their wives and didn't care how often they made them pregnant'.[50] By contrast, Ferris's abortionists—the doctors of the West End—rarely showed sympathy with their clients. Abortion was a medical business, with a turnover of £1 million a year, built on networks of general practitioners, psychiatrists, and abortionists, fed by the middle to upper level of class society: 'typists, secretaries and suburban housewives, to whom £100 or £150 is a lot of money without being an impossible amount to raise in an emergency... Chelsea-type girls—models, secretaries, journalists'.[51] In this world, doctors worried about sailing too close to the wind legally and less about the social meaning of abortion. Dugald Baird, the Regius Professor of Midwifery at the University of Aberdeen, was a rare voice articulating a sense of conscience: 'I have not been able to stand by and see people miserable, without wanting to do something to help.'[52]

Ferris's work turned on the hypocrisy, untruths, greed, and desperation that underpinned the practice of abortion in Britain, whether in the backstreets or Harley Street: '[e]veryday the phones ring, the curtains are drawn, the lies are told, the money changes hands, the women breathe again'.[53] There were forces undoing this situation: the growing acceptance of abortion among doctors and, not least, the ubiquity of the experience wrought by the actions of women themselves. The choice, it seemed for Ferris, was between accepting a modern world, in which abortion might be an affordable service, divorced from lies and hypocrisy, and staying in a 'barbaric' state.[54] Thus, abortion was, like poverty in a welfare society, a leftover problem for a progressive nation. The abortion laws and the persistence of backstreet abortions may have seemed increasingly anachronistic and intolerable in a society in which the consumer magazine *Which?* could publish a supplement on contraceptives. The practice of abortion before 1967 became a critique of contemporary British society, especially its dark corners of insecurity, powerlessness, and exploitation.

---

[49] Moya Woodside, 'Attitudes of Women Abortionists', *Howard Journal* 11 (1963), 107–8.
[50] Woodside, 'Attitudes of Women Abortionists', 109–10.
[51] Ferris, *The Nameless*, 113.
[52] Ferris, *The Nameless*, 168.
[53] Ferris, *The Nameless*, 169.
[54] Ferris, *The Nameless*, 169.

The urgency of the abortion question was brought home in the early 1960s by two kinds of health problems. Reports into maternal deaths in England and Wales between 1952 and 1966 showed that by the mid-1960s unsafe abortion was the leading cause of avoidable maternal death. Highlighted by media reports of the horror of backstreet abortions, these long-term statistics undoubtedly did much to advance the cause of legal and safe abortion. A shocking tragedy in the early 1960s also did much to encourage public support for legal abortion. In the spring of 1961, there surfaced reports of badly deformed children born to mothers who had taken the sedative thalidomide. By 1964, 349 children had been born in Britain with serious deformities. International cases such as those of Sherry Finkbine in the United States and Suzanne Vandeput in Belgium underlined the heartrending choices facing women who had taken the drug. In July 1962, a National Opinion Poll showed that 72% in Britain agreed with legal abortion if there was good reason to suspect a deformity in the foetus. The threat of foetal abnormality became one of the touchstones of the abortion debate in the mid-1960s; indeed, *Abortion Law Reformed*, the 'official' ALRA account of the Abortion Act, was dedicated to 'the thalidomide mothers for whom reform came too late'.[55]

The driving force of abortion law reform in British society continued to be the ALRA. In the early 1960s, the ALRA underwent a significant metamorphosis. In 1961, the Association's annual report noted that '[a] more combative spirit is now apparent among our supporters'.[56] Over the next two years, the organization saw the passing of one generation and the accession of another. In 1963, Douglas Houghton became Chair. The new Vice-Chair was Diane Munday. Madeline Simms, who was the editor of *Fabian News* and a medical sociologist, joined Munday in the day-to-day running of the ALRA. Munday and Simms were a Jenkins and Chance for a more modern age—very much the models of a new generation of pressure group activists—representative, according to Simms's account, of the new blood in the organization: 'in their thirties and either had young children or were newly married'.[57] It is also important to acknowledge that it was the experience of having an abortion herself that had inspired Munday's involvement with the ALRA; getting an abortion involved her being treated 'like a subnormal child who could not be expected to make any decisions for herself'.[58] In this way, Munday's experience was one of the perils of middle-class sexuality, of a middle-class woman at the mercy of the medical profession. Abortion had underlined her lack of individual and gendered power in society. This eventually became a recurring theme in abortion advocacy. From the 1960s on, the message about abortion moved gradually from a connection with working-class sexuality towards the more general problems of female sexuality and women's status.

What we know of the membership of the ALRA in the 1960s suggests that its middle-class composition may have increased and that its links to working-class

---

[55] Hindell and Simms, *Abortion Law Reformed*.
[56] CMA, SA/ALR/A1/3/17, Annual Report 1960–1.
[57] Hindell and Simms, *Abortion Law Reformed*, 112.
[58] Hindell and Simms, *Abortion Law Reformed*, 113.

organizations were less important. A membership survey in the mid-1960s showed that doctors, family-planning workers and teachers formed a substantial minority of the ALRA supporters. Much less evident in the ALRA of the 1960s were the long-standing connections to working-class organizations. One memoir later suggested that about a fifth of ALRA's membership were also members of the Fabian Society, showing a continuing connection to the sphere of Labour politics.[59] Organization-ally, the ALRA enjoyed a new infusion of funds. It was in receipt of substantial support from the American Hopkins Funds Board, to the tune of about $2,000 a year, leaving the ALRA with an annual budget of about £7,000 by the time of the Abortion Act of 1967. Much of this money was spent on opinion polling. The association was more forceful and more scientific than its previous incarnation in gathering information about public and parliamentary support and in contacting the media.

In 1963, the ALRA restated its aims, arguing that a woman should be able to request an abortion from a doctor if it was necessary 'for preserving the physical or mental health of the woman', when there was the risk of a 'defective child', and in cases of sexual offence.[60] Three years later, a 'social clause' was added, which would make abortion legal 'when the pregnant woman's capacity as a mother will be severely overstrained'.[61] There was, therefore, some continuity between the 1930s and the 1960s in terms of abortion rhetoric. Explicit feminist arguments for abortion as the right of women as individuals rarely appeared in statements from ALRA's spokespersons or allies. Instead, eugenic arguments (about 'defective children') were common, or comments that the law itself demanded reform since it was so frequently broken. Class arguments were also notable; Lena Jeger told the 1964 annual meeting, '[t]he well-to-do could safely buy the termination of un-wanted pregnancies while others, often working-class mothers who had already borne several children, either got no help, or took terrible risks with unqualified people'.[62] *In Desperation* was a collection of ten letters sent to the ALRA; four of them were from working-class women.[63] The image of woman as mother was perhaps the most powerful touchstone. This situated woman not as an individual, but rather, as the Labour MP Renée Short wrote in 1966, as the 'foundation of the family'.[64] As in the 1930s, abortion advocacy was not solely directed at giving women rights, but, at least in terms of rhetoric, as a means of protecting the family, thus a kind of sexual maternalism. As suggested in the previous chapter, sexual modernization, at least in terms of reproductive control, represented a series of overlaps rather than a linear progression.

[59] Colin Francome, 'Fabians and Fertility', *Breaking Chains* 11 (January–February 1979).
[60] CMA, SA/ALR/A.1/3/20, annual report 1963–4.
[61] CMA, SA/ALR/A.11/3/15, ALRA, Newsletter 17 (Winter 1966).
[62] CMA, SA/ALR/A.1/3/21, Annual Meeting, 21 November 1964, Kensington Central Library; Lena Jeger, 'Personal Freedom and Social Reform'.
[63] SA/ALR/A.11/3/15, *In Desperation: Letters Sent to the Abortion Law Reform Association* (London: ALRA, no date [1966]).
[64] Renée Short, 'The Case for Legalized Abortion', *Evening Mail and Despatch* (Birmingham), 24 October 1966.

Newer strands were, at the same time, being worked into the argument for the reform of the law. First of all, there was a sense that the difficult access to abortion not only revealed differences between the classes, but also exploited women and either humiliated them or forced them into criminal behaviour. The latter was a point made, for example, by Lena Jeger, the ALRA's vice-president, in her column for *The Guardian*.[65] Abortion was increasingly a question of women's rights generally, rather than working-class women's rights. Those rights were not always placed outside of the traditional context of sexual life—marriage and the family— but it was still a question of gender rights. This emphasis upon rights was also increasingly reflected within the membership. There were a number of comments made about the distance between the ALRA's leadership and elements of the membership who believed abortion to be 'the inalienable right of a woman and her husband and her doctor to make this kind of decision for themselves, asserting that this is an area of private life in which, in a democratic society, the aim of the law has no right to reach'.[66] Abortion law reform was thus also moving from the rights of working-class women to the rights of women generally, and from an argument about class society and the family to one about privacy and individual rights. The adoption of a 'social clause' in 1966, meaning that a woman could justify an abortion for 'social' reasons, rather than as a threat to physical or mental health, might be seen as bringing together both an older rhetoric about class and a newer rhetoric about women's rights, albeit within the context of family life. In other words, two different kinds of protagonists—the working-class mother and the middle-class professional woman or mother—could be brought together in the same frame.

The medical profession was the most affected of all the elite groups discussing abortion. By the mid-1960s, at least at the official level, the medical profession wanted something done about abortion, but was unhappy at the prospect of control over the procedure going out of its hands and into those of ordinary women. There were four main groups involved in the discussion of abortion in this period, prompted by a flurry of parliamentary attempts to reform the law: the BMA, the Royal College of Obstetricians and Gynaecologists (RCOG), the Royal Medico-Psychological Association (RMPA), and the Medical Women's Federation (MWF). In 1966, all four released reports on abortion. Common ground could be seen between the BMA and the RCOG. Though they acknowledged that reform was inevitable, both groups were very reluctant to accept 'social' grounds for abortion, insisting instead upon the risk to life and health of the woman. Both wanted the decision for and execution of abortion to be left with the medical profession, the RCOG more narrowly with consultant gynaecologists, the BMA content with two doctors. In November, the two groups published a joint statement outlining their views. The MWF was similarly cautious, though it did envisage 'taking into account the whole family situation and circumstances past, present and future' as

---

[65] Lena Jeger, 'Law That Fails', *The Guardian*, 24 November 1964.
[66] Judith Cook, 'Interest to Procure', *New Statesman*, 13 November 1964.

criteria for therapeutic, legal abortion.[67] Only the RMPA favoured abortion in 'all social circumstances'.[68]

However sympathetic the medical profession was becoming to the reform of abortion law, it was certainly not on the basis of greater power for women over reproduction. In 1966, for example, a conference organized by the FPA brought together doctors and family planners to discuss abortion. Most of the doctors who spoke favoured a substantial reform of the abortion law. They also stressed the scale of the problem of illegal abortion. The conference concluded by resolving that abortion should be legal and a 'proper part of gynaecological practice' within the NHS.[69] Some of the doctors and family planners at the conference were more concerned with abortion as a health risk or as an uncontrolled procedure rather than as a question of women's rights. Women's voices were not in the forefront of this debate, but when women did speak at the conference, they did redress this imbalance. Rowena Woolf, who had worked in women's reproductive health for almost thirty years, noted a change in the attitude of women in the 1950s and 1960s: '[t]he numbers of women seeking abortion increase continually: they are less timid, less furtive, more determined, and more practical. They say, "I'm determined not to have this baby, and I would like this abortion by a doctor under reasonable conditions; but if I can't have this I will go elsewhere".'[70] Such women, Woolf argued, wanted a 'fifth freedom', echoing Roosevelt's 1941 speech.

Parliament had become the cockpit of abortion law reform in the 1950s. But it was a very different parliament that passed the 1967 Act. The Act began as a private member's bill, from a Liberal MP helped by an avowedly non-partisan group. But it is difficult to see the Act being passed under anything but a Labour government and without the backing of the parliamentary Labour Party. At critical moments, Roy Jenkins and the Labour government intervened to secure passage of the bill by allowing extra parliamentary time. Without this, the bill would have failed like every other previous attempt. The parliamentary Labour Party also played an important role. The overwhelming proportion of the bill's supporters came from the Labour benches. Finally, it was Labour parliamentarians in both the Commons and the Lords—Renée Short, Lord Silkin, and Lena Jeger in particular—that either prepared the ground for Steel's bill by attempting abortion bills of their own or, in Jeger's case, kept up public pressure on the question in parliament and in the media. The Abortion Act was not a Labour reform, but Labour played a large part in its realization.

This is not to say that the Labour Party of the 1960s was an unambiguously sympathetic vessel for either the permissive society or sexual reform. Peter Thompson has usefully pointed out the limits of 'permissive' opinion within the Labour

---

[67] 'Abortion Law Reform: Memorandum Prepared by a Subcommittee of the Medical Women's Federation', *British Medical Journal*, 17 December 1966, 1512–14.

[68] Quoted in Hindell and Simms, *Abortion Law Reformed*, 171.

[69] Resolutions, *Abortion in Britain: Proceedings of a Conference held by the Family Planning Association at the University of London Union on 22 April 1966* (London: Pitman Medical, 1966), 108–9.

[70] Rowena Woolf, 'Changes', in *Abortion in Britain*, 70. Dugald Baird had coined the phrase.

Party of the 1960s, particularly around homosexuality and abortion.[71] In Lancashire, Allan Horsfall's courageous attempt to mobilize Labour support behind the Wolfenden Report's recommendation was met by opposition at the local and national levels of the party.[72] Figures higher up in the party such as Gaitskell and Wilson were dubious about the electoral impact of associating the party with sexual issues. This reflects a wider ambivalence about public opinion and permissiveness. Dominic Sandbrook points to a survey done in 1969 by *New Society* that highlighted some popular disavowal of reforms such as homosexual and abortion law reform.[73]

All of these factors conditioned Labour as a vessel of progressive reform. But there remains little question that reforms such as homosexual and abortion law reform stood a better chance with the Labour governments of the 1960s than with previous governments. In part, this had to do with the sense that such reforms, particularly after Wolfenden, were overdue. In part, it had to do with the quickening efforts of pressure groups like the ALRA. Reform was also based upon contingent factors, such as the thalidomide tragedy. But the culture of the Labour Party also had something to do with it. This was particularly true of the Labour Party at Westminster. The enlarged PLP of 1966 was notably younger and more socially liberal than their predecessors. It has also been suggested that the PLP's frustration at the Wilson government could sometimes be vented through support for socially liberal measures.[74]

What changed within the Labour movement between the 1930s and the 1960s was that the strongest support for abortion moved from the margins of politics to the centre stage. Westminster became the main theatre of abortion politics. If the birth control and abortion movement wanted for utopian idealists like Stella Browne and Dora Russell in the postwar period, it gained something perhaps more prosaic but ultimately more effective: allies in parliament.

Douglas Houghton and Kenneth Robinson have already been noted as supporters of abortion law reform early in the 1950s. Both continued to advocate the cause in the 1960s with greater force. In a remarkable article for the usually staid *Labour Woman*, entitled 'Fulminations of a Feminist', Robinson lectured the women of the party on their feminist failings: 'the Labour movement as a whole . . . has been backward in the fight for sex equality, and for <u>personal</u> as well as political, economic and social freedom for women'. Houghton connected his own feminism directly to sex reform:

> . . . [a]nything which savours of bias against women or detracts from their dignity and equality as individuals and citizens arouses my deepest instincts for battle. I wish

---

[71] Peter Thompson, '"Gannex Conscience"? Politics and Popular Attitudes in the "Permissive Society"', in Richard Coopey, Steven Fielding, and Nick Tiratsoo (eds), *The Wilson Governments 1964–1970* (London: Pinter, 1993).

[72] See Allan Horsfall, 'Wolfenden in the Wilderness'.

[73] Sandbrook, *White Heat*, 190.

[74] Centre for Contemporary British History, *Witness Seminar: The Abortion Act* (London: CCBH, 2001), 36.

enough Labour women felt the same. If they did, our cruel abortion laws would have been reformed.[75]

Notably, he articulated a case for sexual reform that depended upon a rights- or equality-based feminism, rather than a class-based approach. Like Houghton, Robinson was involved in the ALRA at a high level. By the early 1960s, both Houghton and Robinson had risen within the ranks of the Parliamentary Labour Party. Robinson was, for example, Opposition spokesman on health before 1964. Both were poised to become ministers in a Labour government.

Lena Jeger became formally involved in abortion law advocacy in the mid-1950s. Jeger's husband, Santo Jeger, a doctor, had been the MP for Holborn and St Pancras South; on his death in September 1953, Jeger contested and won the seat, which she held from 1953 to 1959 and from 1964 to 1979. She was a graduate of the University of London, who had worked in the Ministry of Information and had edited the Foreign Office's official publication in wartime Moscow, *British Ally*, in which position she had been a colleague of Dora Russell. Jeger became involved in local politics in St Pancras after the war and sat on the London County Council. Once in parliament, she was counted among the Bevanite Left.[76] In 1955, out of the blue, Jeger wrote to Alice Jenkins expressing her interest in the abortion issue.[77] This may have originated in her own experience in local London politics; she may also have inherited the interest from her late husband, who had helped establish health clinics in Shoreditch.[78] Jeger proved a reliable ally for the cause in the Commons, harrying the Conservative Home Secretary, R.A. Butler, with questions on the issue in the House, contacting barristers defending doctors charged with abortion, and urging the ALRA to pursue a parliamentary strategy.[79] She became vice-president of the association in 1958. A year later, she lost her seat in the general election.

Between 1959 and her return to the Commons in 1964, she worked as a staff writer for *The Guardian*. It was as a journalist that Jeger made perhaps her most important public intervention on abortion. In the winter of 1959, before she lost her seat, she wrote a series of articles on abortion for the *Woman's Sunday Mirror*.[80] These not only set out Jeger's argument for abortion law reform (already discussed in the previous chapter), but, perhaps more importantly, reproduced the testimony of some of the many letters sent to Jeger in response to the articles. Most of these responses chronicled the desperation felt by women at their inability to control reproduction. A particular casualty was the happy marriage. In this, therefore, the idealized marital heterosexuality of the 1950s was shown to be an illusion. Again,

---

[75] Douglas Houghton, 'Fulminations of a Feminist', *Labour Woman*, 51/1 (January 1963), 8–9.

[76] See comments in Janet Morgan (ed.), *The Backbench Diaries of Richard Crossman* (London: Hamish Hamilton and Jonathan Cape, 1981), 890.

[77] CMA, ALR/3/4/66, Lena Jeger to Alice Jenkins, 14 July 1955.

[78] See LSE, Lena Jeger Papers, 7/3, Lena Jeger to Rose Heilbron, 14 January 1958.

[79] CMA, ALR/A1/2/2, Annual General Meeting, 22 October 1958.

[80] 'Abortion: Must This be a Word of Shame', 19 January 1958; 'The Operation That's All Right—If You Have Money', 16 February 1958; 'The Day I Tried to Kill My Husband', 2 March 1958.

6.1 'Lena Jeger, early 1960s', unknown date, unknown photographer, copyright London School of Economics

abortion became a critique of the assumptions of the affluent society. Many of the letters also pleaded with Jeger to provide contact information for illegal or legal abortions (which she declined); others acclaimed her as the leader on the issue: 'Thank God we have someone in the Commons who is prepared to fight to have the abortion laws changed.'[81] Back as an MP in 1964, Jeger kept up a column in *The Guardian* and used it to press for abortion reform. In 1964, she argued that the abortion law was a failure, impossible to enforce, widely ignored, and, given the advantage enjoyed by wealthy women, contravening the principle of equality before the law.[82] She also believed strongly that a Labour government committed to 'a programme of progressive law reform' had to think about reform of a situation that discriminated against both the poor and women.[83]

With Jeger, Robinson, and Houghton, abortion had important frontbench and backbench allies. As has already been discussed, in the 1950s, mainstream Labour intellectuals like Tony Crosland and Roy Jenkins had included abortion law reform in a brighter vision of liberal social reform that would loosen the shackles, not only of Victorian social mores, but also Fabian puritanism. Labour came to minority power in 1964 and obtained a parliamentary majority two years later with an influx

---

[81] LSE, Lena Jeger Papers, 7/3, Audrey Humble to Lena Jeger, no date [March 1958].
[82] Lena Jeger, 'Law That Fails', *The Guardian*, 24 November 1964.
[83] CMA, SA/ALR/1/2/21, ALRA Annual Meeting, 21 November 1964.

of younger Labour MPs, who were more socially liberal than their predecessors. Within the Labour governments of 1964 and 1966, key figures were sympathetic to abortion law reform. Kenneth Robinson was Minister of Health and, within the Cabinet, Douglas Houghton was first Chancellor of the Duchy of Lancaster and then Minister without Portfolio. Another sympathizer, Richard Crossman, held the critical position of Leader of the House by 1967. Tony Crosland was within the Cabinet as Minister of Education.

Perhaps the most important factor was the tenure of Roy Jenkins at the Home Office between 1965 and 1967. Lena Jeger remarked in 1965 that 'any private member's bill needs Government cooperation'.[84] Jenkins's predecessor, Frank Soskice, made clear that he would not grant parliamentary time to an abortion bill.[85] Roy Jenkins took over the Home Office in December 1965. He was on record as supporting abortion law reform as part of a larger vision of 'civilizing' Britain. Hoping to let 'some fresh air' into social policy, Jenkins indicated to abortion law reformers that he was in favour of private member's initiatives on abortion.[86] He was determined to grant drafting help and, most important of all, parliamentary time to MPs proposing private members' bills on these questions. He also was happy to lend his own public authority to such bills. The Abortion Act of 1967 of course depended upon the decades-long commitment of the ALRA and the personal courage of David Steel, but we should not forget the role of Jenkins. Jenkins quite rightly suggested that the private members' bills 'would not have got through had not I or some of similar mind been Home Secretary'.[87]

Support for abortion reform was, therefore, centred in Westminster in the early 1960s. In many ways, this situation was the obverse of that before the 1950s. In the 1920s and early 1930s, the Labour women's movement had been an important site both of support for the birth control issue and of controversy over whether birth control was a socialist question. This was much less obvious in the 1960s, even as some aspirations of the interwar period came closer to being achieved. There are several reasons for this. Not least, the ALRA increasingly focused on converting parliamentarians, the elite of the political world, rather than building up a groundswell of support among local women's sections. The ALRA's reliance on using opinion polls also suggested an interest in mobilizing public support outside of partisan structures. The leadership of the Labour women's movement continued to be reluctant to associate itself explicitly with potentially controversial issues like birth control and abortion. At best, the women's sections' leadership vacillated on the question of abortion. The ALRA thought, for instance, that the NLWAC had agreed to circulate two thousand of its pamphlets through the women's sections, but later in the year, the CWO, Constance Kay, declined

---

[84] CMA, SA/ALR/5/1, Lena Jeger to Vera Houghton, 27 May 1965.

[85] CMA, SA/ALR/3/5/280, Report of ALRA deputation to Home Secretary, 2 February 1965; SA/ALR/3/5/287, Memorandum by Vera Houghton, 6 February 1965.

[86] Roy Jenkins, *A Life at the Centre* (London: Macmillan, 1991), 177; CMA, SA/ALR/3/4/262, D.F. Pollack to Vera Houghton, 13 June 1965; SA/ALR/3/4/269, Roy Jenkins to Vera Houghton, 15 June 1965.

[87] Jenkins, *A Life at the Centre*, 208.

to use party machinery to circulate the pamphlets because Labour had not decided its policy on abortion.[88]

It was also difficult to see the Labour women's sections as vibrant a source of support in the 1960s as they had been in the 1920s. The generation gap within the party showed itself in the women's sections. Some sections turned their face against the dawn of a new society. The North Paddington Queen's Park Women's Section was noted to have 'closed its ranks' in 1963 as if battening its hatches against the coming storms of social change.[89] One cannot fail to be moved by the honest indifference of the Merton and Morden Women's Section to the party's attempts at tackling the brave new world: '[n]o one wished to go to the Conference about Labour in the 60s'.[90] And this from a section that, in the same year, sent in a pro-abortion resolution to the women's conference.[91] By the end of the decade, a common lament showed up in the minute books of local women's sections and organizers' reports: ageing members, a lack of new and younger blood, sections eviscerated by members' poor health.[92] The weakness in recruiting younger women for the women's sections had been noted in the wake of the 1959 election.[93]

There nonetheless remained some signs that women's sections and the WCG provided a consistent source of support for abortion law reform within the party. In 1965, the Putney women's section complained that party leaders had to give more attention to 'matters over which women are worried and distressed, among which were listed abortion law reform and birth control'.[94] The ALRA's main partisan political contacts on the ground continued to be mostly with Labour women's sections. And even if generational change was sapping the vibrancy of Labour women's sections and the WCG, they still were the source of friendly resolutions. In 1966, for example, the WCG urged the Labour government to legalize abortion and provide it within the National Health Service.[95] The ACLW passed a resolution espousing the ALRA's aims by 'an overwhelming vote' in 1967 after numerous pro-abortion resolutions were received the previous year from Labour women's sections. Most of these resolutions took the form of supporting the ALRA programme.[96]

Beginning in 1965, Parliament witnessed a small, but perceptible, movement towards abortion law reform. In the Commons, there were two attempts to pass a bill; both failed, but they helped indicate a way forward. In June 1965, the Labour

[88] NLWAC/M/71/12/65: NLWAC, Minutes 2.12.65.
[89] LMA, ACC 2417/H/36/15, North Paddington Queen's Park Women's Section, Regional Women's OrganiSer Report, 17 October 1963.
[90] LSE, Merton and Morden Women's Section, 3/10, Minutes, 28 March 1961.
[91] NCLW, *Resolutions*, 1961, 9, resolution 63.
[92] See, for example, LMA, ACC 2417/H/36/4, Carshalton South Women's Section, Dorothy Clements to Regional Women's OrganiSer, 14 August 1969.
[93] NLWAC/M/November 1959: NLWAC, Minutes, 5 November 1959; see also NLWAC/5/1960–1: NLWAC, 'Women's Organisation and Activities'.
[94] CMA, SA/ALR/A1/2/3, Executive Committee, 25 May 1965; see also *The Times*, 18 May 1965.
[95] See CMA, SA/ALR/5/1/2/4, Cooperative Congress, 26 and 27 April 1966.
[96] CMA, SA/ALR/1/3/23, Annual Report 1966–7, 4 May 1967.

member for North East Wolverhampton, Renée Short, put down a bill that would have legalized abortion in an admittedly narrow context: for the life and health of the mother; in the case of a pregnancy caused by a sexual offence; and when there was a serious chance of a 'defective child' being born.[97] Short's bill died from lack of time, a fate that also met a similar bill put by the Conservative Simon Wingfield Digby in February 1966. Lord Silkin's bill in the Lords was a more sustained and ultimately more productive effort. A bill passed in the Lords had no formal consequence in the Commons, but it would have been an important symbolic victory. In 1966, Silkin published his first bill, drawing heavily upon drafts by Glanville Williams. The most notable aspect of the bill was the attempt to have a 'social' clause, allowing a termination in light of a woman's 'social conditions'.[98] A second draft did go through, but with little formal consequence for the Commons. What Silkin's initiative did highlight was the various hurdles that awaited the passage of an abortion bill in the Commons.

In May 1966, David Steel, the recently elected Liberal MP for Roxburgh, Selkirk, and Peebles, came third in the ballot for private members' bills in the 1966–7 session. He was encouraged by Dick Taverne, Jenkins's Under Secretary at the Home Office, to choose either homosexual law reform or abortion, a clear indication of the Labour government's interest in progressive, sexual reform, if only by proxy.[99] Steel chose abortion.

Steel and the ALRA had a constructive, if somewhat uneasy, alliance over the life of the bill. The ALRA was never quite sure whether Steel was completely onside with their campaign; for his part, Steel was understandably interested in making his own way and his own name with the bill. In the beginning, the ALRA played a critical role in shaping Steel's bill. The drafting committee featured a number of Steel's parliamentary sponsors, as well as ALRA activists such as Diane Munday, Glanville Williams, and Peter Diggory. The bill born of these discussions was 'much as ALRA wanted it', though the organization worried that 'Steel had only a limited grasp of the subject and had not decided for himself which were the central issues'.[100] In the end, this proved an important point. The Medical Termination of Pregnancy bill Steel published on 15 June 1966 proposed four criteria for legal abortion, to be established by two registered medical practitioners. An abortion would be permitted if two doctors believed that the continuance of a pregnancy 'would involve serious risk to the life or grave injury to the health, whether physical or mental, of the pregnant woman whether before, at or after the birth of the child'; if there was a 'substantial risk' of physical or mental abnormality; if the pregnant woman's capacity as a mother will be severely overstrained by the care of a child or of another child as the case may be; and, finally, if the pregnant woman was the victim of a rape, under the age of 16, or 'defective'. With its explicit reference to abortion as a means of protecting maternity and the family, the third criteria

---

[97] *Parliamentary Debates* (Commons), 714, 15 June 1965, cs. 254, 256, 257.
[98] Quoted in Hindell and Simms, *Abortion Law Reformed*, 134.
[99] CCBH, *Witness Seminar: The Abortion Act*, 25.
[100] Hindell and Simms, *Abortion Law Reformed*, 158–9.

reflected abortion advocates' long-standing concern with working-class mothers. At the same time, the first justification offered a fairly wide interpretation of 'health' to include mental factors, echoing the desire of abortion activists since the 1930s. Both provoked attention and controversy. It was clear from the beginning that they encouraged fears that abortions would become too easy to obtain, whether because of the 'social' clause implied in the third criteria, or the wide definition of health suggested in the first criteria. In June 1966, for example, Dick Taverne warned Steel against pushing for a wide (and World Health Organization-inspired) definition of 'health' as meaning 'complete physical, mental and social well-being' because this 'would open the door very widely to abortion on social grounds and this is hardly likely to be acceptable'.[101]

The anti-abortion lobby was caught on the back-foot by Steel's bill, unorganized and surprised by the pace of change. Religious opinion on abortion was divided. The Anglican Church's left-leaning Board for Social Responsibility had published *Abortion: An Ethical Discussion* in 1965, which accepted that abortion might be justified if a pregnancy threatened a woman's life and well-being. Other segments of Anglican opinion, such as the Archbishop of Canterbury, were much more equivocal. The social clause prompted particular discomfort. Unsurprisingly, the Catholic Church in Britain set its face against any grounds for the legalization of abortion. The movement against abortion law reform gained institutional shape with the formation of the Society for the Protection of the Unborn Child (SPUC) in January 1967. This was not formally a Catholic organization, but many Catholics were involved. The Conservative MP, Norman St John-Stevas, was a leading parliamentary opponent of abortion. Opponents of abortion could count on the consistent support of *The Times* and the *Daily Telegraph*. The SPUC did attempt to make the anti-abortion campaign a mass movement, succeeding in gathering half a million signatures on a petition delivered to an (absent) Prime Minister.

For its part, the ALRA tried to rally support for the cause in various ways. It organized meetings and took out advertisements in newspapers. Perhaps the most 'modern' and most effective weapon in its arsenal was opinion polling. Through 1966 and 1967, the ALRA commissioned polls from NOP. It was able to do this entirely due to the American money supporting the organization. All of these polls showed widespread support for the reform of the abortion laws. In July 1966, for example, NOP did a survey for the ALRA of women's experiences, using a sample of about three thousand women. This survey showed a number of things. First of all, it suggested that nearly 600,000 women had likely had mostly illegal abortions since 1946. It also demonstrated that an overwhelming majority of women (75%) wanted easier access to legal abortion and a substantial minority (33%) felt that women should be the sole arbiters of abortion access—abortion on demand, in effect.[102] In February 1967, the ALRA could show that 65% of voters were in favour of abortion on social grounds. The main intended audience for these polls

---

[101] CMA, SAL/ALR/A.15/5, David Steel Papers, Dick Taverne to David Steel, 20 June 1966.
[102] Hindell and Simms, *Abortion Law Reformed*, 160–1.

was, of course, parliamentary opinion. The ALRA had attempted to map parliamentary support for the abortion issue in the three years after 1964. This support seemed to increase with each election in the mid 1960s. In 1965, for example, 150 MPs were thought to support abortion law reform; after the election of 1966, that had risen to 436.[103] Labour MPs formed the large majority of this number and the ALRA found that the PLP was generally supportive. There was a hardcore of opponents, most of which was made up of either Catholic or represented Catholic-dominated constituencies, often in Lancashire and Scotland.[104] Some leading female Labour MPs, such as Bessie Braddock and Barbara Castle, were non-committal on abortion, though the cause did enjoy the support of notable male Labour politicians such as Richard Crossman and Michael Foot. In 1966 and 1967, the ALRA launched an intensive campaign to mobilize MPs in the Commons, led by its lobby organizer Alastair Service, using letters and circulars and old-fashioned buttonholing. The thing that the ALRA wanted to hammer home was that the voters wanted, or at least did not oppose, abortion reform.

The second reading of Steel's bill came on 22 July 1966. Introducing the debate, Steel remarked that in addition to the other confusions and inequities surrounding the bill, the issue of class difference stood out: '[a]ny law which means one law for the rich and another for the poor is in itself unsatisfactory'.[105] The social clause of the bill also gathered round it arguments for abortion law reform that were echoes of the interwar campaigns and more recent discussions of the 'rediscovery of poverty'. John Dunwoody, a doctor and Labour member for Falmouth and Camborne in Cornwall, evoked the maternalist arguments for abortion when he stated that access to legal therapeutic abortion would help 'mothers with large families . . . with low incomes . . . broken down physically and emotionally' to play a fuller maternal role in 'building and maintaining the family unit'.[106] Others, like David Owen, then Labour member for Plymouth, saw the question as: 'a progressive and inevitable outcome of modern medicine'.[107] There was also considerable talk of the problem of 'defective' births. Perhaps the most moving speech was by Edward Lyons, a Labour MP for Bradford East, who spoke powerfully of his wife's long and difficult struggle to find a legal abortion after being told the foetus she was carrying was likely afflicted by the rubella virus.[108] Opposition to the bill came from both sides of the House, from Norman St John-Stevas and Jill Knight on the Conservative benches and William Wells and Kevin MacNamara on the Labour side. The Labour members tended to be Catholic or MPs for predominantly Catholic constituencies. Roy Jenkins made an important contribution to the debate. While emphasizing that the government's position was one of 'neutrality', he also made clear that he saw the state of the current abortion law as 'a major social problem'. In particular, he acknowledged the need to help those 'many women who

[103] CMA, SA/ALR/A1/2/5, Survey of Parliamentary Support, 1965, 1966.
[104] See CMA, SA/ALRA/5/1, Correspondence with Labour MPs, 1964–7.
[105] *Parliamentary Debates* (Commons), 732, 22 July 1966, c. 1071.
[106] *Parliamentary Debates* (Commons), 732, 22 July 1966, c. 1098.
[107] *Parliamentary Debates* (Commons), 732, 22 July 1966, c. 1114.
[108] *Parliamentary Debates* (Commons), 732, 22 July 1966, c. 1090.

are far from anxious to escape the responsibilities of motherhood, but rather wish to discharge their existing ones more effectively'. Jenkins avoided going into the social, economic, or feminist aspects of the question, but did paint the existing law as 'harsh and archaic', one that forced 'law abiding citizens' to become criminals.[109] It is notable that no voice was raised in a feminist argument for abortion law reform. Indeed, Steel made it clear that he and other supporters of the bill had no intention of opening the way for abortion on demand.[110] When the vote was taken, Steel's bill passed 223 to 49. The overwhelming majority of those in favour—some 167 votes—were from the Labour benches. Fourteen of the 'no' votes were Labour. The ALRA was 'greatly surprised' by the size of the majority.[111]

The bill was scheduled to go through the committee stage in January 1967. Between the spring of 1966 and the beginning of 1967, medical opinion organized. The opinions and influence of medical organizations, particularly the BMA and the RCOG, were crucial to the shape of the Abortion Act in this regard. In April 1966, the RCOG set out very strict criteria (based mostly upon risk to physical life or health, or abnormalities in the child) for abortion, to be decided by gynaecologists alone. The BMA followed in July 1966, similarly emphasizing that abortion had to be left in the hands of medical practitioners and discouraging any consideration of social criteria for abortion. In November 1966, the two organizations published a joint report rejecting both the social clause of the Steel bill and the clause dealing with pregnancies as a consequence of rape or sex under the age of 16. At issue was who was to decide a woman's well-being and whether the social context of motherhood had any purchase in the consideration of that well-being. The medical profession clearly wanted to have control over the first and to avoid any connection with the second.

Steel was worried by the strength of medical opinion. Lord Silkin felt Steel was 'getting cold feet' about the social clause.[112] Steel became convinced that the social clause was a liability in a number of ways. First of all, it seemed to invite medical opposition. It also seemed unnecessary as long as doctors were allowed to look at what Steel later called the 'totality' of a woman's situation.[113] Fearing that the social clause would be shaved off the bill in committee or in parliament, leaving no reference to the larger context of a woman's life, Steel took the unusual step of amending his own bill, withdrawing the third criteria (Clauses 1 (I)(c) and 1 (I)(d)), broadening the language of Clause 1 (I)(a)(i) to expand the doctors' consideration of risk to include 'well-being' as well as physical and mental health, and adding a new clause, 1 (I)(a)(2), permitting doctors to consider 'the patient's total environment actual or reasonably foreseeable'. Steel felt that this would placate the medical profession and liberal religious opinion. He also believed it carved out a middle ground for parliamentary supporters. Not least, he thought that the new bill

[109] *Parliamentary Debates* (Commons), 732, 22 July 1966, 1140–2, 1144.
[110] *Parliamentary Debates* (Commons), 732, 22 July 1966, 1075.
[111] Hindell and Simms, *Abortion Law Reformed*, 164.
[112] CMA, SA/ALR/A.16/10, Lord Silkin to Vera Houghton, 29 December 1966.
[113] CCBH, *Witness Seminar: The Abortion Act*, 47.

embedded the meaning of the social clause in the reference to 'total environment', later remarking 'the social grounds are there, buried in the medical grounds'.[114]

But the decision to drop the social clause was a huge disappointment to the ALRA. Vera Houghton complained to Steel that the ALRA attached the 'greatest importance' to the social clause because it was 'really the only significant reform' of existing abortion practice, in other words, the only real extension of what doctors were already doing.[115] Steel defended himself by saying that the social clause needlessly courted the opposition of both the BMA and parliamentary opinion; he maintained that the use of 'well-being' kept the door open for a liberal interpretation of the abortion law. But he was also clear that the point was to 'enable much greater discretion to be exercised by the future generation of doctors'.[116] By contrast, Diane Munday remembered later, 'most of the campaigners believed it should be a woman's right to choose with no kinds of conditions or approvals written into the law'.[117] Despite the grave reservations of many of its members, the ALRA Executive saw no other option but to continue its support for Steel's bill.

For two and a half months beginning in January 1967, Steel's bill passed through the committee stage. The make-up of this committee was determined by the proportions of the second reading vote; thus, there was a preponderance of pro-reform MPs. The bill as Steel had amended it in December 1966 remained largely intact. The ALRA's Peter Diggory played a crucial role in advising Steel through the committee stage.

Once the bill had emerged from committee, its fate rested with the amount of parliamentary time that would be granted for its third reading by the Cabinet. When the issue came up in the spring of 1967, the Cabinet did not discuss any substantive issues beyond whether the bill deserved parliamentary time. Lord Longford, the (Catholic) Lord Privy Seal, and Anthony Greenwood, the Minister for Housing and Local Government, were opposed. Ray Gunter, the Minister of Labour, and William Ross, the Secretary of State for Scotland, thought it was an unpleasant issue. Gunter and Greenwood also stressed that, along with homosexual law reform and the abolition of hanging, giving abortion parliamentary time associated Labour with a 'permissive, not to say beatnik, image which would not go down well in the provinces'.[118] Jenkins and Crossman were abortion's main supporters within the Cabinet, simply arguing that the bill enjoyed the support of the majority of the parliamentary Labour Party. In the end, the majority of the Cabinet agreed that twelve hours would be given the third reading. This was a critically important decision, unprecedented in the history of private members' bills.[119] The Labour government of 1966 did not initiate the Abortion Act, nor did it organize its passage through the Commons, but without the granting of parliamentary time, Steel's bill would have been left on the dust-heap like the bills of

[114] CCBH, *Witness Seminar: The Abortion Act*, 48.
[115] CMA, SA/ALR/A.16/4, Lord Silkin Papers, Vera Houghton to David Steel, 4 January 1967.
[116] CMA, SA/ALR/A.16/4, Lord Silkin Papers, David Steel to Vera Houghton, 8 January 1967.
[117] CCBH, *Witness Seminar: The Abortion Act*, 50.
[118] Hindell and Simms, *Abortion Law Reformed*, 196.
[119] See comments by Steel at CCBH, *Witness Seminar: The Abortion Act*.

Reeves, Short, and Silkin. Labour politics interceded in a complex, but important, way at this moment. It may have been what Jenkins called the 'liberal hour', but this was afforded by a particular kind of Labour government.[120]

The bill had its third reading in June 1967. Once again, the opponents of abortion tried to talk it out. When it appeared that twelve hours would not be enough, the Labour Cabinet again played a critical role in allowing the bill time enough for its passage. On the morning of 14 July 1967, Steel rose to conclude the debate. His closing remarks dwelt less on the opportunities that might be opened up for women and much more on the safeguards and restraints of his bill that would prevent abortion on demand, particularly in the central role played by the medical profession in the delivery of abortion. Steel's hope was not to open up abortion as a right for women, but to end the 'scourge of criminal abortion'.[121] Only the Labour MP Christopher Price painted the passing of the abortion bill as a triumph of women's agency: 'The public opinion behind the Bill is millions of women up and down the country who are saying "we will no longer tolerate their system whereby men lay down, as though by right, the moral laws, particularly those relating to sexual behaviour, about how women should behave".'[122] The bill passed its third reading by 262 to 181 votes. Labour MPs made up the majority of the bill's supporters; Conservative MPs made up the majority of the bill's opponents.

The bill still had to pass through the Lords. It faced some opposition, but survived largely unamended, with one important exception. An amendment by the Lord Chief Justice made the criteria for abortion about determining in good faith the greater risk: the continuance of the pregnancy or an abortion. Even if the continuation of the pregnancy entailed a relatively small risk, therefore, a termination could be justified. The Lords passed the bill in this form on 27 October 1967. Six months later, in April 1968, it came into effect.

The bill that passed the Commons and the Lords in 1967 was significantly different in wording from that which had passed second reading a year before. The new bill permitted an abortion if two doctors agreed:

(1) (a) that the continuance of the pregnancy would involve risk to the life of the pregnant woman, or of injury to the physical or mental health of the pregnant woman or any existing children of her family, greater than if the pregnancy were terminated; or

(1) (b) that there is a substantial risk that if the child were born it would suffer from such physical or mental abnormalities as to be seriously handicapped.

(2) In determining whether the continuance of a pregnancy would involve such risk of injury to health as is mentioned in paragraph (a) of subsection (1) of this section, account may be taken of the pregnant woman's actual or reasonably foreseeable environment.

---

[120] Jenkins, *A Life at the Centre*, 210.
[121] Hindell and Simms, *Abortion Law Reformed*, 200.
[122] *Parliamentary Debates* (Commons), 750, 13 July 1967, c. 1373.

Clearly, an explicit reference to both the social context of abortion and the idea of the 'overstrained' mother had been lost between 1966 and 1967. But this did not mean that it was not implicit in the new bill. It was, for example, notable that (1) (a) suggested (rather than stated outright) that an abortion might be considered if a pregnancy proved injurious to 'any existing children' of the mother's family. Similarly, (2) included the possibility of considering social or economic factors with its suggestion that 'account may be taken of the pregnant woman's actual or reasonably foreseeable environment'. But this would be the decision of doctors, rather than of women themselves.

The 1967 Abortion Act ended one phase of abortion advocacy. The same year also saw another phase of birth control advocacy coming full circle with the passing of the National Health Service Amendment (Family Planning) Act. In 1966, Kenneth Robinson, as Minister of Health, circulated a memo to local authorities authorizing locally run health clinics to provide free contraceptive treatment for 'the benefit of women to whom pregnancy would be detrimental to health'.[123] This led to the introduction of the National Health Service Amendment (Family Planning) Act in 1967, which opened up the criteria on women receiving contraceptive advice; there was no restriction on age or marital status. The Act also opened up the grounds on which such advice could be asked for, now including social as well as medical grounds. Again, it was a private member's bill, this time by the Labour MP for Bebington, Edwin Brooks. Brooks was an academic and former councillor from the Gilbrook ward of Birkenhead whose encounters with 'untold number of working-class women' forced 'to bear children they did not want, or to seek backstreet abortions' inspired him to promote either a bill on abortion or on the provision of contraceptive information.[124] Once Steel had launched his own abortion bill, Brooks was encouraged to pursue a family planning bill by Kenneth Robinson and helped with the bill's drafting by the Ministry of Health. The FPA also quietly provided support. There was little controversy over the bill, at least compared with the abortion campaign. It easily passed its second reading in February 1967 and received Royal Assent in June. *The Times* remarked, '[r]arely can a social reform have had such a loving reception'.[125] The bill permitted (though it did not enforce) local health authorities to provide contraceptive advice free of charge as well as access to contraceptive appliances (although, importantly, these were not yet free under the NHS). As already noted, there were to be no restrictions on marital status or age, though, in terms of the latter, girls under 16 would have to have the permission of their parents.

The debate on the second reading did reveal striking things about the context of the reform. Brooks's introductory remarks set the tone for the debate. Brooks placed his bill in the context of both long-standing and immediate concerns about population growth, about which he later proselytized in his book *This Crowded*

---

[123] Quoted in Cook, *The Long Sexual Revolution*, 302.

[124] Edwin Brooks, *This Crowded Kingdom* (London: Charles Knight, 1973), 102; see also Audrey Leathard, *The Fight for Family Planning*, 132.

[125] Quoted in Leathard, *The Fight for Family Planning*, 135.

Kingdom (1973). In rather melodramatic tones, he spoke of the 'mushrooming cloud' of the world population explosion without the 'pestilence and famine' to discipline 'man's genius for fertility'.[126] In this way, Britain had to act as a model to the developing world by supporting 'responsible and wise parenthood'.[127] But, for Brooks, the threat of fertility was also a domestic one and in this he drew upon concerns about the problem family, resistant to the reforming power of the welfare state and the managed economy, living in 'ghettoes of the underprivileged'. The state had to step in to save 'women on the treadmill of motherhood'.[128] Only Renée Short and Joan Vickers perceived the reform as one that related to women's rights. Responding for the government, Kenneth Robinson argued that family planning was an 'essential aspect of family welfare'.[129]

IV

The Conservative government of Harold Macmillan declined to pursue legislation on the sections of the Wolfenden Report dealing with homosexuality but the report did encourage the organization of homosexual rights advocacy and the gathering of sympathizers from parliamentary ranks. In the spring of 1960, Kenneth Robinson announced that he would press for the adoption of the second part of the Wolfenden Report. This encouraged the formation of the HLRS in May 1960. Though Robinson's bill was defeated, it set in motion a series of parliamentary attempts to reform the law, including those of the Labour MP Leo Abse (March 1962), the Conservative Lord Arran (October 1965), the Conservative Humphry Berkeley (February 1966), Lord Arran again (June 1966) and, finally, Leo Abse (July 1966). This last initiative, the Sexual Offences Bill, was ultimately successful in reforming the law.

The Sexual Offences Act has, like the Abortion Act, been seen as a kind of shorthand for political permissiveness in the 1960s. Its realization has much in common with the Abortion Act. It was certainly a moderate reform. In fact, though it did decriminalize homosexual behaviour in private, the penalties for public sex were made much harsher and the age of consent set high at age 21 (against 16 for heterosexuals). In this way, as Houlbrook and Robinson have argued, the 1967 reform only brought a particular kind of homosexual into political life—respectable, adult, private and civilian—but by doing so, reaffirmed the heterosexual norm.[130] It also left the question of equality and rights for homosexuals largely unresolved, a spur, of course, to reform in the 1970s and 1980s.

The road to homosexual law reform also shared common elements with the abortion law campaign. There was a link between a moderate reforming organization

---

[126] *Parliamentary Debates* (Commons), 741, 17 February 1967, c. 936.
[127] *Parliamentary Debates* (Commons), 741, 17 February 1967, c. 937.
[128] *Parliamentary Debates* (Commons), 741, 17 February 1967, cs. 938–9.
[129] *Parliamentary Debates* (Commons), 741, 17 February 1967, c. 1004.
[130] See Houlbrook, *Queer London*; Robinson, *Gay Men and the British Left*.

and liberal opinion, particularly within the Labour Party; the Labour government allowed the matter to be debated in parliament as a private member's bill, though not perhaps as generously as it had with the abortion law; and homosexual law reform enjoyed an effective parliamentary lobbyist in the figure of Antony Grey.[131] Grey was an effective pressure group reformer within the corridors of power. He worked with the HLRS and the Albany Trust. He was a tireless campaigner both in terms of the general public and, as importantly, the great and good of Westminster. A particularly important connection was with Kenneth Robinson, whom Grey called 'one of the nicest and most straightforward people in politics that I have known'.[132]

More broadly, the reform of the laws on homosexuality turned on the conversion of elite opinion and obtaining the apparent approval of the public. In this case, it was the opinion of some of the established churches that became a reference point. Leo Abse was, for instance, able to speak of the support for moderate homosexual law reform from the Church Assembly, the Methodist Conference, the Church of England Moral Welfare Council, and even the Roman Catholic Welfare Committee, all of which had, in varying degrees, accepted the need for Wolfenden-style reform.[133] In the midst of the 'secularization' of Britain, the churches themselves became agents of permissiveness in 1960s Britain. The 'revisionist' route thus depended upon the confident articulation not of a radical future, but of a modern present already achieved.

Being able to refer to public opinion through opinion polls was also critical, as it had been with abortion. Throughout the twentieth century, politicians were reluctant to speak in positive terms about sexual reform because of the fear of public approbation. This, of course, raised fundamental questions about what politicians were supposed to do in terms of opinion, a point made by Kenneth Robinson in 1960: it was 'frequently the duty of Government to lead and not to follow public opinion, and to do what they know to be right'.[134] But this duty was rarely taken up, at least in terms of sexual issues. Public opinion polls changed all this. In 1958, R.A. Butler, the Conservative Home Secretary, could assert that there was 'a very large section of the population who strongly repudiate homosexual conduct and whose moral sense would be offended by the law' without having to offer any evidence of this.[135] But eight years later, David Owen could use opinion polling to claim that the public, or at least 63% of the public, actually supported a change in the law.[136]

It is important to consider how homosexuality was constructed in the political sphere of Westminster. In fact, most politicians unsurprisingly disavowed much knowledge about either the practice or homosexuality as an identity. Given the

[131] See Antony Grey, *Quest for Justice: Towards Homosexual Emancipation* (London: Sinclair-Stevenson, 1992).
[132] See Grey, *Quest for Justice*, 42; see also obituary of Grey, *The Guardian*, 4 June 2010.
[133] See *Parliamentary Debates* (Commons), 19 December 1966, c. 1072.
[134] *Parliamentary Debates* (Commons), 29 June 1960, c. 1458.
[135] *Parliamentary Debates* (Commons), 26 November 1958, c. 370.
[136] *Parliamentary Debates* (Commons), 19 December 1966, c. 107.

male dominance of the two houses at this time, this is perhaps unsurprising. The Labour MP Eirene White made an acute (and unchallenged) point in 1960 when she said 'that in considering the subject of male homosexuality a number of men consciously or subconsciously are moved to vehement condemnation by some feeling that they have to assert their own virility in the process'.[137] The same might be said of the often-condescending compassion enunciated in favour of reform. The dominant view of the homosexual from supporters of law reform was coloured by pity. There was little discussion of rights (with one important exception) and a greater focus upon compassion rather than condemnation. The main difficulty for these supporters of law reform was that people with a disability, an unexplainable deviance, were being made into criminals for their weakness. The sponsor of the Sexual Offences Act, Leo Abse, caught this approach when he said, in 1966, that parliament were dealing with 'large numbers of people—many of them, apart from this particular aberration, who are totally law-abiding'.[138] This had an echo in abortion law reform, that the law had forced 'good' people, with a weakness, into criminal behaviour. Others saw the laws on homosexuality creating both criminals and victims. The veteran Tribunite G.R. Strauss called the existing laws a 'blackmailers' charter'.[139]

There were far fewer voices speaking of the need to reform the law as a means either of reforming British society more generally or as a means of protecting human rights. Kenneth Robinson has already been noted as an early champion of homosexual law reform as a 'matter of tolerance and common justice'.[140] Support also tended to come from those considered revisionists. Douglas Jay—President of the Board of Trade between 1964 and 1967—was a notable example. In 1960, he remarked that 'our criminal law on this issue at present discriminates against one minority and in doing that . . . it infringes on the essential liberty of the individual'.[141] Two years previous, Jay went so far as to say such discrimination led 'eventually to concentration camps and the persecution of heretics'.[142] It was often pointed out, in this respect, that adulterous heterosexuals and lesbians were exempt from the law in a way that homosexuals were not, even if such behaviour still offended morals. As Roy Jenkins pointed out, this was the law's 'illogical position'.[143] Other Labour figures felt that the laws on homosexuality violated the right of privacy. In 1966, David Owen argued that homosexuals were asking 'not to affect the morals of society, not to live flagrantly or openly, but to live in their private life as their sexual drive dictates to them to do'.[144] It was often pointed out, with respect to both rights and privacy, that only Britain and the Federal Republic of Germany had laws discriminating against homosexual behaviour between consenting adults in private.

---

[137] *Parliamentary Debates* (Commons), 29 June 1960, c. 1468.
[138] *Parliamentary Debates* (Commons), 19 December 1966, c. 1072.
[139] *Parliamentary Debates* (Commons), 19 December 1966, c. 1096.
[140] Grey, *Quest for Justice*, 42.
[141] *Parliamentary Debates* (Commons), 29 June 1960, c. 1490.
[142] *Parliamentary Debates* (Commons), 28 November 1958, c. 450.
[143] *Parliamentary Debates* (Commons), 29 June 1960, c. 1508.
[144] *Parliamentary Debates* (Commons), 19 December 1966, c. 1111.

Kenneth Robinson wanted to bring Britain into line with other European countries; Roy Jenkins wanted 'a reasonable law for a civilized country'.[145]

Labour was also home to a significant body of opposition to any reform of the laws on homosexuality. Often as not, this opposition came in the form of prejudice, a prejudice that was consistent through the period between Wolfenden and the Sexual Offences Act, even if it did diminish in intensity as the 1960s went on. In 1958, it was, however, in full flower. The two main hammers of Wolfenden were Fred Bellenger and Jean Mann. The former called homosexuals a 'malignant canker in the community', a 'cult' that would force humanity to 'revert to an animal existence'.[146] The latter implied that homosexuality was not simply an abhorrent sexual deviance, but a kind of social conspiracy promulgated by the media and the entertaining classes, an 'evil thread [running] through the theatre, through the music hall, through the Press, and through the BBC'.[147] In the 1960s, the Mahon brothers of Bootle, Peter and Simon, took up the cudgel of Labour resistance to homosexual law reform, to the point that they proudly wore the badge of Labour 'reactionaries' presented to them by the *Tribune*. The Labour MP A.D.D. Broughton voiced the fear that homosexuals empowered by the implementation of Wolfenden might actually act like normal people: 'They may go to the extent even of showing some signs of the affection that they have for one another in public. I can envisage men walking along the street arm in arm, possibly holding hands, and at dances perhaps wishing to dance together and even caressing in public.'[148] In his professional life, Broughton was a psychiatrist.

In political discourse at this time, homosexuality provoked both anxiety and pity. It appeared as a condition or pathology that is, at once, a contagion, a conspiracy, an affront to the natural and spiritual realm, and a door into crime or mental illness. The bid to reform homosexuality was coloured not with the expression of community with citizens suffering discrimination, but rather with condescension and pity for victims of an incurable illness. What remained was the unknown quality of the homosexual, homosexual identity, and homosexual activity.

The unlikely champion of homosexual law reform on the Labour benches was Leo Abse, a Cardiff solicitor who had been elected to the House in 1958 for the Monmouthshire constituency of Pontypool. Abse's insistent Freudianism renders his memoir virtually unreadable, but it is clear that this intellectual position afforded him considerable interest in matters of morality and sexuality. Soon after his entry into the House, he began to pursue what he called his 'sex' bills. But Abse was not a sexual liberal in all respects. He was a staunch opponent of abortion law reform. Indeed, he had a savage dislike for abortion reformers, calling them 'intelligent shrill viragos', claiming Janet Chance, Stella Browne, and Alice Jenkins were afflicted with 'pathological disorder' and 'resented their feminine

---

[145] *Parliamentary Debates* (Commons), 29 June 1960, c. 1509.
[146] *Parliamentary Debates* (Commons), 26 November 1958, c. 417.
[147] *Parliamentary Debates* (Commons), 26 November 1958, c. 458.
[148] *Parliamentary Debates* (Commons), 26 November 1958, c. 443.

identity'; Abse nurtured a particular distaste for Browne, calling her a 'loud-mouthed, filthy storytelling ragbag'.[149] But Abse was a strong supporter of homosexual law reform, though he was heterosexual. He introduced a bill in March 1962 and, in July 1966, following Lord Arran's bill in the Lords, introduced the Sexual Offences Bill in the Commons.

What differed between homosexual law reform and abortion law reform was in the relationship between the respective lobbies and their parliamentary sponsors. Anthony Grey has already been noted as the moving force behind the HLRS; he had also written the main clause of Arran's bill in the Lords and had good connections with the Labour Party by the mid-1960s.[150] But he and Abse were not allies in the cause of homosexual law reform. Grey found Abse remote and indifferent to 'pleas for a better Bill . . . he made a virtue of his unsympathetic treatment of us'.[151] For his part, Abse did not want to be the poodle of any lobbying organization.[152] This lack of influence undoubtedly shaped the content and tone of the bill, which seemed to approach homosexuality at best with a benevolent condescension. But, like the abortion law reform initiative, Abse's bill did enjoy the support of the Labour Home Office. Once again, Jenkins helped out with drafting and parliamentary time. The reaction to this was not entirely positive. Richard Crossman remarked that it had 'gone down very badly that the Labour Party should be associated with such a Bill'.[153]

The first clause of the Sexual Offences Bill decriminalized homosexual acts between consenting adults (meaning men over 21). There were significant exceptions to this: the armed services and the merchant navy. Other clauses in the bill actually increased the punishment for homosexual acts. Such acts between men over 21 and consenting youths over 16 would, for example, be punished by a prison term of five, rather than two, years. The bill also extended the law against prostitution to male prostitutes. As Houlbrook and others have suggested, the bill brought a particular kind of queer subject into legitimacy: the respectable homosexual, whose sexual difference, behaviour, and desires remained firmly behind closed doors. It was a bill more about sexual diffidence than difference.

The dominant tone of the parliamentary debate on the Sexual Offences Bill was one of pity for the homosexual and a kind of empathetic distaste for his predicament, rather than an acknowledgement of homosexual rights. Indeed, one might argue that the real subject brought to life in 1966 and 1967 was not the respectable homosexual, but the pitiable homosexual. Abse described homosexuals as 'lamentably different in direction' from heterosexuals. The 'paramount reason for the introduction' of his bill was not to encourage homosexuality but to 'prevent . . . little boys from growing up to be adult homosexuals'.[154] Cleaving closely to his own Freudian perspective,

---

[149] Leo Abse, *Private Member* (London: MacDonald, 1973), 218.
[150] See Weeks, *Coming Out*, 173.
[151] Grey, *Quest for Justice*, 91, 106, 129.
[152] Abse, *Private Member*.
[153] Richard Crossman, *Diaries* II, 172, 407.
[154] *Parliamentary Debates* (Commons), 19 December 1966, cs. 1070, 1078.

Abse maintained that 'mature love' could only be found with a woman.[155] But these impediments to a normal sexual and emotional life for homosexuals could not, in Abse's opinion, be the basis for criminal discrimination. Pity and fairness demanded the abandonment of restrictive legislation against homosexuality. Private, respectable homosexuals were not accorded fair treatment under law, refusing them the choice of living 'out their lives in discretion... away from public view'.[156] As long as homosexuality could be lived off the public stage, the pity Abse felt for homosexuals could be translated into political reform. Other Labour speakers followed a similar line. David Owen made a clear distinction between the '"queer" [and] the "nancy boy"', the 'homosexual who goes about importuning and soliciting' and the respectable homosexual: '[w]e are thinking of the men who live a haunted existence, who are asking through this Bill only for the right to live within the privacy of their own houses as they wish to live'.[157] But Owen also made sure to state that the bill did not condone homosexuality.[158] When Roy Jenkins came to speak, it was again with the tone of pity, rather than empowerment: 'it is a disability and a very real disability for those who suffer it, which greatly minimizes their chances of finding ordinary stable relationships. The question that we have to answer is whether on top of that disability, we should subject these people to the rigours of the criminal law.'[159] Other speakers from the Labour and Conservative benches followed similar lines. The ground of opposition to the bill, particularly in its second reading, rested upon the status of the Merchant Navy and how the bill applied to merchant seamen.

The vote for the first reading saw 244 MPs voting in favour of the Sexual Offences Act and 100 against. Of those MPs voting in favour, 180 were Labour. This represented 74% of the entire vote in favour and, perhaps more importantly, nearly half of the entire PLP elected in March 1966. By contrast, only 20% of the Conservative parliamentary party voted for the bill. Of those rejecting reform, 30 were Labour MPs, of which one third were from Scotland and most of the rest were from northern constituencies. But Conservatives were more highly represented in the votes against. They represented 27% of the entire Parliamentary Conservative Party.

As with abortion law reform, it was Parliament that changed the framework of sexual life in Britain. And, again as with abortion law reform, legal change to homosexuality raised a number of questions about the sexual subjects it brought to legitimacy. As much as we might ask what power women were given over their bodies with the Abortion Act, we have to think about the possibilities afforded homosexuals in 1967. 'Liberation' was limited to the home; only a particular kind of queer man was granted sexual rights. Though it is difficult to see how any other form of homosexual law reform could have occurred in the particular circumstances of the 1960s—in this way, respectability, like maternalism, was an ambiguous, but

[155] *Parliamentary Debates* (Commons), 5 July 1966, c. 261.
[156] *Parliamentary Debates* (Commons), 19 December 1966, c. 1070.
[157] *Parliamentary Debates* (Commons), 19 December 1966, c. 1111.
[158] *Parliamentary Debates* (Commons), 19 December 1966, cs. 1108, 1111.
[159] *Parliamentary Debates* (Commons), 19 December 1966, cs. 1141–2.

important, vehicle of reform—obviously this marked a beginning, rather than an end to the question of homosexual rights.

Even if parliament helped set the framework of homosexual life in 1967, it is important to move the narrative away from Westminster. The story of Allan Horsfall was told at the beginning of this book. Faced with the resistance of his local Labour Party to the pursuit of homosexual law reform, Horsfall persisted with the issue. At the party's Scarborough conference of 1961, he lobbied MPs to support Wolfenden. After moving to Bolton, he challenged police prosecutions of gay men. Not least, Horsfall wanted to 'explode' the idea that working-class culture was naturally homophobic. The 'hard resistance' to homosexuality often spoken about by miners' MPs, for example, he found absurd working within the mining industry and seeing no evidence for it.[160] Horsfall also played a critical role in moving homosexual advocacy out of London. Against the wishes of some in the HLRS, he established the North Western Homosexual Reform Committee (NWHRC), which became the Campaign for Homosexual Equality (CHE). The CHE became an important organization in the post-1967 history of gay rights. In that history, important unresolved questions were tackled, not least equality in terms of the age of consent, the application of the law outside England and Wales, and homosexuality in the armed forces.

Thus 1967 both ended one period of sexual politics and set the parameters for another. It is, however, critical to understand that this was not a clean break between particular traditions or ideologies. As has been suggested in previous chapters, the unfolding of sexual reform was partial and uneven, as much rooted in the past as responding to changes of the present. In 1969, for example, a Divorce Act was passed. Again, this began as a private member's bill, enjoyed cross-party support (though with more proportionally from the Labour Party than the Conservatives) and was granted extra parliamentary time by the Labour government. It was a significant reform, making marital breakdown the main justification for divorce, thus making divorce much easier and less costly for men and women. Sometimes, this has been seen as a product of the permissive society, reflecting 'more individualistic ways of thinking about personal relationships'.[161] This is perhaps what it became, but the Divorce Act was framed in 1968 and 1969 more as a way to 'buttress the security of marriage', to 'encourage family stability', and, not least, to legitimize long-standing 'illicit unions' and encourage people having children within legal marriage.[162] Women were given more power through the Divorce Act, and through the Matrimonial Homes Act (1968), but, as Lena Jeger argued, it was not a conscious blow for women's equality.[163] Thus, the legislative reforms of the 1960s, and particularly those of 1967 affecting abortion and homosexuality, in many ways left open the question of sexual reform, even if whether they did change the ground upon this might be debated.

---

[160] Horsfall, 1, 29.

[161] Adrian Bingham, *Family Newspapers* (Oxford: Oxford University Press, 2009), 48.

[162] Quotes from William Wilson, *Parliamentary Debates* (Commons), 758, 9 February 1968, c. 812; Leo Abse, *Parliamentary Debates* (Commons), 784, 12 June 1969, c. 1858.

[163] See *Parliamentary Debates* (Commons), 758, 9 February 1968, c. 857.

PART 3

ROADS FROM 1967

7

Second Wave Feminism, Labour, and the Defence of the Abortion Act, 1967–90

David Steel's Abortion Act came into effect on 27 April 1968. Its impact was immediate. Emergency admissions to hospitals on account of abortions dropped dramatically in the first year of operation.[1] The number of therapeutic abortions increased; this was perhaps unsurprising given the shadowy statistics on abortion before 1967. In the first year of operation, there were 23,641 abortions performed in England, Wales, and Scotland, three-fifths of which were done in NHS hospitals. The figure was 54,819 in 1969 and nearly 160,000 in 1972.[2] The number of abortions obtained within the NHS plateaued at around 60,000, meaning that most legal abortions were performed at private clinics. The growth in abortions was particularly apparent in women between the ages of 16 and 34.[3] In the first two years of the Act's operation, the vast majority of those receiving abortions (72% in both years) did so under the criteria of a risk to physical or mental health.[4] This remained true over thirty years later.[5] Despite some press titillation that London had become Europe's abortion capital (with 'package' tours for foreign women that included a therapeutic abortion), the actual number of abortions done for foreign nationals was statistically small compared to domestic figures.

Just over a year after the Act went into operation, Norman St John-Stevas attempted the first restrictive amendment to it as a private member's bill; more followed over the next twenty years. Between 1967 and 1988, there were four serious attempts to restrict the Abortion Act: the White (1975), Benyon (1977), Corrie (1979), and Alton (1987–8) bills. Each focused on either the availability of abortion, the definition of 'risk', or the upper time limit of legal termination.[6] None was substantively successful, but in 1990, in part because of continuing pressure from the anti-abortion lobby, the government-sponsored Human Fertilization and Embryology Act changed the upper limit for some abortions from

---

[1] In London, for example, such admissions decreased from 5,178 in 1966 to 3,445 between October 1968 and September 1969.

[2] See Data Base 5777 in http://www.statistics.gov.uk, accessed 18 June 2008.

[3] See Dataset D3459 in http://www.statistics.gov.uk, accessed 18 June 2008.

[4] Statistics from ALRA, *The First 18 Months of the Abortion Act* (London: ALRA, 1969).

[5] See statistics on legal abortions, statutory grounds, Dataset D5779, 2001, http://www.statistics.gov.uk, accessed 18 June 2008.

[6] There were also six minor initiatives.

the twenty-eight weeks set down by the Infant Life Preservation Act (1929) to twenty-four weeks.

In the two decades following the passing of the Abortion Act, the Labour Party became a critical element in campaigns to oppose restrictive legislation. This period also saw the party's treatment of sexual issues open up in ways unimaginable earlier in the century. In 1975 and 1977, the party's annual conference committed Labour to the expansion of reproductive rights, including abortion on demand. In 1982, Labour's programme included policies to eliminate discrimination against homosexuals on the 'principle of sexual equality'.[7] Three years later, the party conference adopted a comprehensive programme to promote gay rights. What had been undercurrents in Labour politics came to the surface with considerable force in the 1970s and 1980s.

Two factors account for this development. There is no question that Labour was changed from outside. Women's liberation and gay liberation—movements not simply outside the mainstream Left, but formed in reaction to its traditions—were powerful influences. If the revisionists of the 1950s had gently unlatched the window of socialist ideology to sexual issues, women's and gay liberation threw it wide open, insisting that socialism should include sexual issues and be about sexuality. As Geoff Eley has pointed out, this represented 'the collision of Left cultures' in Europe.[8] With 1968 acting as a kind of Year Zero, the interaction of women's and gay liberation movements with the Left illuminated a series of fractures about the culture, ideology, strategy, and structure of left-wing politics. Women's and gay liberation posed searching questions about the relationship between sexuality and left-wing politics, notably in the attention given to sexual and gender oppression and individual rights. Feminism challenged some of the fundamental ideas that had shaped the Left's approach to sexuality, notably the nature and role of the family. Animating much of this was the resurrection of an older utopian spirit that preached the foundational and transformative power of sex as a force in human life. Women's liberation and gay liberation were exercises in new forms of democracy. In such ways, both grew out of, and in reaction to, the faultlines and silences of previous socialisms.

The emergence of women's liberation and gay liberation also brought to the fore unfamiliar protagonists in the discourse around sexual reform on the Left: the independent, sexually autonomous woman, unmoored from the family and freed from an assumed heterosexuality, and the 'unrespectable' homosexual, whose sexuality was public and unapologetic. It might be argued that the meaning of sex itself changed in the 1960s and 1970s, becoming more clearly about the axes of pleasure and power. In that, it reflected both the continuities of socialism's engagement with sexuality and the departures witnessed in the 1970s.

But simply narrating the challenge of women's liberation and gay liberation is not an adequate explanation for the changes in the Labour Party's approach to abortion and gay rights in the 1970s and 1980s. Some part of such an explanation

---

[7] *Labour's Programme 1982* (London: Labour Party, 1982), 193–8.
[8] Eley, *Forging Democracy*, 337.

lies with Labour itself. Change also came from within. Two points about the Labour Party between the late 1960s and the early 1980s are particularly apposite in this regard. The first relates to the women's sections, trade unions, and the broader question of women within the party and its ideology. In the late 1960s and early 1970s, the Labour movement grappled with both the problem of discrimination against women in society and the inadequacies of the movement in recruiting and representing women. The outcome of such debates was nowhere near what could be termed second wave feminism, but it did prepare the ground for the reception of feminist arguments on questions such as birth control and abortion. Labour governments also passed two pieces of legislation—the Equal Pay Act (1970) and the Sex Discrimination Act (1975)—that began a formal process of addressing gender inequality. As already suggested, a third act, the Divorce Act (1969), was a private member's bill, but was given parliamentary time by a Labour government. It was also seen as shaping women's lives in the 1970s. The second factor was the general air of crisis that hung about the party in the 1970s. The civil war racking the party between the 1970s and the late 1980s helped open a space for policies on reproductive and gay rights that would have been too radical for the party of the 1940s, 1950s, and 1960s. Thus, the waves of feminism and gay liberation broke upon a shore that was already eroding.

This chapter examines the long defence of the Abortion Act, Labour's role in that defence, and the way that defence changed the party. It sets this analysis in the interaction between second wave feminism and the party between the 1960s and 1980s. The chapter begins with a discussion of the intellectual roots of second wave feminism and the emergence of the women's liberation movement. It then reflects upon the changes in the Labour Party and trade unions with regard to the position of women. Both factors were crucial in the defence of the Abortion Act.

I

Women's liberation was rooted in an intellectual critique of sexual inequality, femininity, and the traditional family. Simone de Beauvoir's *Second Sex* (1949), *The Feminine Mystique* (1963) by Betty Friedan, *The Dialectic of Sex* (1970) by Shulamith Firestone, and Germaine Greer's *The Female Eunuch* (1970) were internationally influential texts guiding this critique, but there were important domestic examples as well. *Women's Two Roles* (1956) by Klein and Myrdal is not often seen as an explicitly feminist work, but it did articulate a central ambiguity of modern women's lives: the tension between their reproductive and productive roles.[9] This was a question that underpinned feminist discussions later in the 1960s and 1970s. In *The Captive Wife* (1966), Hannah Gavron mapped the isolation of many married women in postwar British society, particularly in their

---

[9] See Jane Lewis, 'Myrdal, Lewis, *Women's Two Roles* and Postwar Feminism 1945–1960', in Harold Smith (ed.), *British Feminism in the Twentieth Century* (Aldershot: Edward Elgar, 1990).

roles as mothers; motherhood, Gavron suggested, could be a site of frustration and sometimes despair for women.[10]

With 'The Longest Revolution' (1966), an essay published in the *New Left Review*, Juliet Mitchell became perhaps the most important voice of feminism on the British Left since the 1920s. Mitchell sought to establish women and sexual equality as legitimate subjects in socialist theory. Women's oppression was based upon oppression in four spheres—production, reproduction, sex, and the socialization of children. A particularly heavy weight was the construction of motherhood and the traditional family as 'images of peace and plenty' when, in experience, 'they may both be sites of violence and despair'.[11] The way out of such oppression was to transform each of the spheres affecting women. Two things were critical. First, it was important to 'fragment [the] unity' of the traditional family, replacing it with the 'free invention and variety of men and women'; this would end the 'oppressive monolithic fusion' of the roles facing women within traditional families.[12] Secondly, women had to achieve reproductive control and 'sexual freedom'; the latter, in particular, Mitchell perceived as a possible engine of change towards the end of gender equality.[13] Mitchell's essay has often been seen as the first articulation of the leitmotifs that guided women's liberation in Britain, with its questioning of the family and sexuality and its attempt to marry a Marxist approach with psychoanalytic interests.[14] A much less deferential woman could be discerned through this writing.

The women's liberation movement emerged from the creative intersection of a series of inspirations, events and movements, many of the last produced by the particular radical climate of the 1960s, including the American civil rights movement, the radical student movement, and the anti-nuclear, anti-Vietnam war and anti-apartheid campaigns. The fractal germinations of the radical Left were also crucial, especially in the manifold blossoms of the American and British New Left and the Trotskyite movement in Britain. Of particular importance with regard to the latter were the International Socialists (IS) (which ultimately became the Socialist Workers' Party (SWP) in 1977) and the International Marxist Group (IMG).[15]

Generation was also crucial in the unfolding of women's liberation in the 1960s. Second wave feminism was driven forward by a younger generation of women, shaped by the changing social and political climate of the 1950s and 1960s. The story of Sheila Rowbotham should not, of course, be conflated with that of

---

[10] Hannah Gavron, *The Captive Wife: Conflicts of Housebound Mothers* (London: Routledge and Kegan Paul, 1966); see also Jeremy Gavron, '"Tell the Boys I Loved Them"', *The Guardian*, 4 April 2009.

[11] Juliet Mitchell, 'Women: The Longest Revolution', *New Left Review* 40 (November–December 1966), 11.

[12] Juliet Mitchell, *Women's Estate* (New York: Vintage, 1971, 1973), 159; Mitchell, 'Women: The Longest Revolution', 36.

[13] Mitchell, 'Women: The Longest Revolution', 24, 25.

[14] See, for example, Joan Kelly, 'The Doubled Vision of Feminist Theory', in *Women, History and Theory* (Chicago: University of Chicago Press, 1984), 51.

[15] On the radical British left, see David Widgery, *The Left in Britain, 1956–68* (Harmondsworth: Penguin, 1976); Robinson, *Gay Men and the Left*, 24–30.

Women's Liberation but it does illustrate this point. Rowbotham was the product of a Northern, lower-middle-class upbringing, who went from a grammar school to a history degree at Oxford, along the way encountering the disparate influences of Beat culture and Edward and Dorothy Thompson. By 1966, she was living in Hackney, pursuing a doctoral thesis in history, teaching young working-class men and women in Bethnal Green, and immersing herself in the far Left culture of the Young Socialists and the Socialist Labour League. She also became involved with the Agitprop collective, which used street happenings and visual art to push forward the radical cause. 'The Longest Revolution' prompted Rowbotham to reflect seriously upon women's position.[16] Rowbotham's nascent feminism revolved more around sexuality and consciousness than Mitchell's. Inspired by a variety of texts—the work of Nell Dunn, Doris Lessing, and R.D. Laing—and personal experiences, Rowbotham began thinking through the position of women, the nature of sexuality and the politics of Left organizations in 1968 and 1969. She also discovered the work of Edward Carpenter and Aleksandra Kollontai. In her memoir, Rowbotham recalled the jumble of personal and intellectual influences she was trying to make sense of in thinking through her own womanhood: '[m]e; Hairdressing girl; Brentford nylons; Birth control; Unmarried mothers; TUS USDAW; Ford's women; strip tease girl'.[17] She had joined the International Marxist Group in 1967 and the editorial board of the radical journal *Black Dwarf* a year later. It was at *Black Dwarf* that Rowbotham made a crucial intervention. Asked to edit a special issue entitled '1969 Year of the Militant Woman', Rowbotham gathered articles on equal pay, the Hull fishermen's strike and the women who supported it, child care, birth control and the family, as well as her own editorial, a call to arms entitled 'Women: The Struggle for Freedom'. In this, Rowbotham emphasized that the ground of transformation was not only the theoretical, but the ordinary and experiential: '[r]evolutions are made about little things. Little things that happen to you all the time, every day, wherever you go, all your life.' Women wanted to escape characterization as women, instead 'to drive buses, play football, use beer mugs not glasses'. In an attempt to confront the question of unity among women and economic divisions within the category of women, Rowbotham remarked that women were 'perhaps the most divided of all oppressed groups' and in that oppression, the 'women of the working class remain the exploited of the exploited, opposed as workers and oppressed as women'. But the editorial was not simply about liberating women from an oppressed position; it also followed the same vision espoused by Carpenter, Schreiner, Browne, Russell, and Mitchison, evoking a new society through a new heterosexuality:

> Men! You have nothing to lose but your chains.... There will only be thousands of millions of women people to discover, touch and become, who will understand you when you say we must make a new world in which we do not meet each other as

---

[16] See Rowbotham, *Promise of a Dream*, 115, 230.
[17] Rowbotham, *Promise of a Dream*, 209.

7.1 'Sheila Rowbotham, late 1960s', unknown date, unknown photographer, copyright Sheila Rowbotham

   exploiters and used objects. Where we love one another and into which a new kind of human being can be born.[18]

What differentiated Rowbotham from, for example, Mitchell, was this chiliastic sense of personal transformation between people and through sexuality—to 'touch and become', to 'love one another'—which had also characterized the work of writers such as Carpenter and Russell.

   But for Rowbotham, the road to the emancipation for women continued to be paved with the dismissiveness of left-wing men. Travelling to a radical conference at Essex, Rowbotham's growing feminist commitment was confirmed by the indifference and ridicule of male participants. Rowbotham recalled: 'I remember one left man coming up to me and with a pitying air saying he supposed it had helped me to express my personal problems but was nothing to do with socialism.'[19] Not for the first time, laughter was a radical catalyst. At a meeting of the History Workshop Group in the autumn of 1969, Rowbotham proposed a conference on women's history. This provoked the amusement of some men easily tickled by the broad

[18] All quotes from 'Women: The Struggle for Freedom', cited in Tariq Ali, *Street Fighting Years* (London: Collins, 1987), 232–3.

[19] Sheila Rowbotham, 'The Beginnings of Women's Liberation in Britain' (1971), in *Dreams and Dilemmas* (London: Virago, 1983), 36.

double entendre of Rowbotham using the phrase 'talking about women'.[20] Rowbotham's anger at this reaction, shared by other women, prompted the calling of a women's conference at Ruskin College, Oxford, in the last weekend of February 1970. From this conference, there emerged the four demands of the now more formal Women's Liberation movement. These included equal pay and equal educational and job opportunities and twenty-four-hour nurseries. The demand for 'free contraception and abortion on demand' was crucial in the aim for women's 'freedom' and 'control'.[21] The first formal articulation of women's liberation in Britain thus included an insistence on the transformation of repro-ductive and family life for women. Again, it cannot be said that this was an entirely new message, particularly about reproduction. The control of reproduction was linked to freedom and autonomy for women. What was different was the emphasis upon female individualism. Where in previous advocacy on sex reform, the context had been motherhood and the protection of the family, the argument found in the 'Four Demands' was much more reminiscent of the work of Browne and Russell, with its stress upon individual freedom for women.

The women's liberation movement posed an organizational challenge to the traditions of Left democracy in its insistence on a decentralized organization free from hierarchy, as in the London Women's Liberation Workshop, a loosely organized coalition of some seventy smaller local groups. Unity did not necessarily flow from this. The series of national conferences between 1970 and 1978 led to the addition of new demands—notably the right to a self-determined sexuality—but did little to forge a unified movement into the 1980s.[22]

The women's liberation movement gave voice to a series of important ideological challenges to Left thought on sexuality. One obvious area in this regard was the family. Women's oppression was situated in the structure and ideology of the family, such as the division of sexual labour between men and women and the exclusive association of women with household tasks and child-rearing. The relationship between women's oppression, capitalism, and the family became one of the most important and controversial questions within women's liberation and the feminist movement in the 1970s and 1980s.[23] That this was so underlines the socialist anchoring of women's liberation in Britain. Radical feminists insisted that the family was the primary site of patriarchal male power, immune to reconstruction and to historical change. Marxist socialist-feminists stressed that the family variously promulgated an oppressive bourgeois ideology, by putting a

---

[20] See Rowbotham's description of the origins of the conference in Michelene Wandor (ed.), *Once a Feminist: Stories of a Generation* (London: Virago, 1990), 29, 35.

[21] 'The Four Demands', in Michelene Wandor (ed.), *The Body Politic: Writings from the Women's Liberation Movement in Britain 1969–1972* (London: Women's Liberation Workshop, 1972), 2.

[22] See Eve Setch, 'The Women's Liberation Movement in Britain, 1969–79: Organisation, Creativity and Debate', unpublished PhD thesis, University of London, Royal Holloway, 2000.

[23] The literature on this is voluminous, but see, for example, the arguments set out in Michèle Barrett, *Women's Oppression Today* (London: Verso, 1980); Johanna Brenner and Maria Ramas, 'Rethinking Women's Oppression', *New Left Review* 144 (1984), 33–71; Michèle Barrett, 'Rethinking Women's Oppression: A Reply to Brenner and Ramas', *New Left Review* 146 (1984), 133–8; Jane Lewis, 'The Debate on Sex and Class', *New Left Review* 149 (1985), 108–20.

'brake on trade union militancy', promoting a false ideal of private property and individualism, and perpetuating patriarchy.[24]

This debate was a critical one, informing how feminists saw the relationship between class, capitalism, and gender and setting out particular priorities for feminist action, such as can be seen in the Wages for Housework Campaign. The canvas of feminist debates on the family is too large to examine in detail in this work, but several points can be stressed. These debates changed the meaning of the family in sexual reform. In the 1920s and 1930s, the protection of the family or woman's position within the family was a springboard for sexual reform, such as access to birth control and legal abortion. In the 1960s and 1970s, that springboard was the rejection of the family, not simply in terms of reproductive control, of course, but in terms of women's rights and, as will be discussed in Chapter 8, gay rights. Thinking about oppression and the family highlighted the question of sexual and gendered identity, and put this at the heart of thinking about sexuality. How people were made sexually and in terms of gender through institutions like the family became critical to the outlook and actions of women's and gay liberation.

Marriage and the current state of heterosexuality were also portrayed as traps for women, a 'fundamental form of social control' which contained the 'gross, economic, social and sexual inequalities between men and women', as one speaker told the 1973 Leeds conference on Women and Socialism.[25] Writers like Michaela (later Mica) Nava wanted a realistic recognition (in a way that recalled Mitchison, Russell, and Cole) of the absurdity of life-long sexual fidelity between two people and instead invoked a future that would accommodate all sorts of relationships between men and women, whether parental or sexual. The abolition of marriage would, according to Nava, allow the family to be 'liberated, not eliminated'.[26] Heterosexuality had to be, once again, reinvented, as Florence Keyworth insisted in *Red Rag*: 'Let us say that one of the great hopes for the future is that . . . eventually men and women will meet as free and independent beings.'[27] Keyworth's arguments brought out the common ground between the socialist feminists of the 1970s and those of an earlier period, the belief in the radical transformation of human society beginning with the relations between men and women or through sexuality. Sheila Rowbotham summoned up this lineage in her contribution to *Beyond the Fragments* (1979). Rowbotham's interest was in constructing a socialist feminism that would include a consideration of consciousness and sexual pleasure as much as oppression and exploitation. She asked '[h]ow do we conceive and imagine a completely different society, involving not only change in the external structures but an inner transformation of our consciousness and our feelings?' Part of the answer to this lay in a past tradition of socialism, of figures such as Carpenter and Browne, which had 'stressed the transformation of values and

---

[24] See Judith Brake, 'The Family in Capitalist Society', *Socialist Woman* (July–August 1971), 3–4; Mitchell, *Women's Estate*, 154–61.
[25] Women's Library, London [WL], 5/WSC, Leeds Conference on the Family, 1973; Lee Sanders Comer, 'Functions of the Family Under Capitalism'.
[26] Nava, 'The Family', 42.
[27] Florence Keyworth, 'Women's Role in the Labour Movement', *Red Rag* 1 (1972), 3.

relationships in the process of making the new world' and held out the possibility of a 'spiritual rebirth'.[28]

But, of course, this cannot be described as an untroubled utopian dream. In the 1920s and 1930s, Russell and Mitchison had combined a hope for the remaking of heterosexuality with a sometimes sharp and sombre view of masculinity and the emotional cost of sexual freedom. Feminism in the 1970s was similarly caught between dreams of a new world made through sexuality and the difficulties of relying upon sexuality to build that world. In the 1970s, this ambivalence could be discerned both in terms of male sexuality and the larger question of permissiveness. In 1976, four socialist-feminists reflected upon their own relationships in the light of sexual freedom and feminism. Part of the point made by these women was that sexual freedom afforded an opportunity to 'question male supremacy' and explore different ways of living sexual and emotional lives:

> All four of us feel that we need to know more about the alternatives in practical terms to the blood tie family, possible now, which can cope with non-exclusivity in sexual relations, the concept of the 'central relationship' in a person's life and the concept of the sexual relationship as the primary one and new forms of emotional involvements not burdened by guilt or jealousy.[29]

This was a road already mapped by Mitchison and Russell in the interwar period, of course. Permissiveness itself, even though it had been a handmaiden of important reform, was comprehended ambivalently. In *Socialist Woman*, Nora Vange asked 'can we be liberated at all in this society?' Reflecting upon the 'big business' of sex and the 'trendy underground magazines with their pictures of nude busty girls', Vange asserted that '[t]oday's permissiveness has got about as much to do with women's liberation as the plight of Jackie Onassis'. She noted that woman was the 'erotic symbol' of permissive society and, of course, this was a double-edged sword, at once signalling a newly won sexual power and autonomy and objectification and exploitation.[30]

Whether in terms of the family, marriage or the construction of a new world, abortion and birth control were crucial tools. In 1970, *Socialist Woman* argued that if 'sexual intercourse' shaped women's lives, they could not have the 'fundamental' power to control those lives. In this context, birth control and abortion were a measure of social change:

> When we demand the right for control over our own bodies we are making a demand which is not only poignantly and desperately needed by women now, but also a demand which rocks every assumption about the power of women inside society. Freely available contraception and abortion is a vital demand which has meaning to every female. It also has revolutionary implications.[31]

---

[28] Sheila Rowbotham, 'The Women's Movement and Organizing for Socialism', in Rowbotham, Segal, and Wainwright, *Beyond the Fragments*, 119, 131.

[29] 'Four Sisters: Vell Myers, Anne Mitchell, Adali Kay, Val Charlton', *Red Rag* (Autumn 1976), n.p.

[30] Nora Vange, 'The Permissive Society', *Socialist Woman* (July–August 1971), 8–9.

[31] *Socialist Woman* (July–August 1970), n.p.

Birth control and abortion became all the more important in this context as a means of exploring sexuality, in particular 'a reaffirmation of our right to have heterosexual relationships without suffering from the economic and social consequences of our sexuality'.[32]

As Rebecca Jennings has pointed out, the women's liberation movement lent a platform for the articulation of lesbian politics. This was not inevitable. The Women's Group of London Gay Liberation Front was, for example, rejected for membership in Women's Liberation.[33] But lesbian activists persisted working within Women's Liberation, and in 1974, amid some controversy, a sixth demand was added to the original four, that of a 'self-defined' sexuality and the 'end to discrimination against lesbians'.[34] This arose from discussions about lesbianism and heterosexuality and the first part of the demand, the insistence upon a 'self-defined' sexuality, eventually became the preface to all the demands in 1978.[35] The development of lesbian politics within women's liberation led to a split between separatist feminists, determined to avoid associations with men, and other kinds of feminists. Groups such as the Leeds Revolutionary Feminists asserted that women should be 'political lesbians', resisting sex with men as a form of oppression and violation.[36]

II

In the 1980s, Jo Richardson, then a member of the NEC, MP for Barking, and Front Bench Spokesperson on Women's Rights, recalled that a sea-change in Labour's attitude towards women and its organization of women coincided with the emergence of the women's movement. In the 1970s and 1980s, Richardson was one of the most important Labour women to push for the acceptance of sexual issues within the Labour Party, especially in terms of the defence of the Abortion Act. For her, the change involved a personal epiphany about attitudes within the party: 'I began to see how male-dominated it was actually and how patronizing it all was . . . like having a cataract and suddenly having it done.'[37] In the late 1960s and 1970s, there was a significant change in Labour's approach to women's place in the party and society more generally. This is not to say that Labour anticipated the challenge of the women's movement, but if it lagged behind, it was not by miles. Clearly, this did not win the favour of socialist-feminists in the 1970s, but it did prepare the ground for the reception of feminist arguments, particularly about abortion. The party changed enough internally that it was eventually seen as a suitable vehicle for socialist-feminist aspirations. This was particularly important in

---

[32] Angela Phillips, Dorothy Jones, and Pat Kahn, 'Abortion, Feminism and Sexuality—A Long Hard Look at NAC', reprinted in *Socialist Worker* 6/3 (Spring 1978), 8.
[33] Jennings, *A Lesbian History of Britain*, 174.
[34] Jennings, *A Lesbian History of Britain*, 175.
[35] See Setch, 'The Women's Liberation Movement in Britain', 91.
[36] Jennings, *A Lesbian History of Britain*, 177.
[37] LPA, Hilary Wainwright Papers, 3/6, interview with Jo Richardson, no date [1980s].

terms of campaigns around the abortion issue in the 1970s. Changes occurred both at the level of the national party (especially in terms of the constitution and the party programme) and at the level of the women's conference which encouraged the entry of more radical Labour activists. It is worth starting with the women's conferences.

In the 1960s, as the previous chapter discussed, the women's conference was suffering from a clear lack of energy and was plagued by an apparent inability to attract younger recruits. This problem persisted through the 1960s and early 1970s. The 1968 conference noted an 'ageing membership'.[38] There was little success in engaging young single women or young mothers. In the ten year period between 1966 and 1976, the number of women's sections also dropped by 35%. Female parliamentary representation was also weak. In the 1970 general election, only ten women were elected as MPs, lower than the Tories' fifteen and the lowest tally since 1935; the number of female candidates was also at a half-century low. This disturbed the national party in its aspirations to 'fairly reflect a cross-section of society'.[39] There was, therefore, a clear sense that Labour and its women's sections were adrift as a new age dawned for women.

Younger Labour women questioned the point of the women's sections. By 1972, many believed that Labour women should take a more aggressive stance towards the party leadership on their issues and make alliances with the women's liberation movement. Audrey Wise, the MP for Coventry West, argued that the old mantle of the women's sections should be thrown off and Labour women should 'join with Women's Liberation and other movements in asserting themselves'.[40] As the 1970s went on, there was a less deferential approach to the rest of the party from the women's sections.

To be fair, the party had begun to make an effort to address women's questions more seriously. In 1969, the NLWAC published *Planning for Women at Work*, which castigated the inequality and lack of opportunity for women at the work-place. Three years later, the party circulated a 'Green Paper' on *Discrimination Against Women*, which offered a broad survey of gender inequality. The paper presented a different view of femininity than previous party documents, with a greater emphasis upon women's rights and women's identity outside the family. The paper also promoted the need for reproductive control; sex education and a 'free and comprehensive family planning service' were 'very relevant to women's freedom of choice'.[41] The year 1972 also saw the national party conference discuss 'Women and the Labour Party', which tried to deal with the problem of women within the party in explicit terms. Though the document was sceptical of the women's liberation movement, dismissing the four demands as 'nothing new', its organiza-tion as 'unstructured', and its tactics as sometimes 'outlandish', 'Women and the

---

[38] *ACLW* (1968), 3.
[39] *LPCR* (1971), 17; Roy Roebuck, 'Fewer Women in Labour', *The Guardian*, 2 November 1972.
[40] *ACLW* (1972), 45–6.
[41] Labour Party, *Discrimination Against Women: Report of a Labour Party Study Group* (London: Labour Party, November 1972), 1, para. 11, 2, paras. 5.9, 5.10; 19. See also the important precursor, Margherita Rendel et alia, *Equality for Women* (London: Fabian Research Series, No. 268, April 1968).

Labour Party' did admit that: 'we are a very long way yet from equality for women within the Party'. It was also accepted that the party had long rested on a particular and static view of femininity, 'the woman Party member who has children'. It concluded that Labour had to find 'methods of correcting the balance at all levels' and in 'long term policy action'.[42]

Labour's interest in women's issues was not just about meeting the challenge of feminism. Instead, as Patrick Seyd has suggested, much of the impetus for thinking about women also came from the concerns expressed by the trade union movement.[43] Over the twentieth century, the TUC had done more to incite feminist criticism than support, but in the 1960s it developed a more urgent interest in women's issues. This had to do with the increase in unorganized women workers. In 1959, *The Guardian* noted that only 1.5 million of 8.5 million working women were represented by affiliated unions.[44] Obviously, this was a huge pool of potential recruits to the union cause and the TUC was keen to do something about it. Between 1964 and 1970 fully 70% of the increase in TUC-affiliated memberships were women.[45] Part-time workers were also targets for union organization. It is also apparent that women involved in union activity in the 1960s abandoned the sense of deference that had often characterized their predecessors' work. On issues such as recruitment, training and, most of all, equal pay, the TUC's Women's Advisory Committee and the TUC Women's Conference showed considerable impatience with both the Labour government and male unionists at the slow pace of change within the movement.[46] The TUC magazine *Labour* rather patronizingly referred to female trade unionists as the 'new suffragettes' in 1963, but there is little question that it was the union side of the Labour movement in the early 1970s that provided much of the support for the party's discussions of questions of gender discrimination.[47] In 1963, the Union of Shop, Distributive and Allied Workers (USDAW) put a motion calling upon a Labour government to fulfil the ILO pledge on equal pay; that same year, the TUC's *Industrial Charter for Women* demanded equality of pay and equality of opportunities for women workers. The growth of white-collar unions and a shift to the left particularly in unions like the Transport and General Workers (TGWU) led to greater assertiveness on women's issues. This included a discussion of questions like cervical cancer screening and contraception in 1965, an important step in the opening up of trade unionism to include sexual questions.[48]

The issue of equal pay provided potential ground for the convergence of class-based women's concerns and the women's liberation movement. The most celebrated and important strike came at the Ford Factory in Dagenham in the early

---

[42] *LPCR* (1972), 361–6.

[43] See Patrick Seyd, *The Rise and Fall of the Labour Left* (London: Macmillan, 1987), 47–8.

[44] *The Guardian*, 23 November 1959.

[45] Sarah Boston, *Women Workers and the Trade Unions* (London: Lawrence and Wishart, 1987), 265; see also Wrigley, 'Women in the Labour Market and in the Unions'.

[46] See, for example, 'Demand for Action on Equal Pay', *Labour*, October 1968, 5.

[47] 'New Suffragettes Stake Their Claim', *Labour*, April 1963, 74.

[48] See Boston, *Women Workers and the Trade Unions*, 275.

summer of 1968, when just under 200 sewing machinists closed down the works for three weeks in a demand for equal pay. The 'new militancy' represented by the Ford strike was followed up in organizational connections between unionists and the women's movement through the National Joint Action Committee for Women's Equal Rights (NJACWER), and new forms of activism, like the mass demonstration for equal pay of May 1969.

The most important example of a developing intersection between second wave feminism and the labour movement was the Working Women's Charter. The Charter had its origins as an initiative of the London Trades Council (LTC). In 1974, female unionists within the LTC set out what became a ten-point charter for action on women's issues. For the most part, this comprised industrial issues, such as equal pay and equal opportunities in apprenticeship and training. But the Charter also included a vision of the breadth of women's lives, notably in the support for reconciling women's productive and reproductive roles through the provision of nursery places and maternity leave. With its eighth point, the Charter also ventured into previously uncharted territory for union action, clauses that dealt with sexual life: '[f]amily planning clinics supplying free contraceptives to be extended to cover every locality. Free abortion to be readily available.'[49] As Ruth Elliott has suggested, this made the Charter critical in forging a bond between the industrial and the sexual and between an older tradition of women's trade unionism and the emergent women's liberation movement.[50]

Within a couple of years, the Charter had been adopted by a number of local branches and national unions, particularly those, like the National Association of Local Government Officers (NALGO), with a high proportion of female members. Support for the Charter was a recognition that women had to take their own destiny in hand within the union movement and this included 'the right to organize to discuss problems specific to women workers—such as equal pay, nurseries, abortion, etc . . .'. The thrust of this was a recognition that the association of the personal or sexual and the industrial was the only meaningful way towards true equality, as a journal of the Charter campaign argued: '. . . [the Charter] is an outline of the basic requisites for complete equality at all levels of a woman's social, political and economic life'. And in this, the Charter's proponents took up a women's liberation view of gender oppression: '[t]he source of women's oppression lies in the family, in our dual role as worker on the one hand and as wife and mother on the other'.[51]

Thus, in both the Labour Party and the trade union movement, older institutional structures were eroding not simply in the face of an external challenge from women's liberation, but also as a consequence of changing generations within the Labour Party itself, a new engagement with the problem of gender inequality, and, perhaps most powerfully of all, the working through of changes in the labour

---

[49] *Women's Charter* 1 (Summer 1976), n.p.

[50] Ruth Elliott, 'How Far Have We Come? Women's Organisation in the Unions in the United Kingdom', *Feminist Review* 16 (1984), 65.

[51] *Women's Charter* 1 (Summer 1976), n.p.

market. All of these were important factors in the way the labour movement dealt with questions like abortion and sexual rights in the 1970s.

Another element was the weak state of the Labour Party itself in the 1970s. Between 1970 and 1983, the Labour Party was more prey than usual to internecine warfare.[52] The collapse of its centrist social democratic core in the face of the twin crises of unemployment and inflation created an opportunity for left-wingers intent upon a more radical economic and foreign policy. The experience of Labour government between 1974 and 1979 also forced the two sides apart. More than ever in its history, rank-and-file was divided from parliamentary leadership. Their conflicts were fought on every level of the party, from the constituencies to the party conference, the party headquarters in Walworth Road to local councils, and over the most fundamental issues of ideology, organization, and decision-making. Labour's war had its pitched battles at the party conferences and leadership elections, particularly after the electoral defeat of 1979. Eventually, the new balance of the party—more towards the Left and the rank-and-file than to the parliamentary party—led to the establishment of the Social Democratic Party (SDP) by disgruntled traditionalists, most notably the voice of Labour social liberalism in the 1960s, Roy Jenkins. The civil war of the 1970s and 1980s was clearly a disaster electorally for Labour. But it did create a moment in which the new currents of women's liberation and gay liberation could find their way into party policy and party activism.

Rank-and-file activists tried to assert control over the parliamentary party and the policies of the Labour government. The route to this was through constitutional reform. In 1974, the Campaign for Labour Party Democracy (CLPD) was established by rank-and-file activists on the self-titled 'outside Left'. The CLPD aimed to make the PLP and the party leadership more accountable to the rank-and-file through issues such as reselection in the constituencies and the election of the party leader (which had hitherto been done by the PLP). The CLPD's strength lay first in the constituencies and then in the unions. By 1980, the CLPD could count on a significant measure of union support across a variety of levels.[53] The disaffection between the party leadership and union leaders like Hugh Scanlon of the Amalgamated Union of Electrical Workers (AUEW) and Jack Jones of the TGWU meant that the bloc vote was no longer so clearly in the pocket of the parliamentary leadership. The growth and radicalization of unions such as the National Union of Public Employees (NUPE) also fuelled the rank-and-file movement. In 1979, the aim of mandatory reselection of MPs was achieved and 1981 saw the establishment of a new and more open process of electing the party leader.[54] This was divisive. It witnessed the splitting off of a significant minority of traditional right-wingers such as Shirley Williams,

---

[52] On this, see James Cronin, *New Labour's Pasts* (London: Longman/Pearson, 2004).

[53] David Kogan and Maurice Kogan, *The Battle for the Labour Party* (London: Kogan Page, second edn 1983), 35–6.

[54] See Eric Shaw, *Discipline and Discord in the Labour Party* (Manchester: Manchester University Press, 1988).

David Owen, Roy Jenkins, and William Rodgers who founded the SDP. It also ushered in a long-standing period of tension between the wings of the party, with the rise of the 'soft' Left of Michael Foot and Neil Kinnock acting as a buffer between the old Right represented by Denis Healey and the new Left represented by Tony Benn.[55] Such divisions undoubtedly sapped the party's ability to meet the challenge of Thatcherism in the late 1970s and 1980s. But the arguments about party democracy opened up a space for the consideration of sexual issues. Sarah Perrigo has suggested that the crisis of legitimacy seen in the party in the 1970s and early 1980s allowed outsiders, such as feminists, to come inside the party and to work through constituency organizations, conference and trade unions.[56] The 1982 Labour programme, though ultimately unsuccessful, was a turning point in incorporating more obviously feminist demands.

As we have seen, some feminists outside the Labour Party began to accept the need to move back into the Left's mainstream, to engage with the political centre. Hilary Wainwright has chronicled the importance of this movement in *Labour: A Tale of Two Parties* (1987).[57] Though it operated at the grassroots, this change was also reflected at higher levels within the party. With Joyce Gould as the most dynamic CWO within the party since its inception, an important debate opened up about making the party's internal democracy more dynamic.[58] Policy discussion reflected feminist approaches, such as the rejection of the traditional family, as suggested in these comments from the Women's Rights Study Group chaired by Jo Richardson:

> The Party should not speak of 'The Family' but families and explicitly reject the Tory concept of the family . . . The Study Group should discuss ways of living with children outside the traditional family unit which rejected patriarchy and offered more choice to women.[59]

It cannot be argued that Labour was an unproblematically feminist party by the early 1980s. But the women of the party were a more radical generation than in decades, informed by a different and more radical set of assumptions than previous generations. This change helps establish how the abortion issue was received in the 1970s and 1980s and, indeed, how gay liberation was also received.

[55] See Diane Hayter, *Fightback! Labour's Traditional Right in the 1970s and 1980s* (Manchester: Manchester University Press, 2005).

[56] Sarah Perrigo, 'Women and Change in the Labour Party 1979–1995', in Joni Lovenduski and Pippa Norris (eds), *Women in Politics* (Oxford: Oxford University Press, 1996).

[57] Hilary Wainwright, *Labour: A Tale of Two Parties* (London: Hogarth, 1987); see also Patrick Seyd and Paul Whiteley, *Labour's Grass Roots* (Oxford: Clarendon, 1992).

[58] See LPA, NEC, W13/35/13/82, Submission to Labour Party Commission of Enquiry, 1982; NEC, W13/32/13/82, Joyce Gould, 'A Labour Party Charter for Women to Establish Equality for Women Within the Party', November 1982.

[59] LPA, NEC, Women's Rights Study Group, Minutes, 27, 17 February 1983.

7.2 'Jo Richardson, 1985', Keystone Photography, copyright Hulton Archive/Getty Images 3269780 (RM)

III

The early years of the Abortion Act's operation witnessed what became long-term trends. The first was the considerable regional variation in abortion access. Though the 1946 NHS Act required hospitals to offer a reasonable range of hospital and specialist services, there was no specific obligation in the 1967 Abortion Act committing NHS hospitals to abortion provision. In places like Birmingham, Sheffield, Liverpool, and Leeds, abortions were notoriously difficult to obtain compared with London, the Home Counties, Wales, and East Anglia. This imbalance became a recurring theme of birth control advocacy in the 1970s.

The second trend was a steady stream of parliamentary challenges to the law. This was despite broad-ranging acceptance of the 1967 Act. Opinion polls in the 1970s and 1980s consistently demonstrated wide public support for legal abortion under the terms of the 1967 Act.[60] Surveys of the medical profession similarly showed approval of the Act as it had been originally designed.[61] But, predictably, the

---

[60] In February 1980, for example, *Woman's Own* reported that 53% of women polled wanted the law to remain the same or be made more liberal. *The Times*, 2 February 1980.

[61] See Pat Healy, 'Abortion: Why the Doctors are Closing Ranks Against New Curbs', *The Times*, 8 July 1977.

operation of the Act and the increase in abortions also served to mobilize anti-abortionists. The SPUC became better-organized and better-funded than it had been during the campaign for the Abortion bill, with the Catholic Church firmly in support; it was joined by a more radical group, LIFE. These organizations worked hard to lobby MPs and mobilize grassroots opinion in constituencies.

Media coverage of abortion shifted from the horrors of backstreet abortion to the horrors of late terminations and abuses of the new law. This ranged from abortion touting for tourists to more serious allegations about the number and nature of late-term abortions taking place. In 1974, the *News of the World* featured lurid stories of abortion abuse written by Michael Lichfield and Susan Kentish, which were eventually published with the self-explanatory title *Babies for Burning* (1974). Most of these allegations were later shown to be false, but such coverage undoubtedly fuelled the debate about the working of the new Act and, not least, influenced MPs.

The Tory benches had proved more obviously anti-abortion than Labour and when a new Conservative government established an inquiry into the operation of the Abortion Act in 1971, there was considerable disquiet among abortion supporters. The Lane Committee sat for three years, hearing testimony from a wide spectrum of opinion.[62] Its final report salved the anxieties of pro-abortionists, stating unequivocally that 'the gains facilitated by the Act have much outweighed any disadvantages for which it has been criticized'. This went with a caution that the permissive society had 'been taken by some to unacceptable extremes of individualistic behaviour' and the acknowledgement that there were serious ethical issues around the termination of a foetus. The Committee did suggest that twenty-four weeks should be the upper limit of legal abortion and that medical practitioners had a right of conscience not to perform abortion if they so chose. But even with these provisos, any alternative to the 1967 Act was considered untenable. The report argued that the NHS should fulfil its obligation to 'provide a service for its patients who need abortion'.[63] The last sentence marked an important shift, recognizing the need to make abortion provision a part of the mainstream gynaecological healthcare of the NHS.

Events in the Commons and the growth of a well-organized and funded anti-abortion movement after 1967 led to a new style of pro-abortion campaigning.[64] The ALRA continued its work, but in a different direction. Having achieved the object of its advocacy, the association lost its major funding from the Hopkins Fund and, instead of immediately seeking a more expanded bill, decided that it would become a 'charitable organization for research and public education'.[65] Some of its

[62] See Ashley Wivel, 'Abortion Policy and Politics on the Lane Committee of Enquiry, 1971–1974', *Social History of Medicine* 11 (1998), 109–35.

[63] Cmd. 5579, *Report of the Committee on the Working of the Abortion Act* (London: HMSO, April 1974), paras. 608, 607.

[64] See Lovenduski, 'Parliament, Pressure Groups, Networks and the Women's Movement'.

[65] CMA, ALRA 1/2/4, Executive Committee Minutes, 6 July 1967.

members focused on the problem of regional access. In Birmingham, one of the worst-served areas, an ALRA member founded a Pregnancy Advisory Service, giving advice to its clients on abortion services in the area. This became a national model of coordination through the British Pregnancy Advisory Service (BPAS), for which Diane Munday served as Press Officer in the 1970s. As the number of abortions grew and the gap between NHS and non-NHS abortions widened, the question of access became an increasingly important one.

By 1975 more radical groups such as the NAC superseded the ALRA at the forefront of abortion advocacy. That the 1967 Act remained largely intact, even after the 1990 Human Fertilization and Embryology (HFE) Act, was certainly a powerful testament to the efforts of these groups. But it remained a mixed success. With the struggle so dominated by the defence of the 1967 Act, few realistic opportunities to extend its provisions in law presented themselves. The prospect of extending women's control over abortion was left unrealized. In 1988, faced with the prospect of yet another restrictive bill, one pro-choice activist lamented 'those years trapped in defensive dispute [that] had robbed us of momentum'.[66]

At the same time, even if the defence of the 1967 Act did not advance women's reproductive rights in law, it nonetheless afforded the deployment of a far more radical view of sexuality and gender than had been enjoyed or attempted by previous sex reformers. The struggle for abortion may have been about protecting the limited provisions of the Abortion Act, but that the rhetoric of this struggle featured slogans like 'a woman's right to choose' and 'abortion on demand' suggested a much more ambitious vision of women's rights. The 1970s and 1980s also witnessed a level of public support for abortion rights that would have been unimaginable to earlier generations of abortion campaigners. In June 1975, for example, 20,000 people took to the streets of London in support of the Abortion Act; in October 1979, a similar demonstration boasted at least 40,000. The campaign to defend the abortion law in the 1970s and 1980s served another political purpose, giving some degree of focus to the often-fragmented women's liberation and feminist movements. The defence of reproductive rights lent an albeit ragged unity to a movement that often unfurled in different directions almost as soon as it raised its flag. The abortion politics of the 1970s and 1980s also threw different methods of organizing and democracy into sharp contrast.[67] In such ways, the defence of the Abortion Act in this period served as an arena for the discussion of feminist strategy and sexual issues. There was clearly a disjuncture between the immediate struggle and the space of that struggle—the parliamentary defence of the Abortion Act—and the emergence of a newer style, approach, and space of feminist politics and discourse around women's rights and sexuality, including street demonstrations and an emphasis upon greater freedom and broader rights.

The Labour movement was a focus of the abortion campaign of the 1970s and 1980s. The NAC explicitly targeted the Labour Party and links with the trade

---

[66] *The Guardian*, 24 October 1987.
[67] Lovenduski, 'Parliament, Pressure Groups, Networks and the Women's Movement'.

union movement were critical to its work. Auxiliary groups like the LARC also played an important role. Labour MPs in the House of Commons were at the vanguard of defending the Abortion Act. Most obviously, there was an enormous shift in the party's treatment of abortion. For the first time in its history, Labour formally adopted abortion access as party policy. In 1975, in the context of a discussion on the NHS, the party committed itself to 'extended facilities for pregnancy testing, contraception, and abortion so that they are available to all women on request, free of charge'.[68] The party's programme of 1976 incorporated a commitment to oppose any restriction on abortion. In 1977, with the 1967 Act under serious threat in parliament, party conference expressed overwhelming support for a resolution that promised future legislation ensuring 'women's right of choice on abortion' and 'freely available abortion on request'. This was framed in a now-familiar feminist context— 'the right to control our bodies, our sexuality, our personal lives' as a fundamental right of women—and the aspiration that abortion should be 'one point in a socialist programme'.[69] These commitments were matched by the TUC in 1975. The TUC also organized the abortion march of October 1979. Thus, the very Labour institutions that had long opposed discussion of the question now explicitly promoted abortion. In 1977, for example, the National Joint Committee of Woking Women's Organizations (NJCWWO) encouraged its members 'to support the Labour Abortion Rights Committee either as individuals or through their organizations'.[70]

This change was, in part, an effect of the nascent women's liberation movement, whether in terms of the entry of feminist women into trade unions and the Labour Party or the influence of feminist ideas. The roles played by the NAC and LARC were certainly critical factors in this respect. But Labour's acceptance of abortion had other roots. It was, first of all, a response to events at Westminster. As in the 1950s and 1960s, the pace of sexual reform was very much dictated by events in the Commons and, more precisely, by a series of bills from both Conservative and Labour MPs designed to restrict the Abortion Act. Secondly, it was a consequence of changes in the trade union movement, partly, but not entirely, effected by feminist groups.[71] Nor was this an unqualified feminist triumph. The resolutions and commitments of 1975, 1976, and 1977 would seem to suggest that the aspirations of feminist abortion activists were realized within the Labour movement. But the party's approach to abortion in the 1970s and 1980s was conditioned by differences between the policy adopted by party conference and the positions taken up by some members of the PLP. In party conference, the defence of the Abortion Act became a means of promoting a wider vista of reproductive rights for women. In parliament, the defence of the Act was exactly that: a defence, not an advance. The conference's commitments to a pro-abortion position had to be balanced against the right of conscience on the matter enjoyed by individual Labour MPs. For many party members and supporters of abortion, this

[68] *LPCR* (1975), 235.
[69] *LPCR* (1977), 316–17. The vote in favour of this resolution was over 4.5 million to 70,000.
[70] LPA, NEC Minutes, NJC/M/January/1977, NJCWWO Minutes, 18 January 1977.
[71] See Rowbotham, *The Past is Before Us*, 64–5.

underlined the apparently weak grip of party policy on the actions of the parliamentary party and illustrated a problem of party democracy. One of the leading parliamentary defenders of the Abortion Act, Jo Richardson, reminded her own backbenches: '[a]lthough we acknowledged the right of conscience, successive annual conferences have been clearly on record in support of a woman's right to choose what to do with her own body'.[72] Despite these constraints, the level of Labour support for the Abortion Act is notable, compared with the Conservatives. In the division on the second reading of David Alton's bill in 1988, the vote for Alton was overwhelmingly Conservative, while the vote against was solidly Labour. The divisions on the HFE Act in 1990 similarly reflected a strong sense of partisan difference, even when it was a free vote.[73]

What is most interesting is the interplay between parliamentary and extra-parliamentary forces defending abortion in the 1970s and 1980s. The NAC represented a distinct Left and feminist organization. It often showed an ambivalence toward the Labour movement and the parliamentary route, at once understanding that the struggle for abortion had to be fought in the traditional corridors of power and, at the same time, was deeply frustrated that this involved accepting a style and mode of political action so at variance with feminist ideals and a deep compromise on the ultimate feminist goal of abortion on demand. For their part, Labour parliamentarians were more inured to the compromises involved in defending the Abortion Act, but could also use the campaign and the new energy of extra-parliamentary feminism to highlight other issues of sexual inequality, within Labour and British politics. In this, Labour women such as Jo Richardson and the CWO, Joyce Gould, played a critical role and, indeed, the abortion issue helped forge a collective sense among such women.[74] Thus, the sexual politics represented by the defence of the Abortion Act was an interplay between an invigorated, if, by definition, constrained parliamentary politics on abortion and a newer form of extra-parliamentary politics.

IV

Between 1968 and 1975, abortion advocacy was transformed by events at Westminster. The publication of the Lane Committee's report in 1975 elicited considerable interest from abortion advocates and feminists. Not least it signalled the new openness and radicalism around the abortion question within the ranks of Labour women. In 1974, the NLWAC welcomed the report; the Labour women's annual conference that year also used Lane's conclusions to stress their support for free and accessible abortion within the NHS.[75] Class was part of this, as one delegate

---

[72] *Parliamentary Debates* (Commons), Volume 926, 25 February 1977, c. 1871.

[73] See John Baughman, 'Party, Constituency and Representation: Votes on Abortion in the British House of Commons', *Public Choice* 120 (2004), 63–85.

[74] See Elizabeth Vallance, *Women in the House* (London: Athlone, 1979), 75, 88, 92–3.

[75] LPA, NLWAC, 'Statement to the National Conference of Labour Women, 1974: The Lane Report'.

argued: '. . . the profit . . . made by private practitioners from abortion . . . was a political class issue. The rich could easily get abortions.'[76] The ALRA similarly used Lane to highlight the continuing unequal access to abortion, the persistence of which was of greatest disadvantage to 'those in the lowest social classes'.[77]

In 1975, a much greater threat appeared which led to the refocusing of the abortion campaign. In early 1975, James White, Labour MP for Glasgow Pollok, introduced an amendment to the Abortion Act. His bill was not a full assault on the 1967 Act, but it did challenge the operation of abortion in Britain in substantial ways, focusing on regulating more strictly the private provision of abortion and lowering the upper limit to legal abortion to twenty weeks. White's bill also sought to replace the balance of risk criteria with a more restrictive clause only allowing abortion when there was 'grave risk' to life or 'serious injury' to the mother or existing children.[78] Though he was supported by a number of MPs who had opposed the Abortion Act in 1967 such as Leo Abse, Simon Mahon, and Bernard Braine, White said he was a moderate on the question, positioning himself between those who wanted outright abolition and those who wanted abortion on demand.[79] White attempted to claim a reasonable middle ground on abortion, but it was a middle ground that would have restricted access.

The Commons debate on White's bill put the supporters of the 1967 Act on the defensive. David Steel stressed that there had been a decline in criminal abortions, but did admit that the upper limit of twenty-eight weeks might be reduced. The Wilson government's response to White's bill was a promise to establish a Select Committee on abortion. Supporters of the Abortion Act opposed this because it meant re-opening the entire question. But the proposal to set up a Select Committee was carried by a vote of 203 to 88. The dissenting vote was overwhelmingly Labour—of eighty-eight MPs voting against, only four were Conservative and two Liberal. But the level of parliamentary support for White, particularly from the Labour benches, was nonetheless a shock. Dave Marsh and Joanna Chambers have argued that between 1969 and 1975 Labour MPs were concerned about the considerable rise in abortions and the possibility of abuse, a notable change from the generation that had supported the Steel bill in 1967.[80]

The evidence heard by the Select Committee rejected any change to the abortion law. The BMA, for example, voiced 'grave doubts'.[81] In the end, the Select Committee's final recommendations were anodyne, containing little of significant threat to the 1967 Act, except for a suggestion that abortions over twenty weeks be considered in a special category. The government remained largely non-committal, willing to tighten up the administration of abortion, but little more. The issue for

---

[76] *ACLW* (1974), 77.

[77] Abortion Law Reform Association: A Woman's Right to Choose Campaign, *Abortion: How Much Choice Do We Have?* (London, September 1975).

[78] See HMSO, *Abortion (Amendment) Bill 1974–75* (19), 1975; *The Times*, 31 January 1975.

[79] *Parliamentary Debates* (Commons), 885, 7 February 1975, c. 1756.

[80] Dave Marsh and Joanna Chambers, *Abortion Politics* (London: Junction Books, 1981), 25.

[81] HMSO, *Special Report and Minutes of Evidence of the Select Committee on the Bill with Proceedings (Abortion Amendment) Bill*, 1974–5 (692–11), pp. 178, 181, 76.

the House was whether the Select Committee should continue. The pro-abortion members of the Committee were adamant that the committee was 'deeply and irreconcilably divided' and 'serve[d] no useful purpose'.[82] Again, in this, the parliamentary forces in favour of abortion seemed weak, losing the vote against a reconstitution of the Select Committee by 313 to 172.

The White bill had two legacies. The first was the apparent emergence of a new middle ground in parliament on abortion between what were considered two extremes, abortion on demand and the abolition of abortion. This promised little in the way of an advance on women's reproductive rights, though the parliamentary struggle over abortion did fortify the identification of Labour women with the cause of abortion. Nonetheless, Douglas Houghton remarked that the Commons of 1976 was 'reactionary . . . especially on the Labour side' compared to the Commons of 1964–70.[83] The second legacy was the reorganization of the pro-abortion campaign, one that led to the Labour Party making a formal political commitment to abortion access.

V

White's bill saw a new kind of abortion politics emerging outside the Commons. Even in an older organization such as the ALRA this represented a more radical assertion of women's individual rights. Boasting a new and younger leadership, the ALRA publicized a draft bill to coincide with the White bill that would have effectively allowed abortion on demand up to the first twelve weeks of pregnancy.[84] It also launched a campaign for 'A Woman's Right to Choose', which sought to formalize women's right to abortion by the establishment of NHS outpatient services.[85] The campaign was consciously designed to evince 'a strong women's liberation flavour' through the emphasis upon 'the right to control her own fertility'.[86]

As the debate on White's bill went on within Westminster on 7 February 1975, nearly 800 women protested outside the parliamentary chambers. They came from assorted pro-abortion organizations such as the Women's Abortion and Contraceptive Campaign (WACC), a group rooted in the women's liberation movement and the IMG, and the Women's Right To Choose Campaign, a particular initiative for International Women's Year established by the ALRA.[87] Agitation against the bill helped establish new organizations, the most important of which was the NAC. The NAC was founded in March 1975 by members of the WACC and

---

[82] *Select Committee on Abortion (Amendment) Bill*, xxi, xxii.
[83] WL, Campaign Against Corrie Papers [CACP], SPG M11, Lord Houghton to Hazel Hunkins-Hallinan, 2 July 1976.
[84] LSE, Lena Jeger Papers, 7/2, 'Abortion: A Bill', January 1975.
[85] LSE, Lena Jeger Papers, 7/2, 'A Woman's Right to Choose', 1975.
[86] WL, Co-Ordinating Committee in Defence of the 1967 Abortion Act Papers [CO-ORD], SPG M11, ALRA Memorandum, 4 December 1974.
[87] Marsh and Chambers, *Abortion Politics*, 46.

the Women's Charter Campaign, combining elements of extra-Labour groups, the trade union movement and women's liberation.[88]

The NAC's participatory and hierarchical structure reflected the ideals of women's liberation organizations. Local chapters were autonomous; by 1976, there were 350 groups.[89] At its first conference in October 1975, the NAC articulated a desire to protect existing abortion against any restriction and 'to build a mass national campaign on the basis of a woman's right to choose whether to continue or terminate a pregnancy'. The latter made the NAC a more radical organization than the ALRA in terms of policy. Its campaigning slogans underlined an assertion of the link between feminism, sexual freedom, and abortion: 'Free Abortion on Demand—A Woman's Right to Choose'; 'Our Bodies, Our Lives, Our Right to Decide'.[90] Abortion on demand was to be provided through outpatient NHS abortion clinics.[91] The NAC also changed the space of abortion advocacy, from the Central Lobby to the street; one of NAC's first successes was the organization of a march for abortion rights of 20,000 people, the 'biggest demonstration on a women's issue since the suffragettes'.[92] Hoggart has suggested that the NAC brought together three sometimes contradictory approaches: a defence of the 1967 Act; a 'criticism of the implementation' of the 1967 Act; and 'a feminist critique' of the Act.[93]

There was a strong relationship between socialist and labour politics and the NAC. The LARC was an offshoot of the NAC. In 1976, Labour members of the NAC's Steering Committee thought that it would be useful to have a Labour-dedicated organization, believing that 'a vital aspect of building a mass movement in support of women's abortion rights was consolidating and extending that support in the Labour Party' and in the trade union movement.[94] It had about 200 members, with particular links to the NJCWWO, the National Organization of Labour Students, and unions such as NUPE and the AUEW.[95] The LARC had a two-pronged strategy: first of all, it sought to use activism within constituency parties to build support for abortion; secondly, it cultivated contacts with the parliamentary Labour leadership, such as the Leader of the House, Michael Foot. The LARC established its own annual conference; the first boasted a hundred delegates from sixty-seven Labour constituencies.[96] It also put on fringe meetings at both the annual TUC and Labour conferences, though the success of these was uneven, with attendance sometimes 'very poor'.[97] In many ways, the LARC's

[88] Lesley Hoggart, 'Feminist Principles meet Political Reality: The Case of the National Abortion Campaign', http://www.prochoiceforum.org.uk/al6.php, accessed 4 June 2009.
[89] Marsh and Chambers, *Abortion Politics*, 48.
[90] WL, National Abortion Campaign Papers [NAC], Newsletter, 1975.
[91] See Amy Black, 'The Politics of Motherhood in Post-War Britain: Feminism, Socialism and the Labour Party', unpublished MA thesis, Dalhousie University, 1997, 78.
[92] Marsh and Chambers, *Abortion Politics*, 47.
[93] Hoggart, 'Feminist Principles meet Political Reality'.
[94] LPA, NAC, Newsletter, 'Report to the NAC Conference: Labour Abortion Rights Campaign', no date [1978?].
[95] Marsh and Chambers, *Abortion Politics*, 51.
[96] ALRA, *Breaking Chains* 2 (July–August 1977).
[97] WL, CO-ORD, SPG M15, Co-ord Minutes, 8 September 1977, 9.2.

strategy was similar to that taken up previously in the century by the WBCG and the ALRA. The major difference was the purchase this had with the leadership of the official Labour women's organization. The NLWAC associated itself with the LARC and, in 1981, the NJCWWO affiliated to the LARC.[98] The NAC and the LARC were not the same organization, but they shared membership and in 1981 together held a Labour Movement Conference on abortion, suggesting a porousness between the two organizations.[99]

The LARC's primary aim was to 'establish in law a woman's right to make the decision to have an abortion without any medical or legal restriction'.[100] This meant, first and foremost, securing a place in the party manifesto for abortion and abolishing the parliamentary free vote on the question. The LARC's work was a conscious attempt to meld the work of Labour women with the women's liberation movement.[101] The argument for abortion was steeped in the context of both class and individual rights. The LARC saw abortion as a socialist aim about 'the extension of choice in all areas of life and for the rights of individuals to control their lives'. At the same time, the LARC underlined that '[y]oung women of the working classes' had been principal protagonists in this struggle, 'pushing aside centuries of domination and discrimination and establishing new ideas of what their lives should be', against the 'rich' who had long monopolized this right. '[T]o have other goals in life besides motherhood' was, according to the LARC, of particular importance to these young working-class women.[102] The winding together of class and rights rhetoric was reflected in discussion of abortion at party conference and at the party's women's conference. The most notable strategic aim of the LARC was the commitment to abolish the free vote on abortion. The LARC's supporters believed that the question was really about what it meant to have something as party policy and what party and parliamentary discipline was to be on policy commitments. For Jo Richardson, it was similarly a litmus test of the party's dedication to women's equality: '[e]ither we believe that women should be free and equal members of society or we don't. There are no half measures about it.'[103]

VI

In 1980, while admitting the TUC and the Labour Party were 'not perfect', the NAC argued that 'they could be our best weapons'.[104] After the White bill, Labour

[98] LPA, NJC/M/October/1976, NJCWWO, 19 October 1976; NEC, NAD/M/115/11/76, NLWAC minutes, 26 October 1976; NJC/1/July/1980, NJCWWO minutes, 1 July 1980.

[99] Hoggart, 'Feminist Principles meet Political Reality'.

[100] 'LARC Aims', in LARC, *Abortion: The Struggle in the Labour Movement* (London: LARC, no date), 1.

[101] LPA, Toni Gorton and Anne Kingsbury, 'Fight to Commit the Next Labour Government to Legislate for AWRTC [A Woman's Right to Choose]', 1980, from NAC Newsletter Files, 1980.

[102] LARC Executive, 'A Woman's Right to Choose', in *Abortion: The Struggle in the Labour Movement*, 3, 5.

[103] Jo Richardson, 'The Free Vote', in *Abortion: The Struggle in the Labour Movement*, 21.

[104] WL, NAC, Newsletter, NAC Conference, Leeds, 1980.

and the TUC became spaces from which the Abortion Act was defended, though this was not without ambiguity. The defence of the Abortion Act was, in part, led from the centre as much as it was prompted by the campaigning tactics of the LARC. The NLWAC, for example, took an active role in promoting the defence of the Abortion Act through the mid- to late 1970s. During the debate on the White bill, this took the form of supporting the women Labour MPs opposing the bill and lobbying government members, including the Prime Minister, on the terms of reference of the Select Committee.[105] Later in 1975, the NLWAC gave evidence to the Select Committee, making clear the force of Labour's support for strengthening women's choice in any decision to have an abortion, at least up until twenty-four weeks. It also 'totally opposed' the White bill, the terms of which would 'impose unacceptable views and conditions on the female population'. White's provisions to restrict the operation of abortion in particular circumstances promised only to establish 'two standards for abortion—one for those who have more easy access to the medical profession, largely based on finance, and one for those in the lower income groups who might again be driven to illegal "backstreets" abortions'.[106] Two years later, with the Benyon Bill before the House, the NLWAC similarly used its position to lobby Labour MPs and ministers to oppose the bill.[107]

Perhaps the critical factor in the growing acceptance of abortion as a Labour issue was a change in the attitude of the trade unions. Previously, the trade union movement had acted as a brake on any identification between industrial class issues and sexual issues. But in the 1970s, the trade unions were at the forefront in making that association, albeit sometimes contradictorily. This change was probably more about an increasingly assertive role taken by women within the TUC and trade unions' desire to attract female members than the happy embrace of a new agenda by the TUC leadership.

In the case of abortion, the vessel of this change was the campaign for the Working Women's Charter, already noted as a critical document in the articulation of the links among sex, class, and politics and the connection between sexual and industrial issues. The Charter campaign was not only a bridge between the sexual and the industrial in women's unionism, it also provided organizational common ground between women trade unionists, socialist-feminists, and groups like the NAC. In 1975, the Charter came up for discussion at the TUC's annual congress. Moving the adoption of the Charter, one delegate argued that the Charter was an attempt 'to establish real and proper women's rights, not only in the workplace but throughout society' and that its provisions on contraception and abortion were, in particular, 'a launching pad for a massive campaign to improve women's rights'. Another delegate underlined the point that the Charter 'link[ed] women's situation at work with their situation at home and in the family . . . bridg[ing] what we as

---

[105] See, for example, LPA, NLWAC/M/32/4/75, NLWAC Minutes, 15 April 1975.
[106] LPA, NAD/W/31/4/75, NLWAC, Evidence to the Select Committee on the Abortion (Amendment) Bill, 1975.
[107] See correspondence in LPA, NAD/W/95/9/76.

trade unionists regard as the economic issues...with social issues'.[108] But the General Council opposed adoption of the Charter on the abortion issue alone, its spokesperson stating: '[t]he majority of unions may well be in support of family planning and broadly in support of abortion on demand...[t]here may however...be a sizeable minority of unions which do not consider that these are appropriate matters to be within an official charter for the whole trade union Movement.'[109] In its place, the TUC offered its own 'Twelve Aims for Women at Work', a programme that excluded any statement on abortion. The motion to adopt the Charter was lost at conference, but, as Elliott has pointed out, 'within the next half hour, abortion was to become a "trade union issue"'.[110] This came with the Congress' response to the White initiative. A delegate moved a resolution that calling upon the General Council and all unions to campaign to oppose restrictive legislation and for the right for women to obtain contraception and abortion 'on request...free of charge on the NHS'.[111] It was carried. Thus, contradictorily, the TUC rejected the Charter's commitment to abortion while accepting abortion as a response to events within Parliament. This was a critical shift in what the unions considered was union work, including the sexual as well as the industrial.[112]

The Labour Party conference witnessed similar developments. In 1975, as part of a wider discussion of the NHS, the Labour Party conference affirmed, over-whelmingly, a resolution calling for 'contraception, and abortion...available to all women on request, free of charge and oppos[ing] moves to restrict the availability of abortion on social grounds'.[113] The party thus committed itself to free abortion on demand on social grounds as part of its health policy, a completion of the arc begun in the 1920s. Between this vote and the party conference in 1977, Joyce Gould was a moving force on the issue within the movement. Notably, she encouraged the submission of pro-abortion resolutions to party conference, in order to further commit the party to the question, and coordinated the efforts of the NJCWWO and NLWAC. By the time of the 1977 conference, abortion attracted the third-highest number of resolutions.[114] This led to a strong commitment to abortion. By a majority of 4,666,000 to 73,000, thus with the full weight of the trade union block vote, the party passed the following resolution, setting out a commitment to the defence of the Abortion Act, to future legislation that would 'ensure women's right of choice on abortion', and facilitating 'freely available abortion on request on the National Health Service in all areas of the United Kingdom'.[115] Even if these commitments left in the air the question of individual conscience, abortion provision became formal party policy half a century after the question of birth control was first mooted at national conference. What is also striking is the

---

[108] *TUCR* (1975), 410, 413.
[109] *TUCR* (1975), 415.
[110] Elliott, 'How Far Have We Come', 65.
[111] *TUCR* (1975), 416.
[112] See Elliott, 'How Far Have We Come', 65.
[113] *LPCR* (1975), 235.
[114] Marsh and Chambers, *Abortion Politics*, 65.
[115] *LPCR* (1977), 316.

quickness of the Labour movement's response to both the White bill and, later, the Benyon bill. In 1975, the TUC gave evidence to the Select Committee that the White bill would 'reduce the number of safe, legal abortions', with 'working-class girls and women' those mainly affected.[116] Both the Labour Party and the TUC followed the debate on the White bill with commitments to the better provision of abortion and the expansion of women's rights in this area. The TUC went on to organize a rally on abortion and include free abortion in its 1977 *Aims for Women at Work*.[117] The LARC was the engine driving the resolutions at party conference. Its members worked through constituency parties and trade union branches to rally support.[118] The LARC took much of the credit for the success of the 1977 resolution, arguing that its efforts meant that 'Labour now stands clearly for a comprehensive abortion programme'.[119]

The rhetoric around abortion in the party debates of the mid-1970s is important. If we look at three debates on the issue in the period between 1975 and 1977, what becomes clear is that newer arguments based upon women's rights were joined to an older argument about class. The first represented the integration of a language of women's liberation and second wave feminism. In 1977, for example, Gillian Wilding told the Labour conference that 'the right to control our bodies, our sexuality, our personal lives and to plan our child-bearing, is fundamental to women's rights. Any other freedom of choice without this to us is almost meaningless.'[120] It was no different, in this way, from 'other democratic rights'.[121] But this was also linked to what was perhaps a more familiar concern, that the restriction of abortion rights led straight to the 'backstreet abortionist' for 'one section of the community'.[122] It was, for many, a 'simple class issue', according to a delegate at the 1976 conference of Labour women.[123] Closing the 1977 Labour Party conference debate on this issue was left to Lena Jeger, who recalled her past experiences as the wife of an East End doctor, seeing women who were 'prematurely old', who came in 'with their little calendars of dread and fear'.[124] Past and present thus met in Labour's debates on abortion, the woman of the 1970s asking for rights alongside the woman of the pre-1967 era seeking protection. Given the intersections between the LARC, the NAC, Marxist groups, and the Labour Party, it is unsurprising that some of these sentiments could also be found outside the party. The NAC argued, for example, that 'White's Bill is a piece of anti-working class legislation', which would affect 'thousands of working class women'.[125]

---

[116] *TUCR* (1975), 150.
[117] Marsh and Chambers, *Abortion Politics*, 70.
[118] NAC Newsletter, 1978.
[119] NAC Newsletter, 1977.
[120] *LPCR* (1977), 317.
[121] *LPCR* (1977), 318.
[122] *TUCR* (1975), 416.
[123] *ACLW* (1976), 45.
[124] *LPCR* (1977), 323.
[125] Hackney Archives, Hackney [HA] London, Sarah Mudd Papers [SMP] on the Hackney Abortion Campaign in the 1970s, D/F/SMU/1/2, NAC Conference Bulletin, 'Women's Voice' (no date, but 1975—International Women's Year).

In the wake of the 1977 party conference, Jo Richardson argued that the abortion resolution represented a binding policy commitment for the party and wanted the next step to be a manifesto commitment to abortion on demand up to twelve weeks.[126] But the 1977 commitment also permitted the right of conscience on the abortion issue. A resolution demanding that 'all Labour Members of Parliament should be mandated by the Parliamentary Labour Party to vote against any restrictions on abortion' was lost, probably because it failed to mobilize union support.[127] The success of the 1977 abortion resolution still served to illustrate the problematic link between resolutions generated by the cauldron of party democracy, the conference, and the actions of the parliamentary party.

The resolution came after a year in which the 1967 Act was challenged again, this time by a Conservative MP, William Benyon. In February, he put a private member's bill that would have dropped the time limit for abortion to twenty weeks and restricted the ability of pregnancy advice bureaux to refer women to abortion clinics. Roland Moyle, the Labour Minister of State for Health, opposed the bill, as did a coterie of Labour MPs, mostly women such as Renée Short and Maureen Colquhoun. The fear was that up to 40,000 abortions a year would be prohibited if the bill went through. Labour women filibustered the bill in committee in July, holding it up for over a hundred hours.[128] As Leader of the House, Michael Foot refused to grant Benyon's bill extra time and it duly died on the statute book in July. The bill confirmed that Labour women in the House were the bedrock of support for the 1967 Act. It also showed the growing organization and force of the pro-abortion movement outside of Parliament. This ranged from the lobbying efforts of the LARC and NAC to more militant tactics; an anti-abortion Labour MP was assaulted in his constituency office in March and pro-abortion demonstrators led by the 23-year-old actress Eileen Fairweather occupied the pulpit of Westminster Cathedral in July.[129]

VII

The parliamentary and conference debates on abortion foregrounded a long-standing emphasis on protecting the rights of working-class women, thus underlining the class or economic aspects of the abortion question. In other ways, the defence of the Abortion Act in the 1970s within the NAC, LARC, and other circles allowed the discussion of newer ideas of gender and sexuality with relationship to abortion and different ideas of political action.

What was particularly clear was that abortion was represented as a struggle for the rights of a new kind of woman, one separated from the older context of motherhood. This was an age in which, according to Antonia Gorton, the view

---

[126] *The Times*, 18 January 1978.
[127] *LPCR* (1977), 318.
[128] *The Times*, 9 July 1977.
[129] See *The Times*, 12 March 1977 and 16 July 1977.

of women only as 'housewives and mothers' had been challenged, giving them 'more options than ever before in terms of jobs, education and participation in society'. '[S]exual discrimination and oppression' still frustrated the full realization of women's potential. Lack of control over abortion was the most powerful example of such impediments.[130] Not least, the continuing control enjoyed by doctors over the abortion decision undermined women's rights.[131] Full reproductive control was equated with full rights; reproductive control depended upon abortion. 'We believe', an NAC handbill stated, 'that only when <u>women</u> control whether or not we have babies will we be able to take an equal part in society ... this is the most important and fundamental right for women ... The question of <u>who</u> controls what we do with our bodies and our lives is central to our campaign.'[132] In parliament, female MPs often echoed this belief. During the debate on the Benyon bill, for example, Maureen Colquhoun claimed that '[t]his was the kind of Bill which sought to downgrade women and deprive them of their rights'.[133] The abortion debate had thus gone a considerable distance from the 1960s in terms of being a discussion, not simply about the conditions of motherhood or the health of women, but the nature of femininity and the quality of individual rights for women.

The unspoken context in all of this was a different sexual climate, one in which more women might be experiencing greater sexual freedom. Yet it is striking that the question of sexual freedom or sexual pleasure only occasionally intruded into the debate on abortion in the 1970s. Sheila Rowbotham recalled that European feminists were 'puzzled by the silence in the British campaign: "The right to sexual pleasure is a fundamental issue of women's liberation and yet it is rarely if ever articulated".'[134] The IMG's *Socialist Woman* published a particularly focused criticism in this regard in 1978, in which the NAC was censured for a 'doggedly defensive' posture and an emphasis upon the 'economic aspect of fertility control' which separated abortion 'from its feminist context'. Instead, the authors wanted to make the abortion struggle 'primarily a fight for sexual freedom ... the fight for sexual freedom affects all women; so surely all women can identify with a campaign based around that demand'.[135] IMG women working within the NAC responded by saying: '[i]t is not necessary to have broken with a bourgeois conception of morality ... to see the need for the right to abortion'.[136] The new context for abortion was one that emphasized women's rights, but did not necessarily carry with it an idea of sexual liberation. When the NAC spoke of 'a woman's right to

---

[130] HA, SMP, D/F/SMU/1/2, Antonia Gorton, 'The Fight for Women's Right to Choose', in NAC, *Where We Stand* (London, no date, 1970s), 15.
[131] Berry Beaumont, 'What We are Fighting For', 19.
[132] HA, SMP, D/F/SMU/1/2, NAC Handbill (London, no date, 1970s).
[133] *The Times*, 26 February 1977.
[134] Sheila Rowbotham, *The Past is Before Us: Feminism in Action Since the 1960s* (Harmondsworth: Penguin, 1990), 81.
[135] Angela Philips, Dorothy Jones, and Pat Kahn, 'Abortion, Feminism and Sexuality', *Socialist Woman* 6/3 (Spring 1978), 8, 9.
[136] Judith Awkwright and Sarah Hart, 'Supporters of Socialist Woman Reply', 9.

choose whether to continue or terminate a pregnancy', it was assumed that this right would operate in a number of different kinds of sexual contexts.[137]

The defence of the Abortion Act also witnessed experiments with a new kind of politics. The NAC believed that this would reflect the women's movement's desire to build different kinds of democracy.[138] The NAC's campaign illustrated many of the strengths of abortion politics in the 1970s and 1980s—the ability to build broad alliances, to marshal large public demonstrations, and achieve purchase within a mainstream political party. But the NAC experience also highlighted the ambiguities around the relationship among feminist politics, sexual questions, and political strategy. Much more than their predecessors, the abortion campaigners of the 1970s and 1980s were immensely self-conscious and self-critical about questions of strategy. Even as they became more imbricated in the politics of the Left, some abortion campaigners held deep reservations about the implications of that relationship.

In part, these reservations were rooted in the difficulties of yoking the newer organizational and democratic approaches mooted in the women's movement to a more traditional political campaign. In 1979, Sheila Rowbotham assessed the countervailing tensions within the abortion campaign in this respect: 'we found it difficult to carry over the experience of the women's movement in discussing abortion in relation to our personal experience of our sexuality, our relationships, our attitudes to having children or childcare . . . [w]e could not make these connections in relation to the national campaign for abortion'.[139] One of the most thoughtful reflections on this came with Eileen Fairweather's 'The Feelings Behind the Slogans' published in *Spare Rib Reader* in 1979. As the title suggested, Fairweather wanted to connect the politics of abortion with the experience of women, to weave together the personal and the political. Because attempts at Westminster to restrict the 1967 Act had effectively shaped the pro-choice movement, 'the complexity of abortion and its emotional significance for women somehow got lost'. In part, this was about what Fairweather saw as an understandable sacrifice of a new politics based upon consciousness-raising and small workshops to the demands of a 'nationally-led, focused organization' like the NAC. What Fairweather lamented was the loss of complexity in the meaning of abortion rights for women and the reduction of that meaning in the political cauldron.[140] Writing in 1990, Rowbotham took Fairweather's piece as indicative of a wider trend within the pro-abortion movement that expressed 'contradictory feelings and the complexity of choices, both in an existential sense and in relation to social circumstances . . . [a]bortion as a political issue challenges the scope of existing theories about demands, rights, individuals and society, and social need'.[141]

[137] WL, NAC, Aims (1975), n.p.

[138] WL, CO-ORD, SPG M12, NAC, Paper 1, Gill Butler, Rose Knight, Berry Beaumont, April 1978.

[139] Sheila Rowbotham, 'Women . . . How Far Have We Come?' (1979), in *Dreams and Dilemmas* (London: Virago, 1983), 92.

[140] Eileen Fairweather, 'The Feelings Behind the Slogan', in Marsha Rowe (ed.), *Spare Rib Reader* (Harmondsworth: Penguin, 1982), 339, 340, 341.

[141] Rowbotham, *The Past is Before Us*, 82, 91, 93.

The strengths and the tensions around organizing in defence of the Abortion Act were revealed in the workings of the Co-ordinating Committee in Defence of the 1967 Abortion Act (CO-ORD). CO-ORD was the umbrella organization for those working for the protection of the 1967 Act and, more generally, the promotion of the movement for reproductive choice. It comprised a wide variety of groups, including established and mainstream organizations like the ALRA, the Birth Control Campaign (BCC), the BPAS, the FPA, and the Six Point Group, and groups with explicit political affiliations such as the LARC, the NLWAC, the NJCWWO, the WCG, the National Organization of Labour Students, the SMA, the National League of Young Liberals, and Tories for a Free Choice. The NAC was the most obviously 'new' feminist organization and CO-ORD became not only a valuable means of unifying efforts on abortion, but also a forum for differences on abortion and on strategy. The tension between the two was explicit and accepted. In 1977, for example, Joyce Gould, representing the NJCWWO, said that 'Co-ord's strength lay in its fragmentation, the fact that there are so many different organizations with differing attitudes and political points of view and this should be exploited to the full'.[142] But in 1978, tensions overflowed between constituent organizations with the NAC and ALRA at loggerheads. That year, the NAC conference asserted that there should be no restrictions on abortion. This alarmed other members of CO-ORD; the veteran ALRA campaigner, Diane Munday, called the NAC, for example, the 'wild women of the left' and several organizations threatened to leave CO-ORD, though the controversy ultimately blew over.[143]

VIII

May 1979 saw the return of a majority Conservative government under Margaret Thatcher. There has been some comment on the ideological importance of the assertion of the traditional family under Thatcher, not least in the approach to homosexuality, as the next chapter shall explore.[144] Was abortion affected by this, as it was in the United States in the 1970s and 1980s? The evidence is less clear than in the example of homosexuality, but the return of 339 Conservative MPs certainly meant that the Commons might have been more receptive to some sort of abortion reform. As well, it was also possible that the Conservative government might be more willing to grant time to a private member's bill reforming abortion.

Soon enough into the new parliament, the 1967 Abortion Act once more came under threat from an amending bill. John Corrie, a Conservative MP, proposed a private member's bill that, in its original version, would have dropped the time

---

[142] WL, CO-ORD, SPG 15, Co-ord Minutes, 3 March 1977, 3.2.2.

[143] *Evening Echo* (Liverpool), 26 June 1978; WL, CO-ORD, SPG 15, Co-ord Minutes, 2 November 1978, 6.

[144] Sharon Stephens, 'Introduction', in Sharon Stephens (ed.), *Children and the Politics of Culture* (Princeton, NJ: Princeton University Press, 1993), 3–50; Smith, *New Right Discourse on Race and Sexuality*; Heather Nunn, *Thatcher, Politics and Fantasy: The Political Culture of Gender and Nation* (London: Lawrence and Wishart, 2002).

limit to twenty weeks and introduced the idea that continuing the pregnancy would have to involve 'grave risk' to the life of the pregnant woman or 'substantial risk' to the physical and mental health of her or her existing children.[145] Both were significant challenges to the limit set out by the 1929 Infant Life Preservation Act and the risk criteria established when the Abortion Act went through the Lords in 1967, that the risk of having a therapeutic abortion would always be less than taking a pregnancy to term.

The campaign against the Corrie bill represented the interplay between parliamentary and extra-parliamentary abortion advocacy. Spearheaded by the NAC and a new dedicated umbrella organization, the Campaign Against the Corrie Bill (CAC), forces outside of Westminster kept abortion rights in the public eye, not least through street demonstrations. But an older route for abortion advocacy ultimately defeated the Corrie bill within Parliament. It was in the Commons that the Labour Party proved most important. Several Labour women and men were critical in undermining Corrie's bill and preventing its success. Oonagh McDonald, the MP for Thurrock, Essex, was, in effect, the informal whip for pro-abortion MPs. Jo Richardson was also a strong presence on the Labour benches, while Joyce Gould kept a watchful eye from the Gallery on errant Labour MPs. Two veteran male MPs were, however, also critical. Ian Mikardo (Bethnal Green and Bow) and Willie Hamilton (Fife Central) provided much parliamentary experience and acumen in the Commons and in Committee to undermine Corrie's bill.[146]

When he introduced the bill for second reading in July 1979, Corrie represented himself as a moderate, arguing that the NAC wanted 'abortion on demand' and that the 1967 Act had effectively created this with its provisions for the assessment of risk.[147] Jo Richardson countered, calling his bill 'a great disservice to women'. Richardson underlined both women's opposition to the restriction of the 1967 Act and the political weight of the trade unions and the Labour Party.[148] Willie Hamilton played a familiar theme in raising the question as a 'class matter . . . the working class woman will be affected . . . [the bill] is like the Budget . . . it takes care of those at the top of the social tree'.[149] But the opponents of Corrie's bill lost the second reading on a vote of 242 to 98, allowing the bill to proceed to committee. Particularly notable was the decline in the number of Labour MPs voting against a restrictive bill. Marsh and Chambers have suggested that those supporting the bill in July 1979 or abstaining probably did so out of a belief that the upper limit to terminations should be reduced somewhat, but hoped for little more, thinking that a palatable and moderate compromise would emerge during the Committee stage.

In Committee, the opposing members were the Labour MPs Stan Thorne, Oonagh McDonald, Ian Mikardo, Willie Hamilton, and Jo Richardson. Aided

---

[145] House of Commons, Papers, 1979/80 Bill 7 Abortion (Amendment) Bill, 27 June 1979.
[146] Marsh and Chambers, *Abortion Politics*, 164–5.
[147] *Parliamentary Debates* (Commons), Volume 970, 13 July 1979, c. 892.
[148] *Parliamentary Debates* (Commons), Volume 970, 13 July 1979, cs. 920, 919, 930.
[149] *Parliamentary Debates* (Commons), Volume 970, 13 July 1979, c. 961.

7.3 'Abortion Protest, 1980', photography by *Evening Standard*, copyright Hulton Archive/Getty Images 3324223 (RM)

by lawyers from CO-ORD, they fought a rearguard battle to slow down its proceedings, challenging every clause and putting amendment after amendment, fighting especially around words like 'grave' and 'substantial' and the upper limit.[150] The point of this was not simply to play for time, hoping that the parliamentary clock would run out on Corrie, but also to use the amendments to show the radical nature of the original bill, thus frightening Labour MPs into opposing it.[151]

Outside parliament, the NAC spearheaded a campaign against the Corrie bill. This came largely through the CAC, which was far more focused than its parent organization, in simply being dedicated to the defeat of the Corrie bill. The CAC worked within the TUC in particular to build up Labour opposition to the bill.

Corrie faced opposition from the BMA, the TUC, and the NAC.[152] A consistent theme was the argument that any change to the 1967 bill would prejudice against working-class women. In December 1979, for example, Madeleine Simms said, on behalf of CO-ORD, that 'middle-class women had always been able to obtain abortions for such reasons, but the 1967 Act had opened up such possibilities to working-class women as well'.[153] Such criticisms coincided with 'weeks of action'

[150] House of Commons Sessional Papers, 1979/8, HC 338 Standing Committee C, Minutes of Proceedings of the Abortion (Amendment) Bill.
[151] Marsh and Chambers, *Abortion Politics*, 161.
[152] Marsh and Chambers, *Abortion Politics*, 129.
[153] *The Times*, 29 December 1979.

organized through regional trade union conferences and the CAC, including a demonstration on 5 February that saw 12,000 activists and a Women's Assembly three days later to mark the bill's third reading.[154] A major set-piece of such demonstrations was the TUC-sponsored demonstration against the Corrie bill in October 1979. A meeting of the TUC's General Council in July 1979 had insisted that the 'TUC should take the lead in the campaign against the Bill'.[155] This included organizing a public demonstration on Sunday, 28 October 1979. The demonstration turned out to be a massive one, with estimates of between 45,000 and 60,000 people walking from Hyde Park to Trafalgar Square. Len Murray and other male trade union leaders led the way, with the NAC, CAC, and Women Only following, but this prompted a reaction from some feminists within the London Women's Liberation Movement. They pushed in front of Murray and tried to take the stage at Trafalgar Square. Three were arrested. The feminists believed that the abortion issue was 'a women's issue. But others have leapt on the bandwagon' and that, in particular, men were only interested 'to ensure that they are able to carry on fucking women'.[156] Other women regretted the incident, however. CO-ORD believed it had created 'adverse publicity'.[157] Jo Richardson felt the incident underlined a larger problem of strategy for the abortion and feminist movement: 'you've got to persuade some men on some issues and on the abortion issue it is absolutely vital. Indeed, arising from the TUC demonstration a lot more unions wrote to their sponsored MPs saying: "We hope you will oppose the Corrie Bill"—that was very useful.'[158] Richardson's larger point was that abortion could only be defended by a combination of traditional parliamentary means and outside pressure.

Corrie's bill ultimately foundered in parliament. In a debate in February 1980, a compromise on the number of weeks for a legal abortion was reached—with the House voting 272 to 172 in favour of a reduction of four weeks from the mark set in 1929.[159] After the bill was given extra time, 250 female trade unionists, supported by Len Murray, sent a telegram to MPs 'at this eleventh hour to consider the pain and suffering which will be inflicted on so many women and their families if this proposal becomes law'.[160] In March 1980, Sam Silkin, the Labour MP for Lewisham, successfully put an amendment that would effectively defuse the threat of introducing the word 'substantially' to the calculation of risk between continuing a pregnancy or having a termination. This was supported by opponents of Corrie's bill, such as Ian Mikardo.[161] Reluctant to accept this, Corrie withdrew his bill on 26 March 1980.

[154] Hoggart, 'Feminist Principles meet Political Reality'.
[155] *TUCR* (1979), 140.
[156] Al Garthwaite and Valerie Sinclair, 'The TUC's Right To Choose' (first published in *Wire* December 1979), in Feminist Collective Anthology (eds), *No Turning Back* (London: The Women's Press, 1981), 38, 40.
[157] WL, CO-ORD, SPG M15: Minutes, 1 November 1979.
[158] Interview with Jo Richardson, *Power and Politics*, 148–9.
[159] *The Times*, 9 and 16 February 1980.
[160] *The Times*, 14 March 1980.
[161] See *The Times*, 15 March 1980.

Once again, those defending the 1967 Abortion Act had fought off a restrictive bill. The campaign against Corrie also witnessed a strong alliance forged between the Labour movement and pro-abortion advocates. As Hoggart has remarked, the 'connection of health with class, especially in relation to working-class women, was an important shared concern between NAC and the Labour movement'.[162] For her part, the veteran of abortion struggles, Madeleine Simms, remarked that '[o]nce the trade unions and Labour women were involved it became increasingly difficult for even the Roman Catholic MPs to actively support any restriction of the Abortion Act'.[163] Particularly important in this regard was the support of the trade unions and the activity of Labour MPs, especially female MPs. The defence of Steel's Act became embedded in Labour politics by the beginning of the 1980s. However, this triumph was an ambiguous one. First of all, as the controversy around the demonstration of October 1979 showed, trade union support was not without its own problems. Even the Labour Party's explicit support for abortion was qualified by allowing this to be a matter of conscience for individual MPs. But, as Hoggart has suggested, perhaps the greatest area of ambivalence was for feminism itself. Despite its valuable organizational activity, the NAC was unable to make a connection between the slogans it mobilized behind the defence of the Abortion Act—'a woman's right to choose' and 'abortion on demand'—and the demands of protecting the Act within parliament. 'NAC's feminist politics', Hoggart argues, 'became marginalized within its campaigning activity'; the organization's 'abstract slogans' jarred with the 'complexity of abortion as a political issue'.[164]

That tension might also be seen in the quality of Labour's own commitment to abortion as a political issue. Between the Corrie bill in 1980 and the Alton bill in 1988, there were two developments that underlined for pro-abortion activists, particularly within the Labour Party, the continuing precariousness of the Abortion Act. One was sparked by a profound scientific breakthrough. In July 1978, Louise Brown was born in Oldham, the first child to be conceived through *in vitro* fertilization. Of course, this raised enormous ethical questions. The 1984 Warnock inquiry on the question addressed the problem of infertility and assisted reproduction, balancing the demands of research with protection for the human embryo. The report did not, however, take abortion and reproduction within its terms of reference, even if the 'law in relation of them has been a necessary point of reference in discussions'.[165]

In 1985, pricked into action by research on *in vitro* fertilization, Enoch Powell introduced an Unborn Children (Protection) Bill. Powell claimed that his bill did

[162] Hoggart, 'Feminist Principles meet Political Reality'.
[163] Madeleine Simms, 'Legal Abortion in Great Britain', in Hilary Homans (ed.), *The Sexual Politics of Reproduction* (Aldershot: Gower, 1985), 91.
[164] Lesley Hoggart, 'Feminist Principles meet Political Reality: The Case of the National Abortion Campaign', http://www.prochoiceforum.org.uk/al6.php, accessed 4 June 2009.
[165] Cmnd. 9314, *Report of the Committee of Inquiry into Human Fertilisation and Embryology* (London: DHSS, July 1984), 5, para. 1.3.

not deal with abortion; instead, it was intended to prevent any kind of experimentation on human embryos. But inevitably, the parliamentary debate on the issue brought up questions of foetal viability, permissible limits on abortion, and, not least, the claims of women over reproduction. That forty-four Labour MPs eventually voted for Powell's bill alarmed supporters of the Abortion Act.[166] That same year, Victoria Gillick, a mother of ten, won a legal ruling against the medical profession giving contraceptive advice and prescriptions to girls under 16 without parental permission.

The struggles to defend the Abortion Act, not least in the context of the Powell bill, once again raised the questions of abortion as party policy. Following the party conference's 1977 commitment to the protection and extension of the Abortion Act, the party's 1983 election manifesto had, under the rubric of 'a better deal for women', promised that a Labour government would 'improve NHS facilities for family planning and abortion . . . and . . . remove barriers to the implementation of the existing right of choice for women in the termination of a pregnancy'. This was nonetheless prefaced by the qualification that the party would 'defend and respect the absolute right of individual conscience'.[167] At the 1985 party conference, following Powell's bill and the Gillick ruling, a composite resolution was put which insisted 'that the freedom to decide whether or not to bear children should be a woman's fundamental right' and demanded the abandonment of '"conscience clauses" or free votes on such matters'. The sponsor of the motion asserted that abortion was binding party policy and 'there should be no let offs for those who disagree'. Speaking for the NEC, Betty Boothroyd reaffirmed the party leadership's commitment to 'protect and extend' the 1967 Act, but baulked at giving up the conscience clause, asking for a remittance of that part of this resolution; this was refused and the original motion was carried by 5,305,000 to 611,000.[168] As already suggested, this defiance of the NEC reflected a wider context of the loosening of authority within the party in the 1980s. In 1987, in the run-up to the debate on Alton, the NEC reiterated its support for abortion and for the right of individual conscience; it also placed Alton's bill in the context of Thatcherite attacks upon women's lives such as the closing of hospitals for women, the restriction of maternity services, and declining social and economic provision.[169] A larger framework for such discussions was the increasing emphasis Labour was trying to put on women's policy, debated, for example, in 1986 and resulting in the proposal to create a Ministry of Women in the next Labour government to attack the problem of sexual inequality and discrimination.[170]

---

[166] *Parliamentary Debates* (Commons), 73, 15 February 1985, cs. 637–702.
[167] Labour Party, *The New Hope for Britain* (London: Labour Party, 1985).
[168] *LPCR* (1985), 100, 102, 103.
[169] *LPCR* (1987), 156.
[170] See, for example, *LPCR* (1986), 5–8.

IX

Another serious challenge to the Abortion Act marked its twentieth anniversary. In 1987, the Liberal David Alton drew third place in the ballot for private members' bills. Having attempted a restrictive bill in 1980, he tried again, this time with greater prospect of success. Alton's 1987 bill largely focused on the upper limit for legal abortions, hoping to modify the 1929 Infant Life Preservation Act to twenty weeks. When it became apparent that Alton was to introduce an eighteen- or twenty-week bill, it was pointed out, not least by the RCOG, that nearly 85% of all abortions occurred before the end of the first trimester and only 2% after twenty weeks; concern was also voiced about the number of tests for healthy pregnancies that would be compromised by a twenty-week or, as Alton increasingly talked about, an eighteen-week limit.[171] Stuart Campbell, a Professor at King's College Hospital projected that there would be 500 more children born with spina bifida if an eighteen- or twenty-week limit was enacted.[172] In October 1987, however, a *Guardian*/Marplan poll showed strong support for a reduction, even to eighteen weeks. Strikingly, the strongest support for restriction came from manual labourers, while it was socio-economic classes A and B who favoured maintaining the twenty-eight week limit.[173]

The poll was a surprise to advocates of abortion, underlining an ambivalence in public feeling towards abortion by the end of the 1980s: while access to legal abortion remained acceptable, many seemed increasingly uncomfortable with the idea of late abortions, whether because of the work of anti-abortion groups or improvements in neonatology. *The Guardian* itself, the voice of liberal Britain, caught this ambiguity in its leader comment on the bill, rejecting it but also rejecting a more radical path: '[t]he rhetoric of the Right to Choose lobby is now rather out of tune with the times. There is more of a recoil from "social" abortions.'[174]

Perhaps more than with the Corrie bill, the pro-abortion movement found itself fighting out of a corner with the Alton bill. A leading NAC organizer and former member of IMG, Leonora Lloyd, reflected that the time limit was '[o]ur weakest point' and, taking up a metaphor used by Willie Hamilton in the Commons, feared that, through the time limit, the Abortion Act could be cut back by 'salami tactics . . . slice by slice'.[175] One critical point was that the focus of discussion on abortion moved from the position of the individual women to the question of foetal viability or health. Anticipating parliamentary support for a twenty-four-week compromise and the possibility that Thatcher and her Social Services Secretary, John Moore, were willing to allow parliamentary time to effect this, the Labour

---

[171] *The Observer*, 30 August 1987; *The Guardian*, 27 October 1987.
[172] *The Guardian*, 20 January 1988.
[173] *The Guardian*, 16 October, 17 October 1987.
[174] *The Guardian*, 27 October 1987.
[175] WL, NAC, video, *Campaigning for Choice* (London, no date [1992?]).

women's conference sought to shore up Labour opposition to Alton, demanding a three-line whip on the vote.[176] This was unlikely, at least on the evidence of the views of the Deputy Leader, Roy Hattersley, who not only refused to attend the vote but dismissed '[a]ll this nonsense about a woman's right to choose'.[177] Once again, abortion advocates organized. The NAC and the Women's Reproduction Rights Campaign established Feminists Against the Alton Bill (later known as the Pro-Choice Alliance) and there was also a Fight the Alton Bill umbrella movement.[178]

Alton's bill had its second reading in January 1988. The debate demonstrated that the focus of abortion discussion had shifted from either considerations of access or women's rights to a more specific question about the health of the foetus. This is not to say that either women's rights or class access was forgotten—David Steel claimed, for example, that Alton's bill would return abortion to being a 'law for the rich' (echoing Alice Jenkins's book) and Clare Short made the case that without access to abortion '[w]omen's bodies [would] carry the consequences' of male sexual behaviour, charging that the Thatcher government, like the New Right in America 'are not in favour of public expenditure; they want to push women back into a traditional role and deprive them of the freedom to control their lives'.[179] But the crucial part of the debate centred upon foetal health and viability, whether in terms of when tests could be done effectively and conclusively for particular conditions or the ethics of allowing potentially handicapped or disabled foetuses to proceed to term. It was a difficult and intense debate. Jo Richardson's remarks reflected this change in focus and tone. She made it clear that the 1967 Act did not allow a right to choose and did not represent abortion as contraception; instead, she emphasized how difficult a choice abortion was for women, not solely in terms of social considerations, but in terms of things like foetal abnormality.[180] Alton's bill passed its Second Reading by 296 to 251. It went to Committee, in which Audrey Wise, Joan Ruddock, and Richardson represented the pro-abortion forces. An amendment proposing twenty-four weeks seemed to be gathering general support, but Alton refused to compromise and his bill was talked out in May 1988.[181]

In 1990, the Abortion of Act 1967 and the Infant Life Preservation Act of 1929 were finally amended, ironically as part of legislation dealing with the problem of infertility. In January 1989, the Thatcher government apparently indicated to the anti-abortion Conservative, Ann Widdecombe, that it would bring in legislation and allow parliamentary time for a reduction of the upper limit to abortion; the government's hope was that this would make the abortion issue 'go away' even if the actual legislation would only realize 'already established medical custom and

---

[176] *The Guardian*, 16 October, 16 November 1987.

[177] *The Guardian*, 20 January 1988.

[178] Dorothy McBride Stetson, 'Women's Movements' Defence of Legal Abortion in Great Britain', in Dorothy McBride Stetson (ed.), *Abortion Politics, Women's Movements, and the Democratic State* (Oxford: Oxford University Press, 2001), 140.

[179] *Parliamentary Debates* (Commons), 22 January 1988, cs. 1239, 1260, 1261.

[180] *Parliamentary Debates* (Commons), 22 January 1988, cs. 1273–5.

[181] *The Guardian*, 5 February, 27 April, 7 May, and 14 May 1988.

practice'.[182] It would do so in the context of addressing the questions raised by the Warnock Report on *in vitro* fertilization and embryo research.

The government introduced its HFE bill in the Lords, including within this a proposal to restrict termination to twenty-four weeks, with some exceptions. The HFE bill thus amended both the Abortion Act and the Infant Life Preservation Act. Twenty-four weeks was the limit first mooted by the Lane Report in 1975; the RCOG announced its support for a twenty-four-week limit in 1987. It also seemed the point of most agreement within the House over a number of amendment battles in the 1970s and 1980s. But there was immediate objection in the Lords to human fertilization, embryology, and abortion being discussed together, or to being what the Tory peer Lord Ennals termed 'spatchcocked'.[183] The most vocal critic in this regard was Douglas, now Lord Houghton, who protested at the upper house being 'used...as a remedy for the futilities of the House of Commons procedure' by including the 'gremlin' of abortion in a bill on embryo research.[184] To counter this, Houghton introduced his own Abortion Amendment Bill, which set out a limit of twenty-four weeks, but with many exceptions. When the Commons came to deal with the question in 1990, there was, unsurprisingly, considerable disquiet from pro-abortion MPs at the inclusion of abortion within a bill on embryology. In a complicated debate in April 1990, when different time limits were debated at length, some critics of the legislation, such as Clare Short, seemed to accept reluctantly the twenty-four-week limit but sought to strengthen the exceptions to it; Jo Richardson continued to oppose it as 'threatening the lives and futures of countless thousands of women who may need an abortion now or in the future'.[185] In a previous debate, Richardson had called upon Labour members to honour conference decisions on abortion. It was, however, a libertarian Conservative MP, Teresa Gorman, who was left to make an argument for sexual equality and freedom. The Labour MPs followed an older rhetoric of threat to women's lives and to the protection of the family; Mildred Gordon, the MP for Bow and Poplar, argued for women's 'right to decide what is best for their families'.[186] Voting on the time limit was complicated by the rare use of a 'pendulum' procedure, in which there were several votes in favour of different options, from eighteen to twenty-eight weeks. When none of these succeeded, the original proposal of twenty-four weeks stood. In June, after a great deal of confusion, the bill was read, and carried by 303 to 65, with pro-abortion MPs supporting the legislation restricting abortions to twenty-four weeks under the category of greater risk to the woman or existing children, but with a number of exceptions should there be the prospect of grave injury or handicap. The new Act, given Royal Assent in November 1990, now meant that abortion was legal up to the twenty-fourth week as long as continuing

---

[182] J. Isaac, 'The Politics of Morality in the UK', *Parliamentary Affairs* 47 (1994), 177.
[183] *Parliamentary Debates* (Lords), 513, 7 December 1989, 1012.
[184] *Parliamentary Debates* (Lords), 513, 7 December 1989, 1059, 1058.
[185] *Parliamentary Debates* (Commons), 171, 24 April 1990, 186.
[186] *Parliamentary Debates* (Commons), 171, 24 April 1990, 259.

the pregnancy involved greater risk to the woman or her family than terminating it.[187] There were more similarities than differences between the 1990 and 1967 Acts and the HFE did not substantially alter the practice of abortion. The most obvious change was the twenty-four-week limit, but as most observers of the change noted, this was simply a 'codification of existing medical practice'; in other ways, particularly in the way the Act dealt with potential foetal handicap, the law was more liberal than previous legislation.[188] This did, however, stop the NAC from expressing grave concern about the restriction of the upper time limit; the organization remained committed to abortion as a right and maintained that however regrettable late abortions might be, it was 'essential that they remain legal'.[189]

Between the passing of the HFE Act and the election of the New Labour government in 1997, there was little movement on abortion within the Labour Party. Sarah Perrigo has suggested that the process of modernization in the 1980s and 1990s was a boon to women's issues, but abortion activists within the Labour Party were, in fact, anxious about the leadership of, first, John Smith and then Tony Blair.[190] Smith was believed to be against abortion and, under Blair, activists were concerned that despite discussions of improvements to women's health services (including family planning), little was ventured about the extension of abortion rights under a potential Labour government; in particular, NAC wanted to move on from 1967: 'Labour will have to work hard to convince pro-choice activists that they are committed, wholeheartedly, to a woman's right to choose and can deliver on that commitment.'[191] Though the 1967 Act had been protected, in large part through the Labour Party, the expansion of reproductive rights looked no more certain in the 1990s than it did in the 1970s.

[187] *Human Fertilisation and Embryology Act 1990* (London: HMSO, 1990), section 37, 1 (a), (b), (c), and (d).
[188] John Montgomery, 'Rights, Restraints and Pragmatism: The Human Fertilisation and Embryology Act 1990', *Modern Law Review* 54 (1991), 531; see also M.H. Hall, 'Changes in the Law on Abortion: Won't Produce Radical Changes in Practice', *British Medical Journal*, 301/6761, 17 November 1990, 1109–10; John Murphy, 'Cosmetics, Eugenics and Ambivalence: The Revision of the Abortion Act, 1967', *Journal of Social Welfare and Family Law* 13 (1995), 375–93.
[189] WL, NAC, 'Memorandum by the National Abortion Campaign', *NAC Newsletter* (January 1990), 4–5.
[190] See Sarah Perrigo, 'Women and Change in the Labour Party 1979–1995', in Joni Lovenduski and Pippa Norris (eds), *Women in Politics* (Oxford: Oxford University Press, 1996), 118–31.
[191] WL, NAC, *NAC Newsletter* 7 (April 1996), n.p.

8

A Thirty Years War?
Gay Rights and the Labour Party, 1967–97

Despite the reform of 1967, the relationship between homosexual rights and Labour politics remained uncertain. In the 1950s, as already suggested, Labour revisionists had included homosexual law reform as part of what they saw as a programme to modernize and civilize Britain. But the movement for what increasingly became known as gay (and, later, lesbian) rights had shallow roots in the Labour movement and in the British Left generally.

One difficulty, as argued in Chapter 6, was discursive. The figure of the working-class mother and the image of the beleaguered working-class family inspired greater pathos and, therefore, more sustained political action than the homosexual man or the sexually liberated woman. An idea of individual rights or discrimination was not, as yet, as much a spur to social reform as the condition of working-class life. Homosexuality seemed, in particular, to have far less class purchase. Allan Horsfall's experiences had shown the limits of Labour politics in this regard. The case for homosexual rights often grated with an idea of 'traditional' working-class politics and a received understanding of what or who constituted working-class community. The hostility of such views, whether due to religious conviction, personal bias, social conservatism, or political calculation, is undeniable. In 1985, a local trade union official in Greenwich remarked bluntly that he was 'personally prejudiced' and happened to believe that 'homosexuality is perverted', opinions that he and a colleague suggested might be the 'sincerely held views of the majority of the Workforce, and probably the people of the Borough'.[1] Even where there was not such obvious hostility, there might be confusion. In his memoir of growing up gay in working-class Rotherham, Terry Sanderson recalled that his local Labour MP, Peter Hardy, simply believed homosexuality was a London thing that could not migrate up the M1, unlike, perhaps, the badgers to whom he dedicated a book.[2] Nor did the radical edge of socialist politics help. As Lucy Robinson has shown in her comprehensive history of *Gay Men and the Left* (2007), until relatively late in the century, Marxists tended to view homosexuality as a bourgeois deviation that

---

[1] LSE, Hall Carpenter Archives [HCA], GLC Gay Rights Working Party Papers [GWPP], 1/7, Greenwich Lesbian and Gay Rights Group, Newsletter, April/May 1985; LSE, HCA/GWPP, 1/7, TGWU/ACTSS, C. Maslin and B. Corbett, Notes of Mass Meeting, Greenwich, 11 April 1985.
[2] Terry Anderson, 'Faltering From the Closet', in Bob Cant and Susan Hemmings (eds), *Radical Records* (London: Routledge, 1988), 85–93; Peter Hardy, *A Lifetime of Badgers* (Bristol: Newton Abbott, 1974).

would wither once socialism was achieved. The IS, the Revolutionary Communist
Party (RCP), and the Trotskyite Militant Tendency all proved, at best, dilatory and
sometimes unreliable allies to the cause of gay rights and, at worst, violent
opponents. As late as 1983, for example, members of Militant Tendency kicked
and spat upon gay Young Socialists when the latter dared to raise the issue of gay
and lesbian rights.[3]

Kenneth Robinson and Leo Abse excepted, gay rights also lacked consistent
champions in the Parliamentary Labour Party. In contrast to the abortion issue,
there was no identifiable body of support for gay rights within the ranks of Labour
parliamentarians until the early 1980s. As Robinson has pointed out, it was
impossible to be an out gay Labour politician until the 1980s. In 1977, Maureen
Colquhoun was forced to fight a 'savage' reselection battle in her constituency after
being publicly identified as a lesbian.[4] In parliament, gay rights depended upon the
support of straight Labour MPs, notably Tony Benn and Jo Richardson. Signs of a
thaw in this climate only appeared in the early 1980s. George Morton, MP for
Manchester Moss Side, survived an arrest for gross indecency without being
deposed by his local party. He was pointedly unapologetic about 'the feelings
that gave rise' to his arrest.[5] A real turning point came four years later when
Chris Smith, MP for Islington, began an address to a crowd in Rugby with the
words: 'My name is Chris Smith, I'm the Labour MP for Islington South and
Finsbury, and I'm gay.'[6]

Smith's announcement took an enormous amount of personal courage. It also
occurred against an unfolding context of more certain links between gay rights and
Labour politics. In the early 1980s, there were initiatives from the NEC and the
GLC. In no small part due to the efforts of a grass-roots gay rights movement
within the Labour Party and changes within the TUC, the first gay rights resolutions were achieved at Labour conference in 1985 and 1986, and commitments
made to include such policy in the election manifesto. In 1988, at the beginning of
probably the most important policy review since the 1950s, Labour declared that
gay men and lesbian women 'must have the same freedom from discrimination and
prejudice and the same freedom to live their lives as other people'.[7]

As with abortion, this was not a linear story of progress. Instead, it was coloured
by ambiguity and tentativeness. Bold steps forward were qualified by long periods
of passivity, indifference, and sometimes disavowal. Not least, it is a story, like that
of abortion, driven by defensiveness rather than progress. This was particularly true
in the face of a concerted attack on gay rights by Conservative governments
between 1979 and 1997. Examining Conservative thought on race and sexuality

---

[3] LSE, HCA, Journals, 476J, *Gay Socialist: Journal of the Campaign for Gay Rights* 7 (1983); see also
Weeks, *Coming Out*, 234.
[4] See Maureen Colquhoun, *A Woman in the House* (London: Scan, 1980), 136.
[5] *The Guardian*, 26 August 1980.
[6] Chris Smith, 'The Politics of Pride', in Emma Healey and Angela Mason (eds), *Stonewall 25*
(London: Virago, 1994), 63.
[7] Labour Party, *Social Justice and Economic Efficiency: First Report of Labour's Policy Review for the
1990s* (London: Labour Party, 1988), 37.

in the 1980s, Anna Marie Smith has made a powerful case for what she has called the Conservatives' 'promotion of homosexuality' as a 'legitimating strategy for the exercise of authority and the valorization of the family: Queerness became one of the enemy elements which supported the phantasmatic construction of the family as the antagonism-free centre of the British nation.'[8] In this rhetoric, sexual, racial, and political otherness was gathered together in an attack upon local government; gay and lesbian rights initiatives were portrayed as a threat to traditional ideas of community, nation, and family. When Thatcher told her party, on the morning of the Tories' 1987 election victory, that it was time to 'do something about those inner cities', this was a statement of imminent threat. In terms of gay rights, it became most clear with the passage of the 1988 Local Government Act and its Section 28, which prohibited local authorities from 'intentionally promot[ing] homosexuality or publish[ing] material with the intention of promoting homosexuality . . . promot[ing] the teaching in any maintained school of the acceptability of homosexuality as a pretended family relationship'.[9] Section 28 had been preceded by the 1984 Police and Criminal Evidence Act which gave the police far greater powers against what could be interpreted as acts of indecency. Conservative legislation coincided with more invasive police action against gays and lesbians, which in many instances amounted to harassment; in Manchester, notoriously, the Chief Constable, James Anderton, spoke of the '"degenerate" behaviour of people swilling around in a human cesspit of their own making'.[10]

As Smith suggests, during the Thatcher years, the Conservatives and the police did much to both create and demonize the gay community. In a different vein, Martin Durham has argued that Thatcherite Conservatism represented a conscious backlash against permissiveness.[11] This was most obviously rooted in moral and national anxieties, but it had an economic aspect, as well, in the desire to control the excessive spending of local governments.[12] At the centre of these Conservative anxieties lay an idealized heterosexual family with clearly defined gender roles.[13] Gay and lesbian rights were arrayed against this immutable and, of course, completely constructed truth. Such discussions occurred under the shadow of the developing AIDS crisis. In the early 1980s, AIDS was characterized as a 'gay plague', playing into fears of the lesbian and gay community. In many ways, it was not simply that the Labour Party took up gay and lesbian rights, it was that the Conservatives politicized the issue.

[8] Smith, *New Right Discourse on Race and Sexuality*, 185, 189.
[9] Local Government Bill, 1987/88 Bill 65, clause 27, 27; Lords amendments to the Local Government Bill, 1987/88 Bill 111, clause 28, 2.
[10] Quoted in Durham, *Sex and Politics*, 123.
[11] See Durham, *Sex and Politics*.
[12] See Smith, *New Right Discourse on Race and Sexuality*; Bill Schwarz, 'Conservatism, Nationalism and Imperialism', in James Donald and Stuart Hall (eds), *Politics and Ideology* (Milton Keynes: Open University Press, 1986), 154–87.
[13] See, for example, Heather Nunn, *Thatcher, Politics and Fantasy: The Political Culture of Gender and Nation* (London: Lawrence and Wishart, 2002); Jane Pilcher and Stephen Wagg (eds), *Thatcher's Children? Politics, Childhood and Society in the 1980s and 1990s* (London: Falmer, 1996).

It is hardly surprising, given such vehement attacks by the Conservatives, that the Labour Party became a vessel for the advocacy of gay rights in the political mainstream. Labour was, of course, imperfect in this regard. In the first place, as already noted, the culture of Labour politics was not necessarily hospitable to the articulation of gay and lesbian rights. Secondly, pummelled by four consecutive election defeats, Labour was itself trying to find an effective political identity in the 1980s and 1990s. On the one hand, the gay and lesbian rights campaign offered a potential source of new vitality even as the old certainties of electoral strength such as the working-class vote were apparently ebbing away. On the other, many within the party saw gay and lesbian rights as a symbol of what was preventing Labour from claiming back the middle ground. It was not just the Conservatives that ironically 'homosexualized' politics; Labour identified many of its own failures with what the leadership perceived as the excesses of the gay rights movement. Disastrous by-elections in Bermondsey in 1983 and Greenwich in 1987 plumbed the depths of Labour's ambivalence on the issue. When Labour did adopt gay rights between 1985 and 1987, it did so tentatively. The party acknowledged that lesbians and gay men suffered undue discrimination and that something had to be done about this, but this recognition went hand-in-glove with anxieties about the electoral consequences of being associated with the gay issue. The single most important factor in pushing Labour further towards gay rights was Section 28. This was such an egregious attack upon the civil rights of gays and lesbians and such a vilification of those communities that Labour could move to their defence more easily. In the 1980s, as a means of pushing back against Thatcherite Conservatism, Labour distanced itself from its own statist past by stressing its support for individual rights. This included gay and lesbian rights.

In the thirty years that followed the Sexual Offences Act of 1967, a struggle ensued within the Labour movement to accommodate gay rights. This struggle remained open and incomplete. The present chapter begins with a discussion of the GLF, the CHE, and the Marxist gay Left. Because this story has already been told so effectively in Robinson's work, the present chapter pays greater attention to the emergence of gay rights within the Labour movement at the local and national level between the 1970s and the 1990s.

This chapter also tells the stories of gay men and lesbians together. This is not to conflate the two. Certainly, far more attention has been paid to the politics of gay men in the 1970s and 1980s than those of lesbian women. To a certain degree, gay men did the early running in establishing the context of gay rights, not least because the law affected gay men in a way it did not lesbian women. At the same time, lesbian rights developed both from a distinctive pre-1970 lesbian subculture and within the politics of women's liberation.[14] Much more detailed and dedicated research on lesbian Left politics needs to be done and this account does not pretend

---

[14] See Rebecca Jennings, 'The Gateways Club and the Emergence of a Post-Second World War Lesbian Subculture', *Social History* 31 (2006), 206–25; Rebecca Jennings, *Tomboys and Bachelor Girls: A Lesbian History of Post-War Britain 1945–71* (Manchester: Manchester University Press, 2007); Jennings, *A Lesbian History of Britain*, Chapter 10.

to do justice to that subject. It should be stressed, as this chapter makes clear, that there were moments of intersection and deviation between the political aspirations of gay men and lesbian women. They shared, for example, concerns about job discrimination, access to social services, and the promotion of gay and lesbian culture.[15] On the other hand, lesbians were more concerned, at least in the 1970s and 1980s, about child custody and parental rights, often because of the trajectories of their own lives. Lesbians also made a case for separatism, largely against what was seen as the domineering qualities of both heterosexual and gay men. Bisexuality was also an issue not easily accommodated within gay rights at the outset. But, in the example of the Labour Party in the 1970s and 1980s, gay men, lesbian women, and bisexuals worked together, particularly through the Labour Party Campaign for Lesbian and Gay Rights. The progress of gay and lesbian rights within Labour owes much to the work of gay Labour men like Peter Purton and lesbian Labour women such as Sarah Roelofs.

I

In the autumn of 1970, two developments signalled the emergence of a new kind of homosexual rights movement. In October, the London School of Economics played host to the formation of the GLF. The following month, in what amounted to the first gay rights march, there was a demonstration on Highbury Fields to protest the arrest of the leader of the Young Liberals for importuning. Both events challenged the deferential politics of homophile and homosexual rights organizations of the 1950s and 1960s. If, as Robinson writes, such organizations had 'attempted to negotiate the existing system', gay liberation ignored the system, instead exploring new forms of politics and trying to transform the meaning of the political.[16] In the 1970s, there were competing strands of homosexual politics, the first represented by the liberationist GLF, the second by the more gradualist CHE, and the third by an emerging Marxist gay politics.

Like the women's liberation movement, gay liberation was rooted in the particular milieu of 1960s radicalism. A common reference point in histories of the movement was the Dialectics of Liberation conference in 1967. It also drew from American influences, such as the Black Panther movement and, of course, the Stonewall protests of June 1969. Two young, gay English travellers to America, Aubrey Walter and Bob Mellors, were spectators to these developments and carried that inspiration back across the Atlantic to London in 1970.[17] The GLF also had domestic connections with the revolutionary Left, including the IMG, the IS, and the CP, though each treated gay issues with different degrees of sympathy. Like

---

[15] See, for example, the case brought against South West Trains by Lisa Grant, *The Guardian*, 3 May 1996.

[16] Robinson, *Gay Men and the Left*, 39.

[17] Michael Mason, 'Out of the Closets on to the Streets: Gay Men's History', in Healey and Mason (eds), *Stonewall 25*, 98–9; the best historical account of the GLF is Robinson, *Gay Men and the Left*, Chapters 3 and 4.

women's liberation, the GLF offered a different structural model for activism as much as it presented a new politics of homosexual liberation. Workshops on a variety of social, cultural, and political subjects were put together. The GLF experimented with different forms of organization and living. Consciousness-raising was important, but gay liberation took radicalism a step further with communal living. The 'zap'—an often comic public intervention—was used to confront perceived oppressors, as when GLF members invaded David Frost's television show, protested the distribution of David Reuben's *Everything You Ever Wanted to Know About Sex But Were Too Afraid to Ask* (1969), and interfered with the Christian evangelical National Festival of Light. Lesbian women were involved at an early stage of the GLF, though differences between gay men and lesbian women, and among lesbian women, soon emerged, with some migrating to the women's liberation movement.[18]

The chaotic vibrancy of the GLF ultimately led to its implosion within a couple of years. But the GLF left important ideological legacies. Michael Mason remarked that 'creating a gay politics' unwound from understanding two words: 'liberation' and 'oppression'.[19] The first rested upon the idea of a forceful and staged process of 'coming out', 'coming together', and 'changing the world'.[20] How the last two were to be accomplished proved deeply problematic, but the emphasis upon creating a community and a revolution fired debates within gay politics into the 1970s and 1980s. The interest in the nature of oppression certainly differentiated gay liberation from a previous tradition of homophile organizations. Keith Birch, a veteran of the movement, recalled, in a phrase of eloquent simplicity: '[w]e believed everything would change, even ourselves'.[21] Part of changing the world and the self demanded thinking about oppression. Like women's liberation, gay liberation gave enormous attention to the structures, cultures, and consciousness of oppression and in doing so bore witness to changing fashions in Marxist thought. This point will be developed below in a discussion of socialist gay liberationists, but in its short life, the GLF identified medicine, the law, psychiatry, religion, the self, and the family as sites of oppression and persecution for gays. The family was a particular target and, in its first incarnation, the GLF sought the abolition of the family: '[w]e intend to work for the replacement of the family unit with its rigid gender-role pattern'.[22] This vision was thus a revolutionary one: '[t]he granting of equality to homosexuals in all areas of social life would completely change all social relations between people. . . . Family life as we know it would disappear.'[23]

---

[18] See Jennings, *A Lesbian History of Britain*, 169–77.

[19] Mason, 100.

[20] See Robinson, *Gay Men and the Left*, Chapter 3.

[21] Keith Birch, 'A Community of Interests', in Bob Cant and Susan Hemmings (eds), *Radical Records: Thirty Years of Lesbian and Gay History* (London: Routledge, 1988), 51.

[22] George Lennox in *7 Days*, quoted in Robinson, *Gay Men and the Left*, 76.

[23] *Sexual Politics in Britain* (Brighton: Harvester, 1986), CHE Papers and Publications [CHE]; Don Millington, 'Outsiders: Why I Won't Join CHE', *CHE: The Bulletin of the Campaign for Homosexual Equality*: December–January 1976–7.

The spectacular arc of the GLF in the early 1970s should not mask the continuation of an older tradition of gradualist homophile organization. With the achievement of the Sexual Offences Act of 1967, the HLRS effectively closed down. The initiative was left to Allan Horsfall's NWHRC, a more radical organization than the HLRS, even if it was one that was to appear mainstream in comparison to the new gay liberation movement. The NWHRC became the CHE. In stark contrast to the GLF, the CHE kept a traditional structure. It mustered a large membership, probably around 4,000 in the early 1970s. Like previous homophile and sexual reform pressure groups, the CHE also sought respectability and authority.[24] The CHE's political aims were built on the principle that 'the homosexual has an equal right to self-fulfilment and can make an equally positive contribution in our common quest for the betterment of society and the happiness of all' and that there should be 'absolute equality at law between homosexuals and heterosexuals' against 'all forms of legal or social discrimination against homosexuals'.[25] In practice, these aims were manifested in seeking parity of law between Scotland and England, highlighting discrimination at the workplace and police abuse, and, most of all, pressing for the equalization of the age of consent to 16. The CHE favoured traditional political methods to achieve these aims: public education and parliamentary lobbying.

If the GLF focused upon questions of oppression and positioned themselves outside the existing social and political system, the CHE was unashamedly mainstream. It defined its position as one of 'critical integration', an approach that remained committed to significant political change, but without fundamentally changing society: 'gay people can find equality in society *as it is* without there having to be a fundamental change in the social structure'. Unlike the GLF and, later, the Marxist gay Left, the CHE eschewed any analysis of oppression; its approach was 'gay populism . . . a melting pot, or rather a pot-pourrie [*sic*] of ideas; [that does not contain] any coherent explanation of why gay people are oppressed or how liberation should be worked for'.[26] The CHE made clear a desire to join society, not to change it; homosexuals were 'a recognized minority community like any ethnic or religious minority which is attempting to become part of the varied and heterogeneous structure of modern society'.[27] But the 'legal twilight' in which gays existed impeded this fight for 'dignity and self-respect'. This was an issue of 'fundamental human rights'. The CHE was careful to construct the homosexual subject as respectable and private. Indeed, it distanced itself from more radical forms of homosexual behaviour. The CHE argued that the present state of the law frustrated homosexuals forming stable relationships and thus only encouraged 'less socially acceptable' forms of homosexual culture: 'denied the opportunity of meeting and making friends with compatible and kindred spirits [homosexuals are] compelled to seek refuge in promiscuous chance encounters in

---

[24] CHE, Executive Committee minutes, 18 November 1971.
[25] CHE, *Constitution*.
[26] CHE, *CHE—The Way Ahead*: Southampton Conference Workshop Paper, 1976.
[27] CHE, Submission to the Criminal Law Revision Committee, 1976, para. 12.

public lavatories and other, equally sordid, places'.[28] This approach strained relations between the GLF and CHE.

A powerful after-effect of the GLF's disintegration was the development of a discernible gay Left.[29] Groups such as the Gay Activist Alliance, the Gay Workers Movement, and the Gay Marxist Group had connections with the CP and the IS and emerged out of the embers of the GLF, though, as Robinson points out, this left them with 'a sense of being between a rock and a hard place', with one activist saying 'often other gays are totally against us and we are ignored by most of the revolutionary Left'.[30] A significant criticism of the GLF was its lack of intellectual (read Marxist) rigour.[31] Important figures such as Jeffrey Weeks used the Gay Marxist Group and its short-lived publication, *Gay Marxist*, to explore links between socialist politics and liberationist gay activism. A successor organization, the Gay Left Collective, produced a more enduring legacy with the publication *Gay Left*. This too reflected a greater desire for intellectual and organizational discipline. The first issue of *Gay Left*, for example, dismissed the 'sweet smells of incense, inspiration and home-baked bread' that left 'the power structures of society . . . untouched' and 'the lives of the majority of gay people . . . completely unchanged'.[32] Organizers of a meeting on gay workers in 1975 did not hide their impatience with the 'hopeless confusion' of the gathering, marked by a lack of punctuality and direction, which was attributed to the GLF tradition.[33] In the early 1980s, Simon Watney similarly remarked that gay liberation had been 'politically hampered' by 'romantic Leninist or anarchist myth of Total Revolution' and beguiled by the 'glamourous anarchic possibilities of libertarianism'.[34]

What distinguished gay Marxists from both the homophile tradition and gay liberation was a determination to make sense of gay oppression and map a route towards a gay politics that was neither integrationist nor utopian. Instead, it would be moored in 'a materialist analysis of sexual oppression'.[35] An early articulation of this was published in the first issue of *Gay Left* in 1975. Its understanding of gay oppression was related to 'the links between the family, the oppression of women and gay people and the class structure of society'. The family was a particular object of interest with its 'sharp polarization' of gender roles becoming even more cutting during industrialization. The family became a central ideological plank in capitalism, its gender differentiation serving the economic and class needs of capitalism. At the same time, the family in capitalism was socially constructed but represented as natural. For this reason, the family and capitalism marginalized sexual others: 'gay oppression is a result of the demands on the family by a capitalist society'. The

[28] CHE, Criminal Law Revision Committee, para. 15.
[29] For a detailed discussion of this, see Robinson, *Gay Men and the Left*, Chapter 5.
[30] Robinson, *Gay Men and the Left*, 126.
[31] Robinson, *Gay Men and the Left*, 127.
[32] *Sexual Politics in Britain* (Brighton: Harvester, 1986); Collective Statement, *Gay Left* 1 (Autumn 1975), 1.
[33] Bob Cant and Nigel Young, 'The Gay Workers' Movement', *Gay Left* 2 (Spring 1976), 18–21.
[34] Simon Watney, 'The Ideology of the GLF', in Gay Left Collective (eds), *Homosexuality: Power and Politics* (London: Allison and Busby, 1980), 73, 75.
[35] Collective Statement, *Gay Left* 1 (Autumn 1975), 2.

road out of such oppression depended upon both the rejection of capitalism and the family and the unification of all oppressed classes.[36]

As the 1970s went on, this kind of analysis proved less and less persuasive. In part, of course, it foundered on the links that could be made between oppressed classes, whether on grounds of class, gender, or race. But some gay leftists became increasingly uncomfortable with what the editorial collective of *Gay Left* called the 'narrow and limiting' reliance on an '"economistic" form of Marxism'. In its place, there was a growing espousal of an approach clearly inspired by Foucault, dependent upon an 'understanding of the varied mechanisms by which homosexuality is constructed as a repressive category in our culture'.[37] The most powerful example of this was 'Capitalism and the Organisation of Sex' (1980) by Jeffrey Weeks. Rejecting the idea of sex as a 'natural force' promulgated by Marxist thinkers on sex and the family from Engels to Reich and Marcuse, Weeks instead took up Foucault's argument that sexuality was itself a construct, used to limit and discipline the various pleasures of the body. To understand homosexual oppression, one had to understand the vast panoply of mechanism and situation across a wide field of institutions, knowledge, and historical context. Categories rather than capitalism were the enemy. This may have seemed daunting, but it did free leftist sex reformers from an overdependence upon the family and capitalism as the sites of oppression. Instead, what had to be understood were all the modes of 'organization, regulation, categorization', including the family and the economy, but also comprising the law, medicine, psychiatry, and culture. The political aim of gay liberation was, therefore, liberation from categorization: '[i]t is not just the end of the homosexual or the heterosexual we must demand but the end of the ideology of sexuality'.[38] In this way, politics would begin with the corporeal and plastic pleasures of the body; the barricades of revolution would be built upon the restlessly ambiguous pleasures of the sexual body.

But this proved a chimera. Because of the Conservative government in the 1980s, gay rights activists were driven back to defend the very categories about which they might have had serious intellectual doubts. As Matthew Waites has argued, resistance to Section 28 and support for equalizing the age of consent was dependent upon a notion of sexual identity as fixed.[39]

The arguments of the GLF, CHE, and the gay Left afforded a profound critique of existing sexual ideology, but only the CHE had a more precise programme of political action focused upon Westminster and, in particular, on the protection and expansion of the gay rights established by the 1967 Sexual Offences Act. In the mid- to late 1970s, the priorities were equalizing the age of consent with heterosexuals, removing the sanctions on the armed forces and the merchant navy, and

[36] Collective Statement, *Gay Left* 1 (Autumn 1975), 1–2.

[37] Gay Left Collective, 'Introduction' to *Homosexuality, Power and Politics*, 8.

[38] Jeffrey Weeks, 'Capitalism and the Organisation of Sex', in *Homosexuality, Power and Politics*, 12, 14, 19–20.

[39] See Matthew Waites, 'Equality At Last? Homosexuality, Heterosexuality and the Age of Consent in the United Kingdom', *Sociology* 37 (2003), 637–55; 'Regulation of Sexuality: Age of Consent, Section 28 and Sex Education', *Parliamentary Affairs* 54 (2001), 495–508.

bringing Scotland and Northern Ireland under the provisions of the law in England. Success was mixed. In July 1975, the CHE, the Scottish Minorities Group, and the Union for Sexual Freedom in Ireland collaborated on a draft Homosexual Law Reform Bill, the main proposals of which were the equalization of the age of consent and making the law consistent across the United Kingdom. The Labour Home Secretary, Roy Jenkins, was lukewarm in his response, but agreed that the Criminal Law Review Committee (CLRC) would look at all sexual offences, a process that was not complete until 1981. In the Lords, Arran and Boothby brought two bills, one, Arran's unsuccessful attempt to lower the age of consent to 18, the other a successful initiative to bring Scotland within the fold of the 1967 Act. In 1980, through an amendment by Labour's Robin Cook, the Criminal Justice (Scotland) Act legalized homosexuality in Scotland. Northern Ireland achieved the same result, but through a different route. Britain's membership of the European Community was the key factor here. A human rights case was successfully pursued by a gay man, Jeff Dudgeon. In October 1981, the European Court found in favour of Dudgeon, asserting that Britain's laws on homosexuality in Northern Ireland left it in violation of the European Convention. A change in the law in Northern Ireland soon followed.[40] That same year, the CLRC finally reported, rejecting the equalization of the age of consent to 16 and recommending it be set at 18 for homosexuals, though six members of the committee favoured the lower age.[41]

But attitudes hardened against further extensions of gay rights. There seemed little indication of public support for any improvement of the terms of the 1967 Act.[42] Powerful lobby groups such as the Police Federation remained opposed to a change in the law. Controversy still dogged the question of homosexuality at Westminster. In 1976, the scandal of Jeremy Thorpe's alleged involvement in a conspiracy to murder the male model Norman Scott lent a lurid hue to gay issues. The controversial links between the Paedophile Information Exchange and groups such as the National Council for Civil Liberties also undermined the political efficacy of gay rights groups.[43] In 1977, the deselection of Maureen Colquhoun as an MP for Northampton North demonstrated the limits of Labour's culture in dealing with homosexuality. Colquhoun had been involved with the CHE and with Action for Lesbian Parents.[44] She later complained that the Labour leadership was unsupportive and that even those fellow female MPs who had worked closely together to defend the Abortion Act proved unsympathetic to her plight.[45]

As with the politics of abortion, it was the meaning of the parliamentary reform of 1967 that ultimately pulled gay politics back to the centre, in particular, to

---

[40] Jeffery-Poulter, *Peers, Queers and Commons*, 151.

[41] Cmnd. 8216 Policy Advisory Committee on Sexual Offences, *Report on the Age of Consent in Relation to Sexual Offences* (London: HMSO, April 1981).

[42] Jeffery-Poulter, *Peers, Queers and Commons*, 114–15.

[43] See Robinson, *Gay Men and the Left*, Chapter 5.

[44] See CHE, 4 (1976) AL, Executive Committee Minutes, 14 March 1976; Weeks, *Coming Out*, 211.

[45] Colquhoun, *A Woman in the House*; Jeffery-Poulter, *Peers, Queers and Commons*, 136.

parliamentary politics. Between the late 1970s and the early 1990s, Westminster helped define the trajectory of gay politics and activism, often in a reactionary way. This was particularly true of the attacks upon the extension of gay rights witnessed during the Thatcher years, such as the 1984 Police and Criminal Evidence Act and the 1988 Local Government Act. The old politics continued to shape the new politics.

II

After an advertisement in the *Gay News* for a 'gay labour caucus', the Gay Labour Group (GLG) met for the first time in the CHE offices in early 1975; by the end of the year there were about forty-five members.[46] As with other pressure groups in the sphere of sexual politics, the GLG's individual membership was never overwhelming. By August 1983, there were 200 members, with about ten affiliated CLPs.[47] The relatively small numbers nonetheless belied an impressive level of activity and degree of influence. The GLG began by making its presence felt at the Labour annual conference, attending brains trusts and fringe meetings and asking questions about gay rights. It then began to put on its own fringe meetings and discos at both the Labour conference and the TUC, featuring speakers such as Ken Livingstone, Joan Lestor, Jo Richardson, and Peter Tatchell.[48] Following a well-trodden route, the GLG worked within constituency parties to get a resolution on the agenda of the annual conference, such as the one submitted in 1976 by Coventry North East CLP, which castigated the party for failing 'so far, to demand equality for homosexuals [as] merely a reflection of the general ignorance of the subject at all levels within the Party'.[49] Local government was also a target; one of the early members of the GLG was Chris Smith, then a councillor in Islington. On the spectrum of gay politics, the GLG was initially more closely linked to the CHE rather than the Marxist Left. In 1978, the GLG became the Labour Campaign for Gay Rights (LCGR). In Manchester and Nottingham, there were groups who wanted a more radical approach. At the AGM in Nottingham in July 1982, a new form of organization emerged, with strong regional groups in the East Midlands, Bristol, Manchester, and London and the inclusion of lesbians, so that it became the Labour Campaign for Lesbian and Gay Rights (LCLGR). A National Coordinating Committee organized the regional groups and by the fall of 1982, there were seventy-five members and nine affiliated CLPs and other Labour groups.[50]

The veteran activist and historian of the LCLGR, Peter Purton, has suggested that it flourished in part because it formed alliances with other minority activist

---

[46] LSE, HCA, Gay Labour Group Papers [GLGP], 328, *Newsletter* 2 (Summer 1975); see Peter Purton, *Sodom, Gomorrah and the New Jerusalem* (London: Labour Campaign for Lesbian and Gay Rights, 2006) for a focused history of the GLG and its successors.
[47] LSE, HCA, Robert Crossman Papers [RCP], 3/7, Labour Campaign for Gay Rights, 1982–3.
[48] See, for example, LSE, HCA/GLGP 328, Newsletter 8 (October 1976).
[49] LSE, HCA, GLGP, Newsletter 9 (January 1976).
[50] LSE, HCA/RCP, 3/7, Labour Campaign for Gay Rights, 1982–3.

campaigns such as the black sections campaign, while studiously avoiding any association with identifiably hard Left groups within the party such as Militant Tendency.[51] Militant was, indeed, perceived as an enemy. Within the Militant-dominated Young Socialists, for example, one gay member noted a minor triumph after an annual meeting: '[i]n past years we had been kicked and spat upon by delegates. This year we only had to suffer verbal abuse and threats of violence.'[52] The LCLGR's other perceived allies were a collection of campaigning groups on the 'softer' Left within Labour, such as the Labour Coordinating Committee (LCC), the CPLD, and the Tribune group of MPs, especially Jo Richardson. Unions also lent support.[53] Because there were several cases of discrimination on grounds of sexual orientation in the late 1970s and early 1980s, unions were encouraged to become involved in gay and lesbian rights. Studies by the CHE and Lesbian and Gay Employment Rights also showed that there were increasing numbers of known gay and lesbian workers. Unions such as the TGWU took up gay rights policies. A major boost in this regard came in 1984 when NUPE (later renamed UNISON) affiliated to the LCLGR.[54]

In 1981, two developments suggested the gradual success of this nascent campaign. The first was the commitment of the NEC to develop its policy on gay rights following an intervention by Tony Benn. The second occurred at the level of local politics, when Ken Livingstone, the recently elected Chair of the GLC, announced that the GLC would actively pursue a policy of gay rights. In 1985, the Labour Party conference formally adopted gay rights as a policy, which was reaffirmed as a manifesto commitment at the 1986 conference. But, as with abortion, this was not an uncomplicated conversion.

To a considerable degree, the emergence of gay and lesbian rights brought out the cultural struggle over Labour's identity occurring in the 1970s and 1980s, a conflict that boiled over in the Bermondsey by-election of 1983 and at the level of local government. This was not simply an argument between right and left or old and new. After Neil Kinnock's accession to the leadership following the 1983 election, it also became a conflict within the party's ascendant soft Left, between those, like Livingstone, who wished to revitalize the party through issues such as gay and lesbian rights, drawing upon the inheritance of the 1960s and liberationist politics, and those, like Patricia Hewitt, Kinnock's communication adviser, who feared the electoral consequences of '[t]he gays and lesbians issue'.[55] As with the abortion issue, the campaign for gay and lesbian rights within the Labour Party highlighted the pliable nature of socialism. When Jo Richardson said, at the 1987 conference, 'there can be no genuine lesbian and gay liberation without socialism, and that there is no socialism without lesbian and gay liberation', she was not simply describing an ideal state of affairs, but a set of sometimes conflicting

---

[51] See Purton, *Sodom, Gomorrah and the New Jerusalem*, 39.
[52] LSE, HCA/Journals/476J, *Gay Socialist* 7 (June 1983).
[53] Purton, *Sodom, Gomorrah and the New Jerusalem*, 39.
[54] Purton, *Sodom, Gomorrah and the New Jerusalem*, 40–1.
[55] Hughes and Wintour, *Labour Rebuilt*, 19.

relationships.[56] It was really only after 1988, in reaction to Section 28 and in the process of reshaping the party more widely, that mainstream Labour found a palatable way of articulating its support for gay and lesbian rights. In the early and mid-1980s, it was the fissures opened up by the question of gay rights that were most apparent. As Eley has suggested, this was, in no small part, a tense working-through of the post-1960s struggle between different socialisms and different visions of democracy.[57] After 1988, Labour accommodated gay rights into a rhetoric of equality and individual rights; this did not yet displace an emphasis on the heterosexual family as the normative form of sexual life, but it did represent some kind of advance, a staging point to the reforms of the early twenty-first century.

The boldest and most promising attempt to link Labour politics and gay and lesbian rights came with Ken Livingstone's leadership of the GLC between 1981 and 1986. Most accounts agree that Livingstone's initiative was a deeply subjective one, less rooted in ideology than in Livingstone's own preference for an 'eminently practical' municipal socialism.[58] Livingstone was a lab technician who had moved into radical politics through the anti-war movement in the 1960s. In 1974, he became a fulltime GLC councillor in Brixton, notably the home of a GLF office.[59] Livingstone showed an early commitment to gay rights; as a parliamentary candidate for Hampstead in 1977, he proposed reducing the homosexual age of consent to 16.[60] He was a leading force in the group London Labour Briefing, which sought to create a Labour politics removed both from Trotskyite influence and the old Labour right. What particularly interested Livingstone was moving Labour politics away from class towards new kinds of political identity, such as gender, sexuality, and race.

In May 1981, after Labour gained a majority of seats in the local elections, Livingstone became Leader of the GLC. The following August, spurred on by allegations that police were harassing gays, he announced his support for gay rights, pledging that 'where possible, the GLC would implement' the proposals of gay rights groups and support funding of gay organizations along the same lines as other 'voluntary organizations'. This commitment was controversially framed by his assertion that 'everyone is bisexual'.[61] There was both altruism in this commitment and political calculation. The gay and lesbian rights campaign undoubtedly promised battalions of 'foot soldiers' in campaigning.[62] Supporting the cause of gay and lesbian rights also encouraged the development of a new kind of Labour approach, as Livingstone told Beatrix Campbell in 1985: 'in terms of what we've done in things like the GLC women's committee, ethnic minorities, gay rights, we've had a quite clear idea of where we wanted to get to—breaking down attitudes

---

[56] *LPCR* (1986), 40.
[57] Eley, *Forging Democracy*, Chapters 26 and 27.
[58] Robinson, *Gay Men and the Left*, 143.
[59] Robinson, *Gay Men and the Left*, 144.
[60] John Carvel, *Citizen Ken* (London: Chatto and Windus/Hogarth Press, 1984), 63.
[61] *The Guardian*, 19 August 1981; Carvel, *Citizen Ken*, 91.
[62] Robinson, *Gay Men and the Left*, 145.

8.1 'Ken Livingstone at GLC County Hall, 1981', photography by Popperfoto, copyright Popperfoto/Getty Images 80415348 (RM)

and changing lifestyles . . . there is a real chance that the next PLP will put the issues of race, feminism and sexual politics firmly on the agenda'.[63] Livingstone's biographer described him as the 'product of an age of weakening class loyalties' and this was reflected in his desire to build socialism out of new identities.[64]

The GLC established a Gay Rights Working Party (GWP) and by 1984 had spent £300,000 on grants to gay and lesbian groups and earmarked £750,000 for a London Lesbian and Gay Centre. The GLC also published a Charter for Gay and Lesbian Rights, *Changing the World*. The GWP met from 1982 until the abolition of the GLC in 1986, after which the new Association of London Authorities established a Lesbian and Gay Committee.[65] A Lesbian Working Party operated under the aegis of the GLC Women's Committee. The remit of the GWP was principally to draft what became *Changing the World*. But the committee also worked to develop policy in employment and housing, planned the Gay and Lesbian Centre, and, not least, coordinated the applications for GLC grants from various gay and lesbian organizations such as the CHE, the Hall Carpenter

---

[63] 'The Unity Only Labour Can Provide', *The Guardian*, 6 May 1985.
[64] Carvel, *Citizen Ken*, 26.
[65] LSE, HCA/GWPP, 1/8, ALA Press Release, 3 June 1986.

Archives, the London Gay Switchboard, and smaller groups like Lesbian/Gay Video. The belief that London was a particularly important space for gays and lesbians in Britain was central to the GWP's work: '[y]oung lesbians and gay men come to the metropolis in search of work and a large and diverse gay community which offers support and widespread social and sexual opportunities'.[66] The GLC offered an historically important opportunity to effect political change: '[t]he GLC is in a unique position to pursue policies that counteract discrimination and enable the gay community to develop its own range of services and establish itself as a visible section of the population'.[67] Though the GWP was led by John McDonnell and Andy Harris (successive GLC Grants subcommittee chairs) and organized by Margaret Lally, its meetings were a kind of testament to 1970s-style campaigning, featuring an 'open structure' and a floating membership of lesbian and gay individuals and organizations, sometimes culminating in large consultative meetings.[68] There were two monuments to the work of the GWP. The first was physical, a building, the London Lesbian and Gay Centre, in Cowcross Street off the Farringdon Road. Though there were issues in the running of the Centre about lesbian separatism and the presence of bisexuals, it did provide a focus for social, cultural, and political activity until it closed in 1991.

The second achievement of the GWP was *Changing the World*, a charter for gay and lesbian rights in London, developed by the GWP and endorsed by other GLC committees in 1985. *Changing the World* followed two paths to sexual and social change. It offered 142 specific recommendations for improving gay and lesbian life in London, ranging from anti-discrimination measures in employment, health, and housing through changes in the law on child custody to the equalization of the age of consent. This was a broad programme. Some proposals addressed problems specific to the lesbian community, especially the problem of child custody. Nonetheless, *Changing the World* did capture the scale of the problem of inequality on grounds of sexual orientation. The second path set out in *Changing the World* owed more to the legacy of the GLF and gay Marxism in that it evinced a broad transformative vision. *Changing the World* attacked 'heterosexism', grounded in the belief that fundamental social attitudes about sexuality, identity, and the family had to be changed or abandoned, whether this meant anti-discrimination measures or the promotion of gay and lesbian culture and history (such as erecting commemorative blue plaques to Edward Carpenter and Radclyffe Hall).[69]

Changing the World was intended to be both a clarion call for gay rights in a heterosexual city and a unifying banner for gays and lesbians. There were points where the tensions around this were exposed. Not all gays and lesbians were, for example, happy with the document. The Lesbian Working Party and County Hall

---

[66] LSE, HCA/GWPP 1/1, GLC GWG Employment Sub-Committee, 'The Employment of Lesbians and Gay Men—A Strategy for London', 11 January 1983.

[67] LSE, HCA/GWPP 1/6, GLC Policy Co-ordinating Committee, 'GLC Policy in Relation to Gay Men and Lesbians', 12 March 1984.

[68] LSE, HCA/GWPP 1/6, GWP Minutes, 27 November 1984.

[69] GLC/GLC Gay Rights Working Party, *Changing the World: A London Charter for Gay and Lesbian Rights* (London: GLC, 1985).

lesbian group both expressed criticism of it, stressing instead the potential danger of 'mixed projects' between the gay and lesbian communities, criticisms that were not ultimately accepted.[70]

The work of the GWP and the circulation of *Changing the World* also exposed faultlines within the Labour movement. In Greenwich, local branches of the TGWU, largely manual and white-collar staff of the council, unanimously rejected the document, citing, in particular its proposals for education and residential homes. The leaders of the union branches told the Greenwich Council Leader that '[i]rrespective of what the Lesbians and Gays may think, public opinion is still opposed to their way of life, and the majority of the Workers in Greenwich are likewise'.[71] There were financial objections to council money being spent on gay and lesbian rights issues and ignoring the minimum wage or the thirty-five-hour week, instead of maintaining an older fabric of welfare provisions such as Lunch Clubs, Meals on Wheels, and Home Helps: 'the Gays and Lesbians Centre should not be considered a priority over these services'.[72] This reaction may have been isolated; certainly other unions, notably NALGO, passed counter-motions in support of *Changing the World*. But the GLC intervention in gay and lesbian rights undoubtedly opened up differences within the Labour movement.[73] As Robinson has suggested, 'the GLC . . . sent a message to the traditional Left. It showed how far municipal socialism would integrate parts of the liberation movement.'[74] This contrasted sharply with another form of municipal socialism, that of Derek Hatton in Liverpool, whose Militant Tendency espoused instead a 'hyper-masculinity' that rejected gay, lesbian, or feminist initiatives.[75]

If we look away from the GLC, the career of Bob Crossman gives another, perhaps less spectacular but no less profound sense of how gay politics worked on the ground within local government and, no less, how it was dependent upon particular individuals. From a working class background, Crossman had worked in a gay centre in Manchester, then became involved in tenants' rights. He moved to London in the 1970s and became involved in local politics. Crossman ended up as the deputy mayor of Islington, compared, not always favourably, to the San Francisco politician Harvey Milk and dismissed by *The Sun* as the 'barmiest councillor in Britain'.[76] Crossman was never diffident about his sexual orientation: 'I've always been openly gay. I've taken the gay issue on board as part of my whole politics.'[77] His long-term partner often accompanied him as mayoral consort to social functions. Within Islington Council, the Gay and Lesbian Advisory

---

[70] See LSE, HCA/GWPP, 1/1, Note on Consultative Meeting, 24 August 1982; Note of Open Meeting, 29 November 1984; 1/7, GWP Minutes, 17 January 1985.

[71] LSE, HCA/GWPP, 1/7, C. Maslin and B. Corbett to J. Austin Walker, 18 March 1985; see also *Mercury* (Greenwich), 3 April 1985.

[72] LSE, HCA/GWPP, 1/7, C. Maslin and B. Corbett, 11 April 1985.

[73] For NALGO resolution, see LSE, HCA/GWP, 1/7, Greenwich Lesbian and Gay Rights Group, Newsletter, April/May 1985.

[74] Robinson, *Gay Men and the Left*, 143.

[75] Robinson, *Gay Men and the Left*, 140.

[76] 'New Force Sets the Town Hall Alight', *The Guardian*, 25 May 1985.

[77] *The Guardian*, 25 May 1985.

Working Party tackled issues such as police liaison, sex education in schools, equal opportunities and the establishment of a gay and lesbian centre. A Gay and Lesbian sub-committee worked on an Employees' Charter that would prevent discrimination on grounds of sexual orientation. Progress was not easy; in 1983, Crossman complained that 'very little' had been accomplished on gay rights because of a lack of staffing support, attacks by the media and resistance from the local SDP.[78]

Experiments at the local level such as these were later dismissed as 'appalling gesture politics' by a prominent gay activist and Labour MEP.[79] More predictably, such initiatives invited a backlash both from the Conservatives and from the media. The tabloid press leapt on the grants given to gay and lesbian groups, what David Mellor, MP for Putney, later Arts Minister, Chief Secretary to the Treasury, Secretary of State for National Heritage, and 'minister for fun', dismissed as '[g]roups of freaks and weirdos'.[80] The *Daily Telegraph* claimed that 'GLC handouts favour women and homosexuals... it pays to be a black homosexual or a woman living in Haringey'.[81] Following Anna Marie Smith, it is striking the way that the tabloid press and Conservative think tanks such as Aims of Industry sexualized, or homosexualized, what was a question of government finance: local government rates. When *The Sun* or the *Daily Express* spoke of local government spending, it was invariably in terms of 'a whopping grant for "Big Nancy Boys Against the Bomb"' or 'cash doled out to homosexual groups'.[82] In this way, local government was (negatively) identified with the excess of gay and lesbian rights. In a different context, Jim Tomlinson has charted the near hysteria that accompanied Conservative anxieties about inflation in the 1970s and the way this became associated with trade unionism; similarly, the perceived financial 'inflation' of local government spending was firmly associated with the sexual and moral threat of gays and lesbians.[83] This desire to curb excess achieved legislative form when, in 1984, the Queen's Speech announced that the Thatcher government would abolish the GLC, something it accomplished in 1986.

In late January 1983, *The Guardian* reported on 'The Struggle for Labour's Soul in Dockland'.[84] Two years before, the Labour MP for Bermondsey, Bob Mellish, had announced his intention to resign his seat in order to take up a post with the Docklands Urban Development Corporation proffered by the Conservative Minister Michael Heseltine. Bermondsey had long been a Labour seat, but the local

---

[78] LSE, HCA/RCP, 1/1/7; Gay and Lesbian Advisory Working Party, Islington, Bob Crossman, Memo, 'Gay Rights', 4 March 1983.

[79] The actor, Stonewall co-founder and Labour MEP Michael Cashman, letter to *The Guardian*, 13 November 1999.

[80] *Putney Chronicle*, 5 August 1983.

[81] *Daily Telegraph*, 23 February 1984.

[82] *The Sun*, 2 July 1983; *Daily Express*, 30 March 1984; see also Aims of Industry, 'The GLC Grants Scandal', *Westminster World*, March 1984.

[83] Jim Tomlinson, 'The Politics of Inflation in the 1970s', unpublished conference paper, 'Reassessing the Seventies', London, 7 July 2010.

[84] *The Guardian*, 24 January 1983; for a full account of the Bermondsey by-election, see Robinson, *Gay Men and the Left*, Chapter 6 and 'The Bermondsey By-Election and Leftist Attitudes to Homosexuality', in Matthew McCormack (ed.), *Public Men: Masculinity and Politics in Modern Britain* (Houndmills: Palgrave Macmillan, 2007), 165–86.

party was in decline and politics at the local level was riven between Mellish's allies, notably John O'Grady, and younger, left-wing activists, of whom Peter Tatchell was one. Tatchell had come to England in the 1960s from Australia, in protest at conscription in the Vietnam War. He had been involved in gay liberation, but his political work in Southwark and Bermondsey concentrated instead upon issues such as the preservation of a local hospital against corporate development. Though it was often alleged that Tatchell was a member of Militant Tendency, this was never the case. Buoyed by the support of younger Labour members, he won the nomination for Mellish's seat in 1981.

In an article for London Labour Briefing, Tatchell had advocated extra-parliamentary though peaceful tactics against the Thatcher government. This infuriated the Labour leader Michael Foot. In the first in a series of ill-advised and clumsy moves, Foot told the House of Commons that Tatchell's candidature would 'never be endorsed'.[85] What the Labour leadership would not tolerate was an assumed, though unreal, connection between 'far left opinion and militant association and gay liberation'.[86] On 7 December 1981, Foot met with Tatchell telling him his article disqualified him from standing in Bermondsey; later that day the NEC refused to endorse Tatchell's candidature.[87] Tatchell responded with two articles in *The Observer* defending the original pieces, suggesting their prescriptions were closer to early twentieth-century Labour luminaries such as George Lansbury and Arthur Salter than Militant Tendency. At this point, the argument between Tatchell, Mellish, and Foot was really about the culture of the Labour Party and was informed by the ongoing struggle within it over Militant Tendency. Gay rights was not the central issue. Tatchell did not publicize his homosexuality, nor did he emphasize it in his response beyond saying that 'Labour has to reassert its role as the "natural focus" for all radical ideas and movements, embracing with enthusiasm "new" issues such as feminism, black consciousness, ecology, disarmament and gay rights.'[88] Indeed, Tatchell's statement in the original parliamentary selection meeting did not even mention his work with gay groups; when he talked of 'positive action', it was 'for women and ethnic minorities'.[89] Tatchell walked a fine line between not publicizing his own sexuality and maintaining support for gay rights ('I support gay rights. That's all I'm prepared to say at the moment. You can take it or leave it. A person's individual sexuality is not important'), a balance for which he was criticized by some gay rights activists, while, of course, paying a heavy price in tabloid excoriation.[90] Indeed, as Robinson points out, in Bermondsey, the RCP offered the most explicit support for a specific programme of gay rights.[91]

[85] *Parliamentary Debates* (Commons), 14, 3 December 1980, c. 389.
[86] Peter Tatchell, *The Battle for Bermondsey* (London: Heretic, 1983), 51.
[87] Kenneth O. Morgan, *Michael Foot* (London: HarperCollins, 2007), 422.
[88] *The Guardian*, 11 January 1982.
[89] LSE, HCA, Peter Tatchell Papers [PTP], Peter Tatchell, Statement to Labour Parliamentary Selection Meetings, 1981.
[90] Quoted in *The Guardian*, 22 March 1995; Tatchell, *Battle for Bermondsey*, 63.
[91] Robinson, 'The Bermondsey By-Election and Leftist Attitudes to Homosexuality', 173.

8.2 'Peter Tatchell campaigning in Bermondsey, 1983', photograph by Homer Sykes, copyright Premium Archive/Getty Images 750408 06 (RM)

That Tatchell was gay and that he supported gay rights became shorthand for attacking the Labour Left. The tabloid campaign against Tatchell coincided with the 1982 Labour conference.[92] In Bermondsey, John O'Grady, who served as Mellish's proxy against Tatchell, waged a ground war against the 'left-wing new wave'.[93] This included running Independent Labour and Tenants' candidates in the 1982 local elections, a move Mellish supported, earning him expulsion from the Labour Party. In January 1983, Tatchell was re-endorsed as parliamentary candidate for Bermondsey, which Foot and the NEC reluctantly accepted. The by-election date was set for 25 February 1983.

The campaign unleashed a torrent of homophobic abuse. Within Labour, the argument between Foot and Tatchell had been about tactics and Militant. But the campaign was about homosexuality; Tatchell was represented as an unacceptable symbol of far Left gay politics. The tabloids falsely alleged that he had, for example, attended the 'Gay Olympics'.[94] Supporters of Mellish and the Liberal candidate

---

[92] Tatchell, *Battle for Bermondsey*, 109–11.   [93] *The Observer*, 19 December 1982.
[94] *The Guardian*, 24 January 1983.

Simon Hughes pushed the gay issue with slogans such as 'Which Queen Will You Vote For?' and 'Simon Hughes: The Straight Choice', the latter a particularly delicious irony given Hughes's later admission of his own bisexuality. Tatchell spoke of a 'semi-fascist hysteria' during the campaign, which included verbal abuse and physical threats, including threats to his life.[95] The Labour leadership did little to defend their candidate. Infamously, the heir apparent to Michael Foot, Neil Kinnock, joked when asked about Tatchell and media-driven Militant witch-hunts, 'I'm not in favour of witch-hunts, but I do not mistake bloody witches for fairies.'[96] Kinnock later denied that he made the comment, but, having previously referred to gays as 'woofters' in a profile piece, he had form in this area.[97] After the election, Tatchell remarked that he was utterly confused by the attacks and lack of Labour support: he was campaigning only on local issues; he was not a member of Militant Tendency, and, even if he was gay and supported gay rights, the 'advocacy of homosexual equality' was 'official Labour policy' after the circulation of a 1982 NEC statement.[98] The result was a disaster for Labour. Labour had won Bermondsey in 1979 with 19,338 votes; in 1983, Tatchell obtained only 7,698 votes, leaving Simon Hughes and the Liberals to win it on 17,017.

The irony, as Tatchell pointed out in 1983, was that by the time of the Bermondsey election, Labour was moving towards a formal acceptance of some degree of gay rights. After some years of lobbying by the GLG and its successors, Tony Benn had, in February 1981, suggested that Labour and the unions should campaign for gay rights. This led to a preliminary NEC statement entitled *The Rights of Gay Men and Women* (1982). The statement was neither radical nor detailed. For the most part, it relied upon an articulation of 'broad support' for the CHE's recently published Sexual Offences Bill. Nonetheless, the NEC statement helped establish a tentative framework for dealing with gay and lesbian rights within Labour policy. The context for this was a 'broader campaign for the civil rights of all individuals and the protection of minority groups'. Acknowledging that Labour had not previously 'taken a position on the question of gay rights', the NEC now declared that thought had to be given by socialists to the 'best means of removing the discrimination and uncertainty faced by gay people' as an integral part of a political programme. Following the CHE's draft bill, the NEC statement advanced a consideration of the equalization of the age of consent, tackling the bias in the housing market against single people, broadening anti-discrimination laws to protect gays in employment, and ensuring equality of access to public services as potential future policies.[99]

Gay rights activists within the Labour Party did not extend an entirely positive welcome to the statement. The reference to gay identity as that of a 'minority'

[95] *The Guardian*, 19 April 1983; Tatchell, *Battle for Bermondsey*, 105–6.

[96] Quoted in David Rayside, *On the Fringe: Gays and Lesbians in Politics* (Ithaca: Cornell University Press, 1998), 28.

[97] See letter by Peter Tatchell, *The Guardian*, 27 September 1983.

[98] Peter Tatchell, 'Why I'll Not be Standing in Bermondsey', *The Guardian*, 19 April 1983.

[99] Labour Party, *The Rights of Gay Men and Women: A Labour Party Discussion Document* [NEC] (London: Labour Party, March 1981), 11, 3.

group rankled with one commentator who wanted greater acknowledgement of the power of the gay movement.[100] When, in 1983, material for the general election campaign did not include clear statements on gay rights, there was considerable disquiet within the LCGR and desire for a stronger commitment from the party.[101] There were also complaints that the official Labour publication, *Labour Weekly*, continued to ignore the issue despite the NEC statement and that influential figures like Gwyneth Dunwoody remained antagonistic to gay rights.[102]

But a groundswell of support was nonetheless gathering behind gay and lesbian rights. The miners' strike of 1984–5 was a particularly important turning point, which lent the movement for gay rights within the Labour Party considerable momentum. During the strike, gay and lesbian activists tried to make connections with striking miners to offer their support, as Lucy Robinson has documented. Though the miners were acknowledged by one gay activist to be the 'macho vanguard of the working class', connections were made, to the extent that at the 1984 Labour and TUC conferences, the National Union of Miners (NUM) made clear its support for gay rights.[103]

The support of the NUM and other unions such as NUPE and NALGO provided the foundation for success at party conference for gay activists. At the 1985 Labour conference, Sarah Roelofs, a delegate from Hornsey and Wood Green CLP, rose to put Composite 26. Roelofs identified herself as a 'women's delegate and a Lesbian, and very proud to be here and say that at the Labour Party conference'. She struck a note of defiance in the face of an older Labour culture represented by a former Labour MP 'who said, when asked to support a lesbian and gay rights resolution: "We should be building a new Jerusalem, not Sodom and Gomorrah". We say to you, we want no part in your Jerusalem unless it explicitly includes us. . . . We are out in the Labour Party and we are staying out.'[104] Roelofs was the voice of a much less deferential gay and lesbian activism that could be traced back to the appearance of the GLF in the early 1970s, even if it was working within a mainstream political party. In a combative interview with Tony Benn, a figure sympathetic to some degree towards gay rights, for example, Roelofs had made clear that crumbs from the table were not acceptable, nor was the usual framework of Labour's ethos and ideology, encapsulated for her in the image of Neil Kinnock: '[i]t's also how the Labour Party promotes the family, how Neil Kinnock promotes the family when he accepts bunches of roses and puts one arm around Glenys and there they all are, the happy couple'.[105]

---

[100] Jamie Gough, 'The Rights of Gay Men and Women', *Socialist Challenge*, July 1982, quoted in LSE, HCA/Journals/476J, *Gay Socialist* 7 (June 1983).

[101] LSE, HCA/Journals/476J, *Gay Socialist* 7 (June 1983), Report of the Annual Conference.

[102] LSE, HCA/Journals/476J, *Gay Socialist* 7 (June 1983), Chris Richardson, 'The Labour Weekly Saga—Part 3'.

[103] LSE, HCA/Journals/25E, *Lesbian and Gay Socialist* (Spring 1985), '1985: Big Opportunities, Big Dangers', 1; Tom Swann, 'The Fight Goes On!', 3; for a fuller account, see Robinson, *Gay Men and the Left*, 164–9.

[104] *LPCR* (1985), 267.

[105] LSE, HCA/Journals/25E, *Lesbian and Gay Socialist* (Spring 1985), interview with Tony Benn, 16.

Composite 26 was a comprehensive and uncompromising approach to gay rights. It noted the 'failure' of previous Labour policy to 'meet the legitimate demands of lesbians and gay men'. It called for the end to all discrimination and inequity (in the law, with the age of consent, at the workplace, in housing, and over child custody) against gays and lesbians, and attacked police harassment. The resolution encouraged the implementation of policies such as those being developed in the GLC and other local councils. To achieve these aims, the resolution demanded the establishment of an NEC subcommittee dedicated to gay and lesbian rights.[106] After Roelofs' speech, a lone voice from the floor charged that homosexuality was 'an illness and a sickness. Because of this unnatural act we have this disease of AIDS spreading through the world.'[107] But such explicit homophobia was exceptional at the conference. The NEC's response to the resolution was generally positive. The one thing it did not want to accept was the equalization of the age of consent and, ironically, it was Jo Richardson who had to ask that the proposal be remitted. Roelofs refused. With support from unions like NALGO, NUPE, and the NUM, Composite 26 was passed 3,395,000 to 2,805,000.

Capital Gay called the 1985 Labour resolution 'the greatest single step for lesbian and gay liberation since the emergence of our movement fifteen years ago'.[108] Its importance should not, indeed, be underestimated. For the first time, the Labour Party had committed itself to fighting for equality on the basis of sexual orientation; indeed, for the first time, it had identified equality *with* the category of sexual orientation. Just as the abortion commitments of 1975 and 1977 represented a watershed in the party's approach to reproductive politics, this was a massive sea-change in its attitude to the relationship between sexuality and Labour politics.

But, perhaps predictably, the route forward was not a direct one. Despite the conference commitment, the NEC dragged its feet on putting flesh on the resolution. At several points, Roelofs and Purton had to go to party headquarters on the Walworth Road to confront figures such as Jo Richardson with their inaction.[109] This frustration was deepened with the obdurate refusal of some local Labour councils such as Nottinghamshire country and Glasgow City to follow up on the policy. At the 1986 party conference, another resolution was put to force local authorities to follow Labour policy and to ensure that the next Labour manifesto would have an explicit commitment to gay and lesbian rights. On this occasion, both Chris Smith and Jo Richardson noted the connection between socialism and gay and lesbian rights, the former saying '[s]ome people might regard it as marginal to our concerns as a movement. It is not. It is central to our socialism. It is central because we believe in equality—the equal right of everyone to live their life.'[110] The resolution was carried by 4,793,000 to 1,262,000, forcing the NEC to include a commitment in the election manifesto.

[106] *LPCR* (1985), 265.
[107] Walter Evans, Ogmore CLP, *LPCR* (1985), 269.
[108] LSE, HCA/Journals/25E, *Lesbian and Gay Socialist* (Summer 1986), 14.
[109] LSE, HCA/Journals/25E, *Lesbian and Gay Socialist* (Summer 1986), 9.
[110] *LPCR* (1996), 39.

But the 1987 election manifesto did not contain any mention of gay and lesbian rights, even when it made due reference to women's rights (including the pledge to establish a Ministry of Women), the protection of ethnic minorities from discrimination and general talk about protecting workers from discrimination of any kind. By the fall of 1987, once again gay Labour activists were forced to essentially door-step a Labour official at Walworth Road, this time Larry Whitty, the Party Secretary, with the 'sorry story of unkept promises'.[111] A change waited upon the actions of the Conservative government.

III

In January 1988, *The Guardian* columnist and then-SDP supporter Polly Toynbee asserted that the 'gay movement' had 'nurtured within it the seeds of its own destruction', notably with the 'backlash' represented by Section 28 of the Thatcher government's Local Government Bill.[112] Toynbee argued that the gay movement's 'cardinal error was in allowing the cause to be kidnapped by the far Left', with particular reference to Ken Livingstone's GLC. She also questioned whether there was something as definitive as a 'gay community'.[113] Toynbee's article elicited much critical comment, including the response that '[t]o argue that the movement "has nurtured within it the seeds of its own destruction" by working with the only political grouping which is prepared to offer full support is absurd'.[114]

As that writer suggested, in 1987 and 1988 gay rights activists had little choice in their political affiliation. It was the Conservative government as much as Labour councils that made gay rights a partisan issue. The actions and attacks of the Conservative government also went some way to shoring up the unity of the gay community. Between 1986 and 1988, Conservative politicians and the Conservative government made gay rights a prominent political issue, largely through a concerted attack upon local government and state education. Thatcher herself told the Conservative conference of 1987:

> Too often, children did not get the education they needed and deserved. In the inner cities, too often that opportunity was snatched from them by hard left education authorities and extremist teachers.... Children who needed to be taught to respect traditional moral values were being taught that they had an inalienable right to be gay.[115]

The following spring, Thatcher made much of the allegation that teachers in Brent had been promoting homosexual videos.[116] Conservative groups such as Tottenham Conservative Association (which protested local initiatives in Haringey), the

---

[111] LSE, HCA/Journals/25E, *Lesbian and Gay Socialist* 10 (Summer 1987), 9.
[112] Polly Toynbee, 'Freedom's Roadblock', *The Guardian*, 14 January 1988.
[113] Toynbee, 'Freedom's Roadblock'.
[114] Alison Mitchell-Haynes, letter, *The Guardian*, 18 January 1988.
[115] *The Times*, 10 October 1987.
[116] *The Times*, 9 March 1988.

Conservative Family Campaign, and Christian Action, Research and Education demonized local government interventions in gay and lesbian rights.[117] Between 1985 and 1987, Norman Tebbit, a leading Cabinet minister, made the excesses of the permissive society, including gay rights, the focus of his public ire, to the point where he was perceived as 'outright anti-gay'.[118] The tabloids picked up on this criticism. *The Sun* and *Daily Mail* fostered a myth of ludicrous but threatening left-wing radicalism, especially within the Inner London Education Authority (ILEA). How sexuality was taught within the ILEA became a particularly controversial point. Brent and Haringey became as much creations of the mind as geographic locations, places where, according to the *Daily Mail*, children were 'educated into the lesbian way of life'.[119] A Conservative poster in the 1987 election made such arguments a centrepiece; books such as *Young, Gay and Proud* were portrayed as 'Labour's idea of a good education for your children'.[120]

This attitude fuelled the desire to reform both education and local government after the election victory, to 'do something about the inner cities', as Thatcher remarked in the early hours of her 1987 election victory. This resulted in the Local Government Act and the Education Act, both of 1988. The first enshrined Section 28; the second abolished the ILEA.[121] For his part, Kenneth Baker, the Education Secretary, railed against the 'ideologues who had captured much of the education world'.[122] Even moderate Tories at the Conservative Political Centre felt that the abolition of local authorities and the curtailing of local education authority power was justifiably founded on the political excess of local government, again turning on questions of sexuality: '[o]ne is happy to see an understanding of minority sexual orientations, just as one is happy to see an understanding of minority interests of all sorts. However, when such minority interests are given such prominence and majority interests are taught as being mere aberrations, then the correction of the balance has gone too far.'[123]

Between 1985 and 1987, Norman Tebbit launched broadsides against the 'poisoned legacy of the permissive society', including what he called 'sexual deviation . . . treated as the norm'.[124] This matched grass-roots campaigns by Conservative organizations. In Tottenham, for example, after the local council had made tentative steps to introduce the positive representation of gays and lesbians in schools, groups such as the Tottenham Conservative Association and the Conservative Family Campaign organized protests; in October 1986, parents of a junior school in Tottenham formed the Haringey Parents' Rights Group and kept their

---

[117] Smith, *New Right Discourse on Race and Sexuality*, 187.
[118] *The Guardian*, 10 April 1986.
[119] *Daily Mail* (London), 2 May 1986, 7 May 1986, 25 August 1986.
[120] Smith, *New Right Discourse*, 184.
[121] For an overview of the second, see Stephen Brooke, 'Articulating the Nation: British Conservatism, Race and the 1988 Education Act', *Left History* 14 (2010), 9–30.
[122] Kenneth Baker, *The Turbulent Years* (London: Faber and Faber, 1993), 191.
[123] John Bowis, *ILEA: The Closing Chapter* (London: CPC, May 1988), 29.
[124] *The Guardian*, 9 April 1986.

children out of school in protest.[125] During the 1987 election, a handbill was distributed that read '[m]y name is Betty Sheridan. I live in Haringey. I'm married with two children. <u>And I'm scared</u>. If you vote LABOUR they'll go on teaching my kids about GAYS & LESBIANS instead of giving them proper lessons.'[126] The tabloid press kept up a steady campaign against what was increasingly portrayed as the 'Loony Left' in local government, with the promotion of gay and lesbian rights in schools as a dark flagship issue. A particularly good example of such reporting was the story that a book entitled *Jenny Lives With Eric and Martin* was being pushed on young children.[127] That this was not true was beside the point. The Conservatives encouraged the fear that homosexuality was threatening the family and children. In December 1986, Thatcher went so far as to imply that the spread of AIDS was the responsibility of the gay community.[128]

The Labour leadership's response to these attacks in 1986 and 1987 was passive and lukewarm. Kinnock, the leader since 1983, did little to refute the accusations about local government excess. It is likely that Kinnock was more preoccupied with rooting out Militant Tendency from the party, though this would not have made him particularly sympathetic to gay rights, particularly if they threatened to corrode Labour's traditional working-class foundation or disable an appeal to the 'reasonable' middle ground. In essence, the leadership's passivity conceded the argument to the Conservatives. Ken Livingstone later remarked that Labour 'legitimized the witch-hunt which the press then redoubled'.[129] The occasion that illustrated this was the Greenwich by-election of February 1987. This was not quite a re-run of Bermondsey, but, once again, what was perceived as an unsuitable local candidate, Deirdre Wood, was both savagely attacked by the tabloid press as an example of the Loony Left and placed at arm's length by the Labour leadership. On 26 February 1987, Greenwich was lost to Rosie Barnes of the SDP. The same day, Patricia Hewitt, once a leading light of the LCC and now Kinnock's media advisor, wrote a memo that was circulated to the parliamentary leadership and members of the London Labour Party. In it, she argued that '[t]he gays and lesbians issue is costing us dear among the pensioners, and fear of extremism and higher taxes is particularly prominent in the GLC area'.[130] A month later, the Labour ILEA leader, Frances Morrell, recommended that the London Labour Party be reformed and that scaling back the commitment to gay rights should be a focus of such an initiative:

> ... [the] 'provocative presentation' of the gay and lesbian issue is alienating voters and damaging the interests of minority groups ... [m]any electors, and in particular working-class electors, have formed a fixed impression of Labour's policy priorities. That fixed impression is incorrect, it makes Labour unpopular, and it causes us to lose elections.... many voters ... believe the campaign for gay rights has become the

---

125 *The Guardian*, 14 October 1986; Smith, *New Right Discourse on Race and Sexuality*, 187–8.
126 LSE, HCA/Journals/25E, *Lesbian and Gay Socialist*, 10 (Summer 1987), 16.
127 See Susanne Bosche, 'Jenny, Eric, Martin ... and Me', *The Guardian*, 31 January 2000.
128 Jeffery-Poulter, *Peers, Queers and Commons*, 208–9.
129 Ken Livingstone, *Livingstone's Labour* (London: Unwin Hyman, 1989), 280.
130 Quoted in Hughes and Wintour, *Labour Rebuilt*, 19.

party's principal objective, and that, 'unlike our anti-racism programme, it is being carried forward without consultation'.[131]

The comments of Morrell and Hewitt signalled the limit to which the Labour leadership, in its desire to build a 'new model' party after so many years of electoral failure, was willing to embrace gay and lesbian rights. Instead, Labour looked to recapture the middle ground, a landscape apparently inhospitable to gay and lesbian rights.

After the conference commitments of 1985 and 1986, 1987 thus seemed a step back for the development of gay rights within Labour policy. But at the end of the year, the situation changed once more. Again, this owed far more to the actions of the Conservative government than Labour initiatives. The Conservatives had abolished the GLC in 1986. In 1987, a further Local Government Bill was introduced. In December 1987, during the committee stage, the Conservative MP David Wilshire added an amendment prohibiting the promotion of homosexuality or the publication of material for the promotion of homosexuality, or the promotion of material that taught the 'acceptability of homosexuality as a pretended family relationship'.[132] Jack Cunningham, the senior Labour member of the committee, was apparently 'taken by surprise', but offered no opposition to this; indeed, he remarked 'it is not, and never has been, the duty or responsibility of either local or educational authority to promote homosexuality', a clear attempt to put distance between the parliamentary Labour Party in 1987 and the Labour Party of local government.[133] Wilshire's amendment became Section 28 of the Local Government Bill, the provisions of which have already been noted. Cunningham's initial reaction was perceived by lesbians and gays within the party as nothing less than a 'scandalous capitulation to bigotry, a betrayal of lesbians and gay men, an abandonment of clear party policy', yet more evidence of Labour's determination 'to scapegoat our communities for its election defeat [in 1987]'.[134]

But by the following summer, Sarah Roelofs, hardly a friend of the Labour leadership, felt able to say that 'nowhere else in Europe has the labour movement given such support to lesbian and gay rights'.[135] Despite Cunningham's floundering initial response, Section 28 helped mobilize and focus the campaign for gay and lesbian rights within the Labour movement. This occurred (as in the abortion debate) because it encouraged a defence of those rights in the context of a wider defence of individual rights and equality, rather than as an attempt to advance gay and lesbian rights. On 16 December, the NEC made clear Labour's intention to

---

[131] Quoted in *The Guardian*, 20 March 1987.

[132] *The Guardian*, 8 December 1987.

[133] 1987/88, HC 201 Standing Committee A, Minutes of Proceedings on the Local Government Bill, 50; LSE, HCA/Journals/25E, 'Labour Listens? (sic)', *Lesbian and Gay Socialist* 13 (Spring 1988), 7.

[134] LSE, HCA/Journals, 25E, 'Labour Listens? (sic)', *Lesbian and Gay Socialist* 13 (Spring 1988), 7; Jean Fraser, 'The Shadow of the Clause', *Lesbian and Gay Socialist* 13 (Spring 1988), 22.

[135] LSE, HCA/Journals, 25E, Sarah Roelofs, 'Forward to Conference', *Lesbian and Gay Socialist* 14 (Spring/Summer 1988), 20.

'establish full equality in law and in practice for lesbians and gay men'; Neil Kinnock, not known for his sympathy for gay rights, told a local government conference in January 1988 that the amendment was a 'vicious...pink star clause'.[136] Labour could attack Section 28 because it was a defence of individual rights, rather than an argument for the extension of gay and lesbian rights. Anna Marie Smith has suggested, rightly, that this shaped the gay rights movement in a particular way and some gay activists were annoyed by the 'Wolfenden time-warp' that seemed to descend upon the campaign against Section 28.[137] But it is hard to see any other space for the espousal of gay rights at this time, particularly given the Kinnock leadership's desire to move Labour to the centre.

Labour MPs made a strong defence of gay and lesbian rights in the parliamentary debates on Section 28 in December 1987 and March 1988. Ironically, Jack Cunningham argued that it raised 'fundamental issues of personal liberty and civil rights'. Cunningham was, nonetheless, careful to differentiate between the defence of the 'civil liberties of many homosexual people' and giving such people 'positive rights or preferential treatment'.[138] Others, such as Joan Ruddock, repeated the need to protect 'fundamental human rights—the rights of the individual to express within the laws of the land his or her individual sexuality and still be recognized as an equal citizen'.[139] Joan Lestor warned against what she saw as 'recriminalizing homosexuality'.[140] Ken Livingstone mounted a vigorous defence of gay rights and punctured the facts behind Conservative fears, while Tony Benn read the 1985 Labour resolution to the House in its entirety. What is also striking is the intense rhetoric mobilized by Labour MPs during the debate. Tony Banks, for example, talked of Section 28 as a 'bigots' charter' and 'unalloyed fascism'.[141] This was matched by shockingly intemperate remarks made by Conservative MPs, such as Elaine Kellett-Bowman's refusal to condemn an arson attack on the offices of *Capital Gay* because, she suggested, 'it is quite right that there should be an intolerance of evil'.[142] Opposition attempts to stop Section 28 failed. What was clear from the division lists was the high level of partisan division.

Stephen Jeffery-Poulter has suggested that Section 28 profoundly changed the nature of political debate around gay and lesbian rights: 'regardless of its antecedents...[Section] 28 placed the principle that homosexuality was socially undesirable and inherently inferior to heterosexuality on the statute book in an explicit way for the first time'. Jeffery-Poulter also argues that this brought a bracing clarity to the question: 'for the first time, Parliament faced up to the real issue at the centre of the gay rights debate: whether homosexuality should be

[136] NEC and Kinnock quoted in LSE, HCA/Journals, 25E, 'Labour Listens? (sic)', *Lesbian and Gay Socialist* 13 (Spring 1988), 7.

[137] LSE, HCA/Journals, 25E, Peter Kent-Baguley, 'Clause 28: My Little Bill', *Lesbian and Gay Socialist* 13 (Spring 1988), 16.

[138] *Parliamentary Debates* (Commons), 124, 15 December 1987, cs. 995, 996.

[139] Joan Ruddock, *Parliamentary Debates* (Commons), 124, 15 December 1987, c. 1003.

[140] *Parliamentary Debates* (Commons), 129, 9 March 1988, c. 411.

[141] *Parliamentary Debates* (Commons), 124, 15 December 1987, c. 1022.

[142] *Parliamentary Debates* (Commons), 124, 15 December 1987, c. 1009.

recognized as an alternative lifestyle which had equal validity to heterosexuality'.[143] Section 28 also made clear the partisan divisions around the gay and lesbian rights issues. Whatever Labour's flaws on this issue—and they were legion—gay and lesbian activists had little choice but to choose the Left, and, in particular, Labour, because it was only going to be through parliament that the law could be changed, a prospect that resonated with radical causes for centuries, whether we think of trade union or reproductive rights.[144] Section 28 also encouraged unity within the gay and lesbian rights campaign. *Capital Gay* remarked that this was 'the coming of age of the gay and lesbian movement'.[145] Throughout the parliamentary debates, there were significant public demonstrations against Section 28.

Just as significantly, new campaigning organizations emerged. The most important was Stonewall, the brainchild of the actor Ian McKellen, which worked as an 'insider' organization. Stonewall was particularly good at making Section 28 a question of the state of rights and culture in Britain, bringing onto its side not only politicians, but the great and good of Britain's literary and cultural scene. Peter Tatchell helped establish OutRage in 1989, a more radical alternative to Stonewall, which sought, for example, to 'out' gay and lesbian MPs and public figures. There were echoes of earlier radical campaigns when lesbian activists in the visitors' gallery of the House of Lords abseiled to the floor of the chamber during a debate on Section 28 and interrupted a BBC television newscast. The 1988 Labour conference reasserted its belief in gay and lesbian rights and condemned the Section.

Section 28 also had an effect on the place of gay rights within Labour ideology and politics. On the eve of Labour government in 1997, Angela Mason, a leading light for Stonewall, argued that one effect of the abolition of the GLC and the passing of Section 28 was that it 'showed how dangerous it can be for a cause to be hitched exclusively to one political party—and, indeed, one political tendency. Lesbians and gay men were not going to be able to piggy-back change by capturing sections of the Labour Party.'[146] Ten years before, Morrell's and Hewitt's comments had suggested that gay and lesbian rights had to be placed at an arm's length from Labour policy. But what could be suggested, against both views, was that from 1988, gay rights moved from one end of the spectrum of Labour Party opinion to the centre. The vehicle of this change was, first of all, a major policy review launched in 1988 as a means of Labour remaking itself after three straight election defeats.[147] The policy review laid the foundations for a 'new model party', one that would distance Labour from being identified with older and apparently unpopular associations with statism and trade unionism. It was also the first step towards the emergence of New Labour. One overarching ideological theme running through the review was a greater emphasis upon individual freedoms and rights—the areas where Labour felt that the Thatcherite Conservatives

---

[143] Jeffery-Poulter, *Peers, Queers and Commons*, 236–7.
[144] Jeffery-Poulter, *Peers, Queers and Commons*, 235.
[145] Jeffery-Poulter, *Peers, Queers and Commons*, 234.
[146] Angela Mason, 'Coming In: Lesbian and Gay Politics in the Nineties', *Radical Philosophy* 81 (1997), 3.
[147] See James Cronin, *New Labour's Pasts* (Harlow: Pearson Longman, 2004), Chapter 8.

had stolen a march on the party. The final report of the 'policy review for the 1990s' insisted, for example, that 'our commitment to individual freedom, to a more just and more democratic society' was intrinsic to 'Labour's basic values'.[148]

This was a critical phase in thinking about gay rights within the context of the Labour movement.[149] It provided a framework for gay rights, just as the revisionist arguments of the 1950s provided the context for thinking about the decriminalization of homosexuality. This is not to argue that the policy review afforded the articulation of a radical case for advancing the cause of gay and lesbian rights. Instead, the policy review's importance lies in the way it found a moderate middle ground within which to promote gay rights in the context of equality and modernization. In *Social Justice and Economic Efficiency: First Report of Labour's Policy Review for the 1990s* (1988), for example, employment rights were a focus of a push-back for individual rights and freedoms against the Thatcherite government. This included 'sexuality' alongside gender, race, disability, and economic circumstance.[150] Similarly, anti-discrimination laws were emphasized for 'those groups . . . [who] are especially vulnerable to prejudice abuse and discrimination'; for the most part, this meant children and youth, but also lesbians and gays. Section 28 was singled out for repeal; gay men and lesbians 'must have the same freedom from discrimination and prejudice and the same freedom to live their lives as other people. This requires legislation to prohibit discrimination and unfair dismissal on grounds in any way connected with sexuality or lifestyle.'[151] This was developed in the final report of the policy review in the acknowledgement that existing law 'actually discriminates' against lesbians and gay men.[152] Thus, the argument for the modernization of Labour policy included gay rights as part of a general argument about individual rights, equality, and the creation of a modern society.

By no means can this be considered an explicitly radical step forward. There was, for example, a studious avoidance of the wide-ranging vision of GLC initiatives and attacks upon heterosexism (even if, it should be said, the actual building blocks of anti-discrimination reform were to be found in those initiatives). Reaching further back to the transformative visions of the GLF and gay Marxism, this was not a commitment which offered a 'threat' to the existing 'social and moral order' or promised to challenge the entire concept of sexual categories, the 'end' of the homosexual, the heterosexual and the 'ideology of sexuality'.[153] Sexual identity remained fixed; progress would be achieved through the existing political and social system. Predictably, perhaps, the commitments were born of the CHE, not the GLF. Nor can it be argued that the results of the policy review were accepted with

---

[148] Labour Party, *Meet the Challenge, Make the Change: A New Agenda for Britain: Final Report of Labour's Policy Review for the 1990s* (London: Labour Party, 1989), 5.

[149] See also Perrigo, 'Women and Change in the Labour Party 1979–1995'.

[150] Labour Party, *Social Justice and Economic Efficiency: First Report of Labour's Policy Review for the 1990s* (London: Labour Party, 1988), 33.

[151] Labour Party, *Social Justice and Economic Efficiency*, 37.

[152] Labour Party, *Meet the Challenge, Make the Change*, 64.

[153] Don Millington, 'Outsiders: Why I Won't Join CHE', *CHE: The Bulletin of the Campaign for Homosexual Equality*, December–January 1976–77; Jeffrey Weeks, 'Capitalism and the Organisation of Sex', in *Homosexuality, Power and Politics*, 19–20.

equanimity by gay and lesbian activists within the party. A particular point of conflict was equalizing the age of consent. Though Ken Livingstone, Joan Lestor, and Jo Richardson pressed for this commitment, it was voted down seventeen to eleven, leaving the phrase 'greater equality' rather than 'full equality'.[154] At the party conference of 1989, a majority of 1,285,000 defeated the NEC on a commitment to equalize the age of consent.[155]

Nonetheless, there was, as Lucy Robinson has argued, a clear sense of change under Kinnock: '[w]hile the Looney Left used sexuality to challenge traditional parliamentary democracy and local council politics, Kinnock brought the politics of sexuality firmly into the fold'.[156] Bringing the politics of sexuality into the fold had the potential to change the meaning of Labour's own political ideology. There are several ways to think about this. The first was simply about rights. Rather than the pitiable homosexual of the 1950s and 1960s, the protagonist animating discussions of gay and lesbian rights in the 1970s and 1980s was a more complex one, less deferential, less defined in terms of private space or, indeed, in terms of gender, generation or style. The growth of the gay movement, not least in the prominence of Pride parades in the 1980s, bore this out. What had been achieved was the association between male and female sexuality and the right to make a claim upon rights in a variety of social, economic, and cultural spheres, rather than being *given* legality in private space. The second point rests on what could be claimed once given those rights. As shall be discussed briefly below, a core concept of Labour policy was the family, but what was a family? What kinds of relationships might claim benefits or housing? In other words, bringing sexuality into the fold, as Robinson says, might not simply be accommodation by the centre, but a gradual, but powerful transformation of that centre. I have argued in this book that questions of reproductive politics were at their most effective and radical when they intersected with traditional ideas of femininity and the family because they encouraged a gradual, but radical revision of what women were, what agency they had over the family, and what families amounted to, particularly in the context of working-class life. There is a parallel in terms of gay and lesbian rights. These did not have to be explicitly liberationist to be implicitly liberating and transformative. By 1997, as shall be suggested in the next chapter, so-called 'New' Labour was more associated with the reform of sexuality, extending the rights of gays and lesbians, than any party at any time during the twentieth century.

---

[154] Peter Purton, 'Labour's Policy Retreat—National Campaign Launched!', *Lesbian and Gay Socialist* 18 (Summer 1989), 6.
[155] See *LPCR* (1989), 130, 173.
[156] Robinson, *Gay Men and the Left*, 173.

Conclusion: Endings or Beginnings?
New Labour, Sexuality, and Reproductive Politics, 1997 to 2010

In 2005, Labour's election manifesto proclaimed the following as testament to Labour's belief in a 'fully democratic society':

> We are committed to improving the rights and opportunities of gays and lesbians, that's why we brought in legislation on civil partnerships, reducing the age of consent, repealed Section 28 and reformed the sexual offences legislation so that it was no longer discriminatory.[1]

By this point, the Labour Party had been in power for eight years, swept in on a landslide in 1997. Beginning in 1998, there were a series of parliamentary initiatives that reshaped the place of gay men and lesbian women in British society. In 2000, after a two-year struggle between the Commons and the Lords, the age of consent was equalized at 16 between homosexuals and heterosexuals. The ban on gays and lesbians in the armed forces was also ended that year. A new Immigration Rule permitted same-sex partners to be eligible for residency in Britain. The Employment Equity (Sexual Orientation) Regulation three years later protected workers against discrimination on the basis of sexual orientation. In a new Sexual Offences Act, gross indecency was abolished as an offence. The year 2003 also witnessed the repeal of Section 28. Two laws came into effect in 2005 that transformed the idea of parenthood and partnership, the Adoption and Children Act (which had been passed in 2002), allowing same sex couples to adopt children, and the Civil Partnership Act, which afforded same sex couples the right to formalize their relationships and claim the same benefits as married heterosexual couples. In other realms, the government cracked down on homophobia by defining it as a hate crime and increasing sentences for such crimes, established an Equality and Human Rights Commission, which helped protect gay and lesbian rights, passed a Gender Recognition Act giving transgendered persons legal recognition, allowed fertility treatments for lesbian women on the NHS, and, in the final year of Labour government, introduced the 2010 Equality Act, which brought together nine major and around one hundred minor

---

[1] Labour Party, *Britain Forward Not Back* (London: Labour Party, 2005), 111.

laws involving the realization of equality, including those touching upon sexual orientation.[2]

In many ways, this record seemed to fulfil a prediction made soon after New Labour took power: 'the Government seems keener to remove discrimination than any administration since the sixties'.[3] Though there were Labour dissentients from what was later called 'New Labour's gay-friendly Government', this approach seemed to unify the party and draw partisan divisions between Labour and the Conservative party; the unity of the latter, at least until David Cameron's leadership, was tested by questions such as gay adoption, Section 28, and civil partnership.[4] Reproductive politics were much quieter than the politics of gay and lesbian rights during the New Labour years. In 1990, the HFE Act had reduced the number of weeks at which abortions could be performed, from twenty-eight to twenty-four. Eighteen years later, this was challenged, as part of another HFE Act; that challenge was successfully resisted.

The Labour governments of 1997 to 2010 also witnessed the normalization of gay politicians. The election of 1997 saw a number of openly gay and lesbian MPs elected, including Stephen Twigg, Chris Smith, Ben Bradshaw, and Angela Eagle, who became the first out lesbian MP in September 1997.[5] Peter Mandelson, one of the leading figures in the new government was also known to be gay, though he was not formally out. Nick Brown and Chris Smith were also gay Cabinet ministers. But the meaning of this change is more difficult to judge. Though Bradshaw was forced to fight against a viciously homophobic campaign in 1997, he declared that '[b]eing gay did not matter'.[6] As Stephen Fielding has said, *The Sun*'s suspicions of a 'gay Mafia' were misplaced; the reforms were probably more an end-product of the social liberalism that emerged in the late 1980s and early 1990s.[7]

In these changes, two other factors must be recognized. The first is the effectiveness of Stonewall, the gay rights organization founded in 1989 in response to Section 28. Initially inspired by the actors Ian McKellen and Michael Cashman, Stonewall sought, more in the tradition of the HLRS and the CHE, to be a 'professional lobbying group', rather than following the tradition of the GLF, a route taken by OutRage; the target was to work within the system, to 'put the case for equality on the mainstream political agenda by winning support within all the main political parties'.[8] Stonewall was, as many commentators have suggested, extraordinarily effective, not least with the New Labour government. There has been some criticism of Stonewall for its position as the respectable face of gay politics and its desire to normalize homosexuality within existing institutions (such

---

[2] See complete list on the website of LGBT Labour, http://lgbtlabour.org.uk/therecord, accessed 11 August 2010.

[3] Andy Beckett, 'On the Gay and Narrow', *The Guardian*, 3 July 1997.

[4] David Northmore, 'Gay Potato', *The Guardian*, 13 January 1999.

[5] See *The Guardian*, 12 September 1997.

[6] *The Guardian*, 30 September 1997.

[7] Quoted in Stephen Fielding, *The Labour Party: Continuity and Change in the Making of New Labour* (Houndmills: Palgrave Macmillan, 2003), 201.

[8] http://www.stonewall.org.uk/about_us/2532.asp, accessed 11 August 2010.

as marriage and the law) rather than transform such categories, a division between the 'good gays' of Stonewall and the 'bad gays' of OutRage, but the former's efficacy in gaining reforms in a relatively short time remains striking.[9]

The other factor that must also be acknowledged is the greater visibility of gays and lesbians in national and popular culture. By 2009, the annual gay pride parade in London, Pride London, was attracting nearly a million people. In the 1980s and 1990s, as Frank Mort and others have argued, popular fashion showed a greater influence of openly gay styles.[10] This openness was also reflected in music, film, and television, whether in the success of groups such as Bronski Beat, Frankie Goes to Hollywood, and Culture Club, films dealing with gay themes such as *My Beautiful Laundrette* (1985), or the way that gay relationships were not only dealt with by mainstream shows such as *EastEnders* (in which Michael Cashman's character, Colin Russell, kissed another male character, Barry Clark), but also where they were featured as the main subject, in, for example, the Manchester-set *Queer as Folk* (1999). Gay dance clubs such as the Fridge and the Blitz also set the tone for much music culture in the 1980s and 1990s. Increasingly, as well, the 'pink pound' and the 'pink vote' became important for the economy and politics. The consumer influence of gay people became a common theme in the 1980s and 1990s, not least because gays tended to enjoy higher levels of disposable income.[11] As voters, gays and lesbians also became desirable. In part, this was because of Labour's apparent success in deliberately courting them.[12] In the elections of 1997 and 2001, it was estimated that half of all gay voters supported Labour, a third voted Liberal Democrat and less than ten per cent supported the Conservatives.[13] In terms of the consumer and the political market, gays had arrived.

This is not to be complacent about the level of acceptability of gay rights. In 2009, for example, statistics showed a sharp rise in homophobic attacks; ten years previous, there had been a horrific nail bomb attack upon a gay pub in Soho.[14] Nonetheless, there was no denying the greater visibility of gays and lesbians in national life in the late 1980s and 1990s.

The relationship between the reforms of 1997 and 2008 and New Labour has not yet made it into mainstream histories of the governments between 1997 and 2010, though Angela Wilson's short treatment and Matthew Waites's *Age of Consent* (2005) do provide important dedicated accounts.[15] In many ways, this is

---

[9] See Debbie Epstein, Richard Johnson, and Deborah Lynn Steinberg, 'Twice Told Tales: Transformation, Recuperation and Emergence in the Age of Consent Debates 1998', *Sexualities* 2 (2000), 19.

[10] Frank Mort, *Cultures of Consumption* (London: Routledge, 1996); Shaun Cole, *Don We Now Our Gay Apparel* (Oxford: Berg, 2000).

[11] On the prehistory of the pink pound, see Justin Bengry, 'Courting the Pink Pound: *Men Only* and the Queer Consumer, 1935–39', *History Workshop Journal* 68 (2009), 122–48; for the contemporary period, see Alexandra Chasin's study of this trend in America, *Selling Out: The Gay and Lesbian Movement Goes to Market* (New York: St Martin's, 2000).

[12] See Angela Wilson, 'New Labour and "Lesbian- and Gay-friendly" policy', in Claire Annerley, Francesca Gains, and Kirstein Rummery (eds), *Women and New Labour: Engendering Politics and Politics* (Bristol: Policy Press, 2007), 194.

[13] *The Guardian*, 28 March 2004.

[14] See *The Guardian*, 31 May 2009.

[15] Wilson, 'New Labour and "Lesbian- and Gay-friendly" policy', 193–210; Matthew Waites, *The Age of Consent: Young People, Sexuality and Citizenship* (Houndmills: Palgrave Macmillan, 2005).

not surprising, given the proximity of the history of these governments. However, it is notable how little the question figures in existing work on New Labour.[16] The present chapter concludes this study by thinking about the reforms of the early twenty-first century, first in their immediate context, then in the context of the longer history of sexuality and politics over the twentieth century. It begins by considering the relationship between New Labour and two issues—gay and lesbian rights and gender equality—that helped frame its approach to sexual issues between 1997 and 2010.

I

The years between the 1988 policy review and the majority Labour government of 1997 were, of course, eventful ones for Labour, but they also bear out some of the reflections made in the previous chapter about the place of gay rights.[17] The crushing disappointment of the 1992 election defeat was followed by an even more determined effort to remake Labour for middle England, first under John Smith as leader, then, more obviously, under Tony Blair. The New Labour project did not feature sexual politics as its main focus. Indeed, on the face of it, New Labour was about stressing the importance of the family. In 1995, Blair told party conference that 'a strong country could not "be morally neutral about the family"'; the 1997 manifesto similarly stressed that the party's aim was to 'uphold family life'.[18] In 1996, Roger Liddle and Peter Mandelson, the latter a key architect of New Labour and known to be gay, offered an interesting portrait of Blair in this regard:

> When Blair talks about the importance of strong families, it is because he regards them as the foundation of a cohesive society and of strong communities . . . He became critical of what he felt was many on the left's uninterest in social order and their confusion of liberation from prejudice with apparent disregard for moral structures. Blair argues that the left-of-centre's commitment to racial and sexual equality was entirely right, but the appearance some gave of indifference to the family and to individual responsibility was wrong.

Fortunately, they went on, Blair 'is not judgmental about those friends who are not in conventional marriages or who are single parents, or who are gay'.[19] There were

---

[16] Fielding, for example, gives a paragraph to gay equality, while the question is not covered at all in Steve Ludlam and Martin Smith (eds), *Governing As New Labour* (Houndmills: Palgrave Macmillan, 2004); David Coates and Peter Lawler (eds), *New Labour in Power* (Manchester: Manchester University Press, 2000); Steve Ludlam and Martin J. Smith (eds), *New Labour in Government* (Houndmills: Palgrave Macmillan, 2001).

[17] See Cronin, *New Labour's Pasts*, Chapters 9, 10.

[18] Quoted in Martin Durham, 'The Conservative Party, New Labour and the Politics of the Family', *Parliamentary Affairs* 54 (2001), 460; see also Tony Blair, 'Crime and Family Breakdown' and 'Valuing Families', in *New Britain* (London: Fourth Estate, 1996), 244–8; 249–50.

[19] Peter Mandelson and Roger Liddle, *The Blair Revolution* (London: Faber and Faber, 1996), 47, 49.

also signs that the homogenizing, conformist effect of building New Labour was to smooth out the rough edges of Labour's socialism or candidates, tidying it up into what the late Paul Foot called the 'clean, straight image of Labour'.[20] On the eve of the election victory of 1997, for example, Sarah Boseley remarked that New Labour did not want to talk about gay rights for fear of alienating middle England.[21]

Without offering an apologia for New Labour, perhaps the more difficult truth was that this was a balancing act. To be sure, there were moments that the process of creating New Labour marginalized issues like gay rights, in the same way it buried state economic action. But there were also clear signs between 1994 and 1997 that Labour remained committed to some measure of gay rights. At his first Labour conference as leader, for example, Blair made clear that 'the right to be treated equally as a citizen' included protection against discrimination on grounds of 'sexuality'.[22] Jack Straw, the shadow Home Office minister, promoted the idea of a Bill of Rights at the same conference, one that would tackle the question of the age of consent and prevent discrimination on grounds of sexuality.[23] A turning point was the parliamentary debate in February 1994 on the lowering of the age of consent. Neil Kinnock and Tony Blair made important arguments for equalizing the age of consent to 16, though this depended upon an idea of homosexual identity that was fixed by that age.[24] In Blair's view, sexual equality was not a threat to long-standing social mores, but rather a reflection of them; in an echo of the revisionists of the 1950s, he said how politics treated sexual equality was a measure of both modernity and civilization:

> ...I have no desire to return to a time when women were inhibited from going to work, when sex could not be openly discussed and debated, when young people were not taught at school how life is given and created, and when gay men hid their sexuality in fear.... the most basic civilized value is the notion of respect for other people. That is what creates and sustains any decent society ... It is ... why it is wrong to treat a man as inferior because his sexuality is different. A society that has learned, over time, racial and sexual equality can surely come to terms with equality of sexuality. That is the moral case for change tonight. It is our chance to welcome people—I do not care whether there are 50,000, 500,000 or 5 million; it matters not a damn—into full membership of our society, on equal terms.[25]

The proportion of Labour MPs who voted in favour of reform was 84% leaving thirty-nine MPs voting against. It is striking how isolated these MPs were. At the 1994 conference they were the focus of a critical resolution expressing the 'disappointment, regret and anger of this party that 39 of our MPs voted against equality'. On a card vote, 97.6% supported the resolution.[26]

---

[20] Paul Foot, 'Listen, We Don't Want Any Lefties or Stirrers', *The Guardian*, 31 July 1995.
[21] *The Guardian*, 24 April 1997.
[22] *LPCR* (1994), 103.
[23] *LPCR* (1994), 231.
[24] See discussion in Rayside, *On the Fringe*, 49–51; see Kinnock's speech, *Parliamentary Debates* (Commons), 238, 21 February 1994, cs. 82–7.
[25] *Parliamentary Debates* (Commons), 238, 21 February 1994, c. 100.
[26] *LPCR* (1994), 245.

Thus, gay and lesbian rights had become part of the mainstream of Labour policies, perhaps not in a way that transformed that ideology, perhaps more in a process of accommodation, but nonetheless built into the fabric of Labour policy. There was a clear road forward for the party on the verge of power, a prospect that might have been unthinkable in the 1970s. In 1996's *Looking to the Future*, the party stated: '[i]t is a basic principle of human rights that everyone should be entitled to equal treatment, free from discrimination. Labour will reform the present law and prohibit discrimination on grounds of race, sex, sexual orientation or disability. We will repeal the notorious Section 28 of the 1988 Local Government Act.'[27] This was associated with the idea of 'modernization' or the 'modern'. Blair, for example, remarked that his aim was 'rebuilding a modern view of community' in which 'collective action' would advance 'individual freedom', where Labour's basis of support would be modern and '"value"-based, not simply "class"-based', where 'for individuals to advance you require a strong and fair community behind you'.[28] In 1995, Blair told party conference, in a speech that talked of a 'young' Britain: '. . . there should be no discrimination in our young country on grounds of disability, gender, age, sexuality or race'.[29] We might also associate this approach to gay rights with Labour's emphasis upon social inclusion in the 1990s, to bring within the fabric of community those who had been excluded under the Conservatives.[30] In 1997, Angela Mason of Stonewall commented, hopefully, that 'Blair is trying to create an inclusive, rather than exclusive, moral agenda'.[31]

There was even the sense that the apparently countervailing core idea of the family and parenthood might be changing. In 1994, in a discussion of a possible Bill of Rights, a delegate to Labour's annual conference stated:

> . . . some families are more acceptable than others. Family values is a phrase that has gained much credibility within the Labour Party, but whose families, whose values? Labour must recognize that all family forms . . . are equally valid and normal parts of society.[32]

Ambiguity about the terms of political commitments can, of course, be as mobilizing as certainty.[33] That Labour in the 1980s and 1990s held a commitment to older and newer values suggested a resolution of the struggle it had been engaged in over gay rights since 1967, but it was a dynamic resolution. The 1997 election manifesto made no explicit mention of gay or lesbian rights, but nonetheless made clear the ambiguous programme for modernization stating that '[f]amilies are the core of our society' and, at the same time, 'our attitudes to race, sex and sexuality

---

[27] Labour Party, *Looking to the Future: A Dynamic Economy, A Decent Society, Strong in Europe* (London: Labour Party, 1996), 41.

[28] Tony Blair, 'New Community, New Individualism' and 'The Revisionist Tendency', in *New Britain*, 220, 221, 217.

[29] *LPCR* (1995), 101.

[30] See discussion of the New Labour language of inclusion and exclusion in Norman Fairclough, *New Labour, New Language?* (London: Routledge, 2000), Chapter 2.

[31] Mason, 'Coming In: Lesbian and Gay Politics in the Nineties', 5.

[32] Catherine Hanson, *LPCR* (1994), 245.

[33] See Rose, *Which People's War?*

have changed fundamentally. Our task is to combine change and social stability.'[34] It was that tension, between change and stability, modernization and conservatism, that was, in part, played out with the Labour government's approach to gay rights between 1997 and 2010.

Between 1988 and 1997, Labour had been able to be much more explicit about its attempts to 'modernize' the party in terms of women's rights and gender equality. Sarah Perrigo has suggested that there were three critical periods in the developing influence between feminist activists and the Labour Party: between 1979 and 1983, when the delegitimization of the leadership and Labour right encouraged the movement of feminists into the party; between 1983 and 1987, when tensions existed between the party leadership and feminist activists, for the same reasons as with gay rights activists—their perceived association with the far Left; and, finally, between 1987 and 1995, a period in which the 'party strategy of modernization and the demands of women have become increasingly congruent'.[35] Perrigo has also argued that, as in the 1920s and 1930s, the women's organizations of the party afforded an opportunity for the development of policy, the challenging of 'the masculine culture' of the broader party, and the ability to build networks.[36] A Labour Women's Action Committee emerged in 1980 that repeated the same demands that had been raised in the interwar period about the national conference paying attention to the resolutions from the women's conferences. It was clear that there was a new lack of deference from the women's sections, as Jo Richardson suggested in 1983: 'Till now, women have not been able to play their full part in decision-making in the Party; we will not accept this any longer—the fight for change has begun.'[37] Efforts were also made, beginning in 1988 with the Labour Women's Network, to challenge the imbalance between male and female MPs, not least because polls revealed 'women's perception of Labour as a macho male-dominated Party'.[38] This led to the idea of quotas for women, within the party on bodies like the NEC and CLP management committees, and the longer-term aim of gaining 50% female candidates in winnable seats, with the prospect of all-women short lists if this could not be achieved, an aim that was eventually made impossible by European human rights legislation. The late 1980s and early 1990s also witnessed a commitment to greater gender equality in terms of policy and the wider perception of society. Richardson was appointed Women's Rights Spokesperson in 1984 and helped spearhead policy work within the party.[39] A Shadow Ministry for Women was established, which developed a wide range of policies to tackle gender inequality, including the improvement of women's

---

[34] Labour Party, *New Labour: Because Britain Deserves Better* (London: Labour Party, 1997).

[35] Perrigo, 'Women and Change in the Labour Party, 1979–1995', 119; see Wainwright, *Labour: A Tale of Two Parties*.

[36] Perrigo, 'Women and Change in the Labour Party 1979–1995', 123.

[37] WL, Women's Action Committee, *Women, Discover Your Strength* (London: Women's Action Committee, 1983).

[38] Labour Women's Network, *Uphill all the Way: Labour Women Into Westminster* (London: Labour Party, 1994).

[39] LPA, Labour Party, 'Labour's Ministry for Women', NEC Discussion Document (late winter 1986).

wages, child benefit, education and training for women, and tax benefits, all towards the end of combating the 'fundamental causes of inequality'.[40] It was also proposed that a Ministry of Women's Rights or Ministry for Women would be an integral part of a new Labour government. In an odd way, such reforms recalled the local government initiatives of the early 1980s. There were tensions between the leadership and such attempts to bring equality to the party, but the NEC had itself committed to find ways to 'defend and extend women's rights' in the early 1980s and, in the late 1980s, this became a touchstone of modernization.[41] In 1995, for example, party conference trumpeted a report on 'A Fairer Deal for Women', the prospect of all-women short lists and a Ministry for Women.[42] By 1997, the Ministry for Women promise had been watered down to a pledge to have a Women's Minister in Cabinet. The election of 1997 was famous, not simply for the Labour landslide, but because 101 of the new Labour MPs were women. As Sarah Childs has pointed out, the tension between the commitments of the modernization period and the experience of government was shown up very soon in the life of the new government, when it accepted a reduction in the benefit paid to lone parents in December 1997.[43] One question that should be asked is whether this change in the approach to women from the Labour Party in fact changed anything about its approach to reproductive politics.

II

The equalization of the age of consent to 16 had been a long-standing aim of the gay rights movement since the early 1970s. In 1994, it had been lowered from 21 to 18. The Labour government of 1997 was committed to further equalization, but its hand was forced in the matter in the summer of 1997. Stonewall had lent its support to a human rights case brought by Euan Sutherland and Christopher Morris that was heard before the European Court of Human Rights, a case that would show how isolated Britain was in terms of the equal age of consent. It was indicated to the British government that the European Court would find in favour of Sutherland and Morris and, in order to avoid being in violation of the European Court, an out-of-court settlement between Jack Straw, the Home Secretary, and Stonewall was announced.[44] The settlement included an undertaking to have a free vote on the equalization of the age of consent and to complete this undertaking by the 1998–9 session.[45] One of the major reforms on the books for 1998 was the

---

[40] Shadow Ministry of Women, *Putting Equality Into Practice: A Shadow Ministry of Women Consultation Document* (1991).

[41] LPA, RD 508, Home Policy Committee, 'Note on the Women's Rights Study Group', September 1980.

[42] See *LPCR* (1995), 106; Blair, 'Hearing From Women', in *New Britain*, 151–8.

[43] Sarah Childs, *New Labour's Women MPs: Women Representing Women* (London: Routledge, 2004), 3.

[44] See *The Guardian*, 2 October and 9 October 1997.

[45] *Parliamentary Debates* (Commons), 317, 28 July 1998, c. 180.

Crime and Disorder Bill; an amendment to this bill was planned to include equalization of the age of consent to 16. There was all-party support for this and all three party leaders were in agreement. It was, however, left to a private member to introduce the amendment in June 1998. The Labour MP Ann Keen and other supporters of the bill insisted that the debate on the issue was 'about equality . . . [i]t is fundamental in any democracy that the rights and responsibilities of all citizens are protected equally under the law' and a way, not of encouraging sexuality at 16, but rather 'supporting a community in which responsible people seek to behave within the law'.[46] In this way, the amendment was very much in the context of bringing gay and lesbian people within the ambit of the law—perhaps rewarding respectability, but also in the tradition, according to Keen, of the 1918 Representation of the People Act, the 1975 Sex Discrimination Act, and the 1976 Race Relations Act.[47] The amendment was greeted with a significant amount of Conservative opposition, but the vote was firmly in favour of the amendment, 336 to 129. There were thirteen Labour dissentients, including Gwyneth Dunwoody and Tom Dalyell. But the Lords defeated the amendment on 22 July and this imperilled the entire Crime and Disorder Bill. Rather than abandon that bill, Straw asked the Commons to accept the Lords' vote, but promised to bring in a new Sexual Offences (Amendment) Bill in 1998 and vowed to use the 1911 and 1949 Parliament Acts 'if necessary'.[48] Ultimately this is what happened and the new Sexual Offences Bill was finally given Royal Assent on 30 November 2000. As Matthew Waites has suggested, this legislative process made the age of consent at 16 a 'hegemonic' idea of equality, even though groups like the LCLGR explored more radical concepts, such as an age of consent of 14.[49]

The election manifesto of 1997 committed Labour to the abolition of Section 28. In 1999, the government's hand was forced on the matter, because the newly constituted Scottish executive announced that it would move on abolishing Section 28. In the same Queen's Speech that announced the intention to equalize the age of consent, the government announced it would abolish Section 28.[50] At first, the major impact of this announcement was the sharpening of the partisan divide between Labour and the Conservatives and exploiting differences within the Conservative party between those who were socially liberal, and those still wedded to Section 28. In December 1999, for example, Shaun Woodward, a former Shadow Minister, defected to the Labour Party; he was followed in August 2000 by another Tory, Ivan Massow. Both cited the Conservative leadership's attitude to gay rights and Section 28 in particular as the motivating reason. But the political advantage did not last long for Labour and the government soon became mired in controversy over its plans. First of all, the Scottish Executive began to face a great deal of opposition to its own abolition of Section 28, particularly from religious

[46] *Parliamentary Debates* (Commons), 314, 22 June 1998, cs. 756–7.
[47] *Parliamentary Debates* (Commons), 314, 22 June 1998, cs. 760–1.
[48] *Parliamentary Debates* (Commons), 317, 178, 28 July 1998, c. 178.
[49] Matthew Waites, 'Equality at Last? Homosexuality, Heterosexuality and the Age of Consent in the United Kingdom', *Sociology* 37 (2003), 642, 641.
[50] *The Guardian*, 18 November 1999.

opinion, opposition that seemed to have a popular basis.[51] Fearful of creating the same kind of groundswell in England and Wales, the government began to tread gingerly. The balance the government sought to achieve was between abolishing the discriminatory Section 28 and showing that it was still family friendly. Beverley Hughes, the local government minister, walked this line in a statement made in January 2000 about sex education:

> The guidance in relation to sex education in particular will stress the importance of the context of family values and what children need to grow up, but it will also enable teachers to deal with the real issues that gay and lesbian pupils bring into school and want schools and teachers to help them with.[52]

Throughout 2000, the government tried to square this circle, in a way, ultimately, that seemed to confuse the issue. Sex education became, for example, a way of talking about the ideal sexual form. David Blunkett, who was perceived as an opponent of abolition of Section 28, was, at this point, at the Department for Employment and Education and he and his civil servants indicated in the winter of 2000 that they would continue to stress the 'importance and nature of marriage and family life in bringing up children'; at one point, this was even stretched to a Department of Education and Employment source saying that, in terms of advice on homosexuality, a new education circular 'will guide on the same lines' as Section 28.[53] This caused rifts within the Cabinet, with Chris Smith asking Blunkett whether 'government policy is being shifted towards "promoting" hetero-sexuality'.[54] The Learning and Skills Bill of the spring became the vessel of this balancing act. The government was clearly apprehensive of being ahead of public opinion on the matter. It also tried to tread the same fine line within the party. This proved a stumbling block. At first, Alastair Campbell floated the idea that there would be a free vote on the matter; this met with strong opposition from many in the party, not least John Prescott and Jack Straw, as well as backbenchers such as Ben Bradshaw, who said it would be a 'terrible tactical and moral mistake'.[55] The abolition of Section 28 was introduced in the Lords and on 7 February 2000, the Lords rejected it, following the leadership of Baroness Young, on a vote of 210 to 165, including 15 peers. The following March, a compromise was ruled out by a cross-party alliance of Conservatives, cross-benchers, Christian and Muslim peers and on 23 March, a majority of peers supported a Tory amendment to the Learning and Skills bill that would promote 'marriage as the key building block of society'.[56] In July 2000, the Lords again rejected the repeal, even with the sweetener of amendments that would encourage traditional 'family values'.

---

[51] See Kirsty Scott, 'New Parliament, Same Old Prejudice', *The Guardian*, 21 January 2000.
[52] Quoted in *The Guardian*, 25 January 2000.
[53] *The Guardian*, 28 January 2000.
[54] *The Observer*, 13 February 2000.
[55] *The Guardian*, 27 January 2000; see also *The Guardian*, 26 January 2000; *The Observer*, 30 January 2000; *The Guardian*, 23 March 2000.
[56] *The Guardian*, 24 March 2000.

Blair's own position on Section 28 was difficult to read. In public, he was staunchly opposed to it, believing that Section 28 was 'prejudiced' and that the controversy surrounding it served only to 'exploit anti-gay feelings', and each time it was defeated in parliament he promised to continue with abolition.[57] But a leaked memo from Blair in July revealed that he also believed that the issue of gay rights made Labour look 'weak' on the family.[58] The 2001 election manifesto indeed tried to redress this by articulating 'strong and stable family life'.[59] Other pressures pushed Labour forwards, not least the prospect that Section 28 would leave Britain in violation of the Human Rights Act that was to come into force in the autumn of 2000.[60] In June, the Scottish Executive repealed Section 28. But by the end of 2000, it was clear that repeal of Section 28 was not on the immediate legislative agenda and would be left until after the 2001 election. Through all of this, Stonewall remained patient, perhaps confident that a second Labour majority would see repeal through. The record in 2000 had not been a particularly encouraging one, with the party showing signs of division, and the potential for a popular, socially conservative campaign clear.

Repeal waited until 2003. In January, Nick Raynsford, the Local Government Minister, announced that, as part of a new local government bill, he would support a private member's amendment to repeal Section 28. This amendment was put by Kali Mountford, Labour member for Colne Valley, in March 2003. Like the age of consent debate, the parliamentary discussion of Section 28 was shot through with a sense of the rigidity of sexual identity; Mountford herself caught this, saying '[w]e can no more lop off an arm than change our sexuality'.[61] The vote was overwhelming in favour of repeal, 356 to 127, with mostly Conservatives in the opposing ranks. On 10 July 2003, the Lords accepted the repeal, which came into effect on 17 November 2003.

Ben Summerskill, the chief executive of Stonewall, greeted the repeal of Section 28 as the triumph of gay ordinariness, which gave gay people 'a visibility and a sense of civic respect for the first time': 'they can feel free simply to be naff . . . And ordinary. And—whisper it softly for fear of awakening those who like to monopolise our collective vocabulary—normal. Just like everyone else.'[62] In some ways, this might be seen as completing the arc of rewarding respectable homosexuality begun in the 1950s, but of course, it was not. What Summerskill was referring to was, by contrast, the ability to make public a number of kinds of homosexual identity, whether the flamboyance of gay pride or a more muted identity; the point was that homosexual identity might be as publicly varied or not as heterosexual identity.

A critical part of this equalization within the public sphere concerned the redefinition of two key aspects of thinking about how society and private life was constructed, in terms of parenting and partnership. At the beginning of 2002, in

---

[57] *The Guardian*, 26 July 2000; 9 February 2000.
[58] *The Guardian*, 18 July 2000.
[59] Labour Party, *Ambitions for Britain* (London: Labour Party, 2001).
[60] *The Guardian*, 30 March 2000.
[61] *Parliamentary Debates* (Commons), 401, 10 March 2003, c. 70.
[62] Ben Summerskill, 'We're So Ordinary, It's Frightening', *The Observer*, 20 July 2003.

the context of an amendment to a new Adoption bill, the government somewhat tentatively (given fears of inflaming social conservative opinion) indicated that unmarried couples, gay as well as straight, would be allowed to adopt children. At this point, single unmarried people, including gays and lesbians, could adopt children, but not as part of a recognized couple.[63] This was a move supported by child welfare agencies. It took until May for the government to make the commitment explicit, and this was in the terms, not of gay rights, but of extending the pool of potential adoptive parents.[64] The amendment was passed by a majority of 155, but, in a familiar story, was thrown out by the Tories in the Lords. The gay rights issue was increasingly defining a split within the Conservative party, between diehard opponents, of whom the Tory peers formed an important element, and 'modernizers', who wished to move the party more towards social liberalism. A critical moment in this came with the resignation of John Bercow from the Shadow Cabinet in November 2002 in protest against Iain Duncan Smith's opposition to gay and unmarried adoption. That month, however, the Lords voted in favour of the measure and it received Royal Assent on 7 November 2002, to come into effect in 2004. With the change in adoption law, the principle of parenting changed, unfixed from an idea that parenting was normatively done by a man and a woman. When it was agreed that the NHS would provide fertility treatments for lesbian couples, this was strengthened.

The year that the adoption law came into effect, the government indicated it would present a civil partnership bill, which would, in all but name, give the right of marriage to gay couples. This was not only a symbolic recognition of the right to recognition, but also, just as profoundly, a means of ensuring that gay couples had the same pension and inheritance rights as heterosexual couples. The government made clear that this was 'about equality', not 'special favours'.[65] Stonewall welcomed the news, while OutRage called the failure to grant absolute equality, in other words marriage, a 'sexual apartheid'.[66] It appeared for a time that civil partnership would not follow the same, now tiresome, round of opposition from Tories in the Commons and the Lords. Indeed, in 2004, the Conservatives appeared to be courting the gay vote, holding their first gay summit and making every impression that they welcomed the legislation. However, once the bill went to the Lords in June 2004, amendments were added by Tory peers to include, not just same sex partners as possible signatories to civil partnership, but carers and spinsters who lived together. After, once again, a threat that the bill would stall in the Lords, it passed in November 2004, and came into effect December 2005. In the latter years of the Labour government, the main initiative was an Equality Act (2010) that brought existing legislation on sexual orientation and discrimination within one set of laws.

---

[63] See *The Guardian*, 23 January 2002; 5 May 2002.
[64] *The Guardian*, 7 May 2002; 8 May 2002.
[65] *The Guardian*, 28 March 2004.
[66] *The Guardian*, 31 March 2004.

Reproductive politics witnessed less spectacular changes during the New Labour years, though the Human Fertilisation and Embryology Act (2008) contained an important provision for the rights of lesbian couples with respect to assisted reproduction. The Act also prompted the question of lowering the time limit for abortions, from the twenty-four weeks established in 1990 to twenty or twenty-two weeks. The prospect of the bill also raised the possibility of liberalizing the abortion law and pro-abortion campaigners organized to promote this. In 2003, the ALRA and NAC had merged to become Abortion Choice. Some female Labour MPs, such as Laura Moffat and Christine McCafferty, organized a cross-party attempt, through the All-Party Pro-Choice and Sexual Health Group, to get abortion on demand, which would have removed the requirement for permission from two doctors and left the choice to individual women.[67] In May 2008, there was a public demonstration defending the twenty-four-week limit and demanding more liberal abortion laws.[68] At the end of that month, a close Commons vote saw the rejection of a reduction of the time limit to twenty-two weeks, though three Cabinet ministers—Des Browne, Patrick Murphy, and Ruth Kelly—voted to lower the limit. In the Commons debate, Christine McCafferty argued that it was the right of the woman alone to make the decision to have an abortion: '[w]hy is it so difficult . . . to give the power to decide to those who carry the consequences?'[69] At the time, some commentators noted that the debate once again illustrated a partisan divide between Labour and the Conservatives, with the Conservative leader, David Cameron supporting a cut to the time limit.[70] Later that year, Harriet Harman, as Leader of the House, ruled out discussing amendments that would liberalize abortion; it was suspected that one particular amendment, Diane Abbott's attempt to extend the 1967 law to Northern Ireland, was the influential factor here, because the Labour government feared offending the Democratic Unionists, who were set to support the Brown government's unpopular policy on forty-two-day detentions.[71] The Labour government's record on reproductive control was less spectacular than its work on gay and lesbian rights; it had held the line on the reforms of 1967 and 1990, though it had not extended women's rights.

Compared with earlier periods, such as the 1880s, the 1920s, and the 1970s, the major initiatives of the Labour governments of the twenty-first century had little of the utopian flavour of earlier socialist interventions in sexual issues. Rather, they were presented, sometimes controversially, as part of the fabric of modern society, rather than as the forces that would transform that society. This is not to say that things like civil partnership did not change society, but they may have effected that change from the inside out, from within existing terms. The protagonists of the struggle for sexual reform on the Left in the early twenty-first century were very

---

[67] *The Guardian*, 10 June 2007.
[68] *The Guardian*, 21 May 2008; *Parliamentary Debates* (Commons), 20 May 2008, c. 238.
[69] *The Guardian*, 28 May 2008.
[70] Jackie Ashley, 'This Fight Really Matters, and Lays Bare the Big Party Divide', *The Guardian*, 19 May 2008; *The Guardian*, 25 February 2008.
[71] *The Guardian*, 23 July, 17 October, 21 October, 22 October, and 23 October 2008.

different from their progenitors. In previous periods, as this study has argued, it was the working-class mother, the working-class family, or even the breadwinner male, who were the objects of sexual reform. In the late nineteenth century, the sexually autonomous individual, whether male or female, remained a radical character. By the early twenty-first century, individualism and sexual rights were at the heart of what the Labour government achieved in its sexual reform. This may have also reflected a change in the way progressive politics was perceived at the end of the twentieth century, less about older touchstones such as class and more about the rights and choices of individuals. Sexual reform had been brought into the mainstream and lost some of the emancipatory or transformative promise that it held in the late nineteenth or mid-twentieth century. But this also resonates with another tradition in the relationship between sexual reform and Left politics, that the most powerful and far-reaching change came from the shifting understanding of traditional ideas, such as femininity, masculinity, and the family. It also reflected another theme of the twentieth century, the relationship between sexual politics and changes in Labour's own political outlook, in this case, the smoothing of its edges and the loss of its sharpness as a democratic socialist party. Both sex and politics had changed by the beginning of the new century.

In the late 1950s, Allan Horsfall mused upon a simple but profound problem: how the 'individual conscience' on a matter of sexuality could 'make itself felt' through 'political action'.[72] This book has shown how complex and important that question has been for British politics and, more crucially, for the lives of ordinary men and women over the last century and a half, as it no doubt will continue to be in the future.

---

[72] Horsfall, 'Battling for Wolfenden', 2.

Bibliography

A. UNPUBLISHED PRIMARY SOURCES

Bertrand Russell Archives, McMaster University, Hamilton, Ontario, Canada
   Dora Russell fonds
Brynmor Jones Library, Hull
   Socialist Medical Association Papers
   Women's Cooperative Guild Papers
Contemporary Medical Archives, Wellcome Institute, London
   Abortion Law Reform Association Papers
   Birth Control Campaign Papers
   David Steel Papers
   Janet Chance Papers
   Lord Silkin Papers
Durham County Record Office, Durham
   Durham County Federation of Divisional Labour Parties, publications
   Durham Labour Women's Advisory Council Minute Books
Hackney Archives, London
   Sarah Mudd Papers
International Institute for Social History, Amsterdam
   Dora Russell Papers
   Socialist International Women Papers
London Metropolitan Archives
   Carshalton South Women's Section Minute Books
   East Ham South Women's Section Minute Books
   Feltham Local Labour Party, Women's Section Minute Books
   London Labour Party Papers
   North Paddington Queen's Park Women's Section Minute Books
   South Lewisham Women's Section Minute Books
   West Bermondsey Labour Party, Women's Section Minute Books
   West Middlesex Labour Women's Advisory Council Papers
London School of Economics
   Fabian Society Papers
   Lena Jeger Papers
   Women's Cooperative Guild Papers
Hall–Carpenter Archives, London School of Economics
   Gay Labour Group Papers
   Greater London Council Gay Rights Working Party Papers
   Peter Tatchell Papers
   Robert Crossman Papers
Modern Records Centre, University of Warwick
   Trades Union Congress Papers
National Archives, Kew
   Ministry of Health (MH 71)

People's Museum, Manchester
   Hilary Wainwright Papers
   Labour Party Archives
Women's Library, London
   Co-ordinating Committee in Defence of the 1967 Abortion Act Papers
   National Abortion Campaign Papers
   Women's Liberation Papers

B. MICROFICHE AND MICROFILM COLLECTIONS

Mass-Observation Archive: Papers from the Mass-Observation Archive. Marlborough: Adam Matthew Publications, 2001.
Sexual Politics in Britain. Brighton: Harvester, 1986.
The Left in Britain. Hassocks, Sussex: Harvester, 1976.

C. ONLINE ARCHIVES

Mass Observation Online. Marlborough: Adam Matthew Digital, 2004, http://www.am digital.co.uk/Collections/Mass-Observation-Online.aspx (accessed 2 June 2011).

D. PUBLISHED SOURCES

Journals and Newspapers
British Medical Journal
Daily Mirror
Fabian Journal
Gay Left
Gay and Lesbian Socialist
Gay Socialist
The Guardian
Labour Woman
Labour: The TUC Magazine
The Lancet
Lesbian and Gay Socialist
New Generation
New Statesman and Nation
The Observer
Parliamentary Debates Commons and Lords
Red Rag
Socialist Commentary
Socialist Woman
The Times
Woman's Leader
Women's Charter

Reports
Annual Conference of Labour Women Reports
    Labour Party Conference Annual Reports
    Trades Union Congress Annual Reports

Selected Autobiographies, Biographies, and Published Diaries
Benton, Jill, *Naomi Mitchison: A Biography* (London: Pandora, 1992).
Carvel, John, *Citizen Ken* (London: Chatto and Windus, 1984).
Grey, Antony, *Quest for Justice: Towards Homosexual Emancipation* (London: Sinclair-Stevenson, 1992).
Hall, Lesley, *Naomi Mitchison: A Profile of Her Life and Work* (London: Aqueduct Press Conversation Pieces, 2007).
Hall, Lesley, *The Life and Times of Stella Browne Feminist and Free Spirit* (London: I.B. Tauris, 2011).
Heron, Liz (ed.), *Truth, Dare or Promise: Girls Growing Up in the Fifties* (London: Virago, 1985).
Horsfall, Allan, 'Wolfenden in the Wilderness', *New Left Review* 12 (November–December 1961), 29–31.
Mitchison, Naomi, *You May Well Ask* (London: Gollancz, 1979).
Rowbotham, Sheila, *A New World For Women: Stella Browne—Socialist Feminist* (London: Pluto, 1977).
Rowbotham, Sheila, *Promise of a Dream: Remembering the Sixties* (London: Penguin, 2000).
Rowbotham, Sheila, *Edward Carpenter: A Life of Liberty and Love* (London: Verso, 2008).
Rowbotham, Sheila and Weeks, Jeffery, *Socialism and the New Life: The Personal and Sexual Politics of Edward Carpenter and Havelock Ellis* (London: Pluto, 1977).
Russell, Dora, *The Tamarisk Tree* (London: Elek, 1975).
Tatchell, Peter, *The Battle for Bermondsey* (London: Heretic, 1983).
Wandor, Michelene (ed.), *Once a Feminist: Stories of a Generation* (London: Virago, 1990).
Ward, Harriet, *A Man of Small Importance* (Debenham, Suffolk: Dormouse Books, 2003).

Selected Contemporary Books and Articles
Abortion Law Reform Association, *Backstreet Surgery* (London: ALRA, 1939).
Browne, Stella, 'Women and Birth-Control', in Paul, Eden, and Cedar (eds), *Population and Birth-Control* (New York: The Critic and Guide Company, 1917).
Carpenter, Edward, *Homogenic Love* (privately printed, 1894).
Carpenter, Edward, *Love's Coming of Age* (London: George Allen and Unwin, 1896, 1930).
Carpenter, Edward, *Towards Democracy* (London: George Allen and Unwin, 1883, 1918).
Chance, Janet, *Intellectual Crime* (London: Noel Douglas, 1933).
Chance, Janet, *The Romance of Reality* (London: George Allen and Unwin, 1934).
Chance, Janet, *The Case for the Reform of the Abortion Laws* (London: Abortion Law Reform Association, 1936).
Cole, Margaret, *Marriage: Past and Present* (London: J.M. Dent, 1938).
Crosland, Anthony, *The Future of Socialism* (London: Jonathan Cape, 1956).
Ferris, Paul, *The Nameless: Abortion in Britain Today* (London: Hutchinson, 1966).
Gavron, Hannah, *The Captive Wife: Conflicts of Housebound Mothers* (London: Routledge and Kegan Paul, 1966).
GLC/GLC Gay Rights Working Party, *Changing the World: A London Charter for Gay and Lesbian Rights* (London: GLC, 1985).
Jenkins, Alice, *Law for the Rich* (London: Gollancz, 1960).

Labour Party, *The Rights of Gay Men and Women: A Labour Party Discussion Document* [NEC] (London: Labour Party, March 1981).

Mass-Observation, *Britain and Her Birthrate* (London: John Murray, 1945).

Mitchell, Juliet, 'Women: The Longest Revolution', *New Left Review* 40 (November–December 1966), 11–37.

Mitchell, Juliet, *Women's Estate* (New York: Vintage, 1971, 1973).

Mitchison, Naomi, *Comments on Birth Control* (London: Faber and Faber/Criterion Miscellany, No. 12, 1930).

Mitchison, Naomi, *We Have Been Warned* (London: Constable, 1935).

Morris, William, *News From Nowhere and Selected Writings and Designs* (Harmondsworth: Penguin, 1986).

Myrdal, Alva and Klein, Viola, *Women's Two Roles: Home and Work* (London: Routledge and Kegan Paul, 1956, second edition 1968).

Pearson, Karl, *The Ethic of Freethought* (London: Adam and Charles Black, 1901).

Pember Reeves, Maud, *Round about a Pound a Week* (London: Virago, 1913, 1999).

Rowbotham, Sheila, Segal, Lynne, and Wainwright, Hilary, *Beyond the Fragments: Feminism and the Making of Socialism* (London: Merlin, 1979).

Russell, Dora, *Hypatia, or Woman and Knowledge* (London: Kegan Paul, 1925).

Russell, Dora, *The Right to Be Happy* (London: Routledge, 1927).

Russell, Dora, *In Defence of Children* (London: Hamish Hamilton, 1932).

Schreiner, Olive, *Woman and Labor* (New York: Frederick Stokes, 1911).

Secor Florence, Lella, *Birth Control on Trial* (London: George Allen and Unwin, 1930).

Slater, Eliot and Woodside, Moya, *Patterns of Marriage: A Study of Marriage Relationships in the Urban Working Classes* (London: Cassell, 1951).

Spring Rice, Margery, *Working-Class Wives* (London: Virago, 1939, 1981).

Stopes, Marie, *Married Love* (London: A.C. Fifield, 1918).

Thurtle, Dorothy, *Abortion: Right or Wrong?* (London: T. Werner Laurie, 1940).

Wandor, Michelene (ed.), *The Body Politic: Writings From the Women's Liberation Movement in Britain 1969–1972* (London: Women's Liberation Workshop, 1972).

Women's Cooperative Guild, *Maternity: Letters from Working-Women* (London: G. Bell and Sons, 1915).

Woodside, Moya, 'Attitudes of Women Abortionists', *Howard Journal* 11 (1963), 107–8.

Selected Secondary Books and Articles

Alexander, Sally, *Becoming a Woman and Other Essays in Nineteenth and Twentieth Century Feminist History* (London: Virago, 1994).

Bingham, Adrian, *Gender, Modernity and the Popular Press in Inter-war Britain* (Oxford: Oxford University Press, 2004).

Bingham, Adrian, *Family Newspapers* (Oxford: Oxford University Press, 2009).

Black, Amy and Brooke, Stephen, 'The Labour Party, Women and the Problem of Gender, 1951–66', *Journal of British Studies* 36 (1997), 419–52.

Bland, Lucy, *Banishing the Beast* (London: I.B. Tauris, 1995, 2002).

Bland, Lucy and Doan, Laura (eds), *Sexology in Culture: Labelling Bodies and Desires* (Chicago: University of Chicago Press, 1998).

Bourke, Joanna, 'Fear and Anxiety: Writing About Emotion in Modern History', *History Workshop Journal* 55 (2003), 111–33.

Brooke, Stephen, 'Gender and Working-Class Identity in Britain during the 1950s', *Journal of Social History* 34 (Summer 2001), 773–95.

Brooke, Stephen, 'Bodies, Sexuality and the "Modernization" of the British Working Classes', *International Labour and Working-Class History* 69 (June 2006), 122–43.

Brookes, Barbara, *Abortion in England 1900–1967* (London: Croom Helm, 1988).

Cant, Bob and Hemmings, Susan (eds), *Radical Records: Thirty Years of Lesbian and Gay History* (London: Routledge, 1988).

Clark, Anna, *The Struggle for the Breeches* (London: Rivers Oram, 1996).

Cocks, H.G., *Nameless Offences: Homosexual Desire in the Ninetenth Century* (London: I.B. Tauris, 2003).

Collette, Christine, *For Labour and Women: The Women's Labour League 1906–18* (Manchester: Manchester University Press, 1986).

Collins, Marcus, *Modern Love* (London: Atlantic, 2003).

Conekin, Becky, Mort, Frank, and Waters, Chris (eds), *Moments of Modernity* (London: Rivers Oram, 1999).

Cook, Hera, *The Long Sexual Revolution* (Oxford: Oxford University Press, 2004).

Davin, Anna, 'Imperialism and Motherhood', *History Workshop Journal* 5 (1978), 9–66.

Doan, Laura, *Fashioning Sapphism: The Origins of Modern English Lesbian Culture* (New York: Columbia University Press, 2001).

Durham, Martin, *Sex and Politics: The Family and Morality in the Thatcher Years* (Houndmills: Macmillan, 1991).

Eley, Geoff, *Forging Democracy* (New York: Oxford University Press, 2002).

Fisher, Kate, *Birth Control and Marriage in Britain* (Oxford: Oxford University Press, 2006).

Fisher, Kate, '"Didn't Stop to Think, I Just Didn't Want Another One": The Culture of Abortion in Interwar South Wales', In Eder, Franz X., Hall, Lesley, and Hekma, Gert (eds), *Sexual Cultures in Europe: Themes in Sexuality* (Manchester: Manchester University Press, 1999).

Francis, Martin, 'The Labour Party: Modernisation and the Politics of Restraint', in Conekin, Becky, Mort, Frank, and Waters, Chris (eds), *Moments of Modernity* (London: Rivers Oram, 1999).

Francis, Martin, 'Labour and Gender', in Tanner, Duncan, Thane, Pat, and Tiratsoo, Nick (eds), *Labour's First Century* (Oxford: Oxford University Press, 2000).

Freeden, Michael, 'The Stranger at the Feast: Ideology and Public Policy in Twentieth-Century Britain', *Twentieth Century British History* 1 (1990), 9–34.

Giles, Judy, '"Playing Hard to Get": Working-Class Women, Sexuality and Respectability in Britain, 1918–40', *Women's History Review* 1 (1992), 239–55.

Gledhill, Christine and Swanson, Gillian (eds), *Nationalizing Femininity* (Manchester: Manchester University Press, 1996).

Graves, Pamela, *Labour Women: Women in British Working-Class Politics 1918–1939* (Cambridge: Cambridge University Press, 1994).

Gruber, Helmut and Graves, Pamela (eds), *Women and Socialism/Socialism and Women* (New York: Berghahn, 1998).

Hall, Lesley, '"I Have Never Met the Normal Woman": Stella Browne and the Politics of Womanhood', *Women's History Review* 6 (1997), 157–82.

Hall, Lesley, *Sex, Gender and Social Change in Britain Since 1880* (London: Macmillan, 2000).

Hall, Lesley, 'The Next Generation: Stella Browne, the New Woman as Freewoman', in Angelique Richardson and Chris Willis (eds), *The New Woman in Fiction and in Fact: Fin-de-Siècle Feminisms* (London: Palgrave/University of London, Institute for English Studies, School of Advanced Study, 2001).

Hall, Lesley, 'No Sex Please, We're Socialists: The British Labour Party Closes its Eyes and Thinks of the Electorate', in Battan, Jesse, Bouchet, Thomas, and Regin, Tania (eds), *Meetings & Alcoves: The Left and Sexuality in Europe and the United States since 1850* (Dijon: L'Institut d'histoire contemporain, 2004).

Hall, Lesley and Porter, Roy, *The Facts of Life: The Creation of Sexual Knowledge in Britain 1650–1950* (New Haven: Yale University Press, 1995).

Haste, Cate, *Rules of Desire: Sex in Britain: World War One to the Present* (London: Pimlico, 1992).

Hekma, Gert (ed.), *Past and Present of Radical Sexual Politics* (Amsterdam: Mosse Foundation, 2004).

Hoggart, Lesley, *Feminist Campaigns for Birth Control and Abortion Rights in Britain* (Lampeter: Edwin Mellen, 2003).

Hoggart, Lesley, 'Feminist Principles meet Political Reality: The Case of the National Abortion Campaign', http://www.prochoiceforum.org.uk/al6.php, accessed 4 June 2009.

Houlbrook, Matt, *Queer London* (Chicago: University of Chicago Press, 2005).

Howell, David, *MacDonald's Party* (Oxford: Oxford University Press, 2002).

Hunt, Karen and Hannam, June, *Socialist Women: Britain, 1880s to 1920s* (London: Routledge, 2002).

Jeffery-Poulter, Stephen, *Peers, Queers and Commons* (London: Routledge, 1991).

Jennings, Rebecca, 'The Gateways Club and the Emergence of a Post-Second World War Lesbian Subculture', *Social History* 31 (2006), 206–25.

Jennings, Rebecca, *A Lesbian History of Britain: Love and Sex Between Women since 1500* (Oxford: Greenwood, 2007).

Jennings, Rebecca, *Tomboys and Bachelor Girls: A Lesbian History of Post-War Britain 1945–71* (Manchester: Manchester University Press, 2007).

Kelly, Joan, *Women, History and Theory* (Chicago: University of Chicago Press, 1984).

Knight, Patricia, 'Woman and Abortion in Victorian and Edwardian England', *History Workshop Journal* 4 (Autumn 1977), 56–69.

Koven, Seth and Michel, Sonya (eds), *Mothers of a New World: Maternalist Politics and the Origins of Welfare States* (London: Routledge, 1993).

Koven, Seth, *Slumming* (Princeton: Princeton University Press, 2004).

Langhamer, Claire, 'The Meanings of Home in Postwar Britain', *Journal of Contemporary History* 40 (2005), 341–62.

Langhamer, Claire, 'Adultery in Post-War England', *History Workshop Journal* 62 (2006), 86–115.

Langhamer, Claire, 'Love and Courtship in Mid-Twentieth-Century England', *Historical Journal* 50 (2007), 173–96.

Leathard, Audrey, *The Fight for Family Planning* (London: Macmillan, 1980).

Lewis, Jane, *The Politics of Motherhood: Child and Maternal Welfare in England, 1900–39* (London: Croom Helm, 1980).

Lewis, Jane (ed.), *Labour and Love: Women's Experience of Home and Family 1850–1940* (Oxford: Blackwells, 1986).

Light, Alison, *Forever England: Femininity, Literature and Conservatism Between the Wars* (London: Routledge, 1991).

Lovenduski, Joni, 'Parliament, Pressure Groups, Networks and the Women's Movement: The Politics of Abortion Law Reform in Britain 1967–83', In Lovenduski, Joni and Outshoorn, Jocye (eds), *The New Politics of Abortion* (London: Sage, 1986).

Marsh, Dave and Chambers, Joanna, *Abortion Politics* (London: Junction, 1981).

McKibbin, Ross, *Classes and Cultures: England, 1918–1951* (Oxford: Oxford University Press, 1998).

Mort, Frank, *Dangerous Sexualities: Medico-Moral Politics in England Since 1830* (London: Routledge, 1987).

Mort, Frank, 'Mapping Sexual London: The Wolfenden Committee on Homosexual Offences and Prostitution, 1954–7', *New Formations* 37 (1999), 92–113.

Pedersen, Susan, *Family, Dependence and the Origins of the Welfare State: Britain and France, 1914–45* (Cambridge: Cambridge University Press, 1993).

Perrigo, Sarah, 'Women and Change in the Labour Party 1979–1995', In Lovenduski, Joni and Norris, Pippa (eds), *Women in Politics* (Oxford: Oxford University Press, 1996).

Purton, Peter, *Sodom, Gomorrah and the New Jerusalem* (London: Labour Campaign for Lesbian and Gay Rights, 2006).

Quataert, Jean, 'Socialisms, Feminisms, and Agency: A Long View', *Journal of Modern History* 73 (2001), 603–16.

Rayside, David M., 'Homophobia, Class and Party in England', *Canadian Journal of Political Science* 25 (1992), 121–49.

Rayside, David M., *On the Fringe: Gays and Lesbians in Politics* (Ithaca: Cornell University Press, 1998).

Richardson, Angelique, *Love and Eugenics in the Late Nineteenth Century: Rational Reproduction and the New Woman* (Oxford: Oxford University Press, 2003).

Riley, Denise, *'Am I That Name?' Feminism and the Category of 'Women' in History* (Minneapolis: University of Minnesota Press, 1988).

Roberts, Elizabeth, *A Woman's Place* (Oxford: Blackwell, 1984).

Roberts, Elizabeth, *Women's Work 1840–1940* (London: Macmillan, 1988).

Roberts, Elizabeth, *Women and Families* (Oxford: Blackwell, 1995).

Robinson, Lucy, *Gay Men and the Left in Post-War Britain* (Manchester: Manchester University Press, 2007).

Robinson, Lucy, 'The Bermondsey By-Election and Leftist Attitudes to Homosexuality', in McCormack, Matthew (ed.), *Public Men: Masculinity and Politics in Modern Britain* (Houndmills: Palgrave Macmillan, 2007).

Roper, Michael, 'Slipping Out of View: Subjectivity and Emotion in Gender History', *History Workshop Journal* 59 (2005), 57–72.

Rose, Sonya, *Which People's War?* (Oxford: Oxford University Press, 2003).

Rosenwein, Barbara H., 'Worrying About Emotions in History', *American Historical Review* 107 (2002), 821–45.

Ross, Ellen, '"Fierce Questions and Taunts": Married Life in Working-Class London, 1870–1914', *Feminist Studies* 8 (1992), 575–602.

Ross, Ellen, *Love and Toil: Motherhood in Outcast London 1870–1918* (New York: Oxford University Press, 1993).

Savage, Mike, *The Dynamics of Working-Class Politics: The Labour Movement in Preston 1880–1940* (Cambridge: Cambridge University Press, 1987).

Savage, Mike, *Identities and Social Change in Britain since 1940: The Politics of Method* (Oxford: Oxford University Press, 2010).

Scott, Gillian, *Feminism and the Politics of Working Women: The Women's Cooperative Guild, 1880s to the Second World War* (London: UCL Press, 1998).

Seccombe, Wally, 'Starting to Stop: Working-Class Fertility Decline in Britain', *Past and Present* 126 (1990), 151–88.

Simms, Madeleine and Hindell, Keith, *Abortion Law Reformed* (London: Peter Owen, 1971).

Smith, Anna Marie, *New Right Discourse on Race and Sexuality: Britain, 1968–1990* (Cambridge: Cambridge University Press, 1994).

Smith, Harold, 'Sex vs. Class: British Feminists and the Labour Movement, 1919–29', *Historian* 48 (1984), 19–37.

Smith Wilson, Dolly, 'A New Look at the Affluent Worker: The Good Working Mother in Post-War Britain', *Twentieth Century British History* 17 (2006), 206–29.

Smyth, J.J., *Labour in Glasgow 1896–1936: Socialism, Suffrage, Sectarianism* (East Linton: Tuckwell Press, 2000).

Szreter, Simon, *Fertility, Class and Gender in Britain 1860–1940* (Cambridge: Cambridge University Press, 1996).

Taylor, Barbara, *Eve and the New Jerusalem* (London: Virago, 1983).

Thane, Pat, 'The Women of the British Labour Party and Feminism, 1906–1945', in Smith, Harold L. (ed.), *British Feminism in the Twentieth Century* (Amherst, MA: University of Massachusetts Press, 1990).

Thane, Pat, 'Visions of Gender in the Making of the British Welfare State: The Case of Women in the British Labour Party and Social Policy', in Bock, Gisela and Thane, Pat (eds), *Maternity and Gender Policies: Women and the Rise of the European Welfare States 1880s–1950s* (London: Routledge, 1991).

Thane, Pat, 'Population Politics in Post-War British Culture', In Conekin, Becky, Mort, Frank, and Waters, Chris (eds), *Moments of Modernity* (London: Rivers Oram, 1999).

Thane, Pat, 'Family Life and "Normality" in Postwar British Culture', in Bessel, Richard and Schumann, Dirk (eds), *Life After Death* (Cambridge: Cambridge University Press, 2003), 193–210.

Thomas, Matthew, 'Anarcho-Feminism in Late Victorian and Edwardian Britain, 1880–1914', *International Review of Social History* 47 (2002), 1–31.

Todd, Selina, *Young Women, Work and Family in England 1918–50* (Oxford: Oxford University Press, 2005).

Todd, Selina, 'Affluence, Class and Crown Street: Reinvestigating the Post-War Working Class', *Contemporary British History* 22 (2008), 501–18.

Wainwright, Hilary, *Labour: A Tale of Two Parties* (London: Hogarth, 1987).

Waites, Matthew, *The Age of Consent: Young People, Sexuality and Citizenship* (Houndmills: Palgrave Macmillan, 2005).

Waters, Chris, 'Disorders of the Mind, Disorders of the Body Social: Peter Wildeblood and the Making of the Modern Homosexual', in Conekin, Becky, Mort, Frank, and Waters, Chris (eds), *Moments of Modernity* (London: Rivers Oram, 1999).

Weeks, Jeffrey, *Coming Out: Homosexual Politics in Britain, from the Nineteenth Century to the Present* (London: Quartet, 1977).

Weeks, Jeffrey, *Sex, Politics and Society: The Regulation of Sexuality since 1800* (London: Longman, 1981, 1989).

Yeo, Stephen, 'A New Life: The Religion of Socialism in Britain, 1883–1896', *History Workshop Journal* 4 (1977), 5–56.

Unpublished Theses

Hustak, Carla, 'Radical Intimacies: Sexual Ethics and the Transatlantic Politics of Love in the Sex Reform Movement, 1900–1930', Unpublished PhD thesis, University of Toronto, 2010.

Setch, Eve, 'The Women's Liberation Movement in Britain, 1969–79: Organisation, Creativity and Debate', Unpublished PhD thesis, University of London, Royal Holloway, 2000.

Index

Italicized page numbers refer to Illustrations.